REAL ESTATE
MARKET ANALYSIS

REAL ESTATE MARKET ANALYSIS

Techniques and Applications

NEIL CARN
Georgia State University

JOSEPH RABIANSKI
Georgia State University

RONALD RACSTER
The Ohio State University

MAURY SELDIN
The American University

PRENTICE HALL CCIM

Commercial-Investment Council
Realtors National Marketing Institute®
of the
National Association of Realtors®
Chicago, Illinois

PRENTICE HALL, *Englewood Cliffs, New Jersey* 07632

Library of Congress Cataloging in Publication Data

Real estate market analysis: techniques and applications / Neil Carn
 . . . [et al.].
     p.   cm.
   Includes index.
   ISBN 0-13-763368-8
   1. Real estate business.   I. Carn, Neil G.
 HD1375.R3927 1988
 333.33--dc19

Editorial and production supervision by: Editing, Design and Production, Inc.
Cover Design: Ben Santora
Manufacturing buyer: Margaret Rizzi

© 1988 by Prentice-Hall, Inc.
A Division of Simon & Schuster
Englewood Cliffs, New Jersey 07632

Printed in the United States of America

10 9 8 7 6 5 4 3 2

ISBN 0-13-763368-8

PRENTICE-HALL INTERNATIONAL (UK) LIMITED, *London*
PRENTICE-HALL OF AUSTRALIA PTY. LIMITED, *Sydney*
PRENTICE-HALL CANADA INC., *Toronto*
PRENTICE-HALL HISPANOAMERICANA, S.A., *Mexico*
PRENTICE-HALL OF INDIA PRIVATE LIMITED, *New Delhi*
PRENTICE-HALL OF JAPAN, INC., *Tokyo*
SIMON & SCHUSTER ASIA PTE, LTD., *Singapore*
EDITORA PRENTICE-HALL DO BRASIL, LTDA., *Rio de Janeiro*

CONTENTS

PREFACE

This book emerged from our experiences over many years teaching in academic programs, consulting, and working with professional real estate groups. Real estate is a multidisciplinary field that embraces science and art, economic and social phenomena, and business and professional pursuits. Although traditional forms of business analysis and economic decision-making criteria are, and should be, used in real estate, the field's unusually broad and diverse environment (involving business and financial factors as well as social and governmental considerations) requires that some traditional analytical methodologies be supplemented and modified when applied to real estate.

The material presented in this book distinguishes between real estate market analysis and other forms of real estate analysis. The book summarizes many accepted techniques of examining real estate markets and presents new materials and methodologies for some aspects of analysis. The book provides a fairly comprehensive basis for real estate market research in general, but it does not purport to present detailed analytical techniques for the great variety of specific real estate problems.

In several chapters, the authors present a summary of accepted techniques available from the broad and diverse sources that represent the literature of the field. It has been the authors' purpose to consolidate basic real estate market analysis techniques into a cohesive, readily comprehensible study that includes contributions from others' as well as our own materials. We wish to emphasize, however, that any errors, misrepresentations, omissions, or other mistakes are the sole responsibility of the authors.

We particularly want to acknowledge and extend our appreciation to those who worked directly with us in preparing the book. Mr. Allen Marks, a doctoral student in the real estate program at Georgia State University when the book was written, prepared some parts of Chapter 14 about interview techniques and primary data analysis. Mr. Craig Lacey, a real estate graduate student at Georgia State University, helped prepare reading references, the index and other supporting materials. Finally, Hazel Blankenship, an extraordinary secretary, prepared draft copies of the book. Her superior skills and her handling of the rough materials submitted to her helped us immeasurably in meeting our deadlines and other critical production requirements.

Respected members of both the academic community and the body of practicing real estate professionals reviewed all or part of the manuscript in various stages of production. Their suggestions and recommendations were invaluable to us, and their help was critical to our efforts in completing the work. The list of those who gave time and effort in this endeavor includes:

Joseph Albert
James Madison University
Harrisonburg, Virginia

Frank Bella, CCIM
Bellmoor Commercial Properties
Homewood, Illinois

Donald Bodley
Eastern Kentucky University
Richmond, Kentucky

Victor Bowman
Heery
Atlanta, Georgia

Jerome Dasso
University of Oregon
Eugene, Oregon

John Edwards
RBA Group
Atlanta, Georgia

James Graaskamp
University of Wisconsin
Madison, Wisconsin

Steve Gruner
Coldwell Banker
Washington, D.C.

Oakleigh Thorne
Coldwell Banker
Washington, D.C.

Austin Jaffee
Pennsylvania State University
University Park, Pennsylvania

Bill Mundy
Mundy and Associates
Seattle, Washington

Thomas Pearson
Lomas & Nettleton Company
Dallas, Texas

Thomas Powers
Goodkin Research
Lauderdale-by-the-Sea, Florida

Nathan Schloss
Real Estate Research Corporation
Chicago, Illinois

William Weaver
University of Central Florida
Orlando, Florida

James Webb
University of Texas
Austin, Texas

Marilyn Weitzman
Weitzman Group, Inc.
New York, New York

Finally, we want to express our appreciation to our colleagues for encouraging us as we finished the book. We especially want to recognize the support and sacrifices of Bonnie Carn, Rose Rabianski, and Rachel Seldin and other members of our families who accepted any and all hardships that came while we were preoccupied with our schedules and deadlines.

1

REAL ESTATE ANALYSES THAT FOCUS ON THE MARKET

INTRODUCTION TO MARKET ANALYSIS

Real estate market analysis, as a specialty among various types of real estate analyses, studies the factors which contribute to the demand for and supply of a particular type of property. Market analysis is concerned with the underlying determinants of investment profitability, such as population, households, employment, and income, and with psychographic characteristics of the user of real estate. Market analysis also is concerned with the events in the marketplace such as sales, rentals, occupancy/vacancy rates, and forthcoming supply.

Psychographic characteristics of potential buyers and tenants include their attitudes, tastes, and preferences. These determine, in part, the qualitative aspects of real estate developments, including the amenities that should be provided in a single-family dwelling, the proper tenant mix for a shopping center, or the most advantageous design of an office bulding. Another type of real estate analysis, marketability analysis, probes these user preferences and examines the competition in analyzing the project characteristics which will maximize absorption rates and permit the project to perform well on the market. Marketability analysis is part of the larger set of analyses generally referred to as real estate market analysis.

The real estate analyses in Exhibit 1-1, although separately defined and discussed, are interrelated, with many real estate development problems combining more than one type of study. For instance, when the problem involves the most economically appropriate development on a particular site, all the analyses in Exhibit 1-1 can be involved. This text is concerned with the real estate analyses which focus upon the market. These studies provide the basic inputs into analyses that focus on investment or feasibility analysis.

Analysis of Local Economies

Local economic analysis considers the factors basic to the demand for all types of real estate in a local economy. Population, households, employment, and income are the principal variables in local economic analysis. Past trends and forecasts of these demand determinants are made for a defined geographic area.

Exhibit 1-1 Typology of Real Estate Analyses

Studies That Focus on the Market

Analysis of Local Economies. Studies the fundamental determinants of the demand for all real estate in the market.

Market Analysis. Studies the demand for and supply of a particular property type in the market.

Marketability Analysis. Examines a specific development or property to assess its competitive position in the market.

Studies That Focus on Individual Decisions

Feasibility Analysis. Evaluates a specific project as to whether or not it is likely to be carried out successfully if pursued under a proposed program. May relate to developability. Most often relates to financial feasibility, i.e., ability of the project/program to achieve the specified objectives.

Investment Analysis. Evaluates a specific property as a potential investment. Usually incorporates specific financing in the analysis. May evaluate alternative financing options to select most appropriate financing. May include consideration of income taxes. Emphasis is on evaluation of risk and reward. Risk analysis may use sensitivity measures. Reward analysis may use internal rate of return or net present value among the measures of potential investment results.

Market Analysis

Real estate market analysis also has a geographic frame of reference. Market analysis can estimate the demand for and supply of a particular property type in a community, a region, or the nation. At times, the problem is to analyze the market for a proposed development at a particular location. In this instance, the geographic area to be examined contains properties considered to be substitutes by the users of that type of real estate development. Thus, a suburban office building may be the particular property type, with its location defining the geographic dimension of the analysis. Although analyses may be done for an entire metropolitan area, most market analysis problems are concerned with community-level markets and submarkets because that is where the competitive products are located.

Market analysis involves disaggregation and segmentation of market characteristics. Disaggregation differentiates the subject property from other properties by subclassification into smaller groups with differing product characteristics. Segmentation differentiates the potential users of the subject property from the general population according to defined consumer characteristics. Thus, luxury high-rise condominium units in the central city may be disaggregated as the property type for the market analysis, with the demanders for this type of housing segregated from total households on the basis of demographic and economic characteristics to estimate the demand for such housing in the local economy. Disaggregation and segmentation are the basic techniques used to provide a focus for the market analysis problem and to avoid the extraneous data that are not necessary to the study.

New developments and redevelopments are placed in an existing community replete with an urban infrastructure of public utilities, schools and transportation, an existing pattern of land uses, public regulations, neighborhoods, social patterns, politics, and life-styles. The analyst concerned with the market analysis problem of siting a given property type should be aware of these factors and of the externalities created by the development. These externalities involve the effects of the development and the property's operations on surrounding properties and on the neighborhood or district. Externalities may involve larger issues of public concern, such as the impact on the school system or local ecology. Ignoring these externalities invites public sanctions that can prohibit development or adversely affect its profitability. Although this book stresses the economics of markets which provide the primary impetus for the location and characteristics of real estate development, the demand and supply determinants in real estate markets work within the framework of public policy that regulates the use of land.

The real estate analyst may be given the assignment of selecting the most economically appropriate development for a particular location. In this instance, market analysis becomes an integral part of the overall analysis. Financing, tax, and public subsidies must be considered in conjunction with the underlying determinants of economic productivity embodied in the market analysis. The availability of tax increment financing, Urban Development Action Grants, industrial revenue bonds, subsidies for housing for low- and moderate-income families, and tax incentives for rehabilitation and preservation of older properties can result in development that would be judged to be infeasible solely on the basis of demand and supply considerations revealed in the market analysis. Deregulation of financial institutions which resulted in mortgage interest rates that are competitive with other rates in the capital market, the insistence on equity participations by many lenders, and the present trend to moderate the tax shelters and subsidies enjoyed by many types of real estate have and will operate to cause the determinants of economic productivity to exert a more influential role on real estate development.

Market analysis uses both primary and secondary data. Primary data are originated by the analyst and include surveys of new construction, vacancies, and absorption of space over time. Secondary data are from sources compiled by others. Census data, planning reports, population projections, and other forms of secondary data are secured by the analyst's focus upon the demand for the property type in question. This book provides procedures for the use and analysis of secondary data for residential, retail, and office properties. However, the importance of primary data in a well-done market analysis cannot be overstressed. Reliance solely on secondary data produces an "arm-chair" analysis which is likely to be inadequate because the data most needed to carry out a line of reasoning are not available. The inclusion of some types of primary data is almost always necessary to have a competent market analysis.

Marketability Analysis

The marketability study focuses on a specific property in the attempt to maximize the property's competitive position in the market. The marketability study can be an integral part of a market study, or it may stand alone to answer a specific question. The marketability study incorporated within a market study of a particular property type takes the information in the broader study and relates it to the particular project. The marketability study focuses on the ability of that specific property to generate additional income. This "income" may take the form of additional retail sales for a shopping center, an improved absorption rate in the form of a faster rent-up for an office building, or a faster sell-off for a residential development. Whether the development is retail office or residential, marketability is concerned with the attainment of an appropriate rent or sales price for the development.

The marketability study involves a careful analysis of the specific site and its locational attributes and of the existing or proposed development. Then, it assesses the acceptance of these attributes by potential users of the property. Often this assessment is done by observing the "revealed preferences" embodied in competitive developments that have had strong market acceptance. Subdivisions of homes which sold quickly at attractive prices will be surveyed to ascertain the packages of amenities which were provided. Sufficient data and careful analysis can reveal price or rent differentials for various attributes, such as a basement, fireplace, or premium view. Such detail assists in determining the profitability of offering a particular amenity.

The marketability study may directly involve potential users of the property to ascertain their psychographic characteristics. Shoppers at retail centers may be intercepted and questioned concerning their preferences and attitudes. Surveys may be conducted of residents or tenants at competitive developments. Marketability analysis involves primary data collection that provides:

1. A statement of the characteristics of the product or the service that can be marketed.
2. The price for which the product will sell, or for which it can be rented.
3. The quantity of units that should be offered in the market.
4. The quantity of units that can be sold in the market during a specific period of time (typically referred to as the absorption rate).
5. The nonprice sales terms and the financing terms that will facilitate the best sales performance.
6. A profile of the most likely buyer.
7. The marketing program and methods to reach the target markets most effectively.

When the marketability analysis is completed, the analyst should be able to present to the decision maker an answer to a question or a series of questions calling for the kinds of conclusions noted above. These conclusions should aid the decision maker in the areas of production planning for the type and the quantity of the product, in marketing to a selected population segment, or in establishing the revenues to be derived from the venture.

Feasibility Analysis

Feasibility analysis involves finding out whether a specific project can be successful. Success, in this instance, includes profit sufficient to attract capital to the investment. Since it is the after-tax return on investment that drives real estate development by attracting equity capital to real estate from other investments, feasibility analysis should involve financing and tax considerations as well as market conditions for a specific property type.

When dealing with a specific client, the feasibility analysis can be refined to ascertain whether the project will satisfy the client's objectives and constraints. If the developer can build a maximum of 40 homes a year, the market needs to be capable of an annual absorption rate of only 40 units at an acceptable price for the project to be feasible. The fact that the market would absorb twice that number of completions simply adds to the comfort level of the developer. The feasibility analysis also can put the proposed development in the context of the developer/investor's portfolio, which can influence that individual's investment decision.

Appraisal literature refers to the highest and best use of a particular site as "the reasonable and probable use that supports the highest present value, as defined, as of the date of appraisal," or "the use, from among reasonably probable and legal alternative uses, found to be physically possible, appropriately supported, financially feasible, and that results in the highest land value."[1] From the viewpoint of the investor, the highest and best use is "the most profitable use" of the site.

Highest and best use in the context of the developer/investor, then, is the limiting condition of feasibility; that is, it is the use which not only provides a "satisfactory" profit, but which provides the maximum profit. The appraiser should carefully consider the highest and best use of every site, but typically state the conclusion only as a general category of land use. The report may state that the highest and best use is "single-family residences" or "commercial development."

Investment Analysis

Investment analysis evaluates a specific property as a potential investment. It may involve an after-tax analysis of the risk-return relationships in real estate developments in seeking the highest rate of return commensurate with an acceptable level of risk. The after-tax cash flow and after-tax cash reversion are processed into measures of return on investment such as the internal rate of return, net present value, profitability index, financial management rate of return and others. The risk of the investment may be analyzed by partitioning the rate of return, by sensitivity analysis, and with computer-assisted simulations. Alternative financing and tax assumptions can be incorporated to seek the combination of financing and tax considerations that produces maximum profitability. The effects of these alternatives on the riskiness of the investment also are examined.

Marketability analysis provides a critical component of investment analysis. The magnitude and timing of income are provided by the marketability analysis which indicates rent or price levels, vacancy and absorption rates, and the scale of the project. The subjective probabilities assigned to market-determined variables in a simulation of return on investment also depend upon marketability. The rate of change assigned to rents, prices, and property value over the assumed holding period are based on market evidence and forecasts. Marketability analysis evaluates the characteristics of the specific property which assesses the market-determined variables in the investment analysis, such as rents and net income.

[1] American Institute of Real Estate Appraisers, *The Appraisal of Real Estate*, 8th ed. (Chicago: AIREA, 1983), p. 244.

The types of real estate analyses just identified form a hierarchy beginning with the local economic analysis that provides basic aggregate inputs into a market analysis. Market analysis segregates users and disaggregates the supply of real estate to estimate market conditions for a particular type of property. Marketability analysis refines the specific project in the class of property analyzed by the market study. Feasibility analysis assesses whether this specific project will generate a satisfactory profit; investment analysis probes circumstances that produce the optimum risk-return relationship.

CRITICISM OF MARKET STUDIES

Each type of real estate analysis has potential shortcomings that can be avoided or ameliorated by awareness of their potential occurrence. These problems revolve around the data, statistical analysis, and the analyst-client relationship. A constructive discussion of these problems as they can appear in a market analysis will be helpful in producing work of high quality.[2]

Problems in the Market Analyst-Client Relationship

Several problems can arise in the analyst-client relationship. These problems revolve around conflict of interest, inexperience with market studies, the short-term nature of the relationship, and the unwarranted belief that the uniqueness of the product will somehow bring success.

In the context of a market and marketability study, failure to determine the client's objectives implies that the analyst knows that the client has already determined one or several of the following items: the best product or service to be delivered, the ideal location for the provision of the product or service, the most acceptable price, and/or the best marketing strategy to be utilized. On the contrary, a market analysis should be used to forecast the outcome of certain courses of action so that the client may determine quantity and quality of product, price, location, timing and pace of development, and marketing strategy. None of these factors should be predetermined only on the basis of beliefs or suppositions if successful outcomes are to be realistically expected. Under certain circumstances the client's recent experience and knowledge in the market may eliminate the need for the market analyst's study of some of these variables. But, even in this case, the issue should be addressed by the analyst at the start of the project.

At times the analyst becomes overly optimistic about the project. This occurs when the analyst is swayed by the client's enthusiasm for the product and

[2]This section incorporates discussion from John R. White, "Improving the Quality of Feasibility Studies," *Urban Land*, October 1976, pp. 5–9; Gary W. Eldred and Robert H. Zerbst, "A Critique of Real Estate Market and Investment Analysis," *The Appraisal Journal*, July 1978, pp. 443–452; and Bradford Perkins, "Why Real Estate Feasibility Studies Have Not Worked," *Real Estate Review*, Fall 1979.

begins to believe that the project is unjustifiably unique in character. Once the analyst chooses to take this position (a volitional fallacy), several things may happen in the course of the analysis. Unsupported, above-average absorption rates or substantially lower vacancy rates can be attributed to the project. In other words, the analyst overallocates the percentage of the total market that can be captured by the project. The analyst attributes a greater drawing power or market penetration rate than is warranted and verifiable by the data. The analyst should not be swept up into blindly accepting the client's or employer's unsupported opinion of the development's unique characteristics.

The client should request specific information about the education and the experience of the analyst. Is the analyst trained to do what the job requires? The answer to this question does not lie in the quantity of education, but in the content of that education. Then, if the training is there, does the analyst have the experience in undertaking this line of work? To carry the discussion further, the nature of the experience should also be examined. The phrase, "10 years of experience" can mean different things. On the one hand, the analyst could improve his studies over time as the experience level leads to new understanding and new, improved techniques. On the other hand, the analyst may simply replicate the procedure he has used for 10 years. The list of clients (often one-time-only clients) expands, but the study is static. In this instance the analyst has 1 year's experience for 10 years of work. There are no new techniques, and there is no increased understanding.

Analysts should accept assignments with which they have had no prior experience only after informing the client and obtaining the client's permission. Even then, the analyst should seek assistance from an experienced associate for portions of the study where experience is needed.

At times the market analyst does not act in a professional, independent manner when analyzing the market and reporting the facts. The issue of conflict of interest arises when one party hires the analyst and implicitly or explicitly requests a positive report. This positive report is then submitted to a third party, usually a lender, who mistakenly assumes that it is an independent and professional report.

An aspect of the conflict-of-interest situation arises when the analyst utilizes the most optimistic projections (the "best case" scenario) of revenues, vacancy rates, absorption rates, population growth, disposable income increases, and employment growth even though he or she is aware of less optimistic projections that could also be used. Or the analyst understates operating costs and mortgage interest rates by selecting the lowest estimates. Another aspect of conflict of interest is the unquestioning use of the client's data. Analysts must not choose data that lead to a positive result when their own analyses reveal that a second estimate of the same key variable yields an inconclusive or maybe even a negative conclusion on the feasibility of the development. The analyst must determine if information supplied by the developer is supported in the market.

Conflict-of-interest charges may be avoided if the analyst presents the analysis in light of the best, worst, and most probable occurrences. In this situation, the client and subsequent readers of the study could draw their own optimistic conclusions.

Often the client fails to retain the analyst on a continuing basis. If the development is not undertaken immediately, or if it faces inordinately long delays, the market may change drastically, making the original market study, now perhaps one or two years old, incorrect. In this instance, the market should be reexamined, and, if necessary, the market study should be redone. Successive marketability studies are useful to monitor the changing competitive position of a project even after completion.

For example, a typical planning period for a development may run for 6 to 24 months. If the market study is done at the beginning of this project, several changes can occur, including the nature of the previously identified competitors, the entrance of new competitors in the market, changes in growth rates and patterns of population and income, and finally, alteration in the taste and preferences of consumers.

Data Problems

Historical statistical data are often presented in a market analysis to describe what has happened in the past, with no attempt made to carry the analysis into the future. In this instance, the market analysis can only tell the client what happened, but the report cannot provide a foundation for an intelligent estimate of occurrences in the future.

The data that are used in the market analysis report may not relate to the assignment. A good market analysis should discuss the relationship of any data that appear in the report to the assignment that was given the analyst. The most frequent violation of this operational procedure occurs when the market analyst provides aggregate data for such items as population, housing starts, and retail sales when these aggregate figures are not the data needed in the analysis. For example, the assignment may be an analysis for the demand for new housing in the northern section of the city. Presentation of building permit activity for the entire Metropolitan Statistical Area can be misleading and most assuredly is inappropriate. If aggregated data must be used, then they should be related to the market that is under analysis.

It is not uncommon to see an analyst use a 5 percent vacancy rate in the market study simply because it is viewed as a normal or standard vacancy rate. Any such figure for either the vacancy rate or an absorption rate must be derived from information provided in the market. At times, the vacancy rate for an apartment complex might be 10 percent, while at other times in the same geographic area, the vacancy rate may be as low as 1 percent. The use of a 5 percent vacancy rate in either of these two instances will overstate or understate the revenue-generating capability of the apartment complex.

Market analysis may be presented to the client or employer without a thorough and complete identification of the sources of the data that are used in the report. Without adequate citation, the data are difficult to find and check for accuracy. Therefore, all data presented in a market analysis and a marketability study should be credited to sources in as thorough and complete a manner as possible. When the analyst has generated the data, the analyst (or the analyst's firm) should be cited as the source.

The analyst should realize that often the data available for the performance of a market study or a marketability study are unreliable, outdated, and incomplete. These problems occur with some degree of frequency when census data or data from local sources are used. The problem of unreliability can arise when an apparent consecutive stream of data is collected at different times of the year and with different procedures from year to year. Outdated data can mislead when the analyst draws conclusions about occurrences in the market that have been documented three to five years previously. Often even good data from local sources may not be complete or are not available on a continuous basis. Such data might be collected for two or three years, and then budget limitations preclude their collection for three or four years. Then, the data are collected again for two more years. If these data are used, the analyst must make an assumption about the missing years.

In any event, the use of unreliable, outdated, and incomplete data presents problems. If the problems cannot be resolved through the use of supplemental data, the analyst must address himself or herself to the problems that can arise because inferior data have to be utilized in the market analysis.

Market studies may use data for artificially created areas such as census tracts or counties to represent the market area. In this instance, the market area may not correspond directly with the arbitrary geographic areas. The market area may consist of several census tracts plus only a portion of others. Alternatively, the market area may be only a small portion of the county, or the market area may cross county lines. In each of these instances, the exclusive reliance on data from the most convenient source and in the most convenient form may overstate or understate the magnitude of the market.

Some market studies do not utilize primary data, that is, data gathered to provide important information about the specific project under analysis. These reports concentrate exclusively on secondary data and may try to extrapolate information that cannot by its nature be extrapolated from secondary data. The analysis of most problems addressed by market analysis and marketability analysis can be improved by the generation and inclusion of primary data. Certainly, marketability analysis relies heavily on information obtained from primary data concerning the attitudes, habits, and perceptions of consumers. Marketability analysis identifies consumers' tastes and the explicit nature of their purchasing habits and patterns. Secondary data are unable to provide this type of information and its impact on the subject property or development under analysis.

Inappropriate Analytical Techniques

Market studies may rely on analytical techniques that mislead clients and, in some instances, mislead the analyst. For instance, the market study might focus on a single issue, ignoring items such as transport access to the site, development problems associated with zoning and construction costs, engineering constraints, and geological features of the site. Regardless of the positive conclusions that can be obtained by considering only the pure market issues, these other aspects that affect market factors need consideration because they can have an impact on the revenues and expenses of the property.

The statistical procedures used in the market analysis may be over-sophisticated or undersophisticated. Studies might use straight-line projections of past phenomena into the future without passing judgment on the appropriateness of this extrapolation. Changing economic factors can require judgment and knowledge to forecast changes in direction or changes in magnitude into the future. Other studies may use a technique, such as regression analysis or discriminant analysis, to make projections and to discover associations in the data. Care must be taken that the techniques are used properly and that they do not violate the underlying assumptions and requirements for proper use of the technique. The complexity of regression analysis can obscure the end products of the technique. Regression is a sophisticated way of extrapolating data from the past through the present into the future. However, the extrapolation may be done without making judgments about significant changes that are taking place in the current period. Thus, the end product of regression analysis would be no better than a simple "eyeball" projection that ignores a significant, current economic trend. Indeed, a well-reasoned judgment about changed conditions could provide, along with an eyeball review of recent trends, a better projection than a regression analysis.

Unwarranted and Unspecified Assumptions

The market analysis may not give full consideration to very important phenomena. Studies do not consider changes in the level and direction of the local economy, the regional economy, and the national economy, or the unwarranted assumption may be made that the market analysis is being performed in a "non-recessionary economy" or under conditions of continued inflation. Market analysts have often found it easier to assume that inflation will continue into the future at rates that have existed in the past. Such an assumption is not warranted and must be justified and explained within the body of the report.

As will be evident in the market analysis for shopping centers, the effects of inflation on retail sales must be carefully explained in the report.

Management's Capabilities. Market studies typically are conducted under the implied assumption that management of the property is capable and competent, which is not always the case. Management's capabilities should be investigated by comparison of the operating results of the subject property with industry norms. Situations do arise where the consultant should realize that a change in management may result in a change in revenues, operating costs, and cash flow. Inefficient and ineffective management of the property can be replaced.

Unnecessary Limiting Assumptions. Nearly all marketing studies set out the assumptions under which the report was prepared and under which the recommendations are made. However, in some reports, the primary purpose of these limiting assumptions is to reduce the marketing analyst's liability if a lawsuit is filed. In this instance, the limiting assumptions may greatly distort the accuracy of the study.

Unwarranted Recommendations. The recommendations made by the market analyst may be unsupported. The analyst might be lax in reporting the logic that is utilized to go from initial conditions to the results. The cause-and-effect relationships involved in the study are not discussed. A second aspect of the unwarranted recommendation problem is that the analyst does not offer conclusions and recommendations, but merely confirms the client's initial supposition about the project.

Relevance of Market Analysis

Properly accomplished, market analysis and marketability studies can suggest answers to a variety of real estate development and lending questions. These questions include

1. What is the likely demand for a particular type of real estate?
2. What is the net demand (demand less supply) for a particular type of real estate?
3. What is the most economically appropriate use for a given site?
4. What are the rent levels, amenities, and tenant mix that maximize the competitiveness and profitability of a specific project?
5. What are the most probable absorption rate, market penetration, sell-off period, and occupancy rate?
6. What are attainable rents, prices, and retail sales volumes?
7. What is the attainable increment, in prices or rents, for various amenities provided in the project?

8. What are the prospects of the local economy and how do they contribute to the project's success?
9. What changes in tenant mix, promotional activities, or redevelopment will improve competitiveness and profitability?
10. What subjective probabilities should be assigned to changes in market-determined variables (rents, prices, vacancy rates, absorption rates)?

The central thesis of this text is that a competent market/marketability analysis will make a positive contribution to project feasibility analysis. We are all familiar with real estate that has been developed by "gut" feel, where the market analysis consists of building successive projects until failure occurs, of thoughtless imitation of successful developments, and of uncritical acceptance by lenders of cash flow projections based upon the developer's perception of project success and the pro formas generated by the computer software of the developer's accountant. Market analysis and marketability studies will not assure that every development will be successful or that every loan will be secure. As a component of a more comprehensive feasibility analysis, however, market analysis can increase the probability of a successful development and increase the "comfort level" of developer, lender, and investor.

READINGS

BAILEY, JOHN B., and others, "Market Study + Financial Analysis + Feasibility Report," *The Appraisal Journal*, October, 1977.

BARRET, G. V., and J. BLAIR, *How to Conduct and Analyze Real Estate Market and Feasibility Studies*. New York: Van Nostrand Reinhold Co., 1982.

BARRET, G. V., "Appraisal Should be Market Study: Techniques of Analysis," *The Appraisal Journal*, October, 1979.

BOHLING, J., "Market Analysis A Needed Tool for Better Loan Appraisers," *Mortgage Banker*, February, 1976.

ELDRED, GARY W., and ROBERT H. ZERBST, "A Critique of Real Estate Market and Investment Analysis," *The Appraisal Journal*, July, 1978.

GRAASKAMP, JAMES A., *A Guide to Feasibility Analysis*. Chicago: Society of Real Estate Appraisers, 1970.

PERKINS, BRADFORD, "Why Real Estate Feasibility Analyses Have Not Worked," *Real Estate Review*, Fall, 1979.

SELDIN, MAURY, CRE, "A Reclassification of Real Estate and Market Analysis: Toward Improving the Line of Reasoning," *Real Estate Issues*, Spring/Summer, 1984.

WHITE, JOHN R., "Improving the Quality of Feasibility Studies," *Urban Land*, October, 1976.

2

REAL ESTATE MARKET RESEARCH IN STRATEGIC PROJECT PLANNING

INTRODUCTION

Strategic planning for a real estate project is the process of devising policy guidelines and a program of action to move the project from its inception to completion as a successful investment. Strategic planning for real estate illustrates the relationships among the types of real estate analyses discussed in Chapter 1 and demonstrates the relevance of market analysis to the success of the project.

Strategic planning is a dynamic process which involves continuous evaluation of the market in which the development competes. The definition of project success requires setting goals and objectives for the project. Procedures for developing these goals and objectives are presented later in this chapter. Before examining strategic goals and objectives, the levels and stages in strategic planning are discussed. Then the role of market research in the development of a project strategy can be identified and more clearly explained.

Four Levels of Strategic Planning

Strategic planning occurs at four levels, depicted in Exhibit 2-1. Government agencies engage in their versions of strategic planning in setting the legislative and jurisdictional framework in which real estate development and investing occur. At another level, business management engages in strategic planning to accomplish the mission of the firm. Then, project planning contributes to the mission of the firm by designing a strategy to produce benefits from a real estate project to be developed or acquired by the firm. When the real estate project or investment is the sole undertaking of the firm, entity-level (i.e., corporate- or firm-level) and project-level planning are a single process. When the project is one of several undertakings of the firm, planning and the criteria for success must be formulated at both the entity and project levels, with entity-level planning and criteria acting as guidelines and constraints for project goals. The fourth level of strategic planning—report planning—involves the development of the research design for the studies needed to provide information required to formulate entity and project plans. Real estate market analysis is one of the studies done at the report level of strategic planning. Much of this text is devoted to the research design for proper market analysis as a technical report in project-level strategic planning. This chapter will show the needs for report-level market analysis throughout the planning process.

Stages in Strategic Planning

The strategic planning process, whether at the government, entity, or project level, can be separated into stages. These stages are depicted in Exhibit 2-2 as sequential steps in the process, with identification of the basic decision to be made at each stage. However, the ever-changing environment in which real property exists continually requires revisions of plans and implementation meas-

Exhibit 2-1 Levels of Strategic Planning

Local, State, and Federal Agencies
Produces laws, regulations, and land-use controls which must be considered in strategic planning by the private developer.

Business Entity
Uses strategic planning to accomplish the mission of the firm.

Project Planning
Designs the strategy to produce benefits from a specific project or investment.

Record Planning
Develops the research design for studies providing information needed for project or entity planning.

STAGE	DECISION NEEDED
Statement of Goals and Objectives. Provides direction to subsequent planning and gives the specific target for each component of the plan.	*Definition of Purpose and Refinement of Ideas to Specific Possibilities.* Asks "What criteria define minimum-maximum targets needed for successful completion of specific actions?"
Inventory and Forecast of Material Requirements and Resources Available. Identifies resources available to achieve targeted goals, forecasts, and schedules requirements to complete projects successfully; identifies deficiencies and surpluses.	*Determination of Entity's Capabilities and Level of Resources Required.* Asks "Is the opportunity matched with the entity's capabilities sufficiently to merit commitment to the project or activity?"
Evaluation of Alternatives. Identifies the possible array of actions and resource requirements that can be taken to achieve successful completion.	*Selection of Specific Program to Achieve Successful Completion.* Asks "Which specific program of action is likely to produce the most beneficial package of results?"
Preparation of Plan Elements. Details specific activities for each step required for successful completion.	*Selection of Specific Package of Activities.* Asks "What are the most efficient and beneficial methods that achieve all interrelated goals and objectives in a compatible manner?"
Preparation of Specific Actions to Implement Plans. Identifies, coordinates, schedules, and commits the steps, procedures, and resources required to carry out individual plan elements.	*Selection of Managerial Procedures and Management Control Devices to Execute Plans.* Asks "What specific methods should project management use to execute the specific project activities required for completion within the planned schedule?"
Taking Specific Actions, Monitoring Results, and Revising Plans. Establishes a program for identifying needed changes, revises plans, and schedules specific corrective actions of the ongoing project after initial acquisition and development activities are completed.	*Selection of Specific Activities to Execute Plan Revisions.* Asks "What specific procedures and resources are needed to maintain or enhance project performance?"

Exhibit 2-2 Stages in the Planning Process

ures to accommodate unexpected events. The planning process is continuous and may involve restatement of goals, reassessment of resources, and so on, until final disposition of the project.

Goals and Objectives in Strategic Planning

A goal is a general statement of a desired result. It sets forth in general, but qualified, terms what the entity is trying to achieve and how it is possible to achieve it, recognizing known constraints and opportunities. Objectives are a series of specifically targeted end results, usually measurable, that can be achieved by taking particular actions that will contribute to the accomplishment of goals. Objectives are subordinate to goals, but they may also relate to more than a single goal.

The success of each real estate project depends upon orchestrating a complex set of central and supporting decisions based upon numerous technical components. The unifying element in the procedure is the Statement of Goals and Objectives, which represents a composite of the aspirations of the central decision agent (the firm) and the capabilities of the project. In considering realistic expectations for project performance, the decision-making entity also must consider the expectations and limitations imposed by supporting decision agents and the external world.

Central and Supporting Decision Agents   The central decision agent which moves the project forward is the ownership and/or managerial entity. The central decision agent receives advice from the market analyst and from other technical analysts and planners who have evaluated information and alternatives and determined the specific criteria upon which "success" can be determined. These criteria are married to the goals and objectives of the central decision agent for the project and become the basis for the decision at hand. Thus, the market analyst and other technical analysts and planners develop the decision criteria that enable the managerial entity to distinguish between the likelihood of success and failure for the project and to make the decision that moves the project forward to the next stage.

In addition to the central decisions of the managerial entity, there are at least two major supporting decisions made by outside decision agents which have a direct bearing on the central project decisions. Supporting decisions are made by public officials which grant public acceptance or regulatory consents for the project to go forward and which support the project with essential services and facilities. Public policies and approval procedures thus require decisions parallel to and concurrent with the central project decision for the project to move to the next stage. Real estate market analysis, which evaluates consumer acceptance of the project, provides part of the evidence needed for public sector decisions.

The second set of major supporting decisions are those of the lender. Debt financing typically is a major portion of total project value, and separate lending decisions are often required for each stage of project development. Lenders, then, must also make parallel and concurrent decisions for the project to move forward. Real estate market analysis, as part of the project feasibility analysis, provides information required by the lender in assessing the risk of the loans and in determining the amount and terms of the financing.

Establishing Goals and Objectives   In real estate project planning, there is often little attention paid to the development of a comprehensive and formal Statement of Goals and Objectives. With the exception of vague general statements of purpose and certain financial criteria specifying the types and levels of expected returns, most goals and objectives are implicitly assumed. Development of a Statement of Goals and Objectives, however, forces the decision maker to consider expectations, assumptions, and operating constraints in a manner that gives clear guidance to subsequent strategic and technical planning.

The first step in developing the Statement of Goals and Objectives is to list the goals which the central decision agent believes to be the most important for the entity. Four levels of goals affect the outcome of a particular decision. Each of these levels should be considered when this step in the planning process is encountered. The levels are

1. *External.* The goals of society or the community generally which define the role and relationship of the entity to the outside world. These goals, often established by the major supporting decision agents, may be quite general (such as the need for a pollution-free community) or very specific (such as a significant change in construction loan underwriting policies).

2. *Entity Level.* The goals of the organization that holds and manages the real estate project. These goals may be complex, with several layers of subordination, or may be quite simple, depending on the diversity, size, and organizational structure of the entity. The goals should be categorized so that internal goal competition and conflicts can be identified.

3. *Project Level.* The goals that relate to the expected purpose and performance level of the individual project. These goals should be categorized to guide the various plan elements (market, financial, physical, etc.) and for further analysis to identify goal competition and conflicts.

4. *Report Level.* The goals or purposes which technical information, analyses, and plans are designed to achieve. While seemingly at the most subordinate level of the goal-setting process, the goals here may affect higher-level goals. For instance, lack of information or an inadequate procedure to handle information could result in change in entity-level goals indicating the type and level of risk that the firm is willing to take. Report-level goals are tied to the very specific end results of technical project planning.

There is little convention in the procedures used to construct the Statement of Goals and Objectives. Whatever the process used, however, there are certain questions that are addressed. The following sequence of activities will produce usable guidelines for the project planning process:

1. *Identification and Description of Elements to Be Accomplished.* Designed to answer the question, "What is to be achieved?" The process involves dividing expectations into (a) relevant component parts and level and type of risks associated with each and (b) stating how the element relates to "success."

2. *Qualification and Quantification.* Designed to target how much is needed for successful completion. After establishing qualitatively what the expectation is (high/low, moderate/heavy, etc.), this step involves establishing appropriate ranges and measures for minimum and maximum levels required for success.

3. *Resource Availability.* Designed to determine if internal and external resources needed to achieve targets are likely to be available. The strategist can then initially

specify which productive units and materials should be employed and which specific methods and controls should be used to achieve the goal.

4. *Timing and Scheduling Constraints.* Designed to determine when elements should be accomplished and in what sequence.

5. *Identification of Related Issues.* Designed to show both internal and external phenomena related to the element in question. Complimentary, competitive, and conflicting aspects are listed.

6. *Identification of Decisions Required.* Designed to indicate what must be decided, who must decide, and the decision time. Decisions should be categorized as central, technical, or supporting.

7. *Translation to Definitive Criteria.* Designed to set specific targets to be achieved by the project activity and provide decision rules that distinguish between success and failure.

Properly constructed, the Statement of Goals and Objectives provides definitive direction and constraints to subsequent analyses, planning activities, and decisions. While it is specified as the first step in the planning process, it is important to remember that planning is a continuous process taking place in a dynamic environment throughout the life of the project. Goals and objectives must therefore be updated and revised as new information and changes come about. Definitive criteria are most likely to be changed as more in-depth analyses and technical plans are prepared. The initial criteria identified serve as "hopeful" targets set to optimize or maximize achievement. As new limitations or opportunities are exposed through additional research, these targets are adjusted to reflect more realistic conditions and expectations. Additional review and adjustments should also be performed for these elements listed in steps 3 through 6. On occasion, adjustments to maximum-minimum ranges established in steps 1 through 3 must be made.

An updated set of goals and objectives provides the basic framework for evaluating and choosing alternatives both at the entity and project levels. It does, of course, take time and resources to perform in a formal sense what was previously done on an *ad hoc* or implicit basis. There are several advantages, though, of undertaking an explicit goals and objectives statement as part of the strategic planning process. These include having

1. *Specific targets* set to achieve expectations about what, how much, when, and how a real estate project is expected to produce.

2. *Specific criteria and decision rules* for all major project decisions, thereby converting a complex set of events into an orchestrated and comprehensible process.

3. *Compatible plan elements* coordinated by a consistent set of guidelines and targets in an otherwise disjointed and technically disparate process.

4. *Usable management controls* which convert exposed opportunities to profitable activity by investing required levels of resources and performing other actions specified for success.

Conflict Between Entity and Project Goals. The real estate project being planned may be a singular undertaking, or it may be one of several separate projects under the same entity. If the project is the only activity being undertaken by the organization, there is no need to distinguish between entity and project goals. At other times, the individual real estate project may be but one of several undertakings managed by the same entity, such as an investment group or a corporation which has other holdings. Here a distinction must be made between the more general accomplishments the entity or firm wants to achieve and the specific goals of the project. Criteria for success must therefore be stated at two different levels, the entity level and the project level, with the entity-level criteria acting as guidelines and imposing constraints on the goals being considered by the project itself.

Entity and project goals may conflict. For example, an investment group that holds and manages several office properties may find an unusually good opportunity to purchase an apartment complex. Further investigation could show that the group would have to acquire a different set of property management skills, that they need to gain a much deeper understanding of the multi-family residential market peculiarities, and that income and reinvestment requirements could not be scheduled compatibly with those required for the office buildings in their existing portfolio. None of these conflicts indicates that the apartment project would not produce adequate returns for an investor, but the project requirements imposed on this particular investment group would not produce satisfactory results.

Consistency and compatibility in setting goals and objectives is an initial key concern of the project strategist. Once a comprehensive listing is completed, a consistency check should be conducted to identify an array of potential conflicts. These include inconsistencies arising from

1. Needs of the entity versus needs of the project.
2. Internal conditions and resources versus external world and market realities.
3. Long-term possibilities versus short-term operating requirements.
4. Financial/economic goals versus nonfinancial goals.
5. Incompatible targets and procedures.

REAL ESTATE MARKET ANALYSIS IN PROJECT-LEVEL PLANNING

Real estate market research is generally applicable in project-level planning. A real estate project, like the strategic planning process, can be thought of as progressing through stages until final disposition of the property. Because a real estate project can be acquired and disposed of at any time during development, managerial entities/decision makers may enter or leave the project at any stage.

For the purpose of depicting the sequences of project stages, major decision points, and information required, three principal types of real estate projects can be envisioned:

1. *Initial Development Project*: A "new" project involves development of site and/or buildings to accommodate a specific use or uses. Typically, beginning with "raw" land, the project goes to a maintenance stage when permanent occupancy occurs. Thus, it goes through all initial "life-cycle" stages.
2. *Acquisition of Ongoing Project*: The typical circumstance for investment entities and non−real estate corporations, the project involves considering why current revenue, expense, and profit levels exist and what must be done to maintain or improve them. Thus, while the development process has already occurred, some aspects of physical development planning are necessary to provide a strategy for profitable occupancy during the period the asset is held and managed.
3. *Redevelopment or Expansion Project*: This involves a project which requires additional development effort to extend the asset's economic life and maintain or improve its profitability and value. It may involve fewer developmental stages than a new project, or it may require virtually all developmental stages to be replanned and reimplemented. In some cases additional stages such as demolition of existing improvements may be added.

The typical stages for each type of project as it moves from acquisition to disposition are depicted in Exhibit 2-3. Also shown in Exhibit 2-3 are the decisions required to move the project on to the next stage and the types of information required for such decisions.

Regardless of the type of project, the basic sequence of events or stages that moves the project toward a successful conclusion is similar. Informational input, consequently, requires the same basic focus and arrangement with respect to project decision making for any real estate project, although nuances and specific technical aspects of the decision may be quite different. General market analysis guides subsequent site selection and marketability studies, and those elements, in turn, lay the basis for devising a market plan and a marketing strategy. Because the market concerns are pervasive in every stage of project development, the market analyst plays a key role in overall strategy and decision making.

In any project some form of physical evaluation, planning, and construction must be considered. In the Initial Development Project, physical elements are the major concern of several earlier stages. Once actual construction begins, a "commitment point" is reached because the level of equity capital invested, debt financing, and unretractable resources employed would result in significant losses if the owners were unable to complete the project on a reasonable schedule. Sunk costs resulting from immovable and nonreusable improvements associated with land and building construction account for most of the capital invested in the project at this point. Ultimate revenues to amortize these costs and produce a profitable project are realized only after the project is completed and productive occupancy of the premises occurs. Once the com-

Exhibit 2-3 Project-Level Planning: Stages, Decisions, Informational Inputs

TYPICAL SEQUENTIAL STAGE	DECISION NEEDED TO MOVE TO NEXT STAGE	MAJOR INFORMATIONAL INPUTS REQUIRED FOR DECISION
I. Initial Development Project		
Project inception	Determine need and opportunity to acquire project and undertake actual development	*Market*—general market analysis *Financial*—preliminary economic feasibility *Managerial*—internal resource survey: goals and objectives
Site selection and acquisition	Acquire site and undertake site improvements	*Physical*—site analysis and land capability study; site-selection plan *Legal/regulatory*—conditions of sale; standards, costs, procedures for regulatory compliance and public services; zoning approval *Financial*—plan for financing acquisition
Site planning and construction of site improvements	Determine quality and quantity of land infrastructure to support planned uses on site	*Market*—marketability analysis *Physical*—site-development plan *Legal/regulatory*—plot approvals, utility and service connections *Financial*—acquisition and development loans *Managerial*—site-development construction management plan
Architectural planning and building construction	Determine quality, quantity, and timing of structural improvements to support planned uses	*Market*—market plan, including targets for mix of units, market share, absorption rates *Physical*—architectural plans *Financial*—building construction loan, economic feasibility analysis *Legal/regulatory*—building permit and code approvals *Managerial*—building construction management plan
Marketing to initial permanent owners	Method and conditions of sales/occupancy	*Market*—marketing strategy *Financial*—GAP financing; arrangements for permanent financing *Legal/regulatory*—closing plans and documents
Initial and continued occupancy	Method and conditions of maintenance disposition	*Legal/regulatory*—occupancy and licensing code compliance *Market*—marketing strategy monitoring and updating tenant mix, lease structure *Financial*—permanent financing cash management plan, disposition plan *Managerial*—asset management/ property management plan

Exhibit 2-3 *Continued.*

TYPICAL SEQUENTIAL STAGE	*DECISION NEEDED TO MOVE TO NEXT STAGE*	*MAJOR INFORMATIONAL INPUTS REQUIRED FOR DECISION*
II. Acquisition of Ongoing Project		
Project inception	Determine need and opportunity to acquire project	*Market*—general market analysis *Financial*—preliminary economic feasibility *Managerial*—internal resource survey; goals and objectives
Project selection and acquisition	Project selection and acquisition	*Market*—marketability analysis *Financial*—plan for financing acquisition and improvements *Physical*—locational and architectural capability analysis *Legal/regulatory*—rezoning strategy; code compliance analysis plan
Renovation planning and construction	Determine quality, and timing of improvements to support/maintain	*Market*—market plan *Physical*—architectural improvement plan *Financial*—construction loan; economic feasibility analysis *Legal/regulatory*—building permit and code approvals *Managerial*—construction management plan
III. Redevelopment of Expansion Project		
Project inception	Determine need and opportunity to redevelop or expand project	*Market*—market analysis *Financial*—preliminary economic feasibility *Managerial*—internal resource survey; goals and objectives
Identification and planning of redevelopment/ expansion elements	Determine specific needs, costs, and benefits for redevelopment of expansion	*Market*—marketability analysis *Physical*—architectural alternatives and value engineering studies *Financial*—cost analysis of alternatives *Legal/regulatory*—rezoning strategy; code compliance plan
Demolition and reconstruction	Determine quantity, quality, and timing of improvements to support planned uses	*Market*—market plan *Physical*—architectural improvement plan *Financial*—construction loan economic feasibility analysis *Legal/regulatory*—building permit and code approvals *Managerial*—construction management plan

TYPICAL SEQUENTIAL STAGE	DECISION NEEDED TO MOVE TO NEXT STAGE	MAJOR INFORMATIONAL INPUTS REQUIRED FOR DECISION
III. Redevelopment or Expansion Project—Continued		
Continued and expanded occupancy	Method and conditions for occupancy maintenance and disposition	*Legal/regulatory*—occupancy and licensing code compliance *Market*—marketing strategy, with monitoring and updating *Financial*—permanent financing, cash management plan, disposition plan *Managerial*—asset management property management plan

Exhibit 2-3 *Continued.*

mitment point is reached, the basic risk management technique shifts from information gathering and cost minimization to technical planning and time minimization. Time minimization or optimization is essential to minimize labor costs, the major contributor to total construction costs, and to assure proper timing of the project into the market. Thus, the quantity, quality, and phasing targets established by the market plan guide the schedules, design, and costs of the entire project during these critical periods. The market strategist who establishes and monitors these targets is intricately involved in the managerial strategy and control process.

READINGS

BREALEY, RICHARD, and STEWART MYERS, *Principles of Corporate Finance*. New York: McGraw-Hill, 1984.

BROWN, ROBERT K., *Corporate Real Estate: Executive Strategies for Profit Making*. Homewood, Ill.: Dow Jones-Irwin, 1979.

GRAASKAMP, JAMES A., *Fundamentals of Real Estate Development*, Monograph, Urban Land Institute, Development Component Series. Washington, D.C.: Urban Land Institute, 1981.

HALPIN, MICHAEL C., *Profit Planning for Real Estate Development*. Homewood, Ill.: Dow Jones-Irwin, 1977.

MESCON, MICHAEL H., and others, *Management*. New York: Harper and Row, 1985.

VERNOR, JAMES D., *An Introduction to Risk Management in Property Development*, Monograph, Urban Land Institute, Development Component Series. Washington, D.C.: Urban Land Institute, 1981.

3

ANALYZING THE LOCAL ECONOMIC ENVIRONMENT

ANALYSIS OF THE LOCAL ECONOMY[1]

The market analysis process consists of three major tasks. First, the local economy is analyzed with regard to the nature and size of its economic activity in the current period and a forecast of future activity is made. Second, market demand and supply factors are analyzed to understand current and future market activity for the property market in which the subject property competes. Third, the specific characteristics of the space and services provided by the subject property are analyzed and compared to competitive properties to assess its ability to compete in the market. The first of these three components of the market analysis process is discussed in this chapter. The other two components are discussed in Chapter 4 and in subsequent chapters.

The local demands for housing, retail, and office space are determined in part by the economic growth of the community. Market analysts seldom prepare detailed and complete analyses of local economic conditions. Instead, they generally use studies prepared by planning commissions or other public agencies. The output of such studies usually includes current employment and population estimates and forecasts which encompass changes in employment and population. Such data are basic inputs to the analyses of local housing, retail, and office space needs. The market analyst uses these estimates and forecasts, often with adjustments to reflect updated information or when observable facts and trends indicate that changes have occurred which the published conclusions do not consider. The market analyst should understand the methodology used in the published forecast, so that adjustments can be made, or an independent forecast can be prepared when necessary.

An analysis of the local economy consists of three steps. First, the geographic boundaries of the local economy must be identified. Second, the nature and size of its economic activity has to be identified. Third, the changes in level and composition of the economic activity are forecast. These provide the basis for forecasting the change in the level of demand for space.

Defining the Local Economy

For convenience of analysis, the geographic boundaries of local economy are often defined by political boundaries, such as townships, cities, or counties for which data are available from secondary sources such as the U.S. Census. Sometimes cities cross county lines, or they may be independent entities. But, for the most part, cities are political jurisdictions located within the boundaries

---

[1] Material in this section is taken with permission from Donald R. Epley and Joseph Rabianski, *Principles of Real Estate Decisions* (Englewood Cliffs, N.J.: Prentice-Hall, 1986), Chapter 7, "Housing Market Analysis," pp. 211–215.

of a county. The relationship among these concepts is shown in Exhibit 3-1. The local economy also may be delimited using geographic areas defined by the census, such as the combination of cities and counties referred to as a Metropolitan Statistical Area (MSA) or by a combination of census tracts that comprise part of an MSA. MSAs are referred to as Primary Metropolitan Statistical Areas (PMSAs) when they meet additional criteria. The MSA and PMSA criteria are presented in Exhibit 3-2.

The concept of functional integration is central in the definition of a local economy. Simply stated, functional integration refers to the important economic links that exist between the different political-geographic subareas in

Exhibit 3-1 Census Divisions in Metropolitan Areas.

SOURCE: U.S. Bureau of the Census, Washington, D.C.

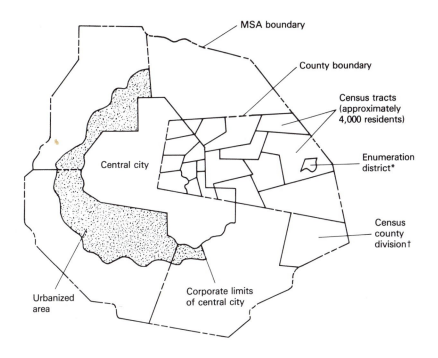

*EDs contain approximately 800 persons or 250 housing units. EDs are revised each census for operational reasons. In urbanized areas the ED counterpart is the block group (BG), which contains approximately 1,000 persons. The BG is composed of census "blocks" that conform to the common use of the work—a physical area that is rectangular or square.

†CCDs are permanent subdivisions of a county. They were established for areas that did not have local political subdivisions such as townships or MCDs (minor civil divisions).

Exhibit 3-2 Metropolitan Area Designations, 1980 Census.

A. *Definition of a Metropolitan Statistical Area*
    The basic criteria for an MSA designation are that the area

    1. Include a city with an urbanized area of 50,000.
    2. Have a total population of 100,000, unless it also contains a city of 50,000. If the city has at least 50,000 population, the 100,000 total population minimum is waived.

    Central counties must have 50 percent or more of their population in the urbanized area of the central city (or cities). They must also have at least 2,500 population in the central city (cities) of the MSA.
    Additional outlying counties are included if any one of the following criteria are met:

    1. Fifty percent of the residents in the county commute to the central county, and the population density is at least 25 persons per square mile.
    2. Forty to 50 percent of the employed workers living in the county commute to the central county, and the population density is at least 35 persons per square mile.
    3. Twenty-five to 40 percent of the employed workers in the county commute to the central county, plus any one of the following:
        a. The population density is at least 50 persons per square mile.
        b. At least 35 percent of the population is urban.
        c. At least 10 percent (or 5,000) of the population lives in the urbanized area.
    4. At least 15 percent of the employed workers commute to the central county, plus any two of the following:
        a. The population density is at least 60 persons per square mile.
        b. At least 35 percent of the population is urban.
        c. Population growth between the last two decennial censuses is at least 20 percent.
        d. At least 10 percent of the population lives in the urbanized area.

    There is a four-tier hierarchy of MSAs.
    Level A: MSAs over 1 million in population
    Level B: MSAs of 250,000 to 1,000,000
    Level C: MSAs of 100,000 to 250,000
    Level D: MSAs of less than 100,000

B. *Definition of a Primary Metropolitan Statistical Area*
    The basic criterion for a PMSA is its inclusion in a metropolitan area as a Level-A MSA. One or more PMSAs can be designated in an MSA if the following criteria are met by a county:

    1. Population equals 100,000 or more.
    2. No part of the central city lies within the county.
    3. Sixty percent or more of the population is urban.
    4. Sixty-five percent or more of the resident workers are employed in the county.

    When a Level-A MSA contains one or more PMSAs, it is designated as a Consolidated Metropolitan Statistical Area (CMSA).

a local economy. As an example, the counties that constitute the MSA are functionally integrated because of a significant commuter flow from the peripheral counties to the central county in the MSA. The definition for the Metropolitan Statistical Area provided in Exhibit 3-2 reveals this important integration concept. Notice that outlying counties are included in the MSA if the level of commuter traffic from the outlying county to the central county is 50 percent under the first condition and 15 percent under the fourth condition. The market analyst may establish boundaries for the market area to be studied by using the geographic area for which data are available or, when necessary, make estimates for split areas.

As part of the local area economic analysis, the analyst examines the characteristics of the local population to get its demographic profile and income characteristics. The U.S. Census is the normal starting point for this part of the analysis. Exhibit 3-3 lists the demographic characteristics contained in the U.S. Census. Exhibit 3-4 lists the social characteristics. Exhibit 3-5 identifies the income characteristics, and Exhibit 3-6 presents the labor force characteristics of the population. These topics are discussed in more detail in subsequent parts of this chapter.

Understanding Economic Activity

A simple economic model known as the circular flow-of-income model provides a concept of major components of the local economy. The relationships in this model are directly related to the concepts of economic base analysis, export base theory, and interindustry relationships (the input-output model).

The Circular Flow-of-Income Model   The internal structure of a local economy comprises three major sectors: the household sector, the business sector, and the government sector. For the sake of simplicity, the government sector, which acts to redistribute income earned by other sectors, is dropped from consideration so that the focus of attention can be placed on the interrelationships between the household sector and the business sector. In this simple model, the local economy is assumed to be a closed economy with no exchange of goods or dollar payments with the rest of the world.

The household sector in the local economy undertakes two activities simultaneously. First, the household sector consists of all individuals and households that own the factors of production. For purposes of analysis, the household sector is assumed to be local residents who

1. Provide labor services to the industries located within the local economy.
2. Own land in the local economy.
3. Own all the capital goods and capital funds, used locally.
4. Provide entrepreneurial talent to local firms.

Exhibit 3-3 Demographic Characteristics in the Census.

SOURCE: U.S. Department of Commerce, Bureau of the Census, *1980 Census of Population and Housing,* Census Tracts, for Atlanta, Georgia.

Census Tracts

	Tract 0501	Gwinnett County
AGE		
Total persons	**12 138**	**166 903**
Under 5 years	886	13 907
5 to 9 years	983	15 606
10 to 14 years	1 123	15 606
15 to 19 years	1 090	13 533
20 to 24 years	1 094	13 087
25 to 34 years	1 930	36 533
35 to 44 years	1 523	25 834
45 to 54 years	1 203	14 441
55 to 64 years	1 017	9 793
65 to 74 years	791	5 547
75 years and over	498	3 016
3 and 4 years	365	5 478
16 years and over	8 922	118 743
18 years and over	8 459	112 926
21 years and over	7 836	105 960
60 years and over	1 763	12 769
62 years and over	1 579	10 871
Median	29 5	28 5
Female	**6 266**	**84 108**
Under 5 years	444	6 758
5 to 9 years	453	7 602
10 to 14 years	550	7 590
15 to 19 years	555	6 704
20 to 24 years	568	6 855
25 to 34 years	951	18 843
35 to 44 years	788	12 475
45 to 54 years	619	6 961
55 to 64 years	550	5 126
65 to 74 years	454	3 165
75 years and over	334	2 029
3 and 4 years	183	2 677
16 years and over	4 701	60 634
18 years and over	4 469	57 807
21 years and over	4 149	54 272
60 years and over	1 056	7 401
62 years and over	955	6 423
Median	30 6	28 8
HOUSEHOLD TYPE AND RELATIONSHIP		
Total persons	**12 138**	**166 903**
In households	12 001	165 937
Householder	4 097	55 227
Family householder	3 336	46 617
Nonfamily householder	761	8 610
Living alone	670	7 002
Spouse	2 790	41 514
Other relatives	4 907	66 207
Nonrelatives	207	2 989
Inmate of institution	123	923
Other in group quarters	14	43
Persons per household	2 93	3 00
Persons per family	3 31	3 31
Persons 65 years and over	**1 289**	**8 563**
In households	1 178	8 108
Householder	782	4 944
Nonfamily householder	328	1 868
Living alone	318	1 802
Spouse	254	1 756
Other relatives	128	1 339
Nonrelatives	14	69
Inmate of institution	111	444
Other in group quarters	–	11
FAMILY TYPE BY PRESENCE OF OWN CHILDREN		
Families	**3 336**	**46 617**
With own children under 18 years	1 745	28 124
Number of own children under 18 years	3 250	50 980
Married-couple families	**2 790**	**41 514**
With own children under 18 years	1 450	25 015
Number of own children under 18 years	2 746	45 869
Female householder, no husband present	**438**	**4 088**
With own children under 18 years	239	2 642
Number of own children under 18 years	429	4 399
MARITAL STATUS		
Male, 15 years and over	**4 327**	**59 626**
Single	991	12 661
Now married, except separated	2 887	42 588
Separated	54	570
Widowed	117	702
Divorced	278	3 105
Female, 15 years and over	**4 819**	**62 158**
Single	807	9 977
Now married, except separated	2 881	42 462
Separated	106	787
Widowed	649	4 478
Divorced	376	4 454

Exhibit 3-4 Social Characteristics in the Census.

SOURCE: U.S. Department of Commerce, Bureau of the Census, *1980 Census of Population and Housing.* Census Tracts, for Atlanta, Georgia.

Census Tracts

	Tract 0501	Gwinnett County
NATIVITY AND PLACE OF BIRTH		
Total persons	12 129	166 903
Native	12 014	164 143
Born in State of residence	9 868	99 067
Born in different State	2 102	64 214
Born abroad, at sea, etc.	44	862
Foreign born	115	2 760
LANGUAGE SPOKEN AT HOME AND ABILITY TO SPEAK ENGLISH		
Persons 5 to 17 years	2 760	40 111
Speak a language other than English at home	37	954
Percent who speak English not well or not at all	–	5.0
Persons 18 years and over	8 480	112 911
Speak a language other than English at home	101	3 231
Percent who speak English not well or not at all	13.9	7.4
SCHOOL ENROLLMENT AND TYPE OF SCHOOL		
Persons 3 years old and over enrolled in school	2 951	48 195
Nursery school	121	2 596
Private	58	2 122
Kindergarten	218	4 020
Private	55	1 369
Elementary (1 to 8 years)	1 710	25 119
Private	28	918
High school (1 to 4 years)	684	10 372
Private	–	403
College	218	6 088
YEARS OF SCHOOL COMPLETED		
Persons 25 years old and over	6 973	95 185
Elementary: 0 to 4 years	480	2 297
5 to 7 years	1 174	5 814
8 years	457	4 116
High school: 1 to 3 years	1 783	14 664
4 years	1 871	31 351
College: 1 to 3 years	706	18 959
4 or more years	502	17 984
Percent high school graduates	44.2	71.7
FERTILITY		
Women 35 to 44 years	785	12 451
Children ever born	1 837	28 832
Per 1,000 women	2 340	2 316
RESIDENCE IN 1975		
Persons 5 years and over	11 111	152 809
Same house	6 046	62 796
Different house in United States	5 005	88 821
Central city of this SMSA	25	3 658
Remainder of this SMSA	3 594	53 547
Outside this SMSA	1 386	31 616
Different SMSA	797	24 183
Not in an SMSA	589	7 433
Abroad	60	1 272
JOURNEY TO WORK		
Workers 16 years and over	5 295	82 419
Private vehicle: Drive alone	3 094	60 094
Carpool	1 907	18 649
Public transportation	46	1 094
Bus or streetcar	5	769
Subway, elevated train, or railroad	–	217
Walked only	144	751
Other means	42	896
Worked at home	62	935
Persons per private vehicle	1.30	1.15
Mean travel time to work ... minutes	26.5	26.4
Worked in SMSA of residence	4 529	75 533
Atlanta city—central business district	41	2 950
Remainder of Atlanta city (pt.)	232	9 294
East Point city	11	238
Remainder of Fulton County	184	2 807
Atlanta city (pt.)	50	1 609
Remainder of De Kalb County	1 007	27 158
Butts County	–	
Cherokee County	–	29
Clayton County	37	748
Marietta city	29	410
Remainder of Cobb County	50	488
Douglas County	–	26
Fayette County	–	6
Forsyth County	65	169
Gwinnett County	2 823	28 873
Henry County	–	51
Newton County	–	24
Paulding County	–	
Rockdale County	–	318
Walton County	–	335
Worked outside SMSA of residence	283	1 768
Place of work not reported	372	5 187

Exhibit 3-5 Income Characteristics in the Census.

SOURCE: U.S. Department of Commerce, Bureau of the Census, *1980 Census of Population and Housing*, Census Tracts, for Atlanta, Georgia.

Census Tracts

	Tract 0501	Gwinnett County
INCOME IN 1979		
Households	**4 116**	**55 339**
Less than $5,000	494	3 471
$5,000 to $7,499	410	2 085
$7,500 to $9,999	388	2 405
$10,000 to $14,999	758	6 895
$15,000 to $19,999	661	7 755
$20,000 to $24,999	598	8 809
$25,000 to $34,999	538	13 631
$35,000 to $49,999	192	7 657
$50,000 or more	77	2 631
Median	$15 054	$22 572
Mean	$16 898	$24 578
Owner-occupied households	**3 045**	**43 449**
Median income	$17 053	$25 175
Mean income	$18 549	$26 773
Renter-occupied households	**1 071**	**11 890**
Median income	$10 826	$15 249
Mean income	$12 202	$16 558
Families	**3 377**	**46 839**
Median income	$16 535	$24 327
Mean income	$18 240	$26 179
Unrelated individuals 15 years and over	**947**	**11 093**
Median income	$6 628	$10 256
Mean income	$8 555	$12 089
Per capita income	**$5 748**	**$8 167**
INCOME TYPE IN 1979		
Households	**4 116**	**55 339**
With earnings	3 452	51 242
Mean earnings	$17 036	$24 425
With Social Security income	1 062	7 614
Mean Social Security income	$4 128	$4 004
With public assistance income	269	1 614
Mean public assistance income	$2 055	$2 200
MEAN FAMILY INCOME IN 1979 BY FAMILY TYPE		
Families	**$18 240**	**$26 179**
With own children under 18 years	$19 019	$26 736
Without own children under 18 years	$17 434	$25 327
Married-couple families	**$19 241**	**$27 372**
With own children under 18 years	$20 636	$28 174
Without own children under 18 years	$17 869	$26 149
Female householder, no husband present	**$12 982**	**$14 867**
With own children under 18 years	$11 423	$13 710
Without own children under 18 years	$15 184	$16 825
ALL INCOME LEVELS IN 1979		
Families	**3 377**	**46 839**
Householder worked in 1979	2 750	42 459
With related children under 18 years	1 899	29 305
Female householder no husband present	468	4 061
Householder worked in 1979	345	3 339
With related children under 18 years	336	2 833
With related children under 6 years	107	839
Householder 65 years and over	431	3 029
Unrelated individuals for whom poverty status is determined	**947**	**11 093**
65 years and over	331	1 868
Persons for whom poverty status is determined	**11 992**	**165 840**
Under 18 years	3 635	53 848
Related children under 18 years	3 628	53 676
Related children 5 to 17 years	2 739	39 804
18 to 59 years	6 680	99 570
60 years and over	1 677	12 422
65 years and over	1 193	8 117
INCOME IN 1979 BELOW POVERTY LEVEL		
Families	**347**	**2 103**
Percent below poverty level	10.3	4.5
Householder worked in 1979	236	1 360
With related children under 18 years	247	1 338
Female householder no husband present	73	467
Householder worked in 1979	48	323
With related children under 18 years	69	375
With related children under 6 years	43	164
Householder 65 years and over	43	415
Unrelated individuals for whom poverty status is determined	**310**	**2 136**
Percent below poverty level	32.7	19.3
65 years and over	141	856
Persons for whom poverty status is determined	**1 616**	**9 269**
Percent below poverty level	13.5	5.6
Under 18 years	578	3 029
Related children under 18 years	578	2 962
Related children 5 to 17 years	438	2 184
18 to 59 years	767	4 204
60 years and over	271	2 036
65 years and over	207	1 598
INCOME IN 1979 BELOW SPECIFIED POVERTY LEVEL		
Percent of persons for whom poverty status is determined:		
Below 75 percent of poverty level	9.9	3.8
Below 125 percent of poverty level	20.3	8.1
Below 150 percent of poverty level	24.3	10.6
Below 200 percent of poverty level	37.7	17.3

Exhibit 3-6 Labor Force Characteristics in the Census.

SOURCE: U.S. Department of Commerce, Bureau of the Census, *1980 Census of Population and Housing*, Census Tracts, for Atlanta, Georgia.

Census Tracts

	Tract 0501	Gwinnett County
LABOR FORCE STATUS		
Persons 16 years and over	8 927	118 836
Labor force	5 816	86 607
Percent of persons 16 years and over	65.2	72.9
Civilian labor force	5 803	86 559
Employed	5 454	83 974
Unemployed	349	2 585
Percent of civilian labor force	6.0	3.0
Female, 16 years and over	4 724	60 714
Labor force	2 649	36 470
Percent of female, 16 years and over	56.1	60.1
Civilian labor force	2 649	36 470
Employed	2 496	35 110
Unemployed	153	1 360
Percent of civilian labor force	5.8	3.7
With own children under 6 years	797	12 658
In labor force	480	6 272
Married, husband present	2 836	41 937
In labor force	1 616	24 641
Civilian persons 16 to 19 years	845	10 601
Not enrolled in school	376	3 490
Not high school graduate	163	1 534
Employed	73	922
Unemployed	19	141
Not in labor force	71	471
OCCUPATION AND SELECTED INDUSTRIES		
Employed persons 16 years and over	5 454	83 974
Managerial and professional specialty occupations	813	21 761
Executive, administrative, and managerial occupations	469	12 861
Professional specialty occupations	344	8 900
Technical, sales, and administrative support occupations	1 462	31 467
Technicians and related support occupations	118	2 812
Sales occupations	405	10 713
Administrative support occupations, including clerical	939	17 942
Service occupations	720	6 614
Private household occupations	36	305
Protective service occupations	126	1 028
Service occupations, except protective and household	558	5 281
Farming, forestry, and fishing occupations	61	609
Precision production, craft, and repair occupations	1 012	11 353
Operators, fabricators, and laborers	1 386	12 170
Machine operators, assemblers, and inspectors	953	6 727
Transportation and material moving occupations	214	2 765
Handlers, equipment cleaners, helpers, and laborers	219	2 678
Manufacturing	1 806	18 744
Wholesale and retail trade	1 068	20 023
Professional and related services	767	12 232
CLASS OF WORKER		
Private wage and salary workers	4 454	69 726
Government workers	668	9 789
Local government workers	368	5 440
Self-employed workers	326	4 172
LABOR FORCE STATUS IN 1979		
Persons 16 years and over, in labor force in 1979	6 218	92 673
Percent of persons 16 years and over	69.7	78.0
Worked in 1979	6 136	92 107
40 or more weeks	4 593	72 826
Usually worked 35 or more hours per week	4 141	66 754
50 to 52 weeks	3 778	62 834
Usually worked 35 or more hours per week	3 456	58 779
With unemployment in 1979	1 003	12 272
Percent of those in labor force in 1979	16.1	13.2
Unemployed 15 or more weeks	324	2 877
Mean weeks of unemployment	12.0	10.4
DISABILITY STATUS OF NONINSTITUTIONAL PERSONS		
Male, 16 to 64 years	3 694	54 369
With a work disability	512	3 811
Not in labor force	261	1 645
Prevented from working	250	1 450
Female, 16 to 64 years	3 917	55 429
With a work disability	455	3 388
Not in labor force	307	2 341
Prevented from working	292	1 910
Persons 16 to 64 years	7 611	109 798
With a public transportation disability	138	1 444
With a work disability	126	1 354
Persons 65 years and over	1 193	8 117
With a public transportation disability	159	1 344
WORKERS IN FAMILY IN 1979		
No workers	365	2 288
Mean family income	$10 562	$10 887
1 worker	974	13 451
Mean family income	$14 896	$21 365
2 workers	1 632	25 312
Mean family income	$19 693	$27 700
3 or more workers	406	5 788
Mean family income	$27 321	$36 760

The factors of production are sold to the business sector. In return, the household receives wages for its labor services, rent for the use of its land, dividends, or [economic rent] for the use of its capital goods, interest payment for the use of its capital funds, and profits for the application of its entrepreneurial ability. These relationships are shown in Exhibit 3-7. Exhibit 3-7A identifies the real flows—the movement of productive services from the household to the business sector. Exhibit 3-7B shows the money flows—the movement of factor payments in the form of wages, rents, interest, dividends, and· profits from the business sector to the household sector.

At the same time that the household sector is providing factors of production to the business sector, it is also purchasing consumer goods and services that the business sector produced. This relationship is shown in Exhibit 3-7A as the movement of goods and services from the business sector to the household sector. It is shown in Exhibit 3-7B as the flow of money in the form of consumption expenditures from the household to business sector.

The business sector, like the household sector, also simultaneously performs two functions in the local economy. First, it uses the produtive resources. Second, it produces the consumer and capital goods and services that are purchased by the businesses and individuals in the household sector.

The circular flow-of-income model presented in this form reveals that the

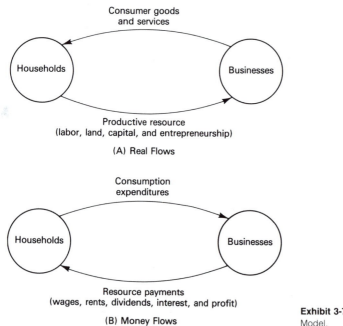

Exhibit 3-7 The Circular Flow-of-Income Model.

local economy is made up of two major sectors and is interrelated by two real flows and two money flows that reflect those real flows. Understanding the composition of the sectors and the composition of the flows is the first and major conceptual step in understanding the nature of the economic activity in the local economy.

The Economic Base of the Local Economy

The economic base of the local economy is the complex of activities that comprise the household and business sectors and the flows in the circular flow-of-income model. The household sector can be described by identifying key variables, such as

1. Size of the population, the number of families, the number of households.
2. Age composition of the population, heads of families, and heads of households.
3. Income composition of the population, families, and households.
4. Size of families and households.
5. Occupational composition of the population.
6. Sex composition of the population.
7. Marital status of the population.
8. Educational level of the population.
9. Other variables needed for specific types of analysis.

This information can be obtained from the *Census of Population.* It is often readily accessible from publications of local planning agencies. Examples of this information have been given in Exhibits 3-3, 3-4, 3-5, and 3-6. These characteristics are very important when analyzing spending patterns and, hence, the demand for space.

The structure of the business sector can be described by identifying the industrial classifications that exist in the local economy. This can be accomplished by means of the Standard Industrial Classification (SIC) system developed and used by the Bureau of the Census. The SIC system identifies industrial activity according to a numerical code of one to four digits that expresses the type of industrial activity that can occur in an economy. Exhibit 3-8 presents a breakdown of the one-digit SIC categories and provides partial information on some of the two-, three-, and four-digit components. The SIC system is important in analyzing employment growth which influences the demand for production space, which impacts household income.

The real flows and the money flows identified in Exhibit 3-7 for consumer goods are closely related. However, it is easier to obtain information on the money flow entitled "consumption expenditures" than it is to obtain a list of the consumer goods and services themselves. Therefore, the information

3 digit	4 digit
201 Meat products	
	2011 Meat-packing plants
	2012
	2013 Sausages and other prepared meat products
	2016 Poultry dressing plants
	2017 Poultry and egg processing
202 Dairy products	
(Remainder of 20 series and 21 to	2021 Creamery butter
34 series omitted here)	2022 Cheese
	2023 Condensed and evaporated milk
	2024 Ice cream and frozen desserts
	2026 Fluid milk
351 Engines and turbines	[4-digit breakdown omitted here]
352 Farm and garden machinery	
353 Construction and related machinery	
354 Metalworking machinery	
355 Special industry machinery	
356 General industrial machinery	
357 Office and computing machines	
358 Refrigeration and service machinery	
359 Miscellaneous machinery	
361 Electric distribution equipment	[4-digit breakdown omitted here]
362 Electrical industrial apparatus	
363 Household appliances	
364 Electric lighting and wiring equipment	
365 Radio and TV receiving equipment	
366 Communication and equipment	
367 Electronic components and accessories	
368 Miscellaneous electrical equipment and supplies	
371 Motor vehicles and equipment	
	3711 Motor vehicles and passenger car bodies
	3712
	3713 Truck and bus bodies
	3714 Motor vehicle parts and accessories
	3715 Truck trailers
372 Aircraft and parts	[4-digit breakdown omitted here]
373 Ship and boat building	
374 Railroad equipment	
375 Motorcycles, bicycles, and parts	
376 Guided missiles and space vehicles and parts	
379 Miscellaneous transportation equipment	
(Remainder of 38 and 39 series omitted here)	

Exhibit 3-8 Standard Industrial Classification.

presented in Exhibit 3-9 can be obtained for Metropolitan Statistical Areas and counties from the *Census of Retail Trade* to describe the composition of this flow. The composition of retail trade for a specific Metropolitan Statistical Area is broken down by two- and three-digit SIC codes.

The nature and composition of the productive resource flow and the resource payments flow can also be obtained from government publications. First, the workers can be identified by the type of industry in which they work.

	1 digit	2 digit
Division A	0 Agriculture, forestry, fisheries	
Division B	1 Mining	
Division C	1 Construction	
Division D	2 Manufacturing (nondurable)	
		20 Food products
		21 Tobacco manufactures
		22 Textile mill products
		23 Apparel products
		24 Lumber and wood products
		25 Furniture and fixtures
		26 Paper products
		27 Printing, publishing industries
		28 Chemicals
		29 Petroleum refining
Division D	3 Manufacturing (durable)	
		30 Rubber and plastics
		31 Leather
		32 Stone, clay, glass, concrete
		33 Primary metals
		34 Fabricated metals
		35 Machinery, except electrical
		36 Electrical and electronic machinery
		37 Transportation equipment
		38 Instruments, photographic goods, optical goods, watches, and clocks
		39 Miscellaneous
Division E	4 Transportation, communication, utilities (electric, gas, sanitary services)	
Division F	5 Wholesale trade	
Division G	5 Retail trade	
Division H	6 Finance, Insurance, and real estate	
Division I	7 Services (personal, business)	
Division I	8 Services (professional, educational)	
Division J	9 Public administration (federal, state, and local government agencies)	
Division K	Nonclassifiable establishments	

Exhibit 3-8 *Continued.*

This method would yield information about the number of workers in the manufacturing industries (durable and nondurable goods) as well as in the retail and wholesale industries. The *Census of Population* provides the number of employees by one-digit SIC codes for MSAs and counties. An example of this information is given in Exhibit 3-6. Similar information can also be obtained from state offices on a county basis. Second, the labor force can be identified by its skill level and job orientation. This method would yield information about the number of

Table 1. **Statistics by Kind of Business for Major Retail Centers, Central Business Districts, Cities With Central Business Districts, and the Standard Metropolitan Statistical Area: 1982**

[For meaning of abbreviations and symbols, see introductory text For definition of SMSA, see appendix D For descriptions of MRC and CBD boundaries, see appendix I]

SIC code	Kind of business	Standard metropolitan statistical area	Atlanta City	Central business district	Major retail centers No 1	No 2	No 3	No 4	No 5	No 6
	Retail stores:									
	Number	16 422	3 534	397	212	188	64	44	146	51
	Sales ($1,000)	11 257 375	2 447 705	245 594	245 456	268 646	38 965	35 890	(D)	58 438
	Annual payroll ($1,000)	1 328 147	344 233	48 338	29 617	29 961	5 667	4 920	20 866	8 865
	Paid employees for pay period including March 12, 1982	151 981	39 758	6 177	3 400	3 391	595	566	2 727	1 134
	Retail stores (establishments with payroll):									
	Number	11 845	2 804	353	204	184	61	41	144	51
	Sales ($1,000)	11 080 896	2 420 369	243 286	244 809	268 524	38 912	35 345	184 256	58 438
54, 58, 591	**Convenience goods stores:**									
	Number	4 630	1 178	137	73	77	11	17	29	4
	Sales ($1,000)	3 733 936	799 038	82 479	89 521	90 025	(D)	18 831	24 955	3 810
53, 56, 57; 984	**Shopping goods stores (GAF)**:									
	Number	3 316	789	159	72	58	39	13	100	43
	Sales ($1,000)	2 776 702	714 722	141 153	61 179	(D)	(D)	11 622	140 365	53 988
52, 55, 59, ex. 591, 4	**All other stores:**									
	Number	3 899	837	57	59	49	11	11	15	4
	Sales ($1,000)	4 570 258	906 609	19 654	94 109	(D)	2 446	4 892	18 936	640
	NUMBER OF ESTABLISHMENTS									
	Retail stores	16 422	3 534	397	212	188	64	44	146	51
	Retail stores (establishments with payroll)	11 845	2 804	353	204	184	61	41	144	51
52	Building materials, hardware, garden supply, and mobile home dealers	509	74	1	7	7	1	1	1	.
525	Hardware stores	151	24	.	3	2	1	1	.	.
52 ex. 525	Other	358	50	1	4	5	.		1	.
53	General merchandise group stores	250	51	11	3	3	3	1	5	2
531	Department stores (incl leased depts)	95	20	3	2	2	1	1	4	2
531	Department stores (excl leased depts)	95	20	3	2	2	1	1	4	2
533	Variety stores	76	20	5	1		1		1	
539	Miscellaneous general merchandise stores	79	11	3	1	1	1		1	
54	Food stores	1 436	306	25	16	16	4	4	9	1
541	Grocery stores	1 121	221	13	7	12	2	2	1	.
55 ex. 554	Automotive dealers	820	121	1	12	9	2	6	3	.
554	Gasoline service stations	1 138	216	5	18	16	-	1	3	-
56	Apparel and accessory stores	1 209	324	82	19	16	16	5	53	20
561	Men's and boys' clothing and furnishings stores	161	53	18	2	2	3	1	7	1
562, 3, 8	Women's clothing and specialty stores and furriers	461	123	19	8	5	4	1	26	14
562	Women's ready-to-wear stores	398	97	14	8	5	3	1	22	10
565	Family clothing stores	107	19	6	2	1		1	3	
566	Shoe stores	381	97	32	4	8	5		16	3
564, 9	Other apparel and accessory stores	99	32	7	3		4	2	1	2
57	Furniture, home furnishings, and equipment stores	894	175	20	25	21	9	1	14	5
5712	Furniture stores	284	46	8	6	2	3		3	.
5713, 4, 9	Home furnishing stores	265	53	3	8	6	2	1	3	5
572, 3	Household appliance, radio, television, and music stores	345	76	9	11	13	4		8	.
58	Eating and drinking places	2 717	780	100	51	55	4	11	17	3
5812	Eating places	2 508	690	99	48	52	4	9	17	3
5813	Drinking places	209	90	1	3	3		2		.
591	Drug and proprietary stores	477	90	12	6	6	3	2	3	.
59 ex. 591	Miscellaneous retail stores	2 395	885	96	47	35	19	9	36	20
592	Liquor stores	353	134	12	5	3	.			1
594	Miscellaneous shopping goods stores	963	239	48	25	18	11	6	28	16
5944	Jewelry stores	183	48	8	5	3	2	1	6	5
5947	Gift, novelty, and souvenir shops	222	77	25	3	4	5	1	8	4
5949	Sewing, needlework, and piece goods stores	101	17	.	3	2		2		1
5992	Florists	227	48	2	3	1			1	.

See footnotes at end of table

Exhibit 3-9 *Continued.*

Table 2. Statistics by Kind of Business for Central Business Districts in the Standard Metropolitan Statistical Area: 1982

[For meaning of abbreviations and symbols, see introductory text. For definition of terms "adjusted" and "unadjusted" and for indication of comparability of 1982 CBD data and 1977 CBD data, see Comparability of 1977 and 1982 Censuses in appendix A. For definition of SMSA, see appendix D. For comparative CBD sales statistics, 1977 and 1982, see appendix H. For description of CBD boundaries, see appendix I.]

SIC code	Kind of business	Establishments		Sales		Annual payroll		First quarter payroll		Paid employees for pay period including March 12	
		Adjusted (number)	Unadjusted (number)	Adjusted ($1,000)	Unadjusted ($1,000)	Adjusted ($1,000)	Unadjusted ($1,000)	Adjusted ($1,000)	Unadjusted ($1,000)	Adjusted (number)	Unadjusted (number)
	ATLANTA CBD										
	Retail stores [1][2][3]	387	388	245 594	238 476	48 338	46 787	12 036	11 719	6 177	6 018
	Retail stores (establishments with payroll) [2]	353	346	243 296	236 304	48 338	46 787	12 036	11 719	6 177	6 018
52	Building materials, hardware, garden supply, and mobile home dealers	1	1	(D)	(D)	(D)	(D)	(D)	(D)	(D)	(D)
525	Hardware stores	.	.	.	.	.	.	.	.	.	.
52 ex. 525	Other	1	1	(D)	(D)	(D)	(D)	(D)	(D)	(D)	(D)
53	General merchandise group stores	11	11	79 852	79 852	11 716	11 716	3 057	3 057	1 449	1 449
531	Department stores (incl. leased depts.) [5][6]	3	3	(D)	(D)	(NA)	(NA)	(NA)	(NA)	(NA)	(NA)
531	Department stores (excl. leased depts.) [6]	3	3	(D)	(D)	(D)	(D)	(D)	(D)	(D)	(D)
533	Variety stores	5	5	(D)	(D)	(D)	(D)	(D)	(D)	(D)	(D)
539	Miscellaneous general merchandise stores	3	3	174	174	52	52	10	10	3	3
54	Food stores [4]	25	24	8 665	8 664	1 261	1 260	312	312	150	149
541	Grocery stores	13	12	6 839	6 838	803	802	203	203	106	107
55 ex. 554	Automotive dealers	1	1	(D)	(D)	(D)	(D)	(D)	(D)	(D)	(D)
554	Gasoline service stations	5	5	(D)	(D)	(D)	(D)	(D)	(D)	(D)	(D)
56	Apparel and accessory stores	82	80	42 517	38 651	7 889	7 537	1 889	1 803	797	759
561	Men's and boys' clothing and furnishings stores	18	18	13 535	13 535	3 171	3 171	728	728	236	236
562, 3, 8	Women's clothing and specialty stores and furriers	19	19	11 189	9 945	1 431	1 334	357	333	226	212
562	Women's ready-to-wear stores	14	14	9 671	9 382	1 312	1 261	329	316	211	204
565	Family clothing stores	6	6	2 967	2 967	656	656	157	157	72	72
566	Shoe stores	32	30	13 068	11 446	2 238	1 983	541	479	207	181
564, 9	Other apparel and accessory stores	7	7	1 758	1 758	393	393	106	106	58	56
57	Furniture, home furnishings, and equipment stores	20	19	7 120	6 788	1 864	1 787	420	405	179	171
5712	Furniture stores	8	7	3 654	3 478	1 366	1 312	291	282	115	111
5713, 4, 9	Home furnishing stores	3	3	(D)	(D)	(D)	(D)	(D)	(D)	(D)	(D)
572, 3	Household appliance, radio, television, and music stores	9	9	(D)	(D)	(D)	(D)	(D)	(D)	(D)	(D)
58	Eating and drinking places	100	99	66 536	63 053	19 237	18 331	4 825	4 656	3 027	2 923
5812	Eating places	99	98	(D)	(D)	(D)	(D)	(D)	(D)	(D)	(D)
5813	Drinking places	1	1	(D)	(D)	(D)	(D)	(D)	(D)	(D)	(D)
591	Drug and proprietary stores	12	11	7 278	7 197	1 070	1 050	257	255	93	92
59 ex. 591	Miscellaneous retail stores [7]	94	95	28 465	28 248	4 833	4 643	1 164	1 120	442	436
592	Liquor stores	12	12	4 925	4 925	409	409	93	93	54	54
594	Miscellaneous shopping goods stores [8]	46	45	11 664	11 449	1 773	1 735	442	431	198	193
5944	Jewelry stores	8	8	4 319	4 319	683	683	177	177	57	57
5947	Gift, novelty and souvenir shops	25	25	3 372	3 372	573	573	133	133	79	79
5949	Sewing, needlework, and piece goods stores	.	.	.	.	.	.	.	.	.	.
5992	Florists	2	2	(D)	(D)	(D)	(D)	(D)	(D)	(D)	(D)

[1] For all establishments, including those without payroll.
[2] Each kind-of-business classification includes leased departments classified in that kind of business as if they were separate establishments. Accordingly, data for leased departments are not consolidated with kind-of-business data for main stores in which they are located. For more information, see Comparability of 1977 and 1982 Censuses in appendix A.
[3] Excludes nonemployer direct sellers, SIC 5963.
[4] Includes sales from catalog order desks located in department stores.
[5] Includes data for leased departments operated within department stores. Data for this line not included in higher level totals.
[6] May include data not covered by SIC 541.
[7] May include data not covered by SIC's 592, 594, and 5992.
[8] May include data not covered by SIC's 5944, 5947, and 5949.

Exhibit 3-9 *Continued.*

Table 3. **Statistics by Selected Kind of Business for Major Retail Centers in the Standard Metropolitan Statistical Area: 1982**

[Data for kind-of-business detail may not add to broader kind-of-business totals. Only those kinds of business without suppressed data are shown. In some instances however, kinds of business for which data are suppressed are included to indicate their relationship to component kinds of business. For meaning of abbreviations and symbols, see introductory text. For definitions of SMSA, see appendix D. For description of MRC boundaries, see appendix I]

SIC code	Kind of business	Establishments (number)	Sales ($1,000)	Annual payroll ($1,000)	First quarter payroll ($1,000)	Paid employees for pay period including March 12 (number)
	MRC NO. 1					
	Retail stores [1][2]	212	345 456	29 617	6 741	3 400
	Retail stores (establishments with payroll)[2]	204	344 809	29 617	6 741	3 400
52	Building materials, hardware, garden supply, and mobile home dealers	7	9 113	1 144	240	99
	Food stores	16	52 288	5 220	1 140	445
541	Grocery stores	7	46 184	4 602	980	354
554	Gasoline service stations	18	30 041	1 383	296	153
56	Apparel and accessory stores	19	18 209	1 798	364	221
562, 3, 8	Women's clothing and specialty stores and furriers	8	3 412	349	66	58
562	Women's ready-to-wear stores	8	3 412	349	66	58
57	Furniture, home furnishings, and equipment stores	25	15 735	1 857	440	146
5712	Furniture stores	6	4 550	412	92	38
5713, 4, 9	Home furnishing stores	8	5 241	722	189	59
572, 3	Household appliance, radio, television, and music stores	11	5 944	723	159	49
58	Eating and drinking places	51	52 318	8 023	1 986	1 413
591	Drug and proprietary stores	6	4 915	518	121	58
59 ex. 591	Miscellaneous retail stores	47	(D)	(D)	(D)	(D)
592	Liquor stores	5	5 638	430	94	41
594	Miscellaneous shopping goods stores	25	(D)	(D)	(D)	(D)
5944	Jewelry stores	5	990	175	28	13
5947	Gift, novelty, and souvenir shops	3	1 396	204	45	29
5992	Florists	3	793	159	43	18
	MRC NO. 2					
	Retail stores [1][2]	185	288 646	29 961	6 712	3 391
	Retail stores (establishments with payroll)[2]	184	288 524	29 961	6 712	3 391
52	Building materials, hardware, garden supply, and mobile home dealers	7	15 431	1 516	337	133
54	Food stores	16	54 868	5 403	1 248	446
541	Grocery stores	12	52 716	5 135	1 186	415
554	Gasoline service stations	16	19 591	892	199	85
56	Apparel and accessory stores	16	11 171	1 193	204	143
562, 3, 8	Women's clothing and specialty stores and furriers	5	4 538	411	87	73
562	Women's ready-to-wear stores	5	4 538	411	87	73
566	Shoe stores	8	1 932	297	64	54
57	Furniture, home furnishings, and equipment stores	21	9 374	1 187	273	96
572, 3	Household appliance, radio, television, and music stores	13	6 459	728	164	61
58	Eating and drinking places	55	30 849	7 618	1 760	1 491
591	Drug and proprietary stores	6	4 508	805	151	86
59 ex. 591	Miscellaneous retail stores	35	16 373	1 867	394	180
592	Liquor stores	3	4 513	158	56	26
594	Miscellaneous shopping goods stores	18	5 863	625	141	75
5947	Gift, novelty, and souvenir shops	4	261	36	8	9
	MRC NO. 3					
	Retail stores [1][2]	64	38 965	5 667	1 285	595
	Retail stores (establishments with payroll)[2]	61	38 912	5 667	1 285	595
56	Apparel and accessory stores	16	5 899	830	170	108
561	Men's and boys' clothing and furnishings stores	3	1 389	259	57	26
562, 3, 8	Women's clothing and specialty stores and furriers	4	(D)	(D)	(D)	(D)
562	Women's ready-to-wear stores	3	1 250	118	29	22
566	Shoe stores	5	1 644	233	49	27
57	Furniture, home furnishings, and equipment stores	9	3 833	495	115	47
572, 3	Household appliance, radio, television, and music stores	4	1 194	197	43	24
58	Eating and drinking places	4	1 185	240	58	45
5812	Eating places	4	1 185	240	58	45
591	Drug and proprietary stores	3	3 877	422	100	53

See footnotes at end of table

workers who are classified as professional; managerial, technical, and service; sales; production; craft; and repair. An example of this information is also provided in Exhibit 3-6. Additional detail and recent updates and changes can be obtained from the Bureau of Labor Statistics.

The demand for space (real estate) generated by the local economy can be described by one or more of the following measures:

1. The number of land units (acres, lots, etc.) and specific use type (residential, commercial, and industrial) can be identified.
2. The area inside existing structures can be stated in square footage available for commercial and industrial users.
3. Sales of vacant parcels of real estate can be enumerated by type of use based on zoning or announced intentions.

Export Base Theory—The Link to the Nonlocal Area The export base model was formulated to analyze the growth of a local economy. The model recognizes that firms in the business sector of the local economy sell to both nonlocal and local consumers but nonlocal sales generate the economic growth. A community's commercial and industrial sectors can generally be divided into two categories—basic and nonbasic activities—that reflect the distinction between nonlocal and local buyers for goods and services produced in the local economy. Basic activities are those industrial and commercial firms that sell a large portion of their products to the nonlocal customers. They are known as the export industries. They make up the basic sector of the local economy. The firms that sell their goods and services primarily to the local customers comprise the service or nonbasic sector of the local economy. In its original formulation, the theory held that an expansion in the basic sector of the economy generated the growth of the local economy. As the export of goods and services grew to accommodate increased demand by external consumers, the local economy grew for two reasons. First, the basic industries needed more employees to meet increased external demand. Second, the firms producing goods for local consumption also had to expand and/or new firms were started to serve the demands of the expanded local labor force in the basic industries. The effect of this expansion on the local economy is an increased demand in the various housing submarkets and in the markets for retail and office space. The increase in demand is brought about by an increase in the number of employed persons and a resultant increase in total local purchasing power.

The significance of the export base theory lies in its signal to the analyst that external factors play a substantial role in the future of the local economy. Export base theory alerts the analyst to the need to find the most significant basic industries and firms, to identify the important external economic variables that affect the basic industry, and to trace the impact of changes in the basic sector on the nonbasic sector of the local economy. These three points are expanded upon next.

The Location Quotient. The most significant basic or export firms and industries can be identified by means of location quotient analysis. The analyst constructs a table which presents the employment data taken from a source such as *County Business Patterns* for the most recent year. The analyst then focuses on the major employers by industry type which employ a significant number of the area's residents. Then, information about these same industries is obtained for the national economy. The analyst calculates the following ratios:

1. The ratio of local employment in a specific industry to total employment in the local economy (e).
2. The ratio of national employment in a specific industry to total employment in the national economy (E).

The analyst uses these two ratios to calculate a third ratio, the *location quotient* (*LQ*). The location quotient is obtained by

$$\text{location quotient} = \frac{e}{E}$$

If the value of the location quotient is greater than 1.0, the industry is considered to be a basic industry. The interpretation of this information is simply that the local economy employs a greater percentage of workers in that industry than the national economy employs in that industry. Consequently, the local economy is assumed to be producing more of the goods or services than the local consumption justifies. Consequently, the industry exports some portion of its output to nonlocal consumers.

The analyst must make a decision about the magnitude of LQ needed to merit further analysis. Should all industries with a location quotient greater than 1.00 be studied, or will only the basic industries with location quotients greater than some value such as 1.50 be studied?

Once the analyst has made the decision concerning what industries to study, the important economic variables that affect that industry must be analyzed. Since the industries under analysis are export industries, the analysis should focus on external factors and economic phenomena that affect the level of activity and economic health of the industry.

Understanding Structural Changes. Employment in the local industries classified as "basic" or "export" is affected by the autonomous demand for their product from outside the local community. This external demand depends upon such general factors as the number and location of consumers, the prices for substitute and complementary products, consumer incomes, tastes and preferences, and other market variables.

The ability of local firms to maintain their market share of this aggregate external demand will depend upon their ability to maintain or improve upon their competitive position in their industry. In the case of durable goods manufacturing, the market analyst may use an industrial analysis service, such as the U.S. Department of Commerce, International Trade Division's discussion of current and short-run market conditions faced by the durable goods industry in the annual *U.S. Industrial Outlook*. The specific local firms engaged in durable goods manufacturing in the community can be found in the *Harris Industrial Directory* for many states, and their competitive position in the industry can be examined by referring to discussion in Standard & Poor's *Standard NYSE Reports*.

For small communities, the analyst may make short-run (three- to five-year) projections of employment in the basic industries by surveying the management of local firms and inquiring about prospects for increased business activity and employment. The quality of information received from management must be judged in the context of information obtained from secondary sources about the industry and firm. For both small and large communities, employment in basic industries can often be forecast by a short-run extrapolation of past trends. Often such forecasts are presented in three scenarios, which represent future employment in the worst case, moderate (most probable) case, and best case. The scenarios should consider the major factors that affect the aggregate demand for the product of that industry and the competitive position of local firms in their industries. The potential variance in employment forecasts is greater for smaller communities than for, say, MSAs. The exodus of a single major employer in a smaller community can negate the most carefully developed forecast. Larger communities are usually less affected by relocation of a single establishment and plant closings.

The key is in understanding the function of the local community as part of a larger economy. With an understanding of the character and function of the community, the exogenous changes in economic activity can be evaluated in light of their impact on the local economy and the resultant demand for space.

The Internal Multiplier Effect Generated by Changes in Basic Employment

When a change in basic employment occurs due to an increase in external demand for the product of the basic industry, the economy also experiences a change in the level of nonbasic employment. Consequently, total employment increases by a multiple of the increase in basic employment. The change in nonbasic employment occurs because the number of basic industry employees increases and/or their local purchasing power increases. This increase in income and/or the number of internal consumers causes an increase in the demand for local goods and services and thus an increase in nonbasic employment. Simply stated, a one-unit change in basic employment causes more than a one-unit change in total employment. This phenomenon is called the internal multiplier effect.

Conceptually, the size of the multiplier can be as small as 1.0, if no feedback effect occurs in the local economy causing a change in nonbasic employment. In other words, any change in purchasing power in the basic industry is spent on imports—all the funds leak out of the local economy. At the other extreme, the internal multiplier can be large if all the funds are spent locally. The magnitude of the multiplier is given by the ratio of total employment to basic employment, but the underlying economic relationship is the reaction of nonbasic employment to a unit change in basic employment. To understand this relationship between basic and total employment, it is helpful to relate historic levels of employment in the basic industries to total employment. If the structure of the local industrial base stayed constant over the recent past, the analyst would find that total employment is a stable multiple of basic employment. The multiplier can be small (1.5 or so) if the basic industries make up the bulk of the industrial structure, or the multiplier can be large (3.0 or so) if the basic industry is a smaller component of the total industrial structure. The numerical value for the multiplier comes from its derivation of total employment divided by basic employment.

Smaller communities may experience less stability over time in the employment multiplier. Industrial relocation, plant/office closings, and start-up firms can affect the magnitude of the computed multiplier. If the local economy has undergone substantial change in its industrial structure, or such change is going to happen, then the analyst has to use judgment concerning the future value of the multiplier. In this case the past can only serve as a reference point for the forecast; a simple projection will not suffice.

Temporal Extensions of the Location Quotient Concept   The location quotient discussed previously provided the analyst with a technique to identify the exporting industries that currently exist. In this sense the concept is useful in and of itself. The change in the local economy's industrial sector over time is also useful information when an analyst makes a forecast. Several techniques to perform such a temporal evaluation have been devised in the past. In general, the full discussion of this topic is typically referred to as shift-share analysis. Other terms are also used.

First, the location quotient (often called the coefficient of localization) is a form of "share" analysis. It measures the local economy's percentage share of an industry relative to its total industrial structure and compares it to the same measure for the nation's industrial structure.

The important question that might need an answer is, "How does this share change over time?" Three concepts have been devised to answer this question. They are the coefficient of redistribution, the proportionality shift ratio, and the differential shift ratio.

Input-Output Analysis   The input-output model is a powerful alternative technique which allows the analyst to combine the concepts of the circular flow-of-income and export base techniques. In its most simple form, the input-output model describes the internal relationships in the business sector and is an alternative to the circular flow-of-income as a descriptive technique for the economy.

The information needed to develop the input-output model is so great that the market analyst is not likely to use this type of analysis. Thus, a discussion of this technique is beyond the scope of this chapter.

Whatever the technique used, the analyst makes a judgment and forecast of salient aspects of the local economy. The forecasts are based on past and current levels and trends of various economic activities. In the next section of this chapter, specific techniques for performing this type of analysis are discussed.

ASSESSING CURRENT AND FUTURE
LEVELS OF ECONOMIC ACTIVITY

To assess and forecast local economic phenomena, the analyst must first understand and describe it. The analyst may then face two additional tasks. First, if the census data are not current (i.e., the analysis is being done in 1986 while the census information reflects the economic relationships of 1980), the analyst must update the key variables such as population, employment, income, and retail sales. Exhibit 3-9 gives the type of retail statistics needed to analyze retail sales. Exhibit 3-6 provided labor force characteristics needed to analyze employment. Other earlier exhibits (3-3, 3-4, and 3-5) discussed population and income. Once the information is updated, the analyst can use this current information, as well as past information, to forecast the level of population, employment, income, and retail sales for future periods.

Employment data need to be examined carefully to determine the most appropriate updating technique. Employment data contained in the *Census of Population* are based on the employee's place of residence rather than on the place of employment. If the geographic boundaries for the local economy and the boundaries for the census of population are coincidental (which is rarely the case), then both statistics by place of residence and place of employment yield the same result. But if the market area or study area comprises only a portion of a larger geographic area in which the local economy functions, the analyst should seek the appropriate employment data for the study, that is, either place of residence or place of employment data. Employment data by industry compiled on the basis of place of employment can be obtained from the Federal Bureau of Labor Statistics, the Census Bureau's *County Business Patterns*, or the Department of Labor in the appropriate state.

If the analyst is seeking the number of employed workers who reside in a market area, employment data by place of residence are the necessary data. If the analyst is seeking the number of jobs in the market area, employment data by place of employment or job site are the necessary data.

There are differences between the concepts of projection and forecast. A projection is simply the extrapolation of the trend of past values for some variable, such as population, through the present period into the future. A forecast, on the other hand, takes data from the past and extrapolates it through the present, but subjects the trend to an analysis that identifies how current factors and conditions are affecting the historic trend. When this analysis is finished, the trend of the variable into the future may be higher or lower than the value would have been from a simple projection. The real estate market analyst is responsible for *forecasting*, as accurately as possible, future changes which are likely to affect a parcel of real property or its income stream.

Often the real estate analyst bases forecasts upon the projections or forecasts made by organizations who perform communitywide studies. Alternatively, population, household, employment, and income forecasts may be purchased from national firms that operate computerized data bases and specialize in selling such data. The real estate analyst also forecasts certain economic trends based upon a projection or a forecast for the national, regional, or local economy. The market analyst may make his or her own forecast by altering the forecasts of others when, in his or her judgment, trends cause economic conditions or current population to vary from the stated forecasts. The market analyst also may develop his or her own updates and forecasts, both to check on the forecasts of others and to use independently in a market analysis. The following sections present some of the traditionally accepted techniques used by analysts to update and forecast secondary data.

Updating Techniques for Households and Population[2]

There are numerous accepted methods for updating population and household data from the most recent census to the current period. Five of these methods—the housing inventory method, the natural increase and migration method, the cohort survival method, the ratio technique, and graphical/mathematical techniques—are discussed in the following subsections.

Housing Inventory Method This updating technique relies on the use of population and household size figures from the previous census. Information from the *Census of Population* and local area data on building permits and demolitions are used. The method of calculating current population is shown in Exhibit 3-10. The 1970 population and the appropriate household size for that geographic area being analyzed (which could be the MSA, the county, or a census tract) are given in line 1 of Exhibit 3-10. Information from the 1980 Census is presented on line 2.

Once these data from the past are given, the trend in household size is updated to the year 1986, and the number of existing households are estimated by using building permit and demolition data from the local community. Adjustments are also made for vacancy changes. This process allows the analyst to produce a population estimate for 1986 and forms a basis for forecasting to 1987 and beyond.

[2]*Ibid.*, pp. 216–218.

YEAR	POPULATION	HOUSEHOLDS	HOUSEHOLD SIZE
1. 1970	10,000	3,570	2.8
2. 1980	14,000	5,600	2.5
3. 1986	15,788	6,805	2.32–2.5

A. *Household Size*
4. −0.3 (−11%)   = change, 1970–1980
5. −0.3 ÷ 10 years = −0.03 (−1%) average annual change
6. −0.03 × 6 years = −0.18 (−6%) expected decrease, 1980–1986

B. *Housing Unit Estimate*

7. Building permits (BPs) issued, 1980–1986	+1,760
8. BPs issued but not used	− 310
9. BPs issued and still under construction	− 270
10. BPs issued in 1979 and completed in 1980	+ 60
11. New units constructed, 1980–1986	+1,240
12. Demolitions	− 30
13. Net conversions	+ 40
14. Change in number of vacant units, 1980 vs. 1986	− 45
15. Net change in housing units, 1980 to 1986	+1,205

C. *Population Estimate*
16. 6,805 × 2.32 = 15,788
17. 6,805 × 2.5 = 17,013

Exhibit 3-10   The Housing Inventory Method to Update Population.

First, household size for 1986 as shown in line 3 is estimated as a continuation of the same direction and annual order of magnitude that took place between 1970 and 1980. Calculations are shown in lines 4, 5, and 6. In this case household size declined by 3 percentage points per year from 1970 to 1980. (See line 9. Line 5 gives the annual change.) Over a six-year period, 1980–1986, this translates into an 18-percentage-point decrease in household size (see line 6). Consequently, the household size figure for 1986 is projected as 2.32 persons per household, shown as household size in line 3. The analyst may modify the trend in this household size projection if local conditions warrant. For example, the census tract may be an in-town neighborhood in which long-time residents, couples in their fifties and sixties, are being replaced by young families, a trend that did not occur prior to 1980. Based on this information, the market analyst believes that the decline in household size will occur at a smaller rate per year than it had in the past. If the relocation trend is substantial enough, the downward trend in household size may have stopped altogether and the household size for 1986 could remain at approximately the 2.5 figure of 1980. In any event, if these phenomena were occurring in the census tract, the market analyst would be able to predict that household size would be no smaller than 2.32 and, more than likely, no larger than 2.5 persons per household.

The next step involves an estimate of households that have taken up residence in this census tract between 1980 and 1986. To obtain this estimate, a logical connection must be made between households and housing units. The household is a group of people who reside within a housing unit. If the number of housing units increases, and if they are all occupied, then the number of households will also increase. The analyst gathers building permit data for new housing unit construction from public records. This figure is adjusted to reflect that some building permits issued in the particular time period are not completed in that period. Also, a certain number of the units are never constructed, even though the building permit is issued, and a certain number of permits issued in an earlier period are completed during the current period. When these adjustments are made, the resulting figure represents the new housing units constructed from 1980 to 1986. Line 11 shows this number as 1240.

The next adjustments take demolitions, conversions, and vacancies into account. The analyst may find that housing units in the area may have been destroyed by fire or removed under eminent domain proceedings. See line 12 for demolitions. The building permit search may reveal that some housing units were converted into nonresidential uses, while certain large, single-family homes were converted into several one-bedroom apartments or condominiums. The net effect of these conversions is 40 additional housing units. (Ninety units were created, 30 units were demolished, and 20 units were converted out of residential use. See line 13.)

A final adjustment must now be made for changes in the vacancy rate for the units. The 1980 Census of Housing indicates that 43 housing units were vacant in 1980; in 1986, 88 units are vacant (by survey). Based on these numbers, the estimate of housing unit construction is converted into occupied units by subtracting the increase in vacancies of 45 units, 1980–1986. See line 14.

The 1205 additional households (line 15) are added to the 1980 total of 5600 (line 2) to get the 1986 total of 6805 (line 3). The population is then estimated by multiplying the number of households by the estimated household size (lines 16 and 17). These calculations yield an estimated population in households for 1986 of between 15,788 and 17,013 people. No estimate has been made of institutional population, such as in college dorms.

Natural Increase and Migration Method This updating technique requires information from the most recent *Census of Population.* The census provides the rudimentary age and sex breakdown presented in Exhibit 3-11. The first important figure is the number of resident females in the 16–45 age category, the primary childbearing years. Given demographic information about the fertility rate of women in this age category, the number of annual births per thousand can be established. If there are 80 births per thousand per year, the increase in population over the six-year period would be 5,760 people (80 births per thousand females times 12,000 females times six years).

The next most important variable is the survival rate, or its complement,

1980 DATA:	AGE	FEMALE	MALE	TOTAL
	0–16	5,500	5,000	10,500
	16–45	12,000	11,800	23,800
	46+	9,000	8,200	17,200
				51,500
Natural increase, 1980–1986				
Total				4,470
Births			5,760	
Less: Deaths			−1,290	
Net migration, 1980–1986*				3,000
Estimated population, 1986				58,970

*Net migration = in-migration − out-migration.

Exhibit 3-11 The Natural Increase and Migration Method.

the death rate, by age category. In this example the age categories are very broad (in actual practice a survival rate is available from mortality tables on a year-by-year basis), and the analyst can assume that on average 97.5 percent of this native population that was alive in 1980 will still be living in 1986. Given this survival rate, approximately 50,210 of the original 51,500 people will survive to 1986.

Based on the figures provided by the application of the fertility rate to the females in the primary childbearing years, and then the application of the survival rate to the entire population, the natural increase in the population over the five-year period of time will be 5,760 minus 1,290, which equals 4,470 individuals. Once this figure is obtained, the next piece of information required to complete the estimate of 1986 population is an estimate of the net migration of individuals into the geographic area.

The topic of migration estimation is discussed later in this chapter. At this point assume that the analyst has been able to estimate that net migration (in-migration less out-migration) is 3,000 people. This figure is added to the net change in the native population (births minus deaths) to get the final estimate for current population.

Cohort Survival Method This population updating technique also utilizes an age breakdown of the population from the most recent *Census of Population*. In this case the breakdown in the age category has to be in five-year intervals because the data are presented in five-year groupings. Exhibit 3-12 provides an example of such an age cohort breakdown. In this technique the fertility rate is used to get the estimate of children between the ages of 0 and 5 in 1986. This is accomplished in the same way as it is in the natural increase and migration method. The number of women in the primary childbearing years is multiplied by their fertility rate to obtain this estimate. As before, assume that there were 12,000 females in the primary childbearing years and that the birth rate was 80 per thousand females per year. This gives us 5,760 births in the 1980–1986 period.

AGE	1980 POPULATION	1980–1986 EST. POPULATION CHANGES	
0– 5	3,500	Births	+ 5,760
6–10	3,500		
11–15	3,500		
16–20	3,600		
21–25	3,800	$3,800 \times 99.6\% = 3,785$	
26–30	3,800		
31–35	4,100		
36–40	4,400		
41–45	4,100		
46–50	4,000		
51–55	4,000		
56–60	4,000		
61–65	3,000		
66+	2,200	Deaths	– 1,290
	51,500		+4,470
		Net Migration	+3,000
		1986 total over 1980	58,970

Exhibit 3-12 The Cohort Survival Technique.

The next step uses the survival rate for these five-year cohorts. If the survival rate for people in the 21–25 age bracket is 99.6 percent, then 3,785 of them will survive the passage of five years. This calculation is performed for each of the age groups, and the surviving members of each age cohort are placed forward in time. In other words, the age group that was 21–25 in 1980 will be in the 26–30 category in 1986. When this adjustment for survival is undertaken for each age group, an estimate for net change in the native population and the 1985 native population are obtained.

The third major component of the cohort survival technique is the calculation of net migration. In this example, there is a net inflow, so this figure is added to the 1986 population estimate shown in Exhibit 3-11. However, a more sophisticated version of the cohort survival procedure would estimate net migration by age group. In this way, the demographers constructing the population estimate can show which age groups are increasing or decreasing due to net migration. Often demographers cannot obtain the age of the individuals in the households that are relocating, particularly from secondary data sources.

Ratio Technique.   The ratio technique allows the analyst to estimate the value of an unknown variable from a known value. The analyst may have past and current data for a larger geographic unit, such as the county, but only past data for the census tract. The task at hand is to obtain an estimate for the population in the census tract. Exhibit 3-13 shows the form of the calculation.

After displaying the data for the county and the census tract, the analyst calculates the ratio of census tract population to county population for 1970 and

Table A The Step-Down Application

	POPULATION COUNTY	CENSUS TRACT	CENSUS TRACT/ COUNTY RATIO	RATE OF CHANGE FOR DECADE
1970	37,000	3,900	0.105	
1980	46,000	4,700	0.102	−0.003
1986	49,000	X	r	

$r = 0.102 - [(0.0003/\text{yr})(6\ \text{yr})] = 0.1002.$
$X = 49,000 \times r = 4,910.$

Table B The Participation Rate Application

	POPULATION	EMPLOYMENT	PARTICIPATION RATE	RATE OF CHANGE FOR DECADE
1970	37,000	15,170	0.41	
1980	46,000	22,080	0.48	+0.07
1986	X	25,235	r	

$r = 0.48 + [(0.007/\text{yr})(6\ \text{yr})] = 0.52.$
$X = 25,235/0.52 = 48,529.$

Exhibit 3-13 The Ratio Technique.

1980, respectively. Then, the change in the ratio from 1970 to 1980 is calculated. In Exhibit 3-13A the change in the ratio is −0.3 percent per decade or −0.03 percent per year. If the analyst examines the growth trends in the county and the census tract, a judgment can be made about the rate of change between 1980 and 1986. If the analyst is satisfied that the 1970–1980 trend holds for 1980–1986, then the value of the ratio in 1986 is 0.102 (10.2%) less 0.018 (0.18 percent). Calculating 6 years × 0.003 yields 0.018. The result is 0.1002 (10.02 percent). Using this ratio in conjunction with the known county population yields an estimate of 4,910 for the population of the census tract.

The ratio technique can also be used to estimate population from employment data by place of residence. An example of this calculation is presented in Exhibit 3-13B. The analyst displays the population and employment data for the county for 1970 and 1980. The employment-to-population ratio is calculated by dividing employed workers by population. The change in the ratio is then computed and analyzed to see if the trend continues through the 1980–1986 period. Assuming that the analyst substantiates this trend, an employment-to-population ratio for 1986 is obtained. The change in the rate from 1970 to 1980 is +0.07 per decade (7 percent) or +0.007 per year (0.7 percent); for 1980–1986 the ratio should increase by 0.042 to a value of 0.52. Dividing this figure into the employment figure of 25,235 yields a population estimate of 48,529 for 1986.

Often the analyst must estimate population for a census tract from current employment data for the county. Exhibit 3-14 shows how this is accomplished. The procedure involves the two ratios used in Exhibit 3-13.

Graphical and Mathematical Techniques. Graphical and mathematical techniques for updating population utilize data from previous periods and project it into the future using either a graph such as that in Exhibit 3-15 or a mathematical equation which approximates the value of the historical curve in Exhibit 3-15. In its most simple form, this technique uses observation to project curve *PA*, the historic population trend, into the future. When this is done, the

Exhibit 3-14 The Ratio Technique: A Two-Stage Application.

	COUNTY DATA			CENSUS TRACT	
	Population	Employment	Employment/ Population	Population	Census Tract/ County Ratio
1970	37,000	15,170	0.41	3,900	0.015
1980	46,000	22,080	0.48	4,700	0.102
1986	X_1	25,325	r_1	X_2	r_2

$r_1 = 0.48 + [(0.007/\text{yr})(6 \text{ yr})] = 0.522.$
$r_2 = 0.102 - [(0.003/\text{yr})(6 \text{ yr})] = 0.1002.$
$X_1 = 25,325 - 0.522 = 48,343.$
$X_2 = [(X_1)(r_2)] = 48,343 \times 0.1002 = 4,844.$

Exhibit 3-15 Graphical Method for Population Projection.

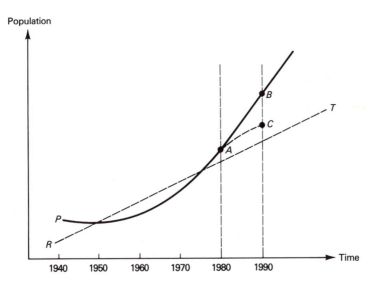

projection will be the *AB* segment of the curve, which shows the population change from 1986 into the future.

A popular mathematical technique for approximating the historical values and projecting them into the future is regression analysis. A detailed discussion of regression analysis is not included here, but the trend line *RT* in Exhibit 3-15 would represent a projection using regression analysis.

Direct observation of past data (the "eyeball technique") and regression analysis can be used to develop projections. If the market researcher used information available during 1980–1986, the trend implied by line segment *AB* could be modified to that shown as line segment *AC*. This modification, which is the forecast, occurs because the analyst realized that some local area factor conditions were limiting population growth. A local condition could be the supply of prime land available for residential construction which has been totally utilized, with only marginal land available for residential development after 1980).

Migration Estimating

The ability to estimate and forecast population and household migration levels is an important skill for the demographer because the level of human migration is an important component in certain population updating techniques. This section of the chapter provides definitions and methods by which estimates of migration can be obtained for a local area, such as a county or an MSA.

Definitions   The U.S. Bureau of the Census and demographers make a distinction between a "mover" and a "migrant." A person who changes residence is a mover. A person who changes residence by crossing a county boundary, that is, moving to a residence in a different county, is a migrant. The real estate analyst is interested in both these individuals, but the type of interest is a function of the study being performed. A study of the aggregate demand for housing in a county would only consider the migrant because the mover is already part of the total demand for housing in the county. However, a study of the demand for new housing in the county should consider both the mover and the migrant.

"Net migration" is defined as the number of migrants into the county less the number of migrants out of the county. Net migration defined in this way can be a positive or a negative number. If the county is growing, net migration is more than likely the cause of that growth, and it will have a positive value. On the other hand, if the county is experiencing a decline in its population level, net migration should have a negative value.

Each of the independent flows comprising net migration is referred to as a "gross migration" flow. If the analyst is concerned with only the people moving into a county, the focus is on the gross in-migration. If, on the other hand, the analyst is concerned only with people moving out of the county, the focus is on gross out-migration. In the vast majority of cases, the real estate analyst is concerned with net migration. However, gross out-migration can become important in a study of the supply side of the resale market for a geographic area such as a census tract or a neighborhood in a census tract. In addition, the real estate analyst, in the manner of the demographer, can use the distinction between a mover and a migrant for a small geographic area of interest such as a census tract. The point to remember is that, in this latter case, the true definitions are based on county lines. Here the terms are just being applied in a conventional manner that is universally accepted.

Migration can be measured directly and indirectly. The direct measure of migration focuses on the migrants and is able to identify and count them. The most usable direct measure of migration is in the U.S. Census. Each respondent writes in the current (April 1, 1980) county of residence and the county of residence in 1975. Thus each household's migration and move can be traced. The data reveal the gross migration flows and the direction of migration among counties, states, and regions.

Indirect measures establish migration as a residual derived from the relationship of other demographic variables. For example, the difference between 1980 and 1986 population for a county consists of births, deaths, and net migration. If the two population values are known, and if births and deaths can be counted or estimated, then net migration is the residual; it is the unknown. Notice that the indirect method only generates net migration; it cannot generate data about the direction of the flows or their respective magnitudes.

Direct Measures of Migration As mentioned in the previous section, the most useful direct source of migration data is the response given by individual households to a census question. However, the census has chosen to publish these data in two different formats between the 1970 and 1980 census. In 1970, the census publication provided data on the number of gross in- and out-migrants to and from each county. This information was presented as a matrix with 3,000 columns and rows, one for each county in the country. The table even provided the number of households who moved from one residence in the county to another residence in the same county during the period. The title of the 1970 publication is *Migration Between State and Economic Areas* PC (2) 2E.

In the publications of the 1980 census, this same information is presented on a net migration basis for each county. The 1980 publication is *Geographic Mobility for Metropolitan Areas*, PC 80-2-2C.

In addition to the census publications, local utility companies may be sources of migration data based on the number of residential connections and disconnections they perform. However, these data are not universally available or applicable. Natural gas utility companies and local telephone companies are excluded as sources of migration data because natural gas is not a universal heating medium. Nor does each household have a single telephone: some households do not have telephone service; other households have two or more telephone lines. Electrical service has the most consistent, one-to-one relationship between the service and the housing unit and is preferred for this reason.

Electric companies generally keep data on a time and location basis on the number of meters in service and the number of new meters installed. The companies know where the meters were installed, but many companies keep their locational data base on company-specific districts and routes which cannot be readily translated to statistical areas such as census tracts. In most instances the conversion is possible, but it may be costly. However, the industry is moving toward consistent recording and reporting by census tracts.

The data that would generate a direct measure of migration are the number of new meters installed for households which did not previously have service in the census tract (new residential meter sets or hookups). If these data are available, the analyst has a direct measure of gross in-migration.

If the analyst also is able to obtain the number of meters disconnected by households which did not have service restored at a different house in the same census tract, a measure of gross out-migration can be estimated. Many electric utilities cannot provide their data in this detailed form, but they can usually provide the number of net new meters installed. These data do not differentiate between movers and migrants; they are only an indirect approximation of net migration.

Another possible source of direct migration is the covered employment surveys maintained by the Department of Labor in each state, although the use of these data has problems. When an employee covered by the social security system changes jobs, the change is reported in the records. Migration can be inferred if the place of employment is consistently recorded as the change of jobs occurs. Problems arise because not all employees are covered by the social security system, and an employee who makes an intracompany transfer may not have to record the change of job because there has not been a change of employer.

Indirect Measures of Migration Only one indirect measure of migration is discussed in this section. It provides an estimate of net migration by using the residual approach. The two versions of this method can be named the *vital statistics approach* and the *life table approach*, depending upon the use of either vital statistics themselves or fertility and mortality rates from published sources. However, the methodology for both approaches is the same. In the following example, the analyst knows the level of population in the county (or census tract) for 1980 from the census. Then census updates, planning department data, or the housing inventory method can be used to estimate population for 1981, 1982, . . . , and 1986. The analyst is able to estimate net migration for each of these years by means of the following formula:

$$POP_{T+1} = POP_T + B_t - D_t + NM_t$$

Rewriting the formula to show net migration can be simply accomplished by moving the terms to the appropriate side of the equation sign. The resulting equation becomes

$$NM_t = POP_{T+1} - POP_T - B_t + D_t$$

where

NM = net migration
POP = population
B = births
D = deaths
T = value of start of the specified year
t = value during the year

The equation is verbally interpreted as saying that net migration during 1981 is equal to population in 1982, minus population at the start of 1981, minus the births that occurred in 1981, plus the deaths that occurred in 1981. This same interpretation can be applied in each of the years 1981 to 1986 to generate an estimate of net migration for each of the years. The generation of this net migration data series allows the analyst to inspect and analyze the historical data.

If the data for births and deaths come from the public records as vital statistics, the net migration equation is known as the vital statistics method to estimate net migration. When fertility rates and death or survival rates are used to estimate births and deaths, the net migration equation is known as the life table method for estimating net migration. If the analyst has a choice between these two approaches, the vital statistics method is preferred because there is one less estimation in the procedure.

Another indirect method to obtain an estimate of net migration utilizes school enrollment data to serve as a proxy for net migration. The underlying premise for this method is that a definite and recognizable relationship exists between the number of school-aged children and the number of people and households. The reliability and accuracy of this relationship is highly dependent on the nature and characteristics of the people in the study area. For example, this technique would be more applicable in a suburban community populated by families with school-aged children. It would be much less applicable, or totally inapplicable, for a study area in the core of a city that is populated by individual or single-person households or a retirement community.

Public school enrollment is readily available because the information is in the public domain. Private and parochial school enrollment should be sought, and, if it can be obtained, it should be combined with the public school data. The technique starts with the analyst obtaining actual total school enrollment data for the study area for the first year of the updating period (i.e., 1980) and first grade enrollments for each year in the updating period. These data are displayed in a table that allows the analyst to trace the movement of those students in the first mandatory year of schooling, let us say, first grade, through the updating time period. Exhibit 3-16 shows how the analyst updates school enrollment information by moving the number enrolled from the age 6 row in the 1980 column (the first-grade student) to the age 7 row in the 1981 column. Similar movements are made for data in each cell in each column. Then the actual total school enrollment in 1986, the current of last year in our updating period, is obtained.

When the elements in the table containing actual enrollment data (*a*) are displayed, the analyst traces the survival of the children over the study period using survival rates from national tables that display the death rate/survival rate

Exhibit 3-16 Procedure to Use School Enrollment Data to Estimate (Net) Migration.

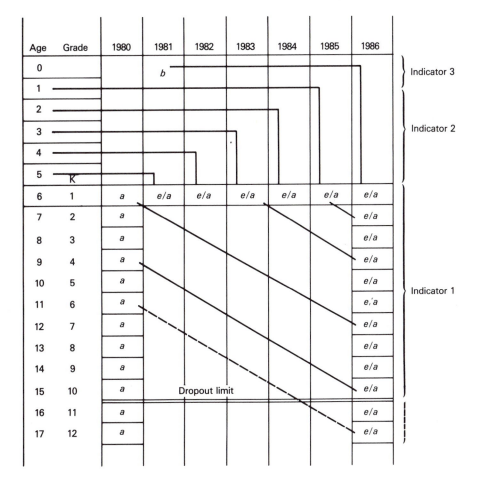

for each age. The analyst follows this same procedure for each grade in 1980 until the upper limiting grade is reached. Depending on the dropout pattern for the high school(s) in the study area, the upper limit could be grade 4 in 1980, which becomes grade 10 in 1986. In this instance, grade 10 in 1986 is the limiting grade because there is a high percentage of dropouts. If, on the other hand, there is little dropping out at 16, then grade 6 in 1980, which becomes grade 12 in 1986, is the limit.

The surviving children who are in the 0–4 age category in 1980 are the first graders as the update period progresses. Exhibit 3-16 points this out. The 5-year-olds in 1980 are the first graders in 1981. The 1-year-olds in 1980 are the first graders in 1985. Thus, if no children died, and if no migration occurred, the number of children in the 0–4 age group in 1980 should be equal to the total of new first graders summed across 1981–1985. Any difference is due to death and net migration.

The first graders in 1986 were born in 1981. The analyst can estimate the number of 1981 births from vital statistics or fertility rates applied to the 1980 female age groups. The survival rate must be applied to these births to get a figure for first graders in 1986.

Using actual enrollment (a) data for 1980 from the school district and the census data for 1980, the analyst calculates the expected enrollments in first grade in 1981 through 1986 and the expected enrollment in each of the grades in 1986. These data are displayed in Exhibit 3-16 by the symbol (e). Net migration of children is obtained from three comparisons in the table shown as Exhibit 3-16. First, the difference in actual and expected enrollments in 1986 summed across all grades used in the analysis is an indicator of net migration. If actual enrollment exceeds expected enrollment, net immigration occurred in this first category.

The second indicator of the net migration of children is the difference between the total number of children in the 0–4 age bracket in 1980 and the sum of first-grade enrollment in 1981–1985. If the total of first-grade enrollments for 1981–1985 exceeds the number of children in the 0–4 age group in 1980, then net immigration of children occurred.

The third indicator of net migration is the difference between the number of children born in 1981 and first-grade enrollment in 1986. In our example this calculation only has to be done once. But if the updating period extends to 1987, the calculation would have to be performed for both years.

When these three separate indicators of net migration are calculated and summed together, the total amount of net migration of children is estimated. This figure is translated to a household figure by using the appropriate number of children per household for the study area. For example, if the household size for the county or the census tract is 3.75, then each 1.75 school children represents a household (assuming all households are two-parent households). But remember that the use of household size data might have to be adjusted for any trends taking place during the 1980–1986 period.

Updating Population with the Natural Increase and Migration and the Cohort Survival Methods

Migration estimation becomes important in the process of updating population when the housing inventory method and the ratio method are not available to the analyst. This could occur if public records for building permit data are not available or flawed, if there is no reputable population forecast or projection, or if the covered employment data are atypical because of a high percentage of employment not covered by the social security system.

When the analyst can use either the housing inventory method or the ratio method, migration estimating remains useful as a means of establishing an alternative updating technique that allows the analyst to cross-check the results with other forecasts.

Another method of migration estimation is based on the nonage-specific net migration, as identified in earlier sections about the natural increase and migration method and the cohort survival method. If the migration estimate requires age distributions, the analyst will have to use an alternative method.

Migration estimating can require establishing a trend between two time periods. The first period (1980–1986, in this example) is the updating time period. The second time period (1975–1979) is the relevant time period immediately before the updating period. The second period is chosen because the economic and social circumstances resemble the updating time period, not necessarily because it is the immediately preceding five years. The NIM or cohort survival population updating technique is first applied to the 1980–1986 period. Then, the migration estimating technique, either direct or indirect, is applied.

If electric meter installation data can be used (a direct measure), then the period for estimating migration is the same as the population updating time period: 1980 to 1986. Here, the analyst only needs to take care to be as accurate as the data permit. The analyst gets the meter installation data for 1980 to 1986, converts it to a migration estimate using appropriate local information, and adds it to the updated native population.

If school enrollment data has to be used, the estimating period for migration is also the 1980–1986 period. So, like the meter installation procedure, the migration estimate is added to the updated native population.

In the event that the migration estimate is taken from 1975 to 1979, and then applied to the 1980–1986 period, the analyst must establish the temporal relationship among the variables that are causal factors in the human migration process. If the economic circumstances causing human migration in the 1975–1979 period are similar in type and magnitude to the economic circumstances in the 1980–1986 period, then the analyst can forecast that migration in the study period should continue at the same annual rate. But, if the economic circumstances in 1975–1979 were better than they were in 1980–1986, then the forecast will have to reflect a reduced annual rate of migration. The factors that affect human migration are revealed in a personal investment decision (a form of investment in human capital) or what can be considered as a private cost-benefit analysis.

The important variables that influence a person's decision to migrate are

1. A positive earning differential.
2. A reduction in the cost of living, income taxes.
3. An improvement in climate, scenery, recreation activities.
4. An improvement in job opportunities such as the potential for advancement, future wage increases.

These benefits to be derived from migration must exceed the costs of migration which the person would have to incur. These costs can be the one-time costs of moving family and belongings, plus any nonmonetary psychic costs that arise from the geographic separation from parents, favored relatives, and friends.

The analyst must be able to judge the relative strength of the attractive aspects of the local economy as it existed during the updating time period and compare it to the time period for which published data exist. So, if the relative attractiveness of the local economy in the 1975–1979 period to a potential migrant was greater than the attractiveness of the 1980–1986 period, then the magnitude of migration in the updating period is estimated at a lower level.

Forecasting Techniques for Households and Population

Each of the updating techniques discussed in the previous section can be used to forecast. The procedure involves an additional conceptual step. The updating task brings the data series to the present; the forecasting task extrapolates the present into the future by analyzing the key variables in each method. The forecast is usually made by a market analyst when there is either a known parameter, such as population forecasts for a larger area, or no forecasts are available elsewhere.

Forecasting from an Existing Prediction[3]   The ratio technique is the simplest method to use if there is a reputable population forecast or projection in existence. Usually such data are provided by some governmental agency. Exhibit 3-17 provides an example of the ratio technique to forecast population for a census tract from a population projection obtained from a state agency.

First, the analyst displays the actual population data from 1970 and 1980 for the county and the census tract. From these data the historical census tract/county population ratios are calculated. The ratios are displayed in the first two rows of the R_1 column. Next, the analyst displays the county population projection from the state agency for 1986, and the census tract population is cal-

---

[3]*Ibid.*, pp. 218–219.

	COUNTY	CENSUS TRACT	R_1	R_2	R_3
1970	37,000	3,900	0.105		
1980	46,000	4,700	0.102		
1986	49,000	4,910	0.1002		
1990	54,000	X_1	0.099	0.1002	0.1025
2000	61,000	X_2	0.096	0.1002	0.106

$X_1 = 54,000 \times 0.1002 = 5,411.$
$X_2 = 61,000 \times 0.1002 = 6,112.$

Exhibit 3-17 A Forecast Using the Ratio Technique.

culated using the ratio technique. Then the population projections for 1990 and 2000 are displayed.

The forecast for census tract population involves the following steps:

1. Forecast the value of the ratio for specified time periods. This is accomplished after examining growth potential revealed from current conditions in the county and the census tract.
2. Apply the appropriate ratio to the projected county population data.

To obtain the appropriate future value of the census tract/county population ratio, the analyst should check the following supply factors:

1. Construction projects underway.
2. Available land zoned for residential construction.
3. The prospects for rezoning from low-density residential to high-density residential, and from nonresidential to residential uses.
4. County plans for road, water, and sewerage system extensions into undeveloped areas.
5. State and county plans for the provision of public services which might require eminent domain acquisition of existing residential units.

The analysts should also check the demand for residential space in the respective areas. A more thorough discussion of these demand variables is presented in Chapter 7.

In the example given in Exhibit 3-17, the analyst may be able to identify any one of a number of interrelationships between the county and the census tract into the future. Three such possible relationships are shown in the exhibit:

1. R_1 — the analyst discovers that the past growth in both the county and the census tract will continue in the same absolute and relative terms. In this event the ratio will continue to exhibit its historical trend.
2. R_2 — the county and the census tract will continue to grow at approximately the 1986 relative rate in the future.

3. R_3 — the county will grow, but the growth rate in the census tract will be substantially higher (the census tract might be the only growth area in the county).

After a thorough analysis, the analyst may determine that the conditions leading to scenario R_2 are the most realistic. Once this is determined, the values of census tract population can be calculated. The resulting population figures for the census tract are 5,411 for 1990 and 6,112 for the year 2000.

Two additional points must be kept in mind when undertaking such forecasts. First, the accuracy of any forecast declines as the forecast period is lengthened. The estimate for 1990 is consequently more accurate than is the estimate for 2000. Second, as the actual population in the current year approaches the projected population level made several years earlier by the state, that population projection is likely to be inaccurate. In Exhibit 3-17 the estimated population level for 1986 fits nicely between the actual 1980 population figure and the projected 1990 figure. However, in rapidly growing areas in which the growth was unanticipated or undervalued, the actual updated population for 1986 and the projected value for 1990 could both be 54,000. In this case the market analyst would have to adjust the state agency's projection for 1990. The adjustment must be logical and based on the facts discovered in the analysis.

Once the level of population is forecast, the number of households can also be forecast. This is accomplished by determining the historic trend in household size for the study area, judging its future size, and dividing this estimate into the population forecast.

Forecasting without an Existing Prediction[4]   If an independent population projection is not available from a reputable government or private agency, the ratio method is not applicable. In this case one of the other techniques must be used. For purposes of discussion, the natural increase and migration method will be used.

Since relatively short time periods are of major concern for small area forecasting, the structure of the natural increase and migration method as displayed in Exhibit 3-11 does not have to be changed. Assuming that the forecast is being made for 1990, the information needed to make the forecast can be taken from Exhibit 3-11. First, approximately 12,000 females are in the primary childbearing years in 1980. The exact number of such women will depend on the relative number of women in the 6–15 age cohort in 1980 who will move into the 16–44 age cohort by 1990 and the number of women in the 26–45 age group in 1980 who will move out of the 16–44 age cohort by 1990. A first approximation would set the inflow equal to the outflow so that the size of the 16–44 age cohort is assumed to be stable at 12,000 women.

[4]*Ibid.*, p. 219.

If this assumption is made, there should be approximately 5,760 births between 1986 and 1990. There should also be about 1,290 deaths between 1986 and 1990. The net effect of the births less deaths will be an increase in population.

But there is complexity with regard to the net migration estimate. The first approximation for new migration could be the simple extrapolation of the 1980–1986 net migration value of +3,000. But an appropriate approach would be an analysis of the 1980–1986 migration figures and the economic and social factors underlying that migration. Then, comparing expectations for the future with the historic economic trends, the migration forecast is made.

If the growth enabling factors in the census tract are still favorable, the historic trend can be readily extended into the future. However, if the ability to grow is retarded because of a factor such as a limited supply of land for residential use, then the future growth will be much less than the historic trend.

Updating and Forecasting Income[5]

Updates and forecasts for income such as median per capita income or household income are usually made by the market analyst since yearly updates from the census year may not be available and forecasts from other sources are rare. The easiest updating procedure requires the analyst to obtain consumer price index (CPI) data that can be applied to study an area. Since the information to construct the CPI is only gathered in a limited number of geographic areas, the best that can be claimed is that the CPI is a relatively good proxy. However, the increase in the CPI can reflect the income change when certain points are kept in mind.

1. When the rate of inflation is small and stable over time, real household and per capita income tend to increase in close proportion to the CPI change.
2. When inflation is large and volatile, real income typically declines.
3. Geographic areas with relatively high median incomes tend to capture all (or more) of the price increase in the form of an income increase.
4. Geographic areas with below-average income levels tend not to capture the full extent of the income change.
5. The change in income tends to lag the change in the price level by about a year.

Assuming that those observations are generally true, an update for income is obtained by multiplying the level of income given in the latest census by the percentage change in the CPI from 1980 to the present. Then this value is added to the 1980 figure.

Forecasting the level of income usually relies on the judicious use of graphic/mathematical and ratio techniques. The historic trend in income for the study area is displayed. Then a year-by-year change in income is also displayed.

[5]*Ibid.*, pp. 220–221.

This data stream could be the figures for per capita personal income in the U.S. gross national products accounts. The ratio technique can be used to see how the historic local area values compare to the historic national figures over time. Once such comparisons are made, the analyst can make a judgment about future levels of local income by projecting reasonable historic growth rates for national income figures. The judgment reflects prior knowledge about many factors. Some of the important ones are the following:

1. The comparison should be made in real terms to eliminate geographic differences in CPI changes.
2. The participation rate affects the level of household income as well as per capita income.
3. Geographic relocation of industry into and out of the area must be considered.
4. The nature of the local economy industrial structure with regard to growth versus stagnant industries must be analyzed.

In conclusion, the level of income can be updated using published data, and the level of income can be forecast by comparing historic values in published data. However, the accuracy of the revised income level is usually not very great in the early years of either the update or a forecast, so it is not accurate in the later years. Yet the income level must be revised because not forecasting income is worse than making a forecast that may be inaccurate.

READINGS

CHAPIN, F. STUART, and EDWARD J. KAISER, *Urban Land Use Planning*. Chicago: University of Illinois, 1979.

DASSO, JEROME J., "Economic Base Analysis for the Appraiser," *Appraisal Journal*, July, 1969.

GOLDBERG, MICHAEL, and PETER CHINLOY, *Urban Land Economics*. New York: John Wiley & Sons, 1984.

HARTSHORN, TRUMAN A., *Interpreting The City*. New York: John Wiley & Sons, 1980.

HEILBRUN, JAMES., *Urban Economics and Public Policy*. New York: St. Martin's Press, 1987.

NOURSE, HUGH O., *Regional Economics*. New York: McGraw-Hill Book Co., 1968.

PITTENGER, D., *Projecting State and Local Populations*. Cambridge, Mass.: Ballinger Publishing Co., 1976.

RABIANSKI, J., "An Alternative to Economic Base Analysis," *The Real Estate Appraiser*, October/September, 1977.

RABIANSKI, J., "Real Earnings and Human Migration," *Journal of Human Resources*, Spring, 1971.

SJAASTAD, L., "The Costs and Returns of Human Migration," *Journal of Political Economy*, Supplement: October, 1962.

4

DEFINING THE MARKET
AND ELEMENTS OF THE STUDY

INTRODUCTION

Understanding three interrelated concepts helps understanding the workings of the market. The three interrelated concepts are (1) the nature of the real estate product, (2) the characteristics of the consumers of that product, and (3) the nature and characteristics of the suppliers/producers of the product. A key concept in understanding the product is a process called market disaggregation. The disaggregation process classifies similar, substitutable types of real estate as a means of identifying a single product traded in a real estate market. Similarly, understanding the consumer in the market requires the use of a process called market segmentation. Segmentation is useful because it clusters buyers according to key characteristics which influence their selection of a product. Both disaggregation and segmentation are employed to identify market forces needed to analyze and forecast those outcomes of critical interest. The first major section of this chapter presents a discussion of the disaggregation and segmentation concepts. In addition, market interrelationships are also discussed because they are a direct result of the disaggregation process.

When these definitions and processes are firmly in mind, the analyst proceeds by analyzing the economic and demographic variables that affect the specific real estate market and its interrelationships with other markets. This analysis requires (1) understanding of demand and supply components, (2) the survey and evaluation of the competition, and, (3) understanding the benefits that can be derived from consumer research. These topics will be the subject matter for the major section of this chapter.

CHARACTERISTICS OF THE MARKET

The market for real estate is substantially different from the markets for other goods, largely because of the fixity of location. The market is fragmented, localized, composed of interrelated submarkets, decentralized. Historically, it has been less organized than other markets. These market characteristics are explained in the following sections and related to the process of market research.

Market Disaggregation[1]

Real estate is not a standardized good. To facilitate analysis, the market for real estate can be broken down into distinct submarkets. The process of dividing a market into smaller, more homogeneous submarkets is called market disaggregation. It is an important step in real estate market analysis because it sharpens the analysis by selecting the submarket to be studied in greater detail.

The first level of disaggregation, once a market area is specified, is by type of land use—residential, commercial, and industrial. Within each of the three major categories, additional distinctions can be identified. Residential real estate is next subdivided by tenure status between owner-occupied and renter-

[1] Material in this section is taken with permission from Donald R. Epley and Joseph Rabianski, *Principles of Real Estate Decisions* (Englewood Cliffs, N.J.: Prentice-Hall, 1986), Chapter 7, "Housing Market Analysis," pp. 175–196.

occupied units. Owner-occupied residences may then be classified by physical type, as single-family detached units, as duplexes, or as townhouses (single-family attached units). The single-family detached housing units can be divided further on the basis of price range, architectural style (ranch, split-level, bi-level), size of the housing unit, size of the lot, the floor plan, number of rooms, number of full baths, basement/attic storage space, fixtures, and so on. The end result of this refinement process is the identification of a relatively standardized class of product that comprises a particular sector of the real estate market in which the determinants of supply and demand are relatively uniform.

Because of the immobility of real estate, markets for real estate are local markets. A property is also affected by its location and surrounding off-site improvements. Thus, even if the impact of these attributes is negative, the property owner cannot escape the environment by moving the real estate to another location.

The consequence of localized real estate markets is that a house located in one urban area can be valued differently from an identical house in another urban area or in different sections of the same urban area solely because of its locational attributes. Moreover, such value differences can also occur in different sections of the same urban area. Therefore, once the market is disaggregated on use, tenure, and physical characteristics, the geographic dimension of the submarket must be specified. The area specification, or market area delineation, could be central city versus suburban, northern suburbs versus western suburbs, neighborhood A versus neighborhood B, for example. However the local geographic area is differentiated, the process of disaggregation by location is another major step.

Newly constructed units must be distinguished from existing units. This distinction can be viewed as market disaggregation among housing units by the age of the structure.

Market Segmentation

Once market disaggregation identifies the specific product, the focus shifts to consumers in the market. Consumers may be classified by groups which have similar characteristics and will express about the same characteristics in their preferences for a specific real estate product. This process of subdividing consumers into smaller groups with similar characteristics is called market segmentation.

Market segmentation can occur on the basis of several consumer characteristics. First, segmentation can occur based on the demographic characteristics of age and sex. The second group of characteristics used in market segmentation are the economic characteristics of the consumer. The most important of these is income. The psychographic characteristics of the consumer present a third segmentation variable that can be used. In this instance, the consumers are divided into distinct groups based upon their attitudes, preference patterns, tastes, and/or behavior. With psychographic variables, the analyst can distinguish among the individuals who are in the same income and age group.

Demand and Supply Relationships[2]

All commodity markets, including real estate markets, are composed of two distinct groups of participants. First, there is a group of individuals who are able and willing to purchase the commodity—the demand side of the market, which represents the consumers. Second, there is a group that is able and willing to produce and make the product available for sale—the supply side of the market. There are distinct and often unique demand and supply characteristics for each specific real estate submarket. Following is a discussion of key demand and supply relationships. In the example used in this discussion, it is assumed the market under study consists of 1- to 10-year-old, moderate-sized, single-family, detached units in the northern section of an urban area.

The Demand Curve   The range of possible prices for the commodity can extend from zero dollars to some finite number of dollars. At each of these possible prices, a different number of households will express interest in the property. These price-quantity relationships are shown in Exhibit 4-1. At a very high price, such as that expressed by P_M, households are not interested in obtaining any of these housing units. At a price of zero dollars, the households in the community are able and willing to buy a large quantity of units, expressed by Q_M. The quantity desired at a price of zero is not infinite because of several limiting factors: (1) the total number of households is finite; (2) some households will not desire this form of housing because it is too small, too cheap, or too far

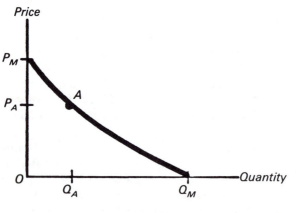

Exhibit 4-1   The demand curve.

²*Ibid.*, pp. 178–181.

from their jobs; and (3) some households will not be able to incur the other expenses of ownership even if the purchase price were zero.

At each of the possible prices between the end points of the curve, a certain number of households are willing and able to purchase this type of housing unit. For example, quantity Q_A will be purchased at price P_A. As the possible price decreases below P_A, the quantity of housing desired will increase as more households are able and willing to buy this type of residential unit. The demand relationship is easily expressed as an inverse relationship between possible prices and quantities desired. As the price declines, quantity desired increases.

The Supply Curve   The demand curve represents only one side of the market—consumer preference and desires for the commodity. The supply curve is the other side of the market. The supply curve expresses the ability and willingness of the owners and builders of residential units to sell their properties. Like demand, the supply of units on the market must be disaggregated by physical and locational characteristics. However, the supply curve explicitly reflects the distinctions between new and used structures, whereas the demand curve treats this distinction as a form of disaggregation. In other words, the demand for new housing units can look like the demand for used or existing units. However, the graph of these curves on the supply side can take a different shape. There are basic supply curves, described in the next sections.

UNITS OFFERED FOR SALE   One supply relationship is the ability and willingness of a particular group of owners to sell their units. For example, assume the units consist of existing, 1- to 10-year-old, moderate-sized, single-family, detached housing units. This relationship is shown in Exhibit 4-2. At a price below P_N, none of the present owners are willing to sell their housing units. The reason is they know that a price of P_N is necessary to enable them to find

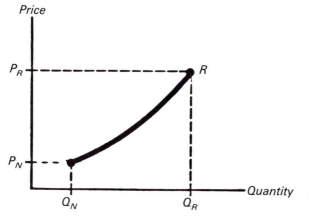

Exhibit 4-2 The supply curve of units offered for sale.

equally suitable housing in some other segment of the market. As the possible sales price increases, the number of these residential units offered for sale increases until point R is reached. At point R, the price is so high that every household unit in this submarket is offered for sale. Q_R is the total number of housing units at this time, so quantities of such housing units above Q_R do not exist. Therefore, even at possible prices above P_R, the quantity of units offered for sale remains at Q_R.

A time element must be kept in mind in analyzing the supply side of the market. In the example, the time span considered is limited to the construction cycle, which can be viewed as 90 days or the length of time during which Q_R (the total stock of existing housing units of the specified type) is constant. As the time period of the analysis lengthens beyond 90 days, more houses become 1 year old, some 1- to 10-year-old houses are destroyed by fire and 10-year-old houses become 11 years old. Thus, for a 180-day-period or a 360-day period, the existing stock of housing can be equal to, greater than, or less than Q_R, depending upon the relative magnitude of new construction, demolition, and aging of the units.

EXISTING STOCK   In addition to the supply of existing units that are offered for sale, the supply side of the market for the type of housing under study could be specified in another way. The total supply (all units in the area whether or not they are for sale) of existing, 1- to 10-year-old, moderate-sized, single-family, detached housing units in the northern section of the urban area can be analyzed. This supply curve for this event is depicted in Exhibit 4-3. It differs from the supply curve in Exhibit 4-2 because it is a perfectly vertical line, reflecting the fact that the total supply of such housing units is perfectly fixed during the time period under analysis. Thus, whether the price of such housing is P_N or P_R, the total number of units in existence is exactly the same; that is, total supply equals quantity Q_R, at this point in time. However, as the time period changes, the existing stock of units can also change.

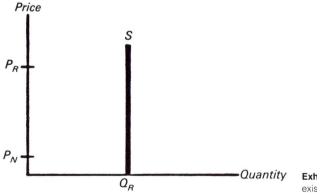

Exhibit 4-3   The supply curve of existing units.

NEW CONSTRUCTION   The third aspect of the supply side to be analyzed is newly constructed units. The new units are similar to others. They are moderate-sized, single-family, detached housing units in the northern section of the urban area. This supply curve is plotted in Exhibit 4-4. The builders of new housing units require that a minimum price be reached in the market before they undertake any construction activity. This minimum price, depicted as P_K, must be high enough to cover the cost of materials, labor, and land that are used in production. Moreover, the price must be high enough to provide some return to the management or owners of the construction company. If the price is less than P_K, no units will be constructed. If the price is equal to P_K, some positive number of units, such as Q_K, will be erected. As the possible price rises above P_K, the quantity of units that the builders are able and willing to build will increase.

The Determination of Price in a Market[3]

The two groups representing supply and demand in the market interact as depicted in Exhibit 4-5, which again represents the market for existing, 1- to 10-year-old, moderate-priced, single-family, detached housing units in the northern section of the urban area.

The market allows both groups of people, as groups but not as individuals, to become simultaneously satisfied. There is only a single point at which the price-quantity relationship producing this mutual satisfaction occurs: point H in Exhibit 4-5. At price P_H, suppliers are willing to supply Q_H and buyers are willing to buy Q_H housing units. At prices above P_H, the suppliers of this type housing as a group are willing to sell more units than potential buyers desire. At prices below P_H, the group of potential buyers are willing to purchase more units than the group of owners are willing to sell. If the market is not encumbered

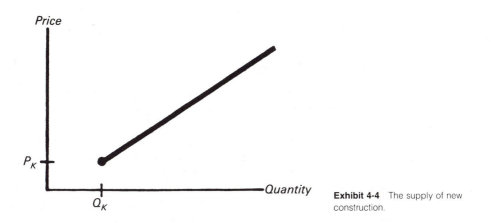

Exhibit 4-4 The supply of new construction.

[3]Material in this section is taken with permission from *ibid.*, pp. 181–182.

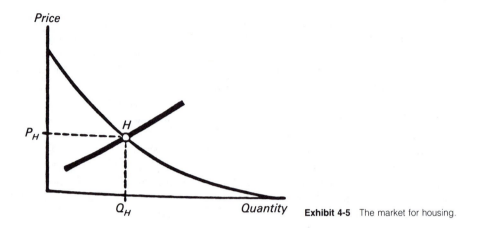

Exhibit 4-5 The market for housing.

in any way, if the potential buyers and potential sellers are allowed to analyze the market and obtain all relevant information, if there is adequate time to negotiate, and if there is no pressure or force exerted on any of the participants, then the market for this housing will clear at price P_H and quantity Q_H.

ACTIVITY IN THE MARKET

The level of activity in a real estate market is influenced by the changes in the economic and demographic factors that underlie demand and supply. Market analysis is basically an examination of these factors to forecast the impact of their changes on the price and the quantity outcomes in the market. A more detailed discussion of demand and supply factors appears in Chapter 7 for the housing market, in Chapter 9 for the retail market, and in Chapter 11 for the office market.

Types of Market Activity

Analysts and others in the real estate industry have used many terms to describe activity in real estate markets. Some of the earliest terms used to describe market activity were a "buyer's market" or "seller's market," "tight market," "balanced market," or "broad versus narrow markets." This section will examine the meaning of these terms, and other more appropriate terms, in the context of demand and supply analysis in a real estate market.

The housing market will be used as the major focus in the following discussion. Two distinct submarkets—new construction and resale—will also be used to point out ambiguities and other aspects of problems regarding terminology.

Activity in the Resale Market[4]

Market analysis can be applied to any specific real estate submarket. One such submarket could be the existing stock of a selected type of housing that is being offered for sale. The analyst knows a historical fact: this type of housing is currently selling for price P_E, and in the current period quantity Q_E units of this type of housing were sold in the market. This fact is shown in Exhibit 4-6. The market analyst undertakes to forecast the price and quantity of sales in the next period. Assume the analyst discovers that over the next three months interest rates on mortgages will decline and there will be a new inflow of households into the market area that prefer this type of housing unit. Based on a forecast of these aspects of the market, the analyst recognizes that the demand for this type of housing will increase, causing the price to rise above that given as price P_E. This higher level of demand will intersect the existing supply curve at point F in the next period. The analyst makes this deduction under the condition that the existing supply of such housing remains unchanged.

However, if new construction exceeds demolitions and no conversions occur, the number of units of this housing offered for sale at each possible price might increase in the next period. The new demand and supply curves can intersect in the next period at a point such as G in Exhibit 4-6. In contrast, if demolitions exceed new construction and no conversions take place, the supply of this housing will be less in the next period. The lower level of supply coupled with an increase in demand will lead to a shift from point E to point H.

When the level of demand increases, and this increase is accompanied by a relatively smaller change in supply (either an increase or a decrease), the

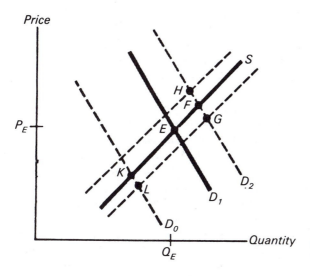

Exhibit 4-6 Market for existing units of housing offered for sale.

[4]*Ibid.*, pp. 191–194.

analyst can forecast an increase in price as well as an increase in the number of units offered for sale. When such price and quantity increases are forecast, the market is referred to as an "active market" for this type of housing unit.

An active market is a market that exhibits increasing levels of demand accompanied by a relatively smaller change (increase, decrease, or no change) in supply. An active market can be initiated by any change in the economic and demographic factors that cause an increase in demand. For example, an increase in the consumer's real income level, an increase in the price of substitute housing, and a reduction in ownership costs could cause the shift in demand.

A dull market would be a market in which the price and the quantity traded decline because a reduction in the level of demand is accompanied by a change (increase or decrease) in supply that is of a smaller magnitude. In other words, a dull market is the reverse of an active market. Graphically, an active market is a movement from point E to points such as F, G, and H in Exhibit 4-6, which represent higher prices with higher quantities traded. A dull market is a movement from point E to points such as K and L, which represent a decline in price accompanied by a decline in the number of units sold.

Active and dull markets are often referred to as a "seller's market" and a "buyer's market," respectively. A buyer's market (dull market) has been defined in the following way: "In a buyer's market properties are offered in great numbers, but the competition among buyers is not keen. Indeed, few buyers appear at any price." This statement is the same as saying that as demand declines, the number of units offered for sale increases. For example, in Exhibit 4-6 this phenomenon is depicted by the movement from point E to point K to point L. However, for all practical purposes, a movement from point E to point K can also be viewed as a buyers' market because the price has declined.

A seller's market (active market) "would result from the opposite conditions. . . . The supply of real estate decreases . . . sales are more frequent . . . (and there are increases) in demand." Graphically, this situation is depicted in Exhibit 4-6 as a movement from point E to point F to point H. But the movements from point E to point F, and even to point G, can also be considered as a seller's market because the price has risen.

In addition to these active and dull market conditions, two other situations can arise in a housing market. Price and quantity sold move in the same direction in both the active and the dull markets. In the active market, price and quantity sold both decrease; in the dull market, the price and quantity sold decrease. However, certain situations in the market can lead to price increases accompanied by a decline in the quantity traded, and to price decreases accompanied by an increase in the quantity traded. These two situations are graphically depicted in Exhibit 4-7. A movement from point E to a point such as R is caused by a decline in the supply of units offered for sale. This situation should occur if demolitions exceed new construction so that the stock of this housing unit declines. Or it could happen if households offer less of these units for sale from the existing stock. The result of these changes is an increased price in the next

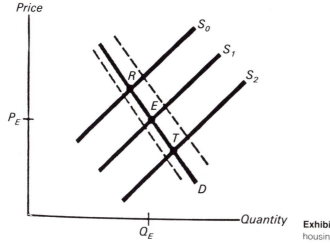

Exhibit 4-7 Market for existing units of housing offered for sale.

period accompanied by a reduction in the number of units offered for sale in that period. In contrast, a movement from point E to point T can be caused by an increase in supply as new construction exceeds demolitions, causing an increase in the stock, or as households offer more units for sale from existing stock. The results of this change are a reduction in price and an increase in the number of units traded in the market in the next period.

Such movements are not called buyer's or seller's markets as previously defined. These changes represent unique market situations that can and do occur in housing markets. By means of the graph in Exhibit 4-8, names can be given to all four types of market changes phenomena. A movement from E as shown in Exhibit 4-6 can take place into any of the four regions shown in Exhibit 4-8. These four regions, and the combinations of demand and supply changes

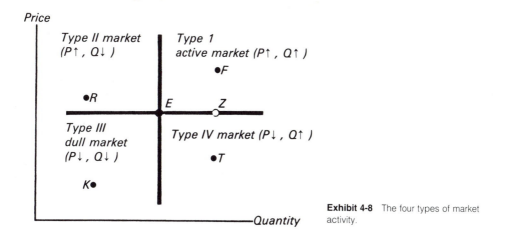

Exhibit 4-8 The four types of market activity.

that cause the movements into these regions, are labeled market activity Types I–IV. The direction of the market movement and its magnitude depend on the direction and magnitude of the shifts in demand and supply caused by changes in their underlying economic and demographic factors.

A relatively infrequent but possible occurrence is the movement from point E to a point on one of the boundary lines. A move from point E to point Z is such a situation. Is this movement a Type I or Type IV movement? For the sake of simplicity, it can be considered a Type I movement. It is an increase in the number of units traded at a constant price in the next period.

Activity in the New Construction Market[5]

The market for newly constructed housing units can be analyzed in the same way as the market for existing housing units. Market analysis can lead to forecasts of an active (Type I), dull (Type III), Type II, or Type IV market phenomenon. The distinguishing feature is that the supply of new housing units is affected primarily by construction costs. As the prices of the factors of production (land, labor, equipment, loans, and materials) increase, the supply in the new housing market decreases. On the other hand, the supply in the market for existing units offered for sale is affected primarily by the size of the existing stock and the expectations/aspirations of the owners of real estate. In addition, economic/demographic factors affect the owners' willingness to sell their existing housing units.

Other Descriptive Terms for Market Activity

In addition to the concepts of buyers' and sellers' markets, there are several other commonly used terms that can be misleading. First, the distinction between a "strong market" and a "weak (soft) market" is the same as the distinction between Type I market activity and Type III market activity, respectively. However, the terms "strong," "weak," and "soft" do not have precise economic meanings. For example, some people might interpret Type II market activity to be "weak" or "soft" because the quantity sold has declined even though house prices have increased. Another person might interpret Type IV market activity as "weak" because house prices have declined even though the volume of sale activity has increased. To add to the confusion, another individual might consider Type IV market activity to be "strong" because volume has increased. So, what is Type IV market activity? Is it a "strong" or a "weak" market? The authors are unable to offer acceptable definitions for these vague terms. A better system of describing market activity needs to be employed to avoid misperceptions and confusion.

[5] *Ibid.*, p. 194.

The terms "broad" and "narrow" should also be avoided. To deal with the terms "narrow" and "broad," recall the discussion of market disaggregation and market segmentation. A "narrow" market describes a general housing market in which only one, or a few, of the submarkets is (are) experiencing market activity. Some users of the term believe it specifies that price and quantity are increasing in a narrow market. This makes a "narrow" market one in which Type I market activity is occurring. A "broad" market would then become a general housing market in which "many" (imprecise) submarkets are experiencing market activity (possibly Type I). Since these terms have no particular or accepted meanings in economic thought, they are not applicable in describing market conditions in real estate.

Terms that are best used to describe tomatoes (soft), muscles (strong or weak), and suit coat lapels (broad or narrow) should be dropped by real estate market analysts in favor of terms that carry market significance in an economic context. The real estate analyst may have to wait for the stock market pundits to abandon these terms. Discussion of such descriptive terms as "tight" and "balanced" markets must await the following discussions about vacancy and absorption analysis. So they will be examined after the next section.

Vacancy Analysis[6]

In the preceding discussion, the assumption was made that, at the prevailing market price, the number of units desired or demanded of a given housing type was exactly equal to the number of units provided; that is, the market cleared. Such a situation is rare in real estate markets. At any given time, there are existing single-family housing units that are vacant and for sale. There are new single-family housing units that have not been sold, while more of these units are being constructed. There are vacant apartments for rent. There are vacant retail stores, offices, and factories. Vacancies occur in the various real estate markets when the prevailing price in the market is greater than the price that would clear the market. In the market for newly constructed housing units, shown in Exhibit 4-9, the prevailing price is P_A and the market-clearing price is P_E. At the prevailing price, the builders of these new units expect to sell quantity Q_S and, therefore, are willing and able to construct this output level. However, at this price, potential buyers are only willing and able to buy quantity Q_D units. Consequently, a fraction of the new units actually constructed are unsold and remain vacant. The actual number of new vacancies is the difference between Q_S and Q_D. Typically, vacancies are stated as a rate or percentage. Vacancies are zero when P_E equals P_A. At this price, there is a single quantity level Q_S because Q_D is equal to Q_E, which equals Q_S.

There is a "desirable" level of vacancies as perceived by the participants in the market. These vacant units facilitate smoothing operation of the real estate

[6]*Ibid.*, pp. 195–196.

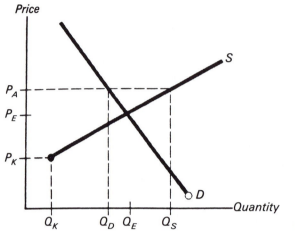

Exhibit 4-9 A market for new housing.

market by allowing for household and business mobility. Deviations from this desirable level of vacancies set in motion forces that can be seen in the market.

Knowledge of the level of vacancy is important to participants on both sides of the market. On the demand side, the consumer should realize that each vacant unit costs the builder the periodic interest payment on the loan used to construct that unit. The higher the number of vacancies, the greater the consumer's bargaining strength in the market and, thus, the greater the consumer's relative ability to obtain a price less that P_A.

On the supply side, low levels of vacancies (below normal vacancies) are to the builder's advantage in the bargaining process. The lower the vacancy rate, the greater the builder's ability to obtain the anticipated price of P_A. More important, vacancy analysis provides a signal to the builder about future construction needs in the market. An increase in the number of vacant new units is a clear indication of excess construction in the submarket. Current vacancies signal the need to produce fewer units in this submarket in the next construction period.

Vacancy analysis is an important part of market analysis because it not only signals changing levels of new construction, it also signals movement of price in the resale market and of changing rent levels in the apartment market. If vacancies are large in the current period, new construction levels in the future periods will decline as builders adjust the pace of new construction. The question of what constitutes "large vacancies" should be considered by the market analyst, who assesses what has been typical in the market in recent periods and what would be necessary in that market in the near future.

Vacancy analysis can also signal price and rent changes in the case of increasing demand in the market. If vacancies are high (above the typical levels necessary for mobility), an increase in demand may not lead to an increase in price until the level of current vacancies declines. If, on the other hand, current levels of vacancy are low, an increase in demand can lead to price and rent increases. This can occur as long as the increase in demand exceeds any increase in supply in the market. Vacancy analysis is an important tool for the analyst because it helps to refine the short-term forecasts of the volume of activity and price or rent level.

Absorption Analysis

Absorption analysis is principally a demand consideration. It attempts to measure the position of the demand curve in a given market which has a time dimension. Economists define the concept of demand as the amount of a product that consumers are able and willing to buy at all possible prices during a given period of time.

An examination of the two panels in Exhibit 4-10 reveals the nature of absorption in the market. In panel A, the prevailing market price is P_a, and the demand is given by the demand curve D_1. The supply curve is also shown as S_1, and it allows for the identification of vacancies. This panel represents the market for new construction. Absorption is shown as 1,000 units during this period of time, usually stated as a year.

Panel B represents the next period of time. Here absorption is 400 units. In these instances the absorption rate is 1,000 units per year in the first year and 400 units per year in the following year.

The example is the simplest occurrence of absorption that can occur. First, the supply in the current period exceeded the demand, so there was current period vacancy. Second, absorption occurred at the same prevailing price level in each year.

Exhibit 4-10 Market absorption.

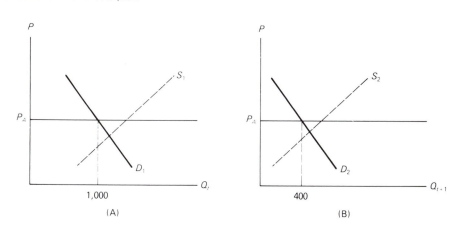

(A) (B)

This situation is not the only way in which absorption can occur. Absorption analysis may have to cross over into the past construction period. For example, consumers may have purchased all the current production (leaving no unsold (vacant) units for the current period) and purchased unsold units that were produced in the previous period and held as unintended inventory. If this situation occurs, absorption exceeds current production.

Notice that in the two situations presented, absorption is never given as current period production levels. In the first instance, absorption (1,000 units in panel (A) and 400 units in panel (B)) was less than the production level given by the intersection of the supply curve with the prevailing price, P_A. In the second situation, absorption exceeded current production by the amount that the builders' inventories were reduced. To measure market absorption, the analyst must look beyond current production.

Exhibit 4-10 contains a simplified example because it assumes that the prevailing price in the market stays the same. The example assumes that the supply curve in the market moves in harmony with the demand curve from one production period to the next. As demand declines, from panel (A) to panel (B), the supply curve also declines to the appropriate level. This keeps the unsold units in each market situation equal. The close matching of demand and supply is very unlikely. Builders may underestimate the decline in demand and drop their production levels, but not by enough to match the change in demand. Unsold units in the second period will increase, and the prevailing price may hold, or the builders will lower their asking price. On the other hand, the builders may overestimate the decline in demand and lower their production. If production is lowered by more than demand indicates, it may cause the sale of all current production and the sale of unsold previous period production. In this situation, builders may raise the prevailing price.

From period to period, a relatively high level of absorption can occur while prices are increasing. When this occurs, absorption figures for the last 5 to 10 years might vary widely, with prices having changed in the market over time. Another complication that may also arise is an increase in the costs of construction labor, materials, and loans, as well as land. These increases can cause the supply curve to change at the same time it is being shifted by the builders' production decisions, which are based on expected levels of demand and consideration of costs.

A big problem with absorption analysis occurs when a naive market analyst presents historical absorption figures for a market area in which the physical product has been changing over time. For example, eight years ago, builders may have been constructing 1,800-square-foot units, whereas today they are constructing 2,600-square-foot units. The historic absorption figures represent the same geographic area, but not the same housing market.

A third point that the analyst needs to keep in mind is that absorption analysis is a concept of the future, not the past. When historical data for past period absorption are used, it can only serve as a way of judging the order of magnitude for the forecasting of the absorption rate. Any manipulation of historic data, regardless of the sophistication of the technique, is just background. The economic circumstances in the future market will be different to varying degrees from the economic circumstances of past market periods. As discussed, analysts should perform forecasts, not projections.

In conclusion, absorption analysis appears to be a demand concept, but in reality it also must consider the effects of supply. Furthermore, it is subject to improper specification if the analyst does not realize that over time, the prevailing price in the market can change. In addition, the submarket being served by the builders may change over time.

Project Specific Absorption Analysis

A specific project in a given market has its own level of absorption, or capture rate, that the analyst may be requested to estimate. In this case, the analyst is asked, "What part of the market's absorption can the project capture?" To make this estimate, the analyst must determine the project's relative attractiveness to the consumer. How does the subject compare to the existing competitive properties and to any new competition that is currently under construction? To start the analysis, the analyst must undertake a survey of the competition—a technique that is described in Chapter 5. Using the survey of the competition in conjunction with absorption analysis allows the analyst to make a judgment about the project's absorption potential, or its capture rate.

Other Descriptive Terms—A Continuation

There are two other pairs of terms which are often confusing. One is the "tight" versus "loose" market distinction. A "tight" market usually refers to a market with a low level of vacancies compared to the level that has been typical for that market. In contrast, a loose market usually refers to a market with a high vacancy level. Tight or loose markets can occur when demand levels are high or low. They depend on how accurately builders estimate the level of demand and, consequently, determine production levels.

In addition, the term "tight" is also used to represent an overall market in which the consumers have little or a low level of choice with regard to available units or space. In other words, supply is adequate for only one or a few of many submarkets.

Markets have also been described as "balanced" markets. But, unfortunately, this term means different things to different analysts. To an economist, a market is balanced when demand is exactly equal to supply in that market. This only occurs at the intersection of these curves. In the context of Exhibit 4-10, the curves intersect at a price that is less than the prevailing price, P_A. The economist refers to this as the equilibrium position in the market. On the contrary, real estate market analysts use the term "balanced" to mean that a "normal" level of vacancy occurs in the market—the situation occurring at the prevailing price in the market.

To add to the ambiguity of the term "balanced," analysts often use it to represent the situation where the overall market can be characterized by several disaggregated submarkets that are experiencing approximately equal levels of sales. In this sense the term "balanced" is being used as the opposite of the term "tight."

5

ANALYZING THE SUBJECT PROPERTY AND ITS COMPETITIVE ENVIRONMENT

INTRODUCTION

In the previous chapter the analysis focused on the market and was not site specific; it was product or use specific. In this chapter the analysis focuses on how a specific property is able to compete in the market. A study which examines how a specific property is able to compete is a marketability analysis.

The data used in the market study and the information derived from it are inputs to the marketability analysis. The marketability analysis extends the market study by adding information derived from the site-specific analysis and ascertaining the competitive potential of a specific project and judging the project's potential for attracting a definable part of market demand available.

A complete analysis of the subject property and its environment requires several major tasks. First, the nature of the subject property must be known. This requires a thorough review of its legal, physical, and locational characteristics. Second, the competition that the property encounters in the market must be known. Third, the reaction of the occupants or user of the property must be understood. (The ultimate user of the property is either the occupant, such as a household in a residential unit, or people who come to the site to perform an activity, such as customers using a retail space.) Then, all this information must be analyzed to judge the effect of these factors on the marketability of the subject property. This chapter addresses three major facets of the market analysis process that feed into the analysis before final marketability conclusions can be reached: (1) analysis of the subject property, (2) competitive survey, and (3) customer research.

ANALYSIS OF THE CHARACTERISTICS OF THE SUBJECT PROPERTY

An analysis of the subject property accomplishes two things. First, it identifies the features of the subject property—desirable and undesirable, curable and incurable. Second, it establishes the items that form the comparison between the subject property and its competition. A discussion of the subject property's characteristics follows.

Legal Characteristics

The legal characteristics of the subject property are important because it is critical for the analyst to know what rights are possessed by the owner and what restrictions apply to these rights. The first concern of the market analyst is a determination of what activity is legally permissible on the subject property. To obtain information pertinent to this aspect of inquiry, the analyst should examine the following:

1. *The zoning of the property*: to identify use restrictions and associated development standards and requirements.
2. *Requirements in the subdivision regulations*: to identify type, design, and standards for required land infrastructure improvements.
3. *Construction code requirements*: to identify minimum design and materials standards for constructing buildings.
4. *Occupancy code requirements*: to identify maintenance and operational standards for occupying buildings.
5. *Environmental and pollution restrictions*: to identify compliance standards in the construction and operation of real property.
6. *Nature and availability of public services*: to determine availability and cost of obtaining essential services.

7. *Deed restrictions:* to identify requirements and compliance actions needed.
8. *Other legal restrictions:* to identify any easements, contracts, or other elements that may restrict property operations.

When the analyst examines these restrictions and requirements imposed by these legal requirements, the legally permissible uses that can be placed on the subject site can be identified.

Physical Characteristics of the Site and the Improvements

Once the legal restrictions are known, the analyst checks the physical characteristics of the property. This includes restrictions on any development imposed by the natural features of the site and any existing improvements. The factors that are analyzed include the following:

1. Site configuration features, including:
   a. Size of the land parcel.
   b. Shape of the land parcel.
   c. Frontage.
   d. Width and depth of the land parcel.
   e. Corner influences.
2. The natural features of the site, including:
   a. Topography (slope and terrain).
   b. Surface soil quality and landscaping.
   c. Subsoil and bedrock characteristics.
   d. Drainage and runoff characteristics (hydrology).
   e. Vegetative cover.
3. Physical characteristics of the improvement, including:
   a. The placement of the structure on the site.
   b. Quantitative and qualitative construction details.
   c. An analysis of the mechanical systems in the improvement.
   d. An analysis of the physical design and layout of the space within the improvement.
   e. Age and condition of the structure.
   f. Special features of the structure such as covered walkways, enclosed entry ways, location of the units within the structure.
   g. Traffic patterns inside the structure, special characteristics of the structure that are viewed as attractive. (This could include design features, floor layouts, positioning window openings, lighting, carpeting, size of the individual units in terms of square footage as well as the type of space being provided bedrooms, bathrooms, living room, dining room, etc.).
   h. Special structural features such as balconies, patios, screened porches.
4. Site amenities, including:
   a. Parking features such as number of spaces, location of the parking facilities relative to the entrance of the structure, and covered area.
   b. Security and safety factors.

These physical features associated with the site and the improvements on the site establish the second set of limiting requirements. A more detailed methodology for performing a physical analysis is described in Chapter 6. Not only must the economic activity be legally permissible, but it must also be physically possible given the physical characteristics of the site and the improvements.

Economic/Financial/Locational Characteristics

In addition to the legal and physical characteristics, the subject property also possesses economic characteristics in the form of location or accessibility features and financial features. The analyst should also identify these features and evaluate their effect on the property. Here is a partial list of these characteristics:

1. Locational or accessibility features, including:
   a. Proximity to employment centers, shopping facilities, entertainment, recreational, and cultural activities.
   b. Proximity to major streets and public transportation.
   c. Proximity to fire and police protection, hospitals.
   d. Proximity to schools especially if the subject property contains residential units.
2. Financial characteristics, including:
   a. Sales prices or rent levels for the space.
   b. Special financial arrangements associated with the sale or rental of the space. This could include price discounts, rent abatement, below-market rate financing, rent escalations, and the provision of special or supplementary fixtures and appliances.
   c. Special charges that may take place in the future. This category can include special assessments for public improvements.

After the legal, physical, and economic characteristics of the subject property are analyzed, many potential uses are eliminated, but some are still possible. These legally permissible, physically possible, and economically supportable uses for the subject property must now be analyzed in greater detail.

A more detailed discussion of these characteristics and their effect on marketability will be presented in the next and subsequent chapters. The purpose of the discussion at this point is to set out a system by which the characteristics of the subject property can be compared to its competition. But before the analysis can move to the comparison, the subject property's competitive area must be determined.

DEFINITION OF THE COMPETITIVE AREA AND THE CONCEPT OF LINKAGES

A definition of the subject property's competitive area is a bridge in the comparison of the subject property and its competition. The competitive area is the geographic space in which the competition operates.

The procedures needed to define the competitive trade area or market area, for housing and for retail activity, contain some common characteristics. Whether the competitive area is for housing or for retail activity, the most appropriate geographic area to analyze is the area that lies immediately adjacent, and in close proximity, to the subject site. Sometimes this area is readily identified because of natural barriers such as rivers, ridge lines, mountains or hills, or fabricated barriers such as railroad tracks, expressways, and open space in the form of parks. For the most part, the geographic extent of the competitive area must be obtained from an analysis of economic variables and consumer behavior.

At its most basic level, consumer behavior is affected by the desire to accomplish two things simultaneously: (1) minimize the disutility of travel and (2) maximize the amenities that can be obtained on the subject property and from the geographic area in close proximity to the subject property.

A more complete discussion of the disutility of travel and the components of the costs of transport consists of a discussion of money and nonmoney travel costs associated with the spatial links are contained in later chapters. In general terms, linkages can be evaluated in terms of money and nonmoney costs. This is true for the trip to school; the trip to recreational, entertainment, and cultural activities; and any other travel the household does.

Each site user wishes to obtain amenities from the subject property itself and from the immediate surroundings of the subject property. The typical suburban household identifies the following:

1. *A relatively large and spacious lot.* A large lot assures a certain measure of privacy, because the typical household sees the space between dwelling units as a measure of privacy. In addition, a large lot provides the household with an opportunity to enjoy the outdoors.

2. *A new housing unit.* The typical residential space user prefers new housing to old housing. Consequently, the newness of the dwelling unit generates benefits that range from increased pride of ownership to increased leisure time as maintenance and repairs are minimized.

3. *High-quality schools and educational opportunities.* The amenity that is being derived from a school system with high educational standards, high-quality teachers, and good students is translated into improved present and future educational opportunities for the children.

4. *Proximity to the schools.* Households typically try to minimize the disutility of the children's trip to school, so they derive satisfaction from being close to school.

5. *Visual attractiveness.* The typical residential land user prefers nonroutine, nonstandard subdivision designs. This desire encourages the use of curvilinear street patterns, design that respects topography and other natural features, and a complementary placement of the structure on the building lot to create visual attractiveness.

6. *Proximity to recreational and other activities.* Households want to be close to the places where they spend their time.

Each household has its own preference pattern for these types of amenities. However, once the household recognizes its preference pattern, it attempts to maximize the benefits that it can derive and to minimize the disutility of travel.

The retail space user can also identify a list of amenities. However, in this instance, the amenities to the retail space user are more intertwined with economic considerations. Keeping this in mind, the retail space user can identify the following list of amenities.

1. *Convenience of access to the site.* The retailer wants people to reach the site of the store easily. In this context, access to the site is related to the existence of good highways and streets, public transportation, walkways to facilitate pedestrian movement, and so on. The amenity or benefit derived by the retailer is increased consumer traffic.

2. *Convenience or access onto the subject property.* Here, the access factor is associated with the movement from the street to the subject property. This movement can be facilitated by things such as appropriate curb cuts, turning lanes, and traffic signals to allow cars to make left-hand turns onto the property, merging lanes to facilitate cars leaving the property, and the like.

3. *Proximity to compatible land users.* In this instance the amenity is the absence of hazardous, noisy, smelly, ugly, and troublesome land uses. The amenity or benefits from the absence of such incompatible land uses is increased consumer traffic.

4. *Proximity to complementary land uses.* Here the amenities are associated with the existence of land users that help attract customers to the subject property.

5. *Visual attractiveness.* The amenities in this sense are the design features of the subject property and the attractiveness of the surrounding area.

Given that the residential land user wishes to minimize the disutility of travel while maximizing the amenities the subject property provides, the competitive geographic area for housing market analysis can be identified as the geographic area that contains households with similarities in proximities to major points, neighborhood features, dwelling unit types, and site sizes and features. These preferences reflect location decisions in which similar costs of friction and amenity trade-offs were made. In general, the households involved in these decisions are similar with regard to their economic, demographic, and psychographic profiles. Consequently, housing market analysis involves the process of defining a standardized product, a homogeneous group of potential customers of homebuyers, and a contiguous geographic area.

The competitive geographic area for retailing is known as a retail trade area. Conceptually, the retail trade area contains the points of origin (usually the residences) of the retail establishment's customers. Frequently, the retail trade area is defined on the basis of its primary and secondary components which are, in turn, determined by either consumer driving time or source of sales of the retail establishment.

As an example, consider the following definitions of primary and secondary trade areas.

1. The primary trade area is the geographic area immediately adjacent to the property and extending out for a definite driving time. Different retail establishments have different maximum driving times to establish the primary trade area. Supermarket trade areas may be defined with driving times of 5 minutes determining the primary trade area, while regional shopping centers may have a primary trade area extending to a driving time of 20 minutes or so.

2. The primary trade area can also be defined as the geographic area immediately surrounding the subject property from which 60 to 70 percent of the retail establishment's total sales are derived.

3. The secondary trade area is the geographic area that is adjacent to the primary trade area and extends away from the site for a predetermined driving time interval. For the supermarket the secondary trade area could be that area lying between the driving time of 5 to 12 minutes from the site. For the larger shopping center, the secondary trade area could be that geographic area lying between 20 and 45 minutes driving time away from the subject property.

4. The secondary trade area can also be defined as the geographic area from which the retail establishment is able to obtain an additional 20 percent of its total sales.

The market analyst must use knowledge and experience to set the geographic limits for the competitive trade area. Typically, the subject property will be at the center of this competitive geographic area, but the shape of the geographic area will seldom be a perfect circle or oval. In reality, the trade area is irregular. It is affected by street patterns, natural and fabricated barriers, consumer attitudes toward travel, and the nature of the product that is being sold. Because of data requirements, the competitive geographic trade area used in the analysis usually conforms to the geographic areas (e.g., census tracts and enumeration districts) for which data are available.

THE SURVEY AND EVALUATION OF THE COMPETITION

After the subject property's characteristics and competitive trade area are identified, the survey of the competition can be performed. Briefly, the survey of the competition is an identification of the properties in the market or trade area that have similar characteristics and attract the same potential buyers or space users. When the survey of the competition is performed, as much information as is practicable is gathered about the competitive properties. If the subject property provides housing units, then the market analyst defines the competitive area and identifies all the comparable properties as well as all the substitutes for the type of housing units on the subject property. If, on the other hand, the subject property provides retail activities, then the market analyst identifies the retail trade area and the direct competitors for the retail establishment located on the subject property.

Nature and Structure of the Survey of Competition

In general, the structure of the information to be gathered in either the residential or the retail case is quite similar. In either case, the information that should be gathered concerning the competitive establishments is given by the discussion of legal, physical, and economic characteristics presented in the first section of this chapter and adapted for the analysis being undertaken.

The market analyst obtains information about the subject property and its competitors to the extent possible given the time and money constraints that may be imposed. The result of the analysis may be the construction of a table, as shown on Exhibit 5-1, which allows the analyst to compare each competitor with regard to each characteristic being evaluated. This table is the starting point for the establishment of a market standard and the identification of a competitive differential for the subject property. These two terms will be discussed in a later section.

Exhibit 5-1 can serve as a model for a competitive survey for housing project on the subject property. Examining the exhibit on the basis of column groupings reveals that the table is divided into four clusters of columns: financial characteristics, structural factors, site characteristics, and neighborhood/location features. The specific columns that can appear under each one of these groups are

1. Financial factors
   a. The rent level per month
   b. The rent for reserved and additional parking spaces
   c. Utilities and division of payments by owner-tenant
   d. Absorption rate of the space or units
2. Structural factors
   a. Age of the structure
   b. Condition of the structure
   c. Size (square footage) of the unit
   d. Number of rooms
   e. Type of rooms
   f. Special amenities such as
      (1) Fireplace
      (2) Patio/balcony
      (3) Built-in appliances
      (4) Utility room/storage
   g. Architectural and design features
3. Site characteristics
   a. Recreational amenities such as
      (1) Swimming pool
      (2) Tennis court
      (3) Health fitness or exercise facilities
      (4) Club house
   b. Landscaping quality
   c. Quality of parking facilities
4. Neighborhood/locational features
   a. Proximity and route environment to employment center

b. Proximity and route environment to shopping centers
c. Proximity and route environment to entertainment, cultural, and recreational facilities
d. Proximity and route environment to and type of public transportation
e. Proximity and route environment to parks and open space
f. Proximity and route environment to major thoroughfares
g. Proximity and route environment to and quality of schools
h. Proximity and route environment to fire, police, and medical services
i. Quality and condition of surrounding structures

When an analyst uses these characteristics to evaluate a subject property, there should be an awareness of (1) how the characteristics will ultimately be

Exhibit 5-1 Survey of the Competition: A Model Form.

	1. FINANCIAL FACTORS a.–d.	2. STRUCTURAL FACTORS a.–d.	3. SITE CHARACTERISTICS a.–f.	4. NEIGHBORHOOD/ LOCATIONAL FEATURES a.–d.
Existing Competitive Properties	1. 2. 3. · · ·			
Competitive Properties Under Construction	1. 2. 3. · · ·			
Vacant Sites That Could Support Competitive Units in Future	1. 2. 3. · · ·			
The Market Standard				
The Subject Property				
Competitive Differential				
Gaps in the Market				

evaluated and used in the analysis and (2) what perspective is needed when the evaluation is performed. First, the initial evaluation should include all the characteristics just listed, plus any additional ones that may be relevant in specific cases. Since these same characteristics are used to evaluate the subject property, the objective here is to be certain that all the factors that can be used for appropriate comparative evaluation are property included. Thus, even if some factors are not present in the subject property, they should be evaluated so their absence will be noted upon comparative analysis. Furthermore, the analyst should know to whom the characteristics are important.

To ensure a consistent and proper perspective, the evaluation of each characteristic should be performed as though one were viewing it from the perspective of the potential consumer or customer coming to the site as well as from the perspective of the space user or occupant. On frequent occasions, part of this evaluation may involve direct contact and interviews with customers to ensure an unbiased and more expansive evaluation. This is discussed further later in this chapter, under customer research.

Examining Exhibit 5-1 on a row-by-row basis reveals that the survey of competition focuses on existing residential properties, competitive properties that are currently under construction, and sites that have the potential for becoming competitive residential properties in the future. Data for the existing competitive properties are obtained by firsthand inspection of the competitive project and questioning the property managers. Data for the competitive properties being constructed can be gathered from a variety of sources.

First, financial features may be obtained from the leasing agent if she or he is attempting to prelease units. Data concerning the structural factors can also be obtained from the leasing agent. Site characteristics can be obtained by examination of the property as well as by direct questioning of the leasing agent. And, finally, neighborhood features can be determined by examining public planning documents and by direct field observation.

Potential for future competition is estimated by gathering information about the availability of vacant land in the market area or immediately adjacent areas that can legally and physically support the construction of a new competitive facility. In addition, the analyst can also check to see whether the local political jurisdiction is likely to allow rezoning of vacant land in the market area to more intense use categories.

Exhibit 5-1 can also serve as the model for the survey of competitive retail establishments. In this case the four column groupings of financial, structural, site, and neighborhood/locational features take into consideration the following types of factors.

1. Financial characteristics
    a. Rent per square foot and the type of rental agreement (net lease, percentage lease, etc.)
    b. Rent abatement concessions and other lease provisions

2. Structural factors
   a. Square footage of retail space
   b. Age of space
   c. Condition of space
   d. Degree of tenant improvement
3. Site characteristics
   a. Quantity and quality of parking (e.g., number of parking spaces per thousand square feet of retail space, condition of parking lot surface)
   b. Quantity and quality of lighting fixtures in the parking area
   c. Existence of security measures
   d. Enclosed or covered walkways from parking facility to retail space
   e. Access to the street system
   f. Adequacy of loading facilities, fire lanes, and so on
4. Neighborhood/locational features
   a. Relationship to main arterials
   b. Proximity to daytime pedestrian traffic associated with employment in close proximity to the retail facility
   c. Age and condition of retail establishment in close proximity to the subject site (if the retail establishment is a free-standing store, this focuses on the age and condition of other stores in the commercial district; if the retail establishment is a shopping center, this variable focuses on the age and condition of the center itself)
   d. The number and type of other stores in close proximity or in the shopping center

Just as in the competitive survey for housing activity, the retail survey is also designed to capture information about existing competition, the competition under construction, and the potential for the creation of competition in the future.

The economic potential for the construction of new retail space as well as the expansion of existing retail space can be obtained in a similar fashion by analyzing the availability of vacant land with commercial potential and the rezoning probability. In addition, the market analyst has to establish the level of unmet demand for retail services within the trade area for the category of product or the type of retail activity that will take place on the subject property.

Evaluation of the Competition

When the competitive survey is performed and the information displayed in tabular form, as shown in Exhibit 5-1, the analyst can examine the facts on a column-by-column basis. The analyst can then identify what the market picture is with regard to (1) financial features, such as rents; (2) structural characteristics, such as unit designs; (3) site characteristics, such as parking; and (4) neighborhood/locational features that currently exist. The analyst should also estimate how these characteristics are likely to change in the future as new properties are developed and become competitive units on the market. Synthesizing the information in this manner allows the analyst to establish the quantity and quality of each characteristic that is being provided by the properties in the market. This synthesizing process is known as the establishment of a *market standard* for each characteristic. From this information the analyst can identify such things as design features that should be incorporated in the structure or pricing and leasing strategies that will help to increase the subject property's market acceptability and its revenue-generating potential. The process of identifying the special features that gives one property a competitive edge over another is known as the process of establishing a *competitive differential.*

When the information gathered in the survey of competition is examined, the analyst may discover something that is not being provided in the market. For example, a housing submarket in a particular city comprises primarily one- and two-bedroom apartments, but an examination of demographics reveals an influx of young professional families (two wage earners and a young child) that would like three-bedroom apartments or two bedrooms with a den. Other units that would fill market gaps might include

1. In-town condominiums that have two master bedroom suites on each side of a common living/kitchen area, designed to accommodate two unrelated individuals who occupy and jointly own or rent a single unit (a design-oriented gap).
2. Condominium units in college towns that can be purchased as housing for the young adult while attending college and then kept as investment property or resold.

The retail market may also contain gaps. For example, there may not be enough restaurants or a specialty clothing store that handles designer fashions in an in-town neighborhood that has recently undergone "regentrification."

In each of these instances the "gap in the market" is discovered by comparing what is currently provided versus what the demographic and economic analysis of consumers reveals as being desired. In addition, a gap could be identified by comparing what is currently being provided in the market and what is currently being provided in markets in other geographic sectors to approximately the same population mix. The bottom two rows of Exhibit 5-1 provide space in which the analyst can highlight the competitive differentials that should be created and the gaps in the market that can be filled.

In summary, the market analyst must understand the nature and structure of the competition that exists in close proximity to the subject property. To accomplish this, he or she surveys the competition, uses the information to develop a market standard, and then uses the market standard to identify features that can create a competitive differential for the subject property. In addition, the analyst searches for "gaps" in the market.

CONSUMER RESEARCH

The data gathered in the survey of the competition directly identify the various characteristics of competitive and substitute properties. However, in an indirect fashion, the data gathered from the survey of the competition also identify current consumer tastes and preferences. The analyst is able to obtain this information by examining which specific financial structural, site, and neighborhood/location characteristics are associated with acceptable absorption rates. Presumably, the dwelling units in the comparable properties that best satisfy consumer tastes and preferences will have the higher absorption rates, given the relative price of the property. So the market analyst can start the process of creating competitive differential by advising the client to design the subject property to include features that are at least as good as those in the properties with the highest historical absorption rates. In this way the analyst can make the judgment that if consumer tastes and preferences are constant, or at least very similar, then consumers will select those properties that yield the same amenities as the properties with the high absorption rate.

However, information about consumer tastes, preferences, and attitudes taken from the survey of competition is indirect knowledge. The analyst infers present and future taste and preference patterns from past taste and preference patterns. Situations will occur in which the analyst will want direct knowledge about current consumer attitudes, habits, tastes, and preferences, particularly to determine how they are changing. The only way this information can be obtained is through the process of consumer research. The analyst must go to the potential consumer and ask questions that will reveal the pertinent information about what consumers would like to have and what they are willing to pay or trade off to get amenities, space services, and so on, when they make a decision to occupy the subject property.

Four examples in which consumer research can be beneficial are

1. *The construction of contemporary-styled housing in a section of the market area that contains only traditionally-styled housing.* To obtain pertinent information, the analyst can interview two distinct groups of people. First, the individuals living in the immediate area who have chosen the neighborhood and locational characteristics can be interviewed to see if they would have an interest in contemporary-styled housing instead of the traditional-styled housing that they did buy. Second, the analyst can identify residents who currently live in contemporary-styled housing in different portions of the metropolitan area. From this group of individuals, who have chosen particular structural and site characteristics, the analyst can obtain information about their level of interest in similar kinds of housing on the subject property.

2. *The establishment of a specialty clothing shop in a geographic area served only by traditional department stores and free-standing clothing stores.* The analyst would survey residents in the retail trade area around the subject site to see whether the product line to be offered by the specialty shop on the subject property is desirable.

3. *The construction of a small office building to house medical services.* In this instance the analyst can interview two groups. First, the analyst should interview doctors and dentists who have office space in nearby structures. From this group the analyst can determine their desire to move to the new complex. If the analyst finds that enough are interested in moving to new offices, the information search process can stop. If, however, no such demand exists from the survey, the people in the market area can be surveyed to see whether they would be willing to patronize medical offices on the subject property instead of driving out of the

trade area to obtain these medical services. For example, the analyst may discover that the population in the trade area is driving across town to visit an eye, ear, nose, and throat specialist and an ophthalmologist. If this is the case, then the analyst can advise the client to seek doctors who specialize in these two medical areas for the new medical office complex.

4. *In the case of a condominium conversion, the analyst may obtain information on the number of potential buyers of the converted units by surveying the tenants in the structure that will undergo conversion.* The analyst can also survey the tenants in apartment buildings in the vicinity. Apartment dwellers are chosen as subjects for the research because they are the most probable, potential buyers of the converted units.

After the market analyst recognizes the need for direct consumer information, the appropriate techniques of consumer research must be identified. Briefly, the decisions that the analyst must make, and the important techniques that may have to be utilized, are identified in the following list of activities:

1. Identify the necessary information to gather.
2. Decide on observational versus questionnaire techniques to obtain the data.
3. If a questionnaire is chosen, select the method of communication (e.g., personal interview, a telephone interview, or a self-administered questionnaire).
4. Identify the appropriate population for the interview (e.g., the analyst must ask questions of individuals who represent the target market, either directly or as surrogates).
5. Select the kind of questions that should be used (e.g., open-end or closed-end versus questions).
6. Establish the wording of the questions.
7. Establish the sequence of questions within the body of the questionnaire.
8. Determine whether the study should be designed as a probability or a non-probability sampling technique.
9. Determine the required sample size to make valid statistical inferences about consumer attitudes, tastes, and preferences.
10. Determine how nonresponse error (and other nonsampling errors) will be resolved.
11. Determine the accuracy and precision of the results of the survey.

Each of these activities must be performed by the market analyst in the process of designing, administering, and interpreting the information gained from the consumers. Discussion of each point is beyond the scope of this chapter. A discussion of the process of consumer research is presented in Chapter 14.

READINGS

ANDREWS, RICHARD B., *Urban Land Economics and Public Policy.* New York: Free Press, 1971.

LLOYD, P., and P. DICKEN, *Location and Space.* New York: Harper and Row, 1972.

6

THE PHYSICAL ELEMENTS: LOCATION AND SITE ANALYSIS

INTRODUCTION

Location is one of the basic ingredients of real estate that makes the commodity more or less valuable to the space consumer. The physical product of real estate comprises two principal components: (1) site-specific physical elements, including the natural site characteristics, man-made land infrastructure, and structural improvements such as buildings that are permanently affixed to the land; and (2) locational attributes, which tie the site to the external world and permit the nontransferable spatial service provided by the site to be consumed by the space user.

Because each site occupies a specific point on the earth's surface that can be occupied by no competitor, the locational attributes provided by the site are unique—they cannot be duplicated anywhere else. The use to which the site is put, consequently, captures locational benefits or liabilities denied to similar uses on alternate sites and make the subject use more or less competitive and valuable.

Physical elements of real estate can generally be modified and adapted so that a site is better able to accommodate a particular use. Often, however, typical modifications to make a site competitive can be accomplished only at great cost. Careful analysis of financial costs and benefits must be performed to determine if it is economically feasible to make a site physically competitive for a particular use. On the other hand, basic locational characteristics are not changeable and must be considered as more or less fixed, at least in the short run. The site user must devise a strategy to maximize the locational advantages and overcome the locational disadvantages rather than change locational characteristics in the physical sense. Actions and improvements may be required to utilize locational attributes, however, and such a program also involves incurring cost.

In any meaningful feasibility analysis of a particular use or project, there are strong interrelationships between locational factors and site factors. To understand the impact of these factors on operational objectives, costs, and other investment objectives, it is usually necessary to evaluate locational and site characteristics jointly. For example, an analyst may consider the proximity between a subject site and nearby complementary uses as purely a locational characteristic. To be valuable from the standpoint of site usage, however, a visual linkage and building orientation along with site access between the subject site and complementary uses may have to be established. The subject site's physical characteristics, such as topographic conditions and street frontage conditions, may impose such significant problems and costs to take advantage of the proximity that there is no resulting advantage in making the linkage. Thus, while many specific characteristics can be identified and measured independently, it is often necessary to evaluate factors jointly to be able to estimate impacts.

A location and site analysis is performed as part of the market research process to ascertain the "attract and hold" capabilities of a particular property or group of properties. Potential occupants must be able to ascertain that a specific property's characteristics are not only capable of physically supporting the use, but are also appealing to those who would patronize the use once it is established. Subsequently, those who are attracted to the property should also be able to complete their intended business satisfactorily and have a desire to return when there is a need to repeat the activity. Location and site analysis, in general terms, measure the ability of specific physical and geographic factors to satisfy operational and functional objectives of a particular use and management entity. The results are used to ascertain a property's competitive capability in the market and, therefore, its relative productivity and potential returns. There are many possible forms of analysis. A particular methodology with multipurpose applications will be identified in this chapter.

There are three general purposes that locational and site analyses may accomplish for a real estate feasibility decision maker:

1. *Establishing development potential and costs*: Is the subject property capable of adequately supporting the use at a reasonable cost that can be amortized over a holding period?
2. *Identifying competitive differentials*: How do the subject property's locational, site, and other physical and legal characteristics give the subject use specific advantages and disadvantages over the properties that support competitive uses?
3. *Evaluating site selection*: How do the characteristics of a particular property satisfy development and operational objectives of a specific use compared to other available properties, to permit the decision maker to select the best among available alternative sites?

THE CONCEPT OF LINKAGES

Linkages are the spatial relationships that exist between different land users. The household, the user of residential land, maintains a link or a spatial relationship with an employer or an industrial or commercial land user. The household also has other links. In the case of a retail establishment, there are links between the commercial land user and households as customers. Households, as providers of labor services, represent another link. Office uses often depend on both nearby households and nearby businesses to patronize the services provided in offices, thereby generating the demand for office space at a particular location.

These two examples point out the economic nature of a linkage as well as its spatial relationship. A linkage also denotes the movement over space that is necessary to maintain the spatial relationship. The household must commute to work. The shopper must travel to the store. The act of moving over space can only be accomplished when costs of friction or transfer costs are incurred by the individual who has undertaken the move.

Linkages for individual land uses will be discussed further in the chapters containing information on specific market research techniques peculiar to those uses. Residential linkages are discussed in Chapters 7 and 8, retail linkages in Chapters 9 and 10, and office linkages in Chapters 11 and 12.

Considerations in Evaluating Linkages

There are three principal considerations in analyzing the quality of a linkage on the development potential of a site: costs of friction, amenity, and convenience. Information gained from the analysis is used by the land-use decision maker to make a locational decision and to select a site.

Costs of friction, or transfer costs, are travel costs that users of a site must incur to maintain the linkages identified. The first of these costs are the direct money or pecuniary costs of travel. These include the dollar costs of

1. The price of a vehicle allocated over its economic life.

2. Fuel costs.

3. Insurance.

4. Maintenance and repair.

5. License and inspection fees and taxes.

6. Parking.

7. Tolls and other user fees.

8. Price of public transportation.

9. Other direct costs of travel.

There are also nonmoney or nonpecuniary costs of friction. Basically, nonmoney costs of friction can be measured by identifying the value of time spent in traveling to complete the links. The value of time varies with the individual type of traveler and may be very expensive if considerable productive time is consumed in traveling. In other cases, such as transportation of school children, cost of travel time is relatively unimportant. Besides the relinquishing of leisure time spent traveling, however valued, the other basic nonpecuniary cost is the anxiety, aggravation, and frustration of encountering congestion and delays—often called distress costs. These costs are very difficult to measure but are very real concerns that must be taken into account. Proxies such as traffic volumes and operational characteristics are used to estimate the impact of these types of factors.

Site users attempt to minimize costs of friction in two ways. First, each user must identify the relative importance of each type of trip and establish a priority to determine when a trip for a singular purpose is necessary. Then, controlling the frequency of trips and combining trips can be accomplished to minimize costs. The relative importance of trips, or links, and the frequency each type of trip must be taken provides a major consideration in selecting a desirable location.

Amenities and convenience are defined later in this chapter. Each site user establishes a preference pattern for certain sets of amenities. The preferences are used by the land-use decision maker in analyzing the trade-offs and costs associated with the operation of a specific site. Some amenities, such as a panoramic view, are locationally specific, while others, such as architectural features, can be provided to almost any site. Convenience is usually associated with the proximity, access, and visibility a site has relative to surrounding features. It deals with the relative freedom of movement from off-site areas to on site. Convenience is more important for certain uses such as retail facilities than for such things as houses because of the number of site users that are affected and the capability of site users to go elsewhere if site visitation becomes inconvenient or problematic. Thus, the importance of convenience ranges from critical to minor depending on the use and the preferences and needs of the site user.

FORMAT OF THE ANALYSIS

A location and site analysis may be performed for a particular purpose or a combination of purposes. The format and procedures used should be designed so that a single field observation about a particular characteristic can be used to satisfy the requirements of multipurpose analytical methodologies. It should be noted that this type of analysis is site specific and is designed to evaluate particular factors at a given time. While there are some secondary data sources, such as soil maps, most of the information for the analysis is obtained through primary data gathering techniques.

There are several key points the analyst should observe *ex ante* when he or she prepares to undertake the task of collecting and analyzing the data:

1. *Understand thoroughly the purpose and specific objectives* the task is supposed to accomplish and how the specific methodologies will achieve those objectives.
2. *Select from a comprehensive listing of factors only those items that are relevant* for analyzing the problem at hand.
3. *Identify the most appropriate measure and types of observations* that will be needed to perform the different types of evaluations required to fulfill requirements of the specified methodologies.
4. *Determine which observations and evaluations can be performed* by the analyst given his or her level of skills and which ones may require special technical assistance from other sources of technical guidance.

Most of the analysis can be performed by economic analysts trained to make specific types of observations, but a specific problem often arises that requires greater expertise to evaluate than the analyst possesses. Some of the types of technical assistance normally available from other sources are

1. *Site planners, landscape architects, and environmental specialists.* For such elements as site design and layout, capabilities of natural site elements, impact of improvements on natural features.
2. *Transportation planners and traffic engineers.* For such elements as accessibility, parking, internal circulation, and transportation facilities.
3. *Architects, civil engineers, and construction managers.* For such elements as placement and design of improvements and costs and impact of alternative designs. Regardless of the specific situation governing the study design, the basic form of the analysis and the individual factors included are usually consistent from study to study.

The general techniques discussed here can be applied in all situations identified, although specific factors may be added or deleted and depth of analysis for particular purposes may be increased substantially. Some specific applications will be mentioned later in the chapter.

There are two basic steps that comprise location and site analysis following the *ex ante* preparation identified earlier. Each is discussed in the sequence in which they should be performed.

Observation and Evaluation of Specific Factors: Step 1

This step breaks down major elements into individual factors and measurable components. An initial ranking, or weighting, is performed to identify how important this specific factor is in coming to a conclusion about the performance of the study element. Then the analyst judges how well the individual factor is functioning compared to a norm or performance standard by ranking it on some scale that shows its performance as being above or below the expected operational norm. A final evaluative activity involves providing a synthesis of the preceding steps and identifying types of corrective actions needed to compensate for problems identified.

Exhibit 6-1 provides a summary of the activities to be undertaken in step 1. There are two different scales used in the weighting activity and the ranking activity, respectively. The weighting scale is an ordinal 1 to 5 assignment where

$$1 = \text{unimportant}$$
$$2 = \text{somewhat important}$$
$$3 = \text{normal or average importance}$$
$$4 = \text{very important}$$
$$5 = \text{critically important}$$
$$100 = \text{absolutely essential}$$

This last weight may be given to a vital element that is not present or doesn't function. It demonstrates that this factor alone renders the project infeasible. It distorts the analysis to use it in any other manner.

The second scale used in ranking assigns a 0 to an item functioning "normally" with a positive ranking for items functioning above standard. A negative ranking is given to items functioning below standard. A recommended range for the scale is from -2 to $+2$ where

$$+2 = \text{performs much above average}$$
$$+1 = \text{performs above average}$$
$$0 = \text{performs average}$$
$$-1 = \text{performs below average}$$
$$-2 = \text{performs much below average}$$

This scale is used so that, when the weight and rank of each item are multiplied together, the synthesized value is positive for those items that provide benefits for the property and negative for those items that pose liabilities.

Exhibit 6-1   Step 1 Activities: analysis of individual factors.

A. ITEMS TO BE MEASURED AND EVALUATED

1. Study Element	2. Factor	3. Component	4. Standard/Norm
Refers to the major concern being evaluated.	Refers to the individual item being evaluated.	Refers to that part of an item which can be measured.	Refers to the minimum standard or expected level of capability of the individual component.
Example: Regional access	*Example:* East-west thoroughfares	*Example:* Traffic volume: _____ Roadway capacity: ____ Congestion level: _____ Specific obstacles: ____	*Example:* Not to exceed 80% of capacity. 10,000 vehicles per day (two lanes) Level of service "C." No impediments to turns. No excessive delays at control points. No obscured visibility at 35 m.p.h.

B. MEASUREMENT AND EVALUATION (-2 to $+2$)

1. Specific Measure/ Observation	2. Weighting (1–5) Importance to Study Element	3. Ranking (-2 to $+2$) Compared to Standard/No	4. Verbal Comment
Precisely identifies the manner the item evaluated fulfills or completes its function	Answers the question, "How important is the item in evaluating the total study element?"	Answers the question, "How well does the item complete its function compared to the expected standard of performance?"	Provides direction for how a problem can be resolved or compensated for.
Example: *Traffic volume*: 9,000 vehicles per day, 90% of capacity. *Roadway capacity*: 10,000 vehicles per day. *Congestion level*: Level of Service "D." *Specific obstacles*: 1- to 1½-minute delays at two consecutive intersections.	*Example:* Weight = 4. East-west thoroughfare is very important.	*Example:* Rank = 1. East-west thoroughfare functions below standard due to excessive congestion.	*Example:* East-west thoroughfare has a comparative value of -4 and is a serious impediment. Impediments are correctable.

Numerous other scales and evaluative techniques could be used for this type of analysis. The advantage of the technique demonstrated here is its simplicity combined with its capability of leading the analyst to a fairly clear conclusion.

Consolidated Analysis of Factors' Impact on Operational Objectives: Step 2

This step consists of consolidating the individual observations performed in step 1 so that conclusions may be drawn about how a particular factor functions to benefit or detract from the potential of the development. To evaluate how the different factors and study elements affect the subject property's development potential, the analyst must explicitly state the property's operational objectives. The objectives must be stated so that the following three questions can be answered about each item's capability of fulfilling that objective:

1. How important is the item's contribution to overall performance level of the factor under consideration? To answer this question, the analyst assigns a weight reflecting each item's relative importance to the factor, using the weighting scale in step 1.
2. How well does the item perform in achieving the objective? To answer this question, the analyst ranks the performance of the factor in achieving the objective by the ranking scale in step 1.
3. What specific observations need to be identified to clarify ranks or weights or to point out specific problems that may require further action?

The evaluations performed in step 1 are used to perform the evaluations in step 2, although the ranking and weighting assignments made in step 2 are designed to answer different questions from those in step 1.

Using step 2 allows many qualitative judgments made about individual aspects of a property to be translated into quantitative terms. This is done to facilitate the comparison of one property's characteristics to another's and to identify in a systematic way those aspects of the property that contribute to or detract from the property's development potential. If there is no intent to perform further comparative analyses, and if specific design and development strategies are already established, there is little benefit from this approach.

Exhibit 6-2 shows the results of some of the activities in step 2. Three levels of ranking and weighting are involved. First, individual items are evaluated and the results are used as input for subsequent higher-level analysis. Second, specific factors included are ranked and weighted according to their level of involvement in the study element. Third, the study element is ranked and weighted using lower-level evaluations as a guide. The ultimate purpose of the three-tier evaluation system is to make systematic judgments about the study element toward the major objectives of the property. The lower-level evaluations simply

Exhibit 6-2 Step 2 activities: consolidated analysis of factors' impact on operational objectives (Partial example).

CONVENIENCE OBJECTIVES

Study Element	MINIMIZES VEHICULAR TRAVEL TIME			MINIMIZES PARKING AND BUILDING ENTRY TIME			MINIMIZES VEHICULAR TRAVEL FRICTIONS			MINIMIZES PARKING BUILDING ENTRY FRICTIONS		
	Ranking	Weight	Comment	Ranking	Weight	Comment	Ranking	Weight	Comment	Ranking	Weight	Comment
Location Analysis												
Regional Access	?	?	—	X	—	—	?	?	—	X	—	—
A. Thoroughfares	0	5	—	X	—	—	-0.5	4	—	X	—	—
1. Level of access provided	+1	5	From all directions	X	—	—	0	3	—	X	—	—
2. Adequacy of design capability	0	4	—	X	—	—	X	—	—	X	—	—
3. Level of driving impediments	-1	3	Two intersections	X	—	—	0.1	4	—	X	—	—
4. Adequacy of road conditions	0	3	—	X	—	—	0	4	—	X	—	—
5. Level of congestion	-1	5	On primary E/W route	X	—	—	0.1	5	—	X	—	—
B. Mass transit	+1	2	—	X	—	—	0	2	—	X	—	—
1. Adequacy of rail service	+2		In service 4 to 6 months	X	—	—	+1	3	—	X	—	—
2. Adequacy of bus service	0	2	—	X	—	—	0	3	—	X	—	—

X = Not applicable.

sharpen the judgments used in drawing conclusions about the property's development potential.

An alternative but similar analysis could be performed by ranking each item only once and then weighting it for each objective.

Specific Factors Included in the Analysis

Whenever a location and site analysis is performed, there is always the question of which specific locational and site elements should be evaluated and which should be treated lightly or ignored. The objectives of the study, the budget available, the specific expertise of the analyst, the specific conditions of the site and use, and the presence or absence of particular factors are considerations in selecting specific elements for analysis. Each project has some unique features, and it also has certain other features that are common to most properties of its class. The analyst must select both unique and common features that are relevant to the problem at hand and must then determine the depth of analysis for specific factors necessary to satisfy the study objectives and stay within budget limitations.

Exhibit 6-3 lists the factors that are normally considered in location and site analyses. It also contains a brief statement of purpose for the specific type of analysis and the type of data collection activities normally required. It can be used as a guide in selecting specific factors and preparing checklists and field sheets for specific measurements and types of information.

Items for analysis are categorized under six major factors in Exhibit 6-3. Regional access is a logical point of beginning because it attempts to answer the questions, "Where are users of the site coming from?" and "How are they going to get to the site?" The specific items included then provide necessary information needed to evaluate the quantity and quality of transportation elements that can make the trip to the site a desirable or pleasant experience. This evaluation of the quality of the route environment is an important consideration for most land uses.

Items listed under "General Locational Characteristics" help to establish the pattern of linkages to be evaluated and provides critical time and distance information for various types of site visitations or outward-oriented trips from the site. Of particular importance for most nonresidential uses is the location of competitive sites and "intercept" locations, that is, those competitive locations that are first encountered and first seen by potential users of the subject site and which, by virtue of their favorable exposure, may divert activity or capture part of the market being sought by the competitive sites.

The next two factors, site access and visibility, are elements that are critical for the site to take advantage of the locational qualities previously identified and for the site to perform its intended functions adequately. Analysis of site access focuses on the quality and efficiency of connections between the site and the abutting street system. Both entering and exiting movements must be examined. It is often necessary to identify turning movement conflicts and congestion when a single access point serves both types of movements. Subsequent items included under site access provide data to analyze conditions affecting internal circulation and parking and the level of service these ancillary uses provide to the site's principal buildings and uses.

Analysis of the site's visibility concentrates on those elements that provide the potential site user with essential information about activities and conditions on the site. First views and impressions are often critical determinants in a user's decision to patronize site activities. Subsequent views of the full spectrum of the site's principal and supporting uses, signs and information about the activities, access conditions, and internal site connections contribute significantly to a continued affirmative decision to utilize the site. The items included in this category provide this user decision information by identifying (1) phenomena that cause visibility to be good or bad, (2) points from which visibility must be effective, and (3) specific activities and site elements that need to be seen. Most of the information needed from this analysis is gathered by the analyst in the field. Firsthand experience is required to reach conclusions about visibility conditions. Varying elevations of the terrain and nearby buildings are often critical determinants of good views. Topographic maps and three-dimensional models (available from secondary sources) are common tools for this analysis.

The last two factors, physical features and design elements and other site features, contain items designed to provide information about the site's development potential as well as the site's relative attractiveness to potential site users. These items relate to the site's capability of holding or retaining the site user's interest after the user is attracted to the site. Physical features and design elements pertain to the manner in which the site's activities function to provide a valuable service to site users. The contribution of each site element to total use can be analyzed, and recommendations can be made to correct those dysfunctional elements that cause the site to lose its competitive capability. Because of the technical nature of many of the items included in this category, the analyst must often rely on technical standards and expertise provided by other experts.

Other site features include those items that provide essential supporting services and approvals for the site to accommodate its uses. Most of the information required for this analysis is readily available from field inspections and public records. Some specific information, such as the route and cost of installing a utility line, may be provided by others.

Types of Operational Objectives

Exhibit 6-2 provides a format to evaluate the impact of specific items on the operational objectives of the subject property. It illustrates how a particular type of objective can be subdivided into individual, measurable components and evaluated by ranking and weighting each component. In establishing research goals and objectives (see Chapter 2), the analyst determines what type of

Exhibit 6-3 Locational and site factors.

FACTORS AND ITEMS TO BE MEASURED/ANALYZED	PURPOSE OF ANALYZING FACTOR	PRINCIPAL SOURCES OF INFORMATION

1. Regional Access
  a. Major thoroughfares
    (1) Number and location (direction) by type/size of roadway
    (2) Planned improvements and new/expanded routes
  b. Thoroughfare design characteristics
    (1) Number of lanes, widths, speed zones, design capabilities
    (2) Traffic controls, by type
    (3) Major turning movements
  c. Thoroughfare operational characteristics
    (1) Traffic volumes by direction of flow and time of day
    (2) Points and levels of congestion
    (3) Incidence of traffic accidents
  d. Physical road conditions
    (1) Surface conditions
    (2) Parkage clutter and visibility
    (3) Frequency of curb cuts (access to abutting properties)
  e. Mass transit facilities
    (1) Routing, frequency, and costs by mode
    (2) Location of and distance to nearby pickup and discharge points
    (3) Level of usage by day of week and hour of day
	To determine the amount and quality of access capability from all parts of a surrounding area to a subject site.	Primary Data
		(1) Field observations specifically authorized
		(2) Traffic counts specifically authorized
		(3) Traffic planning studies
		(4) Driver/passenger interviews
		Secondary Data
		(1) Traffic engineering references and standards
		(2) Thoroughfare plan documents and supporting studies
		(3) Local transit studies and supporting data
		(4) State and local traffic counts and studies
		(5) State and local facility design studies
		(6) Environmental impact studies

2. General Locational Characteristics
  a. Linkage Patterns
    (1) Number and type of links
    (2) Ranking of importance of links
    (3) Frequency of linkage connections
  b. Proximities: Time, distance, and route to
    (1) Central or focal point of market/trade area
    (2) Specific boundaries of market/trade area
	To determine the specific elements of a site's geographic position within a designated area that enhance or restrict the interaction of activities on the site with those of the surrounding area.	Primary Data
		(1) Field observations
		(2) Measurements of driving distances and times
		(3) Delineation of market area
		Secondary Data
		(1) State and local land use and thoroughfare maps

108

Exhibit 6-3 Continued.

FACTORS AND ITEMS TO BE MEASURED/ANALYZED	PURPOSE OF ANALYZING FACTOR	PRINCIPAL SOURCES OF INFORMATION

(3) Competitors or competitive sites
  (a) Intercept locations
  (4) Complimentary activities
  (5) Activity nodes
  (6) Other linkage points
		(2) Regional and local base maps with major features

3. Site Access (ingress/egress points) a. Number, location, and function of ingress/egress points b. Size, capacity, and congestion level of ingress/egress points (1) Turning movements required for entering and exiting traffic c. Distance and route to buildings and primary site activities d. Distance and route to parking facilities e. Distance and route to internal circulation features f. External traffic conditions at ingress/egress points	To evaluate specific conditions that affect the free-flowing movement of vehicular and pedestrian traffic onto and off the site from the immediate approaches to the site and to assess the impact of site-access features on internal site movement and activities.	*Primary Data* (1) Field observations (2) On-site traffic counts and studies *Secondary Data* (1) Site maps and plot plans (2) Traffic engineering and site design standards and references (3) State and local facility design studies of approaches (4) Traffic counts and studies on abutting streets

4. Visibility
a. Conditions of site approaches (first views)
  (1) Elevational conditions from viewpoint
  (2) Level of roadside clutter
  (3) Specific impediments to visibility
    (a) Bridge railings and other sideline obstructions
    (b) Setback distances of buildings adjacent to site
    (c) Setback distance of subject site's activities
    (d) Number, location, size, and type of competing signs
    (e) Density of traffic flow and curb parking on access thoroughfare
b. Location of viewpoints
  (1) Initial viewpoint of first view, by direction
	To evaluate the specific conditions that affect the visual contact between specific site elements and critical nearby points off the site and to determine which improvements are critical to facilitate views to assure that the site's activities will function adequately.	*Primary Data*
		(1) Field observations
		Secondary Data
		(1) Site maps and plot plans of subject sites and critical viewpoints
		(2) Topographic and land-use maps depicting grades and elevations

Exhibit 6-3 *Continued.*

FACTORS AND ITEMS TO BE MEASURED/ANALYZED	PURPOSE OF ANALYZING FACTOR	PRINCIPAL SOURCES OF INFORMATION
(2) Initial viewpoint of first full view		
(3) Initial viewpoint of site access		
(4) Initial viewpoint from pedestrian route		
c. Level of visibility to critical site features		
(1) Principal building or activity (storefronts, entrances, etc.)		
(2) Total site activities (principal plus ancillary uses)		
(3) Site ingress/egress points		
(4) Signs and identification elements		
5. *Physical Features and Design Elements*	To evaluate the specific onsite features that affect the capability of the property to perform its designed functions and to identify those specific components that require improvement for the site to realize its development potential	*Primary Data*
a. Site configuration and layout		(1) Field observations
(1) Boundaries and shape of site		(2) Site engineering studies
(2) Size—area, street frontage, etc.		(3) Planning, design, and cost evaluation studies
(3) Buildings and supporting features		*Secondary Data*
(a) Location		(1) Site maps and plot maps
(b) Size and configuration		(2) Site planning and engineering standards and references
(c) Architectural features		(3) Architectural and space planning standards and references
(d) Physical conditions		(4) Industry or trade and corporate design standards for specific uses
b. Natural features		
(1) Topography		
(2) Geologic condition		
(3) Soil conditions		
(4) Hydrology and drainage		
(5) Vegetation		
(6) Microclimatic conditions		
(7) Biological communities		
c. Internal circulation features		
(1) Capacity for vehicular movements		
(2) Location and condition of pedestrian facilities, by type		
d. Parking facilities		
(1) Distance to major bays from critical site activities		
(2) Number of spaces by bay		
(3) Parking layout features		
(a) Angles and aisle widths		

Exhibit 6-3 *Continued.*

FACTORS AND ITEMS TO BE MEASURED/ANALYZED	PURPOSE OF ANALYZING FACTOR	PRINCIPAL SOURCES OF INFORMATION
(b) Length and width of spaces (c) Number and location of handicapped spaces (d) Special features—large/small-car delineations, etc. (4) Turnover characteristics (5) Physical condition of parking facilities (6) Special facilities and amenities (7) Regulatory and parking design standards e. Building features (1) Architectural styles and coordination (2) Entrance attractiveness (a) Entranceway design (b) Lighting features (c) Display windows/areas (d) Signs, informational and directional (3) Pedestrian traffic patterns among (a) Principal and supporting activities (b) Principal buildings/uses (4) Physical conditions and maintenance 6. Other Site Features a. Adjacent property characteristics (1) Types and uses of building/sites (2) Types of principal and supporting activities (3) Physical conditions and maintenance (4) Location and conditions of ingress/egress points (5) Depth of building/structural setbacks b. Site specific service and facilities—availability, type cost, capacity of (1) Power (2) Natural gas (3) Communications (4) Water (5) Sanitary sewer (6) Drainage facilities (7) Solid waste treatment	To evaluate those specific features of the supporting site infrastructure and institutional environment that affect the capability of the site to perform its designed functions and to identify the specific requirements, procedures, and activities. Required for the site to be able to operate at designed activity levels.	*Primary Data* (1) Field observations (2) Specific adjacent site building inspection of legal and public records *Secondary Data* (1) Property maps (2) Public utility studies and cost information (3) Community facilities plans (4) Public regulatory documents (5) Public property records

Exhibit 6-3 *Continued.*

FACTORS AND ITEMS TO BE MEASURED/ANALYZED	PURPOSE OF ANALYZING FACTOR	PRINCIPAL SOURCES OF INFORMATION

(8) Police protection
(9) Fire protection
(10) Other
c. Regulatory conditions—limitations, requirements, procedures with
  (1) Zoning
  (2) Platting (subdivision regulations)
  (3) Building and occupancy codes
  (4) Other environmental regulations
  (5) Licensing
  (6) Other—historical, educational, etc.
d. Other governmental/institutional features
  (1) Jurisdictional boundaries and tax rates
  (2) Right of way, easements, reservations
  (3) Special districts and assistance programs
  (4) Environmentally sensitive zones
  (5) Other designated districts
e. Legal and title conditions
  (1) Deed covenants
  (2) Other contractural conditions/agreements
  (3) Quality and condition of title or interest
  (4) Lease restrictions
  (5) Other encumbrances or conditions		

objectives are relevant. In this step, the analyst verbalizes the specific item to be accomplished and establishes its priority of accomplishment by weighting it.

Exhibit 6-4 lists the operational objectives that Exhibits 6-2 and 6-3 introduced. The objectives are classified as either convenience objectives or amenity objectives. These objectives relate to the manner in which the site with location and design fulfill the required and desired operational standards specified by the property owners and/or dictated by conditions on competitive sites. The analyst must identify the quantitative measures needed to perform the analysis through a careful review of technical standards, the property's design specifications, and a knowledge of the design standards and specifications used on competitive sites.

In general terms, convenience objectives focus on the need to minimize the travel time, distance, and distress the user experiences to utilize the site. These objectives consider both movements to the site and movements on the site. Amenity objectives comprise those items that contribute to the user's perception of well-being, the ease of carrying out intended on-site activities, and the user's pleasure and enjoyment while on this site. Some amenities, such as handicapped facilities, not only contribute to operational objectives, but may also be required.

Specific objectives for an analysis should be established individually for each site and situation. Exhibit 6-4 should be used only as a guide in establishing the framework for analysis.

USE OF LOCATION AND SITE INFORMATION IN REAL ESTATE DECISIONS

Real estate market research is concerned with the demand and supply for a particular type of space in a specific geographic area. It may comprise a market study focused on a broad geographic area, such as residential space in a com-

Exhibit 6-4 Types of objectives.

A. Convenience Objectives
1. Minimize travel time to subject site.
2. Minimize time to park and enter principal activity area.
3. Minimize or avoid sources of friction in travel routes.
4. Eliminate or minimize obstacles causing delays or hazards in entering or using parking facilities.
5. Minimize travel distances to the site.
6. Minimize user on-site time by providing service facilities.
7. Maximize intercept capability.
B. Amenity Objectives
1. Maximize level of visual attractiveness of site.
2. Maximize level of visual attractiveness of buildings.
3. Maximize level of facilities to enhance on-site movements.
4. Maximize level of facilities to enhance user safety and protection.
5. Maximize level of facilities to accommodate special user needs and enjoyment.

munity or retail space in a trade area. Alternatively, it may be a marketability study and concentrate only on the amount of space that can be reasonably expected for a particular project or site. Location and site information are essential elements of a market analysis that provide the analyst with critical information about the physical components of a real estate market. This chapter describes how location and site data can be collected and analyzed as part of the market research process.

The three general real estate decision situations in which information about the physical elements of real estate markets is of most critical concern are

1. The development potential of a particular site or group of sites and the costs involved in accommodating and operating particular uses on the site.
2. The critical differences, or competitive differentials, in physical and operating characteristics of a use at a particular location compared to those same characteristics of similar uses at competitive locations.
3. The final selection of a site or project that can best satisfy a real estate decision maker's locational, design, and operational objectives after considering the trade-offs associated with alternatives.

For a decision maker to become involved in site or project selection, he or she must have certain information about both development potential and costs as well as competitive differentials. Many types of decisions, however, require only considerations of a particular site. In these types of situations, such as when a site or project has already been acquired and is being planned or when a strategy for an acquired project is being developed to increase its profitability, the analyst limits the analysis to an examination of development potential comparison of competitive characteristics. When the scope of the study is thus limited, the analyst proceeds with much greater detail than when it is performed for a site-selection process.

Examination of the development potential of a site involves determining both the maximum capability of the site for supporting planned uses and the degree to which that capability can satisfy the goals and objectives established for the project. There are three basic inputs to a development strategy that flow from this analysis:

1. The site's physical and legal limitations to development.
2. The degree to which favorable design and other technological inputs can expand the development supporting capability of the site.
3. The costs and other effects on development objective of carrying out particular development plans.

Evaluating competitive differentials is a comparative analysis in which the attributes and liabilities of a subject property are compared to those of competitors'. The analysis involves not only locational and physical characteristics, but also other market data, financial data, and managerial/operational policies that affect the ability of the property to perform in a competitive environment. This type of analysis contributes to both development strategy for the property and an operational strategy for the use.

It is critical in retail space market analysis to identify a project's market penetration capabilities and market share potential. To accomplish this analysis, the analyst performs three basic tasks:

1. Delineate the market or trade area for the subject property, or the specific area from which competitive properties will be taken.
2. Examine the competitive environment by determining which competitors to evaluate, identifying competitive trade areas and overlaps, evaluating all salient characteristics of competitors, and identifying planned and potential growth of competitors.
3. Establish, in as precise terms as possible, the degree of difference between the subject property and each competitor for each characteristic, including locational, site, structural, financial, and managerial/operational characteristics.

Undertaking a site-selection analysis is also a comparative analysis in which a particular parcel is determined to be the most feasible alternative among the sites currently available to support a project. The focus here is which sites have the most favorable set of characteristics to satisfy particular project objectives, rather than evaluating which characteristics certain sites have that are better than those of other sites. Again, the analysis involves more than locational and physical site elements. To perform this analysis, the analyst typically proceeds through four basic tasks:

1. Establishing finite selection criteria, including site, structural, locational, financial, and managerial/operational factors based on project goals and objectives, by which each alternative can be objectively evaluated.
2. Identifying available sites along with problems of assemblage and acquisition prices, terms, and other acquisition factors.
3. Evaluating the capability of each available site to satisfy selection criteria and other goals and objectives.
4. Determining project feasibility for particular site or sites selected, and ascertaining the site or sites, if any, to be acquired.

READINGS

ALONSO, W., and J. FRIEDMANN, *Regional Development and Planning.* Cambridge, Mass.: M.I.T. Press, 1964.

ANDREWS, RICHARD B., "Situs: Variables of Urban Land Use Location," in *Urban Land Economics and Public Policy.* New York: The Free Press, 1971.

BARLOWE, R., *Land Resource Economics.* Englewood Cliffs, N.J.: Prentice-Hall, 1978.

GOODALL, B., *The Economics of Urban Areas.* New York: Pergamon Press, 1972.

GUEST, A., "Patterns of Family Location," *Demography*, February, 1972.

HARRIS, R., G. TOLLEY, and C. HARRELL, "The Residence Site Choice," *The Review of Economics and Statistics*, May, 1986.

HUBBARD, E., "A Commentary on Site Selection," *Atlanta Economic Review*, March, 1978.

7

HOUSING MARKET ECONOMICS

Land Serviced for Residential Use
Site Plan Approvals
Analysis of Pipeline Land Available for Development
SUMMARY

INTRODUCTION

The real estate market analyst must understand the market process in order to develop a logical, defensible estimation and forecast of demand and supply for each type of real estate. In a housing market analysis, this understanding encompasses the nature of housing as a real estate commodity, the characteristics of the consumers of housing, and the nature and characteristics of suppliers. Because housing demand and supply must be forecast, the dynamics of the local market should be understood. Because supply is forecasted and demand is segmented in the analysis of particular housing submarkets, the factors critical to this disaggregation and segmentation should be delineated.

The materials in this chapter deal with basic concepts underlying housing market analysis. The application of these concepts is presented in Chapter 8. In applied analysis, the real estate market analyst may select appropriate surrogates to represent the variables that can simply be assumed in the conceptual analysis and must cope with the uncertainties and lack of knowledge common to all real estate markets moving through time. First, however, the analyst needs to understand the economics of the market that will be examined in the empirical study.

BASIC HOUSING MARKET CHARACTERISTICS

Household: The Basic Unit of Demand

The basic consuming unit in the housing market is the household. As defined by the U.S. Census, a household is the person or group of people who jointly occupy a dwelling unit and who constitute a single economic unit for purposes of meeting housing expenses. Households may be families, two or more persons living together, or individuals. The Census defines nonhouseholds as individuals who occupy group quarters containing facilities (kitchens, baths, etc.) shared by others occupying other housing units in the same complex. As shown in Exhibit 7-1, a household can be either a family or a nonfamily (a single person or individuals who are living independently in shared quarters). The household is the decision-making entity that occupies a housing or dwelling unit.

A. Households (Occuping a Dwelling Unit)
   1. *Families:* (People Related by Blood or Marriage)
      a. Young marrieds (with no children)
      b. Launching families (growing in size with young children)
      c. Maturing families (stable in size with older children)
      d. Extended families (two or more adult generations within same household)
      e. Empty nesters (mature couple with at least one spouse employed)
      f. Retired families (older couple with neither employed full time)
   2. *Nonfamilies* (People Not Related by Blood or Marriage)
      a. Singles (individuals living alone)
        (1) Working single or student
        (2) Retired single
      b. Shared quarters
        (1) Unrelated individuals (persons living independently but sharing same household)
        (2) Unmarried couples (two unmarried persons living as a couple in same household)
        (3) Related individuals (two related persons living independently in same household)
B. Nonhouseholds (Occupying Group Quarters)
   1. Dormitory residents
      a. Institutional (quarters administered by colleges, hospitals, etc.)
      b. Noninstitutional (quarters open to the public)
   2. Retirement or nursing home residents
   3. Other (laborers' quarters, jails, and miscellaneous)

Exhibit 7-1 Types of housing consumers.

Housing Unit: The Basic Unit of Supply

A housing unit is a general term that denotes the area a housing consumer occupies to carry out normal living functions (sleeping, eating, bathing, etc.). It generally implies private and exclusive control by the occupant over the sleeping quarters but does not necessarily imply exclusive occupancy of kitchen, bathroom, and living areas. Technically, the term "dwelling unit" refers to a housing unit that contains private kitchen and bathroom facilities as well as private sleeping and living areas that are exclusively occupied by the household.[1] In a housing market analysis, since the term "housing unit" encompasses "dwelling unit," it is often used as the unit of supply. Each household, by definition, occupies one housing unit.

Allocation of Households among Housing Units

Several determinants operate simultaneously to allocate households among available housing units in the local market. Following is a list of some of these determinants.

[1] This definition of a dwelling unit conforms to typical zoning definitions. For example, the *Zoning Code of the City of Tallahassee and Leon County Florida* defines a dwelling unit as: "A room or rooms connected together, constituting a separate, independent housekeeping establishment . . . containing sleeping, bathing and toilet and cooking facilities."

1. Number of households in the market.
2. Economic characteristics of households.
3. Demographic characteristics of households.
4. Tastes and preferences of households.
5. Prices and availability of substitute goods.
6. Prices and availability of complementary goods.
7. Expectations about the future levels of housing prices, interest rates, and household income.

The supply of housing units in the market are allocated to households on the basis of the household's ability and willingness to pay for housing. Ability to pay depends upon present and expected income and assets; willingness to pay depends upon

1. The prices of other goods and services.
2. The price of housing.
3. Expectations about future levels of prices/rents.
4. The availability and cost of mortgage money.

The willingness to spend is tempered by tastes and preferences, which reflect household size; the household's age, stage in the family cycle, occupation, and status; and other demographic characteristics of the household.

The theorist, when explaining the household allocation process, abstracts from the qualitative characteristics of the local housing stock by measuring supply in terms of ubiquitous "housing services." Each housing unit, given its location, size, and amenities, provides a certain quantity of housing services. A market price is established for each homogeneous unit of housing service. This market price can be thought of as the rent per unit of housing service paid by the tenant to a landlord, or the implicit rent per unit of service paid by the homeowner. Thus, the 5,000-square-foot single-family detached house by the golf course may produce 100 times the number of housing service units as the 1,000-square-foot walk-up flat in the inner city and sells for 100 times the price.

A housing market analyst does not have the luxury of conceptualizing the supply side of the market in terms of housing services. If called upon to perform a submarket analysis, the supply of units must be qualitatively disaggregated and the demand must be segmented.

Thus, supply may be disaggregated by tenure, by price or rent, by location, and, at times, by other characteristics of the unit, such as form of ownership (condominium) and so on. Except for general market analysis, where only the quantity of units may be considered, housing market analysis always requires the critical qualitative supply dimensions to be stipulated and then the demand for that component of supply to be estimated.

Housing Submarkets

The allocation process creates housing submarkets. A housing submarket typically is defined in terms of a homogeneous supply of housing units. This group of similar units is occupied by a relatively homogeneous group of households. The emphasis here is on the word "relatively," in that the households found in any group of similar housing units, such as new townhouses selling for $50,000–65,000 in the northeast sector of the metropolitan area, will vary by income; age of head of household; stage in family cycle; place of employment; and other economic, social, and demographic characteristics.

However, these households will be a relatively homogeneous subset of the total population of households in the market. Typically, in identifying the prospective demand for a particular type or subset of housing units, the analyst sorts households by income on the assumption that households in an identifiable income class will be able to afford those units and that these households on average spend an identifiable portion of income on housing. An analysis of the demand for a federally assisted project for elderly households may require demand to be segregated by age of head of household and by income. Still other analyses (of condominiums, mobile homes, etc.) may require consideration of other variables to differentiate the relatively homogeneous subset of households that are most likely to be "in the market" for a particular type of housing unit. As shown in Chapter 8, the lack of empirical data from secondary sources prevents identification of subsets of households disaggregated by multiple characteristics.

Market Disaggregation

The process of identifying a standardized submarket from a more general, less standardized market is called market disaggregation. It is the first step in real estate market analysis because it identifies the submarket to be studied.

For residential real estate, a logical breakdown is between owner-occupied and renter-occupied units. Owner-occupied residences can be classed as single-family detached units, as duplexes, or as townhouses (single-family attached units). Single-family detached housing units can be divided further on the basis of architectural style (ranch, split-level, bi-level), size of the housing unit, size of the lot, floor plan, number of rooms, number of full baths, basement/attic storage space, fixtures, and so on. The result of this refinement process is the identification of a relatively standardized commodity by use, tenure, and physical characteristics that form a submarket in which the determinants of supply and demand are relatively uniform.

Once the market is disaggregated on use, tenure, and physical characteristics, the geographic dimension of the market must be specified. Because of the characteristic of immobility, a property is affected by its location and surrounding off-site improvements. Consequently, the market for real estate is local.

The same parcel of real estate located at different points in space would have a different perceived value-in-use and value-in-exchange due to these locational attributes. The consequence of localized real estate markets is that a house located in one urban area can be valued differently from an identical house in another urban area or in different sections of the same urban area solely because of its locational attributes. The area specification or market area delineation could be central city versus suburban, northern suburbs versus western suburbs, neighborhood A versus neighborhood B, and so on. However the local geographic area is differentiated, the process is the second aspect of disaggregation.

Next, newly constructed units must be distinguished from existing units. This distinction is important because newly constructed units are typically viewed as being more desirable than used or existing units. New units possess current standards of attractiveness. They may be concentrated at the fringe of the urban area where open space and larger lots are available. This distinction can be viewed as market disaggregation among housing units by the age of the structure. Categories such as newly constructed, 1 to 5 years old, 6 to 10 years old, . . . , 41 years and older can be established.

The practical complexity of differentiating supply is illustrated in Exhibit 7-2, which identifies the choices confronting the household and the detailed disaggregation that can result.

The housing market analyst has difficulty in directly estimating the demand for a multidimensioned submarket defined by the cross-classifications in Exhibit 7-2. Secondary data do not exist in the detail that permit an independent estimation of the demand for "resale condominiums with high-income amenities located in a new stable suburban neighborhood in an unincorporated area of an urban county." Interviews with occupants of such units may permit specification of the "typical" purchaser, which may be households in the $70,000-and-over income category, aged 50–65. Identification from secondary data of households in the local market with the head of household in the 50–65 age category by income categories are not generally available. The analyst, in order to estimate directly the total potential demand, would have to undertake a time-consuming, expensive collection and analysis of primary data, which is usually beyond the budgetary limitations.

Market Segmentation

Once market disaggregation is accomplished, the analyst separates consumers into groups that have similar characteristics and will express about the same level of demand for a specific real estate product. This process is called market segmentation. The first step in consumer research involves the separation of consumers into distinct groups. For example, if the market analyst is attempting to identify the demand for single-family housing units in the $100,000 range, there is a certain income level below which consumers are unable to afford to buy these units. Present mortgage underwriting guidelines establish the max-

TYPE OF CHOICE	VARIABLE	TYPICAL VARIABLE CATEGORY
A. Life-style choices	1. Tenure status	a. Fee simple, owner occupied
		b. Condominium, owner occupied
		c. Cooperative, owner occupied
		d. Privately owned, renter occupied
		e. Investor owned, renter occupied
	2. Building type	a. Single-family detached
		b. Single-family attached
		c. 2–4 unit, single building
		d. Multiple-family low rise (nonelevator)
		e. Multiple-family high rise (elevator)
		f. Mobile home
		g. Group quarters
	3. Amenity level (implies a ranking with defined facilities)	a. Very high
		b. High
		c. Moderately high
		d. Moderately low
		e. Low
		f. None
B. Construction status choices	1. Age category	a. New, never been occupied
		b. Resale, modern design with previous occupancy
		c. Old, nonmodern design (usually worth renovation)
		d. Old, deteriorated
		e. Newly rehabilitated
C. Economic choices	1. Amenity level of housing unit	a. Low income, basic shelter
		b. Middle–low income
		c. Middle income, average amenity level
		d. Middle–high income, above-average amenity level
		e. High income, all available amenities
		f. Very high income, all available amenities with numerous extra features

Exhibit 7-2 Basic housing choices and market disaggregation variable.

imum monthly mortgage payment for principal, interest, property tax, and casualty insurance so that it does not exceed 28 to 30 percent or so of a household's monthly gross income. Households earning less than $40,000 per year are, for the most part, excluded from the market for $100,000 houses. So, in this case the market analyst can separate households earning less than $40,000 into one group and households making more than $40,000 per year into a second group. The second group contains the potential buyers or the market segment that can buy the units offered for sale.

On a conceptual level, segmentation yields distinct groups in which the individuals within the group are similar, while individuals in other groups have very different characteristics. In the previous example, the similarity occurred

TYPE OF CHOICE	VARIABLE	TYPICAL VARIABLE CATEGORY
	2. Neighborhood status	a. New,*expanding or building
		b. New, stable
		c. Modern,* stable
		d. Modern, declining
		e. Modern, rehabilitating
		f. Older,* stable
		g. Older, declining
		h. Older, rehabilitating
		i. Older, dilapidated
D. Geographic choices	3. Locational status	a. Inner city
		b. Close-in
		c. Suburban
		d. Outlying (urban fringe)
		e. Ex-urban
		f. Rural
E. Municipality	1. Jurisdictional status (provider of public services)	a. Incorporated
		b. Urban county
		c. Nonurban county
		d. Public service district
		e. Other

*Neighborhood status categories may be defined as follows:

New: a residential area in which most housing units are 0 to 5 years old, where there has been substantial recent construction.

Modern: a residential area where street design and land infrastructure characteristics substantially meet current subdivision standards; most housing units constructed during post–World War II era, but with little or no new construction in past 15 to 20 years.

Older: a residential area where street design and land infrastructure are well below current subdivision standards; most housing units constructed before World War II with virtually no new construction except replacement or renewal activity.

Exhibit 7-2 *Continued.*

because the first group had an income of less than $40,000 while the second group had an income of at least $40,000.

Market segmentation can occur on the basis of several consumer characteristics. First, segmentation can occur based on the demographic characteristics of age and sex. For example, the population could be divided into different age cohorts that define life-cycle periods for housing unit consumption. Most single-family homebuyers may be found in the 25–44 age bracket. If a study of the single-family dwelling unit market is being undertaken, this age group should be identified and differentiated from the group that is 24 years and younger as well as the group that is 45 years and older because housing demand among younger and older households is quite different.

The second group of market segmentation characteristics are the economic characteristics of the consumer. The most important of these is income. To undertake a market study for the demand for new single-family detached housing, the analyst may choose to segment the population into three groups: households earning less than $20,000 per year, households earning at least $20,000 but less than $40,000 per year, and households earning at least $40,000 per year. With this segmentation based on household income, the analyst can obtain a first approximation of the number of potential buyers for differently priced houses.

When the consumer population is segmented both on age and income, the market analyst has a second approximation of the size of the potential demand for houses in a certain price range.

The psychographic characteristics of the consumer present the third segmentation variable that can be used. In this instance, the consumers are divided into distinct groups based upon their attitudes, preference patterns, tastes, and/or behavior. With psychographic variables, the analyst can distinguish among the individuals who are in the same income and age group. For example, some individuals who are 35 years old and have an income of $30,000 per year choose to live in the suburbs, while others choose to live in town neighborhoods. The distinguishing factor is not age, and it is not income; rather it may be attitude toward urban versus suburban living, taste for new versus existing dwelling units (assuming that the prices are comparable), preference for shorter versus longer commuter trips, life-style, and so on. Without direct information from the consumer, the market analyst is unable to utilize this third segmentation variable. It is directly linked with the process of consumer research by means of survey techniques—questionnaire design and sampling. These topics are discussed in detail in Chapter 14.

Interrelationships Among Submarkets[2]

The housing units within any particular submarket can have many different substitutes. For example, the new single-family, detached housing unit of predetermined structural characteristics in the northern suburbs has the following substitutes.

1. Used single-family housing units of the same type in the northern suburbs.
2. New and used single-family, detached units in the nonnorthern suburbs, which could include some fringe areas of the central city.
3. New and used duplexes or townhouses in the northern suburbs.
4. New and used apartments in the northern suburbs.
5. New and used single-family houses that are slightly bigger or slightly smaller.
6. New and used single-family houses of different architectural style.
7. New and used duplexes, townhouses, and apartments in the nonnorthern suburbs.

Changes in the economic and/or demographic variables in any of these submarkets can affect the new single-family detached housing submarket. The analyst must determine which of these substitute products are the most signif-

---

[2]This material was taken with permission from Donald R. Epley and Joseph Rabianski, *Principles of Real Estate Decisions* (Englewood Cliffs, N.J.: Prentice-Hall, 1986), p. 176.

icant substitutes. Then, changes in the market for the substitute products must be monitored.

It is very important to recognize substitutions among interrelated submarkets. Dealing with these substitutions explicitly provides the analyst with more accuracy in forecasting demand levels and absorption rates for a particular type of real estate. For example, when the analyst measures the decrease in demand for single-family detached units as a result of a rapid price increase, he or she may also be able to forecast what percentage of the consumers substitute townhouses when they can't afford detached units. Thus, knowledge of the interrelationships between these submarkets enables the analyst to predict better demand levels in both submarkets.

DYNAMICS OF THE HOUSING SUBMARKET

The Market for New Construction[3]

The economic and demographic environment of a parcel of real estate affects its value. The impact of the environment can be analyzed and the resulting effect can be shown by using demand and supply analysis. Changes in the economic and demographic environment affect the position of the demand and supply curves. In other words, various economic and demographic factors affect the ability and willingness both of buyers to purchase and of suppliers to provide units of housing at various prices in the market. First, the effect on demand is analyzed; then the effect on the supply side is considered.

Demand Factors

The economic and demographic factors that affect the level of demand are as follows:

1. Net household formation. → more 18+ living at home today
2. Age composition of the household.
3. Household income.
4. Credit conditions.
5. Prices of substitute units.
6. Ownership costs.
7. Expectations about the future.
8. Seasonality.

Each of these variables is examined to identify the changes that will cause an increase in demand for a selected type of housing unit. The movement of

[3]This material was taken with permission from *ibid.*, pp. 182–188.

the demand curve is depicted in Exhibit 7-3 as the shift from D_1 to D_2. This shift represents the fact that potential buyers as a group are willing and able to buy more units of housing at each possible price.

Net Household Information   As time passes, the number of households in an urban area changes for several reasons. First, children reach the age of maturity (18 years in most states) and choose to reside apart from their parents. When a young adult establishes a physically independent existence, an additional or new household is established. This new household requires living space and causes an increase in demand for some type of housing unit. Second, many households will move into the urban area. These new or additional households require living space and thus cause an increase in demand. These two major types of additions to the number of existing households are the first component of net household formation.

At the same time that new household units are being formed through maturation and in-migration, the number of existing household units is being reduced by out-migration from the urban area, death, and the decisions made by adults to share a dwelling unit. The reduction in household units brought about by these circumstances must be subtracted from the new households formed to obtain net household formation. If the resultant figure is positive, the effect will be an increase in the demand for housing.

Age Composition of the Household   Households of different ages tend to prefer different types of housing. The younger households, 18 to 25 years of age, typically choose rental units, and households in the middle years tend to choose owner-occupied housing. Because different urban areas can have different age compositions of households, the markets for various types of housing will be different in each urban area.

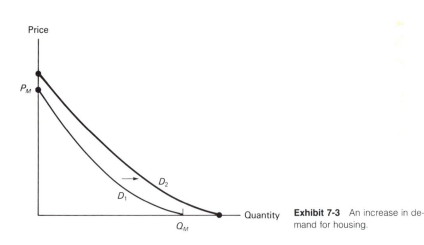

Exhibit 7-3 An increase in demand for housing.

As time passes, the age composition of households changes. Single-person households marry to form multiple-person households. Young households become middle-aged households. Such changes over time bring about changes in future housing demand. Moreover, migration of households from one geographic area to another brings about a compositional change in both areas. As a general rule, households headed by young adults and single-person households have a greater propensity to move. Consequently, the market for rental units and smaller houses can increase at the destination and decrease in the area from which these households moved.

In addition to the age composition, the size of the household can affect the type of housing submarket that the household enters. A household whose head is in the middle years can have children or can be childless. This difference in the size of the household can affect a decision about the size of the housing unit desired. The household with two children may require a moderate-sized, three-bedroom, single-family house, whereas the household without children may require a smaller, two-bedroom, single-family house or even a two-bedroom apartment.

Currently, the size of the typical household in this country is decreasing. This compositional change will have an impact on the demand for housing in the future. Demand for smaller housing units will be increasing relative to the demand for large housing units.

Household Income Determining the impact of income changes on the real estate market involves two steps. First, the type of income must be identified. Then the effect of the change on the demand curve can be determined. The majority of households received an income from the sale of labor services. This income can be identified in several ways. It can be the gross income—a measure of the full payment for the work performed—or it can be a net income figure—the dollars remaining after federal and state income taxes and social security taxes are deducted. This net income figure, known as disposable income, underlies the household's ability to buy all commodities, including real estate.

Disposable income can be stated in nominal terms or in real terms. The nominal income is the household's actual dollars in hand. The real income, or purchasing power, is stated in terms of goods and services that can be bought with those dollars. At two different points in time, the number of dollars a household receives can be the same, but the purchasing power can be different. As the price of a consumer good increases, the real income (purchasing power) of each individual dollar decreases, and fewer units of goods and services can be purchased. Consequently, real disposable income is the demand variable to be examined.

A distinction also must be made between current income and future income. When a household enters into a decision to purchase real estate, it typically commits itself to a stream of future repayments of a loan taken out to purchase the commodity. If the parcel of real estate is a single-family housing unit, the future income stream of the household is an important consideration because it determines the ability to repay the loan. Consequently, for single-family residential property, the level of future real disposable income should be the income variable that determines the level of demand.

In many instances, nominal gross income is used to analyze the demand for real estate. Because this figure is a proxy for the theoretically preferable income figure, the following assumptions are inherent in its use.

1. Future nominal income will be at least as great as current nominal income.
2. Future nominal income will increase at a rate equal to the rate of inflation so that current and future levels of real income will be the same.
3. The tax burden in the future will not be greater than that in the present, and thus the levels of future and current nominal disposable income will be the same.

Once the type of income to be examined has been identified, the impact of a change in the income figure can be determined. In traditional economic theory, as the income level increases, the demand for a typical commodity will increase as shown in Exhibit 7-8. An example of this typical situation is the market for T-bone steaks. As the consumer's income increases, the demand for T-bone steaks increases. In general, the aggregate beef market consists of T-bone steaks, sirloin steaks, round steaks, chuck steaks, hamburger, and beef organ meats. As the income of consumers increases, consumers tend to reorient their purchases from the "low-grade" to the "high-grade" cuts of beef. In other words, as the consumers' income increases, other things remaining constant, they upgrade the quality of beef they buy. Similar upgrading can occur in the housing market. In the case of beef, as income rises, some consumers reduce their purchases of beef organs and shift to hamburger; the demand for beef organs falls and the demand for hamburger rises. In addition, the rising income levels enable some consumers of hamburger to shift their expenditure pattern in favor of steaks. Therefore, different impacts occur in different submarkets for beef. As income rises, the lowest grade declines in demand, the middle grades of beef simultaneously increase and decrease in demand, and the highest grade of beef increases in demand. The market for medium-grade beef is difficult to project because the net effect of the demand change must be determined.

In addition to the shift of consumer expenditures to the market for higher-grade beef, an increase in demand occurs in each of the submarkets for beef as a result of the increase in income. Consumers who never bought beef can increase their consumption of both hamburger and steak. Demand in a submarket can increase for two reasons: present consumers in the submarket buy more, and more new consumers enter the submarket than leave the submarket.

Demand in housing submarkets increases for the latter reason. As income levels rise, people change from one submarket to the next highest submarket. This shift is detected as an increase in demand for the submarkets that represent the more desired forms of housing, and a reduction in demand for the less desirable forms of housing. In a specific housing submarket, however, there is no increase due to an increase in absolute quantity of housing bought by a single consumer. As income levels rise to twice their former level, the typical consumer does not buy two existing, moderate-sized, single-family, detached housing units in the northern suburbs of the urban area, This consumer might buy a bigger house or a new house in the same area, or the extra dollars might be turned to the purchase of a second home or a vacation home in another geographical area that is a different submarket.

Credit Conditions   One of the economic characteristics of the real estate commodity is the fact that its price is a multiple of the buyer's yearly income. The buyer typically must borrow money to purchase the property. The availability of funds for real estate loans and the financial terms associated with the loans therefore are important determinants in the market. On the demand side, as the interest rate on a mortgage loan decreases or as the loan's maturity lengthens, the size of the monthly mortgage payment decreases and more people can enter the market as potential buyers. The consumer's ability to buy has increased. The same result occurs as the down payment requirement drops. Thus, any of these three changes can cause the increase in demand shown in Exhibit 7-3.

Prices of Substitute Units   Each type of real estate has several substitutes. Therefore, each type of housing is affected by changes in the market for its substitutes. As an example, consider a particular type of housing called type X housing. Substitutes for type X housing are the housing alternatives mentioned in the section on interrelationships among submarkets. Call these alternative housing units type Y housing. As the price of any of these residential alternatives increases because of some demand or supply change in their submarket, demand for type X housing increases. This increase in demand for type X housing occurs because the increased price of type Y housing makes that kind of housing unit unavailable to some consumers as a result of income and mortgage loan considerations. Therefore, as the price of type Y housing increases in relation to the price of type X housing, the number of potential buyers of type X housing increases because of a shift of some consumers from type Y to type X units. This increase in demand for type X units is shown in Exhibit 7-3.

Ownership Costs   An individual who owns real estate incurs a series of expenses related to the operation of utilization of the property. A list of these ownership costs follows.

1. The property tax bill and any assessments made against the property for improvements to the land.
2. Property insurance payment.

3. Maintenance and repair costs.
4. Utility costs, including heating, cooling, water, and sewage disposal.
5. Mortgage payment, specifically the interest payment component.

These expense items must be incurred by the property owner because failure to pay the property tax, the assessment, or the mortgage payment will lead to the exercise of a specific lien against the property. Failure to insure the property could result in a substantial financial loss. Failure to maintain and repair the property could lead to a reduction in the property's value. Failure to pay for utilities would cause a reduction in some of the physical and psychic benefits or revenue that the property could generate.

In traditional economic theory, these costs of ownership are incurred to provide goods and services that are complementary goods to housing. Housing cannot be utilized without these complementary expenditures. As the magnitude of these ownership costs decreases, the demand in the market will increase as shown in Exhibit 7-3. A reduction in these costs of ownership allows more potential buyers to enter the market, even if their income level remains constant.

Expectations about the Future The housing market consumers' expectations about economic occurrences in the future can greatly affect the level of demand in the market. The two most critical variables are the future prices of the house and the mortgage interest rate. If the consumer expects either of these two variables to increase in the next period, they will be motivated to purchase during the current period. This temporal shift in purchase patterns (if it occurs) will cause the level of demand in the current period to increase and the level of demand in the future period(s) to decline. The underlying conditions that allow for the consumer to act on these expectations are the existence of the necessary down payment and a sufficiently current income level to qualify for a loan at the currently quoted mortgage interest rate.

Seasonality The level of demand varies with the season of the year. Households seek housing changes in the summer more than any other season because

1. They want to move without interrupting their children's school year.
2. More household formation occurs in June and July due to wedding plans.

The first reason affects the owner-occupied market almost exclusively, while both reasons can affect the rental market.

The preceding discussion of demand factors relates them to increases in market demand. An increase in net household formation, income levels, credit availability, and the prices of substitutes will cause an increase in market demand. Conversely, a decrease in the costs of ownership, which include interest payments, causes an increase in market demand. The directional change in these economic and demographic factors can be used to predict a change in market demand for a selected type of housing.

Supply Factors

An examination of the supply side of the real estate market must be accomplished by examining new construction separately from the existing stock. This approach is required because these two commodities are viewed to be different by consumers and the supply of each is affected by different economic variables.

New Construction   The economic variables that affect the supply side of the market for new construction are

1. The prices of the factors of production used in the construction process.
2. Productivity of the factors of production and technology.
3. The number of builders in the market.
4. Builder's expectations about sales in the near future.

An increase in the supply of newly constructed units is shown in Exhibit 7-4 as a shift of the supply curve from position S_1 to position S_2. This movement can be explained in two ways: Builders are willing and able to construct the same number of units but offer them at a lower price. The second situation is shown as a shift of the minimum price from P_{K_1} to P_{K_2}.

The increase in supply depicted in Exhibit 7-4 is brought about by a reduction in the prices of the factors of production used in the construction industry. As the wage rate for construction labor, the price of building materials, the interest rate for construction loans, the price of construction equipment, and the price of raw land decline, the supply of new construction increases. In addition to declining factor prices, improvements in labor productivity and advances in construction technology can cause an increase in supply. Improvements

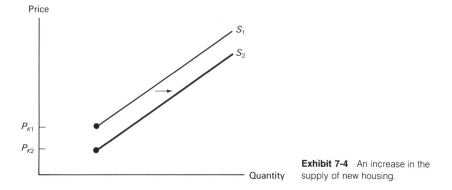

Exhibit 7-4 An increase in the supply of new housing.

in productivity occur if construction laborers become more experienced and make fewer errors, work faster, and utilize more construction equipment that increases output more than costs. Advances in construction technology could be the use of newer and more sophisticated construction equipment and the adoption of prefabrication techniques that can reduce overall construction costs.

The supply of newly constructed units will also increase as new builders enter the market. Typically, new builders will have approximately the same cost structure as the builders already in the market. If so, supply curve S_2 will not extend below the price of P_{K_1}. The builders who enter the market are willing and able to provide new units on the same terms as the present builders; in other words, the minimum supply price of P_{K_1} will apply to all builders, both the new entrants and the present firms.

Finally, builders have expectations about future sales levels. If they are optimistic about the future, more units will be built this period than were built in the last period because each builder expects that the additional units will sell. This will cause the supply curve of new construction for the current period to increase. On the other hand, if the builders are pessimistic about the future, fewer housing units will be built and the supply curve will decrease.

Residential Resale Market[4]

In the resale market, the demand variables are the same as those identified for demand in the market for new construction. The important difference between the markets is the nature of supply. In the resale market, supply is *not* a function of production-oriented variables such as input prices, number of builders, and so on. On the contrary, supply is a function of nonproduction, economic, and demographic variables.

The challenge for any analyst in this situation is facing the strong possibility of confusing market supply with market demand. This can occur because, on the surface, the variables appear to be similar. Demand is a function of the number of households in the market that desire the product and are able and willing to purchase it. Supply in the resale market is a function of the number of households in the market that desire to sell their house.

Transactions in the resale market occur when the desire of the potential buyers regarding physical, locational, neighborhood, and financial features are matched or fulfilled by the physical, locational, neighborhood, and financial attributes of the properties offered for sale. The important supply-side question to answer is, "Why are properties offered for sale?" Or, alternatively, "What factors cause properties to be put on the market?"

What causes the supply of units in the resale market to be offered at a rate that will satisfy demand levels at a prevailing price? Three sets of factors

---

[4]This material was taken with permission from Joseph Rabianski, "The Residential Resale Market," *Real Estate Appraisal and Analyst*, Fall 1985, pp. 5–9.

help to explain resale market supply levels. These are economic factors, demographic factors, and seasonality.

The following outline illustrates the economic factors:

Economic Factors Affecting Supply of Resale Units

A. Unemployment due to
   1. Temporary layoffs
   2. Severance
   3. Firm's relocation to another geographic area
B. Reduction in the households' purchasing power due to
   1. Elimination of overtime or extra compensation
   2. Unemployment of second wage earner
   3. Increase in mortgage payments relative to disposable income when adjustable rate mortgages and graduated payment mortgages are involved
C. Real income life cycle of household
D. Company- or corporation-initiated transfers due to
   1. Personnel changes
   2. Firm's relocation to another geographic area
E. Geographic relocation initiated by the individual that are
   1. Interregional (voluntary job transfer to another geographic area)
   2. Intraurban (job transfer to another section of the metropolitan area)

The occurrence of any one of these economic factors can cause an increase in supply in the resale market. The effects of factors A, B, and C are felt through a change (usually a decrease) in income, while the effects of factors D and E are felt through a change in the number of households that choose to reside in the housing units in the market.

Income and the number of consumers are also supply-side as well as demand-side determinants in the resale market, but there is a substantial difference between the supply-side and demand-side aspects of these variables.

In different geographic areas, different economic factors will dominate the resale market. The analyst must determine which economic changes are occurring, and which of these have the most substantial effect. Just as it can change over space, the relative importance of these economic factors also can change over time.

The demographic factor that operates on the supply side of the resale market is typically referred to as the family life cycle. The demographic variables associated with this factor are identified next.

Demographic Factors Affecting Supply of Resale Units

A. Family life cycle
   1. Age of adults
   2. Size (number of children and other dependents)
   3. Age of children
   4. Sex of children
B. Taste and preference pattern changes

1. Density preferences
2. Tenure preferences
3. Efficiency preferences (size and structural qualities)
4. Amenity preferences
   a. Educational characteristics
   b. Occupational characteristics

The family life-cycle hypothesis argues that a family (or household) has different needs and desires at different stages of its development. A young (25–34) two-person family may buy a relatively small unit as its first home. Then, as the family ages and has children, they sell their first home (a supply change in the resale market for small houses) and buy a larger home (a demand change in the resale market for larger houses or in the market for new construction). Next, when the children leave home, the older, two-person family may sell its large home (supply change in the resale market) and purchase a condominium or a smaller house (demand change).

The family life-cycle relationship just depicted is an age-of-adult, number-of-children, and age-of-children interrelationship. But the sex of the children can also affect the family's need for space. Two teenage boys or two teenage girls can share a bedroom, and there may not be a need to acquire a larger house. But, if there is a teenage son and a teenage daughter, the typical family desires to provide each child with a separate room. Thus, there is a need to change to a larger house.

The life-cycle concept also involves the family's income level. As the wage earners mature, their level of real income tends to increase, allowing them to make the house purchases. They buy their first home and then trade or move up to the larger house. The income aspect of the family-cycle relationship is typically identified under the economic factors.

The household's taste and preference pattern also enters the supply side of the resale market and is affected by the life cycle. Housing tastes and preferences are affected by the income, age, and size of the family as well as by its educational and occupational status. In addition, preferences for the physical structure and the neighborhood can change even if life-cycle status remains constant. A family may find reasons to dispose of their house sooner than originally envisioned if technological advances render it functionally obsolete or if external conditions deteriorate to make the location less desirable.

Investigation of these family life conditions can also affect resale housing demand variables. Households that decide to sell their housing unit because of a change in the factors just discussed will also seek a replacement housing unit.

Seasonality Seasonality is another factor that operates on the supply side of the resale market. Most households prefer to move when it is least disruptive because of school, weather, or other conditions. Consequently, most moves are made at particular times of the year. Sellers desire to place their properties on the market at the time that buyers are seeking to purchase houses. Consequently, seasonality on the supply side coincides with seasonality on the demand side of the resale market. The factor that affects demand the most is the start of school. Since most families prefer to move without interrupting a child's school year, more houses are offered for sale in spring and summer than in the fall or winter.

In summary, analysis of the effect of changes in the major economic and demographic aspects of supply in the resale market reveals that supply will increase when (1) employment increases; (2) the household's purchasing power declines; (3) a family life-cycle mismatch with the attributes of the structure, the neighborhood, and/or the location occurs; and (4) tastes and preferences shift away from the structure, the neighborhood, and/or the location. Further investigation of these variables reveals several causes for increased unemployment, purchasing power reducton, and the family life-cycle mismatch.

Nonexclusive Variables in the Resale Market There are variables that operate on both supply and demand in the resale market. The two principal variables are (1) the mortgage interest rate and (2) the price of substitute housing units. On the demand side of the resale market, there is an inverse relationship between the mortgage interest rate and the demand for houses; that is, demand declines as interest rates rise. On the supply side of the resale market, this same inverse relationship holds because suppliers (owners of existing units) anticipate the decline in demand and defer their plans to sell until stronger demand can maintain price levels, and because owners of existing units must become buyers themselves when their existing unit is sold. If the family life cycle creates a need (demand) for a larger house, the family may defer a move until the mortgage interest rate declines. When this decision is made, the supply in the resale market also declines. Then, when the mortgage interest rate declines, the supply in the resale market increases as households seek a replacement unit in a different market. So, in the resale market, an increase in the mortgage interest rate will cause a decline in demand and a decline in supply.

The price of substitute housing has a direct effect on demand in the resale market. As the price of substitute housing increases, demand in the resale market under analysis increases as consumers desert the higher-priced substitutes. On the supply side, the price of substitute housing has an indirect effect. As the price of substitute housing increases, supply in the resale market under analysis shifts vertically. This movement reflects the fact that the existing quantity of houses for sale will be offered at a higher price after the price of the substitute increases. This vertical shift has the same effect as a decrease in supply; at all possible prices in the market, fewer units will be offered for sale in the resale market being analyzed after the price of substitute housing increases. So, in the resale market an increase in the price of substitute housing will cause an increase in demand and a decrease in supply.

The Market for the Existing Stock[5]

There is a direct connection between the market for new construction of type X housing and the existing stock of type X housing. New construction increases the supply of existing units. It shifts the vertical supply curve shown earlier in Exhibit 4-3 to the right. Other factors also can affect the position of the supply curve for the stock of existing units. Casualty losses due to fire and other forms of destruction, as well as intentional demolition of units, cause the supply to decrease—a leftward shift of the curve. The process of conversion also affects the supply curve. Type X housing might be upgraded by means of a room addition or modernization/renovation work into type Y housing. Such upgrading causes not only an increase in the supply of type Y units, but also a reduction in the supply of type X housing units. Moreover, a lesser form of housing can be upgraded into type X housing, causing the supply of type X housing units to increase. Consequently, the supply of existing housing in any submarket depends on new construction, casualty loss, demolitions, and conversions to or from that type of housing.

Vacancies in a Dynamic Market

The various factors causing demand and supply to change over time in a housing submarket cause the number of vacant units in the submarket to increase and decrease as the submarket adjusts to a new equilibrium price. Given time sufficient for all adjustments to be made, the vacancy rate will return to a "normal" or typical level. Price in the submarket, however, may be higher, lower, or the same. As a practical matter, the market analyst monitors the level and direction of change in the submarket vacancy rate as a leading indicator of a change in price and as an indication of the need for new construction.

In a dynamic market, the analyst must consider the flow of available units to and from the supply over the forecast period. First, the analyst assesses the capability of the existing stock to satisfy current and forecast levels of demand; then, the focus of the analysis switches to new construction or rehabilitation. If there are insufficient units in certain categories in the existing housing stock, the analyst determines if there will be a sufficient amount of new construction or rehabilitation to make up or exceed the deficit. In this way, the analyst concludes how well housing supply is likely to meet expected demand levels over the forecast period.

In some instances the analyst may find there are excess units available for certain time periods. A first concern then is to determine if these excess units are in current inventories (existing stock, vacant for sale or rent) or are newly constructed units that are unsold. If there is an increase of unsold new

[5] This material was taken with permission from Donald R. Epley and Joseph Rabianski, *Principles of Real Estate Decisions* (Englewood Cliffs, N.J.: Prentice-Hall, 1986), p. 189.

units, there is likely to be a downward pressure on prices of competitive units in the existing housing stock, and a reduction in new construction.

The relationship between units in the existing housing stock and new construction must always be considered when housing supplies are analyzed. The first step in the analysis, however, is to investigate each supply source separately, beginning with existing inventories.

Vacancy Analysis of Existing Housing Stock   The focus of a vacancy analysis of the existing housing stock is on the number of vacant units that are available on the market, which is added to the number of occupied units listed for sale on the market. These units are then compared to expected demand levels to determine the level of unmet demand, if any. This unmet demand creates the need for new construction or rehabilitation and exerts an upward influence on price.

Ideally, the steps in a vacancy analysis are

1. Obtain total vacancies in the existing stock and disaggregate by price range and geographic market area.
2. Obtain total vacancies of new construction (unsold inventory) and disaggregate by price range and geographic market area.
3. Reduce total vacancies in the existing stock obtained in step 1 by the following vacancy categories:
   a. Vacancies resulting from seasonal occupancy.
   b. Vacancies awaiting demolition.
   c. Vacancies awaiting rehabilitation or conversion.
   d. Vacancies from other reasons.
4. Sum the adjusted vacancy count in the existing stock (step 3) and the vacancy count in new construction (step 1) to get total available vacant units in each market.
5. Combine available vacancies with an estimate of occupied units offered for sale.

Disaggregation of an overall vacancy rate into submarket rates requires primary data collection that is often prohibitive in terms of cost and time required. Consequently, the market analyst concerned with an existing vacancy rate surveys only the submarket under analysis.

The Dynamics of New Construction: Pipeline Analysis

The supply of new housing in the form of completed construction may be viewed as a flow from a pipeline. Housing completions come out of the pipeline; land development and construction are inputs to the pipeline.

At any point in time there is a stock of units in each of the stages of land development and construction. The size of this stock controls the flow of supply that can emerge from the pipeline during any period of time.

The pipeline's two initiating inputs are (1) land to be developed and (2) authorizations or permits required to enable a builder to build on the land. There are stages of development through which the developer and builder must pass. The pace of supply is controlled by the time it takes to complete these stages.

An analyst can begin an analysis of the pipeline by collecting data on certain local government approvals. The stages of approval by local government vary somewhat among municipalities, but can be classified as follows:

1. Land to be developed
   a. Land planned for residential use
   b. Land zoned for residential use
   c. Land serviced for residential use
   d. Site plan approvals
2. Construction authorizations or actions
   a. Building permits issued
   b. Starts
   c. Completions

Each of these stages is described in the following sections. First, the types of land to be developed are identified.

Land Planned for Residential Use   Land planned for residential use is land so designated on public planning documents, specifically, the community's land-use plan. These documents show public intention to regulate and encourage residential development but give no time frame for it.

Land Zoned for Residential Use   The zoning code legally defines the type of use the landowner can build on the land. Developers and builders frequently find it necessary to seek "rezoning" or zoning changes to gain permission to build the type or density of housing (or other types of structures) they want to build. Land may be planned for one density yet zoned for a less intense use waiting until the "time is right."

Land Serviced for Residential Use   To get a building permit, certain services such as sewer and water are required. When local government controls the provision of services, it controls the pace at which land may be developed. Local government may also use subdivision regulations to restrict development by requiring minimum levels of services prior to the commencement of construction. The level of services may relate to transportation as well as utilities, and may even include the adequacy of other public facilities such as schools or parks. This control over the infrastructure limits development to land appropriately "serviced."

Site Plan Approvals   This stage of the approval process refers to approval of the various elements involved in engineering the land for a specific subdivision plat or other site plan that specifically identifies the location and type of improvements.

Once data on the amount of residential land available and the potential residential units that the acreage represents have been collected, the analyst then reviews public records to ascertain how many units are in the pipeline. The following data are compiled.

1. *Building permits.* The number of building permits issued on the basis of approved construction plans are first identified. The units represented by these building permits may not be completed or even started.

2. *Starts.* A start is the beginning of construction of a housing unit. Inspection records identify units that have been started but not completed.

3. *Completions.* The building is completed when it has a certificate of occupancy or has passed final inspection under the building permit. Other work may be done on the building, but the building may now be legally used as a dwelling and viewed as a unit coming out of the pipeline. Exhibit 7-5 graphically demonstrates the pipeline concept.

Exhibit 7-5 Pipeline analysis.

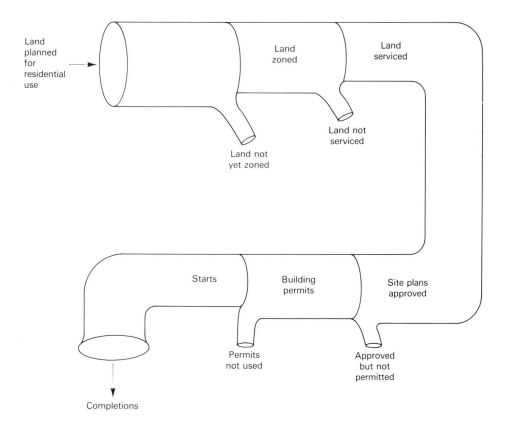

Analysis of Pipeline Land Available for Development

In measuring the number of housing units that could be put in the pipeline during a particular time frame, the first measure is the site plan approval. Depending on the time frame, land for additional units may also be approved. But the timing of development is then up to the builder. The builder's decision to go ahead will be marked by the building permit.

Thus, the first indicator of the number, type, and location of new housing units that could enter the pipeline is the number of units allowed by the approved site plans. The first indicator of what units have entered the pipeline is the number of housing units for which building permits have been issued.

The issuance of building permits is not completely dependable as an indicator of units that will be shortly completed. Under some circumstances, builders may stockpile building permits well in advance of construction, perhaps in anticipation of a regulatory change. Also, market conditions may change, with the result that permits are allowed to lapse.

The most reliable leading indicator of housing units to come out of the pipeline is "starts." The number of units started are generally reported in federally gathered statistics based upon local data. In the final analysis, however, the number of starts must be compared to the number of completions. The difference between starts and completions during a specific time period is reflected by the change in the number of units under construction, adjusted by units in abandoned projects, if any.

Pipeline analysis provides the analyst with an estimate of the potential supply of new units over the time period in the market forecast of demand. As described already, pipeline analysis covers all potential residential construction in the market. The analysis may be disaggregated geographically (considering land planned, zoned, and serviced) and by type of improvements (indicated by site plan approvals and building permits) to estimate forthcoming supply in a submarket.

SUMMARY

The competitive, dynamic housing market solves the complex economic problem of allocating an heterogeneous collection of households among the diverse array of housing units. In this process, rents, prices, vacancy rates, and the density of occupation are determined. New construction and rehabilitation are stimulated.

The real estate market analyst must understand the economics of the dynamic housing market to develop a logical, empirical analysis and forecast of housing demand. As with all forms of empirical real estate market analyses, appropriate proxies must be selected for many variables to obtain usable data. There are frequently no data for many variables used in a conceptual economic analysis of the market process.

Demand in the housing market is measured in terms of households; supply is quantified in housing units. Households are allocated among available housing units on the basis of income and other economic, demographic, and psychographic characteristics that determine their willingness to spend on housing versus other goods and services.

The local housing market can be conceptualized as interrelated submarkets. Housing submarkets are defined as a group of similar housing units occupied by a relatively homogeneous group of households that consider this group of housing units to be closer substitutes, one for another, than for other housing units in the market. The formation of submarkets requires segmentation of households and disaggregation of the supply of housing units. Submarkets are interrelated in that a decrease in the price in one submarket causes a decrease in the demand for units in a submarket of housing units considered to be close substitutes.

As in all markets, demand and supply interact to determine price and the quantity demanded. In a housing submarket, where households are occupying housing units at the going price (or rent), the vacancy rate for the submarket also will be determined. The economist typically casts the conceptual analysis over time in terms of supply conditions. In the market time period, the supply of units is given and demand (households) fluctuates to determine prices and vacancy rates. In the intermediate or short-run time period, the supply of units can change within the capacity of the existing homebuilding industry through new construction and rehabilitation, and both demand and supply vary in the determination of price. In the long run time period, the construction industry can increase its capacity, resulting in further changes in supply in response to long-run changes in demand.

The housing market and its linked submarkets interact to exert forces toward equilibrium prices and vacancy levels. However, the dynamic market is in continuous flux as the number of households and their economic, demographic, and psychographic characteristics continuously change. Other factors influencing the demand for housing also fluctuate, including credit conditions, ownership costs, prices of other goods and services, and expectations about future prices. On the supply side of a dynamic submarket, units can be supplied when existing households move or when units are added by new construction or rehabilitation. But, excess supply overshoots the would be equilibrium points.

READINGS

EPLEY, DONALD, and JOSEPH RABIANSKI, "Housing Market Analysis," in *Principles of Real Estate Decisions*. Englewood Cliffs, N.J.: Prentice-Hall, 1986.

KAU, JAMES B., and C. F. SIRMANS, "The Housing Market," in *Real Estate*. New York: McGraw-Hill, 1985.

MCMAHON, JOHN, "Residential Land Uses," in *Property Development*. New York: McGraw-Hill, 1976.

RABIANSKI, JOSEPH. "The Residential Resale Market," *Real Estate Appraiser and Analyst*, Fall 1985, pp. 5–9.

SUMICHRAST, MICHAEL, and MAURY SELDIN, III, *Housing Markets*. Homewood, Ill.: Dow Jones-Irwin, 1977.

8

EMPIRICAL RESIDENTIAL MARKET ANALYSIS

INTRODUCTION

The principal tasks of the analyst in a housing market analysis are to forecast the level of demand for and supply of particular categories of housing units. The availability of existing housing units and the production of new units are considered in determining how well the forecast levels of demand can be met. The result of the housing market study is the estimation of the rate of absorption for categories of housing over a particular time period. The rate of absorption is defined as the number of units (by type, market segment, price) that are expected to be occupied (purchased or rented) within a specified period of time (a month, a quarter, or a year) at prevailing prices.

Three major levels of housing market studies are commonly performed. Each subsequent level of analysis builds on information provided by the prior study, so that the most detailed level of analysis, the site-specific level, is built on the assumption that general housing demand and supply factors are already known. The three levels of housing market analysis are the following:

1. *Analysis of the General Housing Market.* This aggregate type of study focuses on the demand and supply of housing units within an identified study area. The factors common to the demand and supply of all types and price ranges of housing units are considered. A general housing market analysis usually is performed for a local housing market, such as a Metropolitan Statistical Area or a county, but may also be performed for a state, a region, or a nation. The study shows the strength of the demand for housing and the unmet housing needs for all types of housing within the area under study. If disaggregated housing market forecasts are required, this study serves as the foundation by providing aggregate demand and supply data that can subsequently be broken down into more specific market components, where each component can be separately evaluated and forecasted.

2. *Analysis of Housing Submarkets.* The housing market analysis is a market-specific and/or product-specific analysis where various categories of housing may be examined independently of one another. Housing submarkets may be identified by geographic boundaries of a market area; by physical characteristics (such as building type, size of unit, and amenity level or quality of unit); by economic characteristics (such as tenure—owned or rented—and price range); and by user characteristics (second homes, low-income, etc.). The study then examines demand and supply factors to estimate the level of unmet demand expected in various time periods for the housing submarkets. At this level of analysis, the unmet demand for new rental and owned units by rent and price range may be forecast or a variety of special-purpose studies can be performed, such as the market for mobile homes, congregate housing, federally assisted housing (for the elderly or for open occupancy), second homes, and so on.

3. *Site-Specific Housing Marketability Study.* The site-specific study deals with the capability of an identified group of housing units offered at specific locations to be absorbed by the market. Using a submarket forecast of demand for specified housing with particular physical and economic attributes within narrowly defined market area boundaries, the analysis examines the ability of the individual project to compete with similar housing units on the market. The study takes into account the competitive characteristics of all existing and expected supplies of units in the identified submarket and concludes how well and how quickly a specific supplier can expect to market the units. The forecast level of project absorption assumes the effectiveness of particular marketing strategies, or a recommendation for a marketing strategy is given in the study. This level of analysis requires current information about general housing market condi-

tions and conditions in specific local submarkets as well as the competitive attributes of a given project. The steps in a marketability analysis are described in Chapter 5, Analyzing the Subject Property and Its Competitive Environment.

EMPIRICAL HOUSING MARKET ANALYSIS

The discussion in Chapter 7 provided a conceptual and informational setting in which the housing demand-supply decision is made. Both the nature of the housing product and the nature of the housing supply-demand decision were discussed. In this chapter the process of performing the empirical analysis and its varied dimensions are discussed.

Specifying the Problem

The analyst's first task is to identify precisely the decision maker's problem. The analysis can then be structured and the data required to perform the study can be specified. Starting with the decision maker's knowledge, perceptions, and constraints, the analyst strives for a thorough definition of the problem. A discussion with the client might follow this sequence:

> Builder asks analyst to discern the future level of demand for housing in Able County and the level of competition. Reason for the analysis: Should the builder shift some (or all) of his construction activity to Able County?

How flexible are the builder's construction capabilities?

> Builder says he is able to produce (or only desires to produce) single-family detached units in the $90,000+ range.

Has land been acquired?

> Builder says land has not yet been acquired, but he has options on several parcels already zoned.

What kind of study is needed?

> Analyst says, "It seems that you need a market analysis for long-term housing demand in the county for the product line and then a site-specific study for each of the sites."

What kind of study is performed?

> Analyst prepares a plan to do a five-year market study for $90,000+ single-family detached housing (physical and tenure disaggregation) in Able County (geographic disaggregation).

Housing market analyses and the problems they hope to solve range from deciding to construct federally assisted housing for low- or moderate-income households in projects and restricting it to elderly occupancy, or making it available for open occupancy, to analyzing demand for mobile homes, second homes, or resort units. The analysis may also need to be geographically disaggregated if the site is specified. These various problems produce the types of analysis shown in Exhibit 8-1.

Structuring the Analysis

Once the analyst and the client narrow the focus of the study, the analyst must outline the components of the study. The following scheme is one form of working outline that allows the analyst to accomplish the disaggregated study requested by the client. In the following discussion, the client has indicated that the appropriate study will be an analysis of effective demand for new single-family housing by price range in Able County for the next five years. To estimate this effective demand, the analyst would

1. Review the relevant local economic variables that will determine the future of Able County. The most significant variables are
   a. Employment in the metropolitan area (or in the subject and adjacent counties).
   b. Accessibility of Able County residents to the major job sites in the metropolitan area.
   c. Locational amenities in Able County and its surrounding area.
   d. Public services, especially the quality of the school system.
2. Review the historic trend in household formations and prepare a forecast of household growth in the near future (analysis of household growth).
3. Calculate unmet demand in Able County (analysis of the unmet demand for housing).
4. Segment household growth on the basis of income required to purchase the house that the builder is supplying to the market. This task may require the following actions:
   a. Calculate the minimum-priced house that can be constructed in Able County.
   b. Calculate the minimum income required for buyers to enter the market.
   c. Relate the builder's price range to the appropriate income categories that can purchase the house(s) being supplied.

Exhibit 8-1 Type of Market Analysis.

General market analysis	All types of housing units
	Total local economy
Submarket—disaggregated market analysis	Specific product type
	Specific age category of unit
	Specific market area
	Specific market segments
	Specific price ranges
Site-specific/product-specific market analysis	Site-driven analysis
	Use or market-driven analysis
	Capital-driven analysis
	Entrepreneurial-driven analysis

Components of Analysis

Several steps are required to examine supply and demand components. These are described using the logical sequence with which they are performed.

Analysis of Local Economy   The full array of demographic and economic variables describing the local economy were discussed in Chapter 3, including the techniques for updating and forecasting those variables. As a practical matter, the budget available to perform a market study typically precludes a detailed analysis of the local economy. However, the analyst is cautioned not to omit local economic considerations from the solution to a market analysis problem. All forecasts of market demand depend upon the basic health of the local economy. The analyst must achieve an understanding of the local economy sufficient to be able to ascertain probabilities for key variables that must be forecast.

When budget considerations are restrictive, an analysis of local economic factors can be most efficiently accomplished by first identifying key variables in the market and then gathering only the data necessary to evaluate and forecast these variables. This approach avoids presentation of unimportant or irrelevant data that have no value in a market study. In the majority of studies, the key variables fall into the following categories:

1. *Demographic*: change in the number of households, household size, household age structure (age of household head)
2. *Economic*: change in income distribution of the households—offer price of product (a supply-side concept based on production costs and quality of materials, workmanship, and fixtures); mortgage interest rates; price of substitute housing.
3. *Physical*: construction constraints imposed by lot size and shape, topography, drainage capacity, and so on.
4. *Legal*: police power constraints such as zoning, subdivision regulations, building codes, and the like.

The key variables used should be fully understood. Historic trends should be analyzed, current changes should be spotted, and future values of the variables should then be forecast.

Analysis of Household Growth   Able County households are to be forecast over the five-year period. The analyst may use reliable forecasts or projections of population and households for the market area in question prepared by reputable sources. The state or a regional planning agency may project population, and in many instances an employment projection may also exist, or the information may be obtained from a commercial research organization that maintains a comprehensive data base, a trade or industry organization, or others. If an adequate population study exists, the analyst extracts from it the population, number of households, household size, and employment data to be used.[1] The source of such secondary data is cited, and the analyst ratifies the judgment, if appropriate.

Exhibit 8-2 provides one of many possible formats for the display of historic and projected population and household data. A series of tasks must be performed to complete the table, depending upon the analyst's need to develop forecasts from available information:

1. Task (a) involves the application of the housing inventory technique to develop an estimate of the number of households in 1986. (See Chapter 3.)
2. Task (b) involves the forecasting of the historic trend in household size from 1980 to 1986 and then into the future. The issue of forecasting household size was discussed in Chapter 3. At this point the analyst must check current period information to forecast future values.
3. Task (c) is the estimation of current population by multiplying the household estimate by the household size estimate.

Exhibit 8-2 Population and Household Estimation: Able County.

	POPULATION				HOUSEHOLD			HOUSEHOLD SIZE	
	Actual	Estimated	Projected	Adjusted Projection	Actual	Estimated	Forecast	Actual	Estimated Forecast
1970	8,000	—	—	—	2,800	—	—	2.06	—
1980	10,000	—	—	—	4,000	—	—	2.5	
1985	—	11,400 (d) (e)	12,000		—	—	—		
1986	—	11,760 (c)	12,400		4,900 (a)				2.4 (b)
1990	—	—	14,000	13,300 (f)	—	—	5,375 (g)		2.35
1995	—	—	16,000	15,200 (f)			6,755 (g)		2.25

Tasks: (a) Derive figure using housing inventory method in Chapter 3.
     (b) Forecast historic trend in household size (see Chapter 3).
     (c) Multiply number of households times household size.
     (d) Make an "off-table" calculation to estimate previous year's population.
     (e) Rationalize estimated population into projected population.
     (f) Adjust population projection for indicated overstatement.
     (g) Divide adjusted population by forecast household size.

[1]If a second home/preretirement/investor market is analyzed, such as resort condominiums, household formations in the local market provide only a portion of total demand, that is, the demand from permanent residents in the market. To estimate the other, often more significant, component of demand, the analyst may rely on historic trends of households and housing units reported in the 1970 and 1980 censuses. If 1,000 households were formed and 3,000 additional units were occupied, 1970–1980, a demand for 2,000 units can be attributable to the second home/preretirement/investor component. Caution must be exercised in projecting a continuation of this demand component, which is influenced by credit conditions, tax factors, national economic prosperity, and the rate of inflation. The analyst should compare the historic trend indicated by the census or other reputable secondary sources with primary data collected on recent purchases of units by nonresident user/investors.

4. Task (d) may or may not be necessary. In some localities a regional, county, or city planning department might be able to provide an estimate for population in the metropolitan economy on an annual basis. If these data are available for use, the analyst can use the ratio technique to step down from the metropolitan economy to the county level to have an estimate of population for the study area (the county) for the previous year. Task (d) is symbolized as an off-table calculation.

5. Task (e) starts with a display of the county population projection for 1985, 1990, and 1995 obtained from a regional planning commission. The 1985 projection of county population is compared to the 1986 estimate obtained from the housing inventory method. This comparison reveals that the planning commission's projection was too optimistic. The published projection can be analyzed by breaking it down or extrapolating it on an annual basis. Some agencies will explain the projection methodology, so the analyst can use that methodology to construct the 1986 projected population value. Other agencies will not reveal or are unable to explain adequately the projection technique. In this instance, trends detected from published data can be used to create the projection for 1986. Display the projections for 1985, 1990, and 1995 on graph paper and fit a curve or curves to that data. In our example, the three points are connected by a straight line, showing that the population projection in 1986 is 12,400 and that there is a projected population increase of 400 persons per year.

Comparing the estimated population figure generated by the housing inventory method to the planning commission's population figure gives the analyst a first approximation of any excessive optimism in the population projection. In this instance, the projection overstates population by 5.3 percent, calculated using the midpoint formulation shown in Exhibit 8-3.

If a population estimate for 1985 is available for the county from the application of the ratio technique, then a second check for an optimistic projection can be made. In this case, the midpoint formulation will provide a 5.1 percent measure of the excessive projection.

6. Task (f) involves a respecification of the planning commission's population projection based on the indicated margin of error in the projections. In this case, the analyst would have to deflate the 1990 and 1995 population projections by at least 5 percent. This is shown as the adjusted population projections in Exhibit 8-3.

In practice, the analyst should try to use every reasonably available source of data to correct for errors in projections. One such technique is shown in the appendix to this chapter. The authors used internal data provided by *Sales Marketing and Management* magazine for a county cloaked as Baker County; the name is fictitious, but the data are real.

7. Task (g) involves the translation of the adjusted projection into a projection of household data by using the forecasted household size. The 1990 adjusted projection of 13,300 is divided by household size of 2.35 to obtain a forecast of 5,375 households.

	ACTUAL	ESTIMATED (P_e)	PROJECTED (P_p)
1985	—	11,400	12,00
1986	—	11,760	12,400

Growth rate, midpoint formulation: $\dfrac{(P_p - P_e)_{1985}}{(P_p + P_e)_{1986}} = \dfrac{640}{12,080} = 5.3\%$

Exhibit 8-3 Population Adjustments.

An issue that may need attention by the analyst is the population in households versus the population in group quarters. The household size variable is obtained by dividing population residing in households, not group quarters, by the number of households. If the people living in group quarters are not subtracted from the total group figures, the household size variable is increased. Usually the population in group quarters is a very small percentage of the county population. But a situation can arise where the distinction between these two components is important. In typical counties, the inclusion of people in group quarters in the population figure causes a change in the hundredths (the second decimal) of the household size number. In an area where group living arrangements are a high percentage, as in a college town with dormitories, the error can be substantial.

Employment data could be used to update population and, thus, household data. The analyst must know the nature of the employment data available. Unlike population and household data, which are provided on a place-of-residence basis, employment data can be provided on a place-of-residence or on a job-site basis. The census provides employment data on a place-of-residence basis. On the other hand, local and regional planning agencies present employment data on both a place-of-residence and a job-site basis. State labor departments also present "covered" employment data on a job-site basis, which is a major subset of total employment.

If the area of analysis is large enough, these two sets of employment data are virtually the same. For example, if the earth were considered, total employment by residence is the same as total employment by job site. But as the area gets smaller, these two employment concepts move apart. For example, a high percentage of the people who live in a county may not work in that county. There is no one-to-one correspondence between residence site and job site, even if by chance the two numbers are equal.

This distinction between residence-site and job-site employment is made because the analyst may wish to use the labor participation rate to translate employment into population and household data. The labor participation rate is employment by residence site divided by population. However, the "participation rate," often used in population updating, is "covered" employment by job site. The conceptual validity and the accuracy of this hybrid ratio is greater at the metropolitan level than it is at the county level.

If a projection of employment by residence site is available, it can be used to generate a participation rate at any level of geographic disaggregation. If, on the other hand, a projection of employment by job site is available, it should only be used for the entire metropolitan area.

Analysis of the Demand-Supply "Gap"   The unsegmented demand forecast for housing begins with the household figures from Exhibit 8-2. Assume that the housing demand forecast is for 1990; Exhibit 8-4 shows the structure

ROW		1980–1986	1987	1988	1989
Annual Demand					
1	Household change	900	158	159	158
2	Losses through demolition	210	10	8	5
3	Other losses (act of nature)	35	5	5	5
4	Net conversions (+ or −)	+49	+7	+7	+7
5	Annual demand (sum of rows 1–4)		180	179	175
Construction					
6	Pipeline completions		200	20	0
7	Output to meet minimum production × intended inventory or		0	40	60
8	Forecast construction (rows 6 and 7)		−200	60	60
9	Unmet demand (+) or overbuilding (−) (row 5 minus row 8)		−20	119	115
Vacancy					
10	All existing vacant units in market caused by market forces		220	150	150
11	Frictional vacancies		100	100	100
12	Unintended vacancies (row 10 minus row 11)		120	50	50
13	Net unmet demand (+) or excess vacancies (−) (row 9 minus row 12)		−140	69	75
14	Annual construction to meet unmet demand		0	0	4

Exhibit 8-4 Annual Demand Forecast: Unsegmented Analysis.

of this procedure. The data for the first row are generated from the forecast of households shown in Exhibit 8-2.

ROW 1   The change in the number of households from 1980 to 1986 is estimated to be 900. The forecast for households in 1990 is 5,375, an increase of 475 households over the 1986 level. The increase of 475 is assumed to be evenly distributed over the next three years of 1987, 1988, and 1989. (This distribution might also be an extension of a trend developed over the 1980–1986 period.)

ROWS 2 AND 3   The second and third rows in Exhibit 8-4 present the data for intentional demolitions (row 2) and losses by "act of nature" (row 3). Demolition permits often must be obtained in advance, and a search of the building permit records will reveal the extent of demolitions over time and in the near term. Destruction of units by acts of nature are somewhat predictable through the use of actuarial tables. Casualty insurers can provide secondary data on the percentage of housing units expected to be destroyed by fire annually.

ROW 4 The fourth row contains information on net conversions in the unsegmented housing market. In most communities, conversions require building permits, enabling permit data to be used. There are many forms of conversions that the analyst must keep in mind. The most typical is the conversion of apartments to condominium units. Condominium conversions usually yield one new unit for each existing unit converted, but sometimes the number of existing units can diminish as two or more small units are combined for a larger condominium. In some markets residential space is converted to commercial space. In other areas, older homes are converted to apartment units.

The analyst must examine the exact nature of the conversion to determine its effect. In this example the analyst discovered that housing units were being lost as residential space was being converted to small office space and small residential units were being converted to larger condominium units. The analyst found that 49 housing units were lost in the last seven years (1980 to 1986). This fact translates to the analyst's judgment that the recent trend will continue into the future at 7 units being lost per year. The loss of the units signifies a need for 7 replacement units—therefore the conversion value carries a positive sign.

ROW 5 The addition of demolition and conversion data yields an estimate of replacement demand that, combined with changes in household formations, provides an estimate of annual housing demand shown in row 5 of Exhibit 8-4. Remember that this is an unsegmented and highly aggregated demand analysis. No consideration is given at this point to housing unit composition, interest rates, income levels, relative prices, and other significant market variables. Figures for annual demand for 1987, 1988, and 1989 are provided in Exhibit 8-4.

ROWS 6 AND 7 These rows contain data on construction from the "pipeline" for the next period (row 6) and an estimate of intended inventory holdings by the builders in the market to meet marketing and production needs (row 7). Pipeline analysis (discussed in Chapter 7) reveals that 200 housing units are permitted and under construction for 1987 and 20 housing units for 1988.

An analysis of local builders reveals that they plan to maintain at least a certain minimum scale of operation to keep key personnel in all divisions of their operation. In addition, the builders plan to have inventory that will serve as model homes. These two desires are translated into a minimum production level that will be maintained during each planning year. In the market being analyzed, the analyst discovers that 60 units of output represents this minimum output level required by the builders in the market. In 1987 the pipeline production of 200 units exceeds this minimum. In 1988 pipeline construction is 20 units, and thus 40 more units will be needed to maintain key personnel and to hold units as models. In 1989 minimum production is set at 60 units.

The information on minimum production and desired inventory holdings can be obtained by surveying (quite possibly informally) the largest builders in the market and interpreting the situation for the smaller builders, or the value for row 7 can be stated as the extrapolation of the low points in a historic series for new construction in the market area. (The assumption being made here is that the low points over time indicate the minimum requirement for continuity of operation of local builders.)

ROW 8   Row 8 exhibits the analyst's forecast for future construction levels. These values represent the plans in effect and under construction plus the impact of minimum construction necessities.

ROW 9   Row 9 provides an estimate of unmet demand or overbuilding. A positive number represents unmet demand, while a negative number indicates overbuilding. In concept, row 8 indicates the amount of housing units that must be provided after pipeline and desired minimum production levels are met. It represents the number of new units the market can absorb over volume of current construction and planned construction.

ROW 10   Row 10 brings the vacant stock of housing into the analysis. If households need housing units and new units are not available, households will seek out vacant units from the existing stock in the market area as substitutes. Thus, there is a reduction of vacancies in existing housing as a result of unmet demand for new construction. However, if the analysis is being undertaken for a subarea of the market, then the analysis might be clouded by the fact that the unfilled demand may lower vacancies in some other subarea and leave the subject market area's vacancies unaffected. The underlying reasons for insufficient new construction could be the arrival of in-migrants with financial resources and different preferences. Vacant housing in the subject market area might be too expensive, or it might be inexpensive but offer too few of the desired amenities. The vacant housing might be located in undesirable neighborhoods that have poor-quality schools, safety problems (either perceived or real), and other drawbacks.

Consequently, vacancies cannot be inserted into the analysis without a check by the analyst of the characteristics of the vacant stock and correlation of the vacant stock with the characteristics of consumers in the market, especially in-migrants.

The figures in row 10 represent total vacancies in the market area's existing housing stock. Since the analysis is highly aggregated and unsegmented, no distinction is made for owner- versus renter-occupied units or price-versus-rent levels. However, based on off-table analysis, the analyst may know that there is a match between the characteristics of the vacant stock and the in-migrants.

The vacancy estimates are forecast numbers that combine history and judgment. One way of generating the vacancy forecast is to (1) prepare a display of historic vacancy numbers or percentages, (2) observe the pattern of the data, (3) project and observe the trend into the future (say, from 1987 to 1989), and (4) then convert the projection into a forecast by analyzing the current events that will affect future vacancies and making the appropriate adjustments.

A second way to handle row 10 is to make an estimate of 1987 vacancies from 1986 data. Vacancies at the beginning of 1987 will be the vacancies at the beginning of 1986 plus new construction less demolitions, plus or minus net conversions, plus or minus household change in 1986. This way is recommended because it enables the analyst to detect any short-term anomaly in the historic mean of vacancy levels.[2]

ROW 11   Row 11 presents data on a market phenomenon that is an economic reality as well as a necessity. There are always vacant units in the market because of operational inefficiencies (such as leasing problems) and pricing strategies. All this speaks to the need of some minimum vacancy level in the market. This minimum level is called the frictional vacancy level because it symbolizes the same phenomenon that the term "frictional unemployment" symbolizes. Neither unemployment nor vacancies are desired, per se, but frictional unemployment is a measure of the unemployment that occurs because laborers are out of work while they change jobs or job locations. Frictional vacancy represents the vacancy that occurs because of market imperfections, administered pricing policies, and inventory holdings. These vacancy levels vary among local markets.

In calculating frictional vacancies, the historic trend of the vacancy levels or rates is developed, and the low points of the cyclical pattern are observed and projected over the forecast period. The underlying argument for this tactic is that the low point is established as builders act to increase current inventory, and as administered prices are raised. These two actions cause an increase in vacancies. Very often, analysts will use the term "normal" vacancy to represent the phenomenon. The term is not the issue. The measure used to represent the phenomenon, however, is a major concern. Many analysts simply use the historic average for vacancies to represent this frictional or normal vacancy. When the average is used instead of the low-point trend as the basis for a forecast, the level of such desired vacancy is overstated.

ROW 12   This row represents the unintended vacancy level that the analyst forecasts for the market. It is existing vacancy net of fractional vacancy (i.e., row 10 minus row 11). This unintended vacancy can be used to supply any unmet demand for housing. So positive levels of unintended vacancies reduce unmet demand. Operationally, these row 12 values are negative numbers.

[2]In resort areas where a substantial component of demand is accounted for by nonresident demand (investor/second home), this technique is not appropriate.

ROW 13 Row 13 presents the figures for net unmet demand, or excess vacancies, depending on the sign of the term. In the example of Exhibit 8-4, overbuilding of 20 units and unintended vacancy of 120 yields excess vacancies for 1987 of 140 units. This aggregate analysis suggests that additional construction beyond that in the pipeline would not be warranted in 1987. In 1988, the same calculation reveals continued unintended vacancies of 50 but a need for any additional construction of 69 units. In 1989 a need is also indicated for 75 units of additional construction. Operationally, row 13 is row 9 less the value in row 12. Conceptually, it represents overbuilding (minus in row 9) augmented by unintended vacancy. Or row 13 represents unmet demand (plus in row 9) reduced by the unintended vacancies.

ROW 14 Finally, row 14 provides the forecast for annual housing construction. The values in this row require a cumulative interpretation across the years of the forecast period. In 1987 pipeline construction in conjunction with annual demand yields overbuilding of 20 units and total excess vacancies of 140. Thus there is no need for any additional construction over existing plans.

In 1988, row 13 reveals the need for 69 units. But since there are 140 units classified as excess vacancies, there is no need for additional construction above the planned level of 60 shown in row 8. In 1989, there is need for 75 units of housing, but there are still 71 units classified as excess vacancies (i.e., 140 less 69). So only 4 additional units of construction are needed above the planned level of 60 units. It is important to note that the analysis at this point is at the aggregate level.[3] Market opportunities for new construction can exist even in overbuilt situations if the units supplied do not match segmented demand.

The nature of the forecast will change if any of the variables in the analysis changes. For example, the analyst may wish to calculate the annual construction needed for unmet demand, given that 1987 vacancies are 155 units. What would happen if 1987 vacancies were established as 70 units? Would the values for row 9 in 1988 and 1989 change? Would the values in row 11 change?

Segmentation Analysis

After the analyst forecasts the growth in households and calculates the aggregate unmet demand, segmentation of the market can take place. The level of unmet demand is a key factor at this point. First, if there is little unmet demand for the next few years, the builder might not want to enter the market. However, a survey of the existing stock and the pipeline can reveal a gap in the market. For example, a survey of developers with projects in the pipeline may

---

[3]This example was adapted from a version presented in Michael Sumichast, "Housing Market Analysis," in *The Real Estate Handbook*, ed. Maury Seldin (Homewood, Ill.: Dow Jones-Irwin, 1980), pp. 315–337; and in Michael Sumichast and Maury Seldin, *Housing Markets* (Homewood, Ill.: Dow Jones-Irwin, 1977), p. 315.

reveal that the price range that the builder wishes to produce is not in the pipeline. (The analyst should not use property values derived from building permit data to estimate the values of properties in the pipeline. Builders understate values by varying amounts, making the data unreliable indicators of value.) In that event, the builder may want to enter the market even if unmet demand is low. To determine if there is sufficient demand for the specific product, a segmentation analysis should be performed.

Segmentation analysis consists of three steps:

1. Calculating the minimum price at which new houses are being provided
2. Calculating the income level needed to buy the lowest-priced house
3. Matching the income levels to the house price ranges

These tasks are discussed in the next sections.

Calculating the Minimum Supply Price of Housing

Once the size of the potential market is known, the next step in analyzing the new, single-family housing market is to estimate the minimum price for a unit that can be obtained in the market. As a practical matter, the analyst examines houses recently constructed and sold or offered for sale in the market. The lower end of the scale of new construction will be new houses which just meet zoning and building code regulations, with basic amenities, located in the lowest-land-cost neighborhood available for new construction.

Because the lowest-cost houses being provided may not be the lowest cost that *could* be provided, the analyst should compute the cost of a house constructed on the lowest-cost developable land in the market. If the computed cost of house and lot is below that observed being offered in the market, the computed cost will be used as the minimum-priced house. The analyst will find that developers in an active competitive market typically will be serving the full range of potential buyers, including households with incomes at the margin of homeownership.

In computing the minimum-cost house, the analyst starts with physical and legal requirements of the site and the market area. In the process of analysis he or she may determine that the zoning ordinance requires a minimum quarter-acre building lot and certain minimum standards for the type and quality of materials. In addition, the minimum-sized housing unit may be either specified by the zoning ordinance or by market preferences. If the analyst discovers that the minimum-sized house is 1,600 square feet and the market will accept an average-quality structure, and the lot size must be at least 10,000 square feet (configured in the range of 60 × 165 feet or 75 × 135 feet), then the analyst can determine the minimum price for which the structure can be placed on the market by the typical builder. The sales comparison technique can be used to get the value of the land. An appraisal cost estimation procedure can be used in conjunction with certain characteristics of the housing unit to obtain a re-production cost figure per square foot of house.

The task at hand now requires that the analyst multiply the number of square feet (1,600) times the per square foot cost ($48 per square foot) to get a structural value of $76,800. This value can be adjusted upward for any extra structural amenities the house provides (e.g., $2,200 for a second fireplace). Then the value of the land ($13,000) is added to this figure to get the builder's stated price of $92,000. This is considered a normal profit price because the per square foot cost of $48 includes the level of overhead and profit that is sufficient to keep the builder in this line of endeavor. Based on this analysis, the analyst knows that the lowest asking price will be $92,000, could be $90,000, and might, under adverse market circumstances, drop to the $85,000 level. However, the feasible minimum price of new housing units in the market under normal con-ditions is $92,000. Exhibit 8-5 illustrates the steps in this analysis.

Builders, lenders, and market analysts typically work with per unit costs in computing the end cost of the house and lot. An example of this computation for the minimum-priced house is given in Exhibit 8-6. In Exhibit 8-6 land density is the maximum, and square footage per unit is the minimum for new construc-tion.

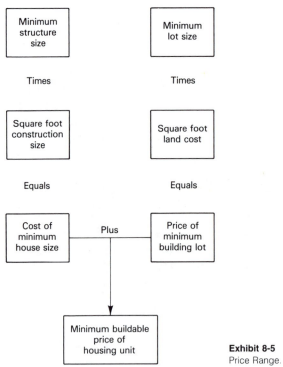

Exhibit 8-5 Steps in Determining Buildable Price Range.

1. Land cost per unit ($3,250,000 sales price for 100 acres at a density of 5 units per acre) $ 6,500
2. Development cost per lot (water, sewer, roads, engineering fees, etc.)   3,000
3. Building construction cost (1,600 square feet at $34 per square foot hard cost)   54,400
4. End cost of house and lot ($63,900 ÷ 0.70) (profit, general and administrative, marketing, and miscellaneous soft costs are typically 29–32% of the selling price; profits are 7–11%)   91,250

Exhibit 8-6   Calculation of Minimum-cost House.

Calculating the Minimum Household Income to Enter the Market

When the minimum price for the new units is established, it is necessary to determine how many households meet minimum income qualifications to ascertain the size of the market. The first step in the process of calculating the minimum level of household income needed to buy the lowest-priced new house is gathering mortgage loan underwriting standards from the lending institutions that serve the market. After interviewing representative mortgage lenders, the analyst will accumulate the following needed information:

1. Interest rate on a fixed rate, 30-year mortgage loan: 12 percent
2. PITI (payment for principal, interest, taxes, and insurance) to gross monthly income: 28 percent
3. PITI plus monthly payments for other long-term debt to gross monthly income: 36 percent
4. "Typical" loan-to-value ratio: 90 percent

This information is assembled in the following manner:

1. Since the minimum new house price in the market is $92,000 and since the loan-to-value ratio is 90 percent, then the maximum loan is $82,800.
2. The monthly principal and interest payment for a 30-year loan at 12 percent is $843.26 (using a calculator or loan tables).
3. Property tax and homeowner insurance on a $92,000 home are found to be $1,800 and $240 per year, respectively, or $150 and $20 per month.
4. Total monthly PITI is $1,013.26.
5. The underwriting standard for PITI is PITI = 28% of gross monthly income so, PITI divided by 28% ($1,013.26 ÷ 0.28) = gross income of $3,618.80 per month, or $43,425 annual household income.

If the market is offering graduated payment mortgages and/or adjustable rate mortgages that start with a 9 percent initial-year interest rate, then the necessary household income to buy the lowest-priced new home that can be built in the area will fall to $35,836 per year. The lowest possible income for the typical market purchase and loan arrangement establishes a house value to annual household income relationship of $92,000 ÷ $35,836 = 2.57.

This is the first step in the process of income segmentation. Households with incomes below $35,000 per year form a segment of the total households that cannot enter this market for new construction even for the lowest-priced new house. The segment that concerns the analyst is that portion of total households that earn $35,000 or more on an annual basis.

Matching Household Income to House Price

Taking the information generated for the minimum-priced house and the minimum household income needed to purchase, the analyst can construct a table such as that shown in Exhibit 8-7 to match income to price range. This table can be constructed by relating monthly income to PITI as shown in part A of the exhibit, or the analyst can use a shorthand version shown in part B.

Part B assumes that the house value-to-household income ratio of 2.6 (calculated at a house price of $92,000 in the previous panel) is constant across the upper-income categories. In reality, the ratio will more than likely fall as the more affluent purchasers can put more than 10 percent down. Also, higher-income groups do not choose to consume housing in proportion to their higher incomes. Holding this ratio constant across the income categories is an assumption of the analyst that somewhat overtakes house prices in the higher-income categories, but that is not critical to the analysis.

The income categories presented in Exhibit 8-7 would be ideal to use in the analysis. However, the readily available secondary data in the census only provide two categories of income above the figure $34,999. The two categories are $35,000 to $49,999 and $50,000 or more. The analyst is left with two choices, that is, either (1) use the two category breakdown provided in the census or (2) construct a distribution of households inside of the categories.

Assuming that the census categories are insufficient, the next step is to create a plausible distribution. The first thing that the analyst must do is spread the 1980 households in the $35,000-to-$49,999 category into the three subcategories. Then the $50,000-and-more category must also be spread across the eight subcategories shown in Exhibit 8-8. To create a theoretical but realistic distribution, the analyst must rely on certain statistical concepts. First, the income categories are in the upper tail of what can be assumed to be approximately a normal distribution. Thus, as the level of income increases, the number of families in each successive category decreases.

There are several ways to proceed after the households are distributed in the expanded income categories. The simplest assumption is that the distribution will remain constant over time as the households experience a change in their nominal income level due to real productivity changes and inflationary changes. Simultaneously, it is assumed that the new households are distributed in the same manner as the original households. (This last assumption can be relaxed if relevant market information can be brought to bear on the issue from building permit data.) Therefore, as the market moves from 1979 to 1986, two

A. Monthly Income to Price Range

HOUSE PRICE	LOAN (L/V = 90%)	PI MONTHLY PAYMENT	PROPERTY TAX	INSURANCE	PITI	NECESSARY INCOME	PRICE/ INCOME
$ 90,000	$ 81,000	$ 652	$1,800	$240	$ 822	$35,228	2.6
92,000	82,800	666	1,800	240	836	35,828	2.6
95,000	85,500	688	1,900	250	867	37,157	2.6
100,000	90,000	724	2,000	260	912	39,086	2.6
110,000	100,000	804	2,200	280	1,011	43,329	2.6
120,000	108,000	869	2,400	300	1,094	46,886	2.6
125,000	112,500	905	2,500	310	1,139	48,814	2.6
140,000	126,000	1,014	2,800	340	1,276	54,686	2.6
160,000	144,000	1,159	3,200	390	1,454	62,314	2.6
200,000	180,000	1,448	4,000	400	1,820	78,000	2.6

Assumptions:
Loan 9%, 30-year fixed rate mortgage.
Property tax = 2% of house price.
Insurance = $240 for $90,000 + $10 per extra $5,000.
Necessary income = PITI = 28% × 12.

B. Shorthand Version of Exhibit 8-7A Calculations

HOUSE PRICE	RATIO	NECESSARY HOUSEHOLD INCOME
$ 90,000		
92,000	2.6	$35,800
95,000	2.6	
100,000	2.6	38,910
110,000	2.6	
120,000	2.6	
125,000	2.6	48,638
140,000	2.6	54,475
160,000	2.6	62,257
200,000	2.6	77,821

$$\text{Necessary household income} = \frac{\text{house price}}{2.6}$$

Exhibit 8-7 Matching Household Income to Housing Price.

things happen. First, the existing households move up the income category ladder, and, second, new households from net inmigration increase the size of the categories. The new in-migrants may be assumed to have a distribution like the original households or may affect only higher-income categories in the distribution.

By investigating the trends in locally applicable consumer price indices, the analyst can judge the change in prices from 1979 to 1986. This information can be confirmed by checking the wage and salary increases given by a sample

Exhibit 8-8 Estimating Distribution of Household Income Categories.

HOUSEHOLDS BY 1980 CENSUS CATEGORY	INCOME CATEGORIES	DISTRIBUTION OF 1979 HOUSEHOLDS	1979 NUMBER OF HOUSEHOLDS	1980–1986 NET MIGRATION	1986 NUMBER OF HOUSEHOLDS	1986 INCOME CATEGORY DISTRIBUTION	1987–1989 NET MIGRATION	1990 HOUSEHOLDS
3,470 (6.3%)	Less than 5,000							
2,080 (3.8%)	5,000– 7,499							
2,400 (4.3%)	7,500– 9,999							
6,900 (12.5%)	10,000–14,999							
7,750 (14.0%)	15,000–19,999							
8,810 (15.9%)	20,000–24,599							
31,410 (56.8%)	31,410 + 3,974							
13,630 (24.6%)	25,000–	6,815 (12.3%)	6,815	+ 861				
	30,000–34,999	6,815 (12.3%)	6,815	+ 861	= 7,676			
	35,000*–	3,400 (6.1%)	3,400	+ 427	= 3,827	6.1%	165	3,992
7,650 (13.8%)	40,000†	2,550 (4.6%)	2,550	+ 322	= 2,872	4.6	124	2,996
	45,000–49,999	1,700 (3.1%)	1,700	+ 217	= 1,917	3.1	84	2,001
	50,000	1,000 (1.8%)	1,000	+ 126	= 1,126	1.8	49	1,175
	55,000	700 (1.3%)	700	+ 91	= 791	1.3	35	826
	60,000	400	400					
2,630 (4.8%)	65,000	200	200					
	70,000	100 (1.7%)		+ 119	1,049	1.7	46	1,095
	80,000	80						
	90,000	75						
	100,000	75						
55,320 (100.0%)		55,320 (100.0%)	55,320	+ 7,000‡				12,085

*Income to buy new house given mortgage terms and builder's offer price in 1980.
†Income to buy new house given mortgage terms and builder's offer price in 1986.
‡From the housing inventory method.

of the community's dominant industries or firms. Based on such investigation, the analyst discovers that a 4 percent simple growth rate represented wage trends in the market. The amount each household is earning in 1986 is 1.25 (1 + 0.04 (6) = 1.24) times its earnings in 1979. Based on this assumption, households earning $25,000 in 1979 are earning $31,250 in 1986, households earning $30,000 in 1979 are earning $37,500 in 1986, and households earning $45,000 in 1979 are earning $56,000 in 1986. By performing these calculations, the 1979 households can be moved through time and placed in the appropriate 1986 income category. The process is analogous to the cohort survival process. (For the sake of simplicity, we are not applying a survival rate to these income cohorts.)

Net migration can now be handled. The number of net migrating households is obtained from the housing inventory technique. These migrants are found to be younger and better educated and to possess higher skill levels. Thus, migrants will be distributed in higher-income categories than will the native population. For purposes of this analysis, it is assumed that there are no migrants in the lowest two income categories (less than $5,000 and $5,000 to $7,499) as stated in 1979. The migrants who would have been mathematically distributed to these lowest income categories will be equally divided among the next two income categories ($7,500 to $9,999 and $10,000 to $14,999). This initial assumption does not require a change in the first net migration estimate of 3,974 (56.8 percent of the 7,000 migrants from the previous period). There is simply a redistribution within the less-than-$5,000-to-$24,999 income categories. Since this group is not part of the segmented market, this first assumption has no substantive effect.

The direct effect of the migration assumption is felt in the $30,000-and-more income categories. The distribution is established by moving the native households in 1979 forward in time by means of the historical CPI information. Then the associated distributional percentages are applied. For example, there were 3,400 households in the $35,000-to-$39,999 income category in 1979. Given the 4 percent simple growth in CPI over the 1980–1986 period, these households will be in the $40,000-to-$44,999 income category in 1986 ($35,000 × 1.25 = $43,750). The 12.3 percent distribution of households in this income category is then applied to the 1980–1986 net migration estimate of 7,000 to get the net migration value of 861 migrant households in this income category. This same process is used to complete the net migration column in Exhibit 8-8.

The original relationship between new house prices in the market and household income was performed using the 1980 data. The analyst must recalculate that relationship for 1986. Assume that construction costs have increased 10 percent for the 1979–1986 period and that current interest rates are the same as they were in 1979. When the 1986 calculation is made, the result is that the builders' selling price for this house has increased to $101,200 and the minimum household income to buy this house has increased to $38,460. The same income categories are applicable in 1979 and 1986.

However, a substantial change may occur in the market that can either add the $30,000–$34,999 bracket or subtract the $35,000–$39,999 bracket from the market. For example, consider the situation where the mortgage market terms stay constant (or happen to be the same value in 1979 and 1986), but the price of building sites and construction labor push the price for the minimum-sized house from $92,000 in 1979 to $115,000 in 1986. This is a 4 percent simple growth over the six-year period. In this instance, the minimum household income to buy the minimum-sized house is $42,710. This establishes a new house price-to-household income ratio of 2.69.

The meaning of this elimination of the $35,000–$39,999 income category is that approximately 860 migrants and 6,015 native household cannot enter the new housing market in the market area.

Exhibit 8-7 sets the stage for a income/price-segmented forecast of households. Assume that households in the $35,000+ income categories can buy the $92,000 house in 1986. Now, the analyst must forecast four variables:

1. Net migration for the 1987–1990 period
2. The increase in construction costs
3. The increase in household income
4. Any change in the mortgage interest rate

The increase in construction costs and the change in the mortgage interest rate that are forecast will determine the minimum price for the house in 1990 and the minimum income required to buy that house. The analyst applies the same techniques shown in the previous sections. The important analytical input at this juncture is the forecast value for 1990 mortgage interest rates and construction costs. Forecasting interest rates is risky business, at best, and generally inaccurate. The way through this maze for the real estate market analyst is to use the judgment of experts in that area. Magazines and newspapers typically contain articles on expert opinion (economic forecasters at universities, commercial banks, major financial consulting companies) concerning near-term interest rates. The analyst uses these to develop market-specific mortgage interest rate forecasts.

Construction cost forecasts are easier to make. First, construction wages tend to follow changes in the CPI; material prices tend to follow the changes in wholesale prices in general. Land prices present the biggest problem. But the analyst can rely on recent local experiences in the land market to draw judgments that translate into the land price forecast.

Forecasting the increase in income of the native population in the county requires interpretation of several relationships. First, household incomes rise as the CPI increases and as productivity advances. The CPI change can be established by calculating the average or typical annual change in the recent past and then using that rate as the annual change. The productivity change can be established by determining the average or typical change in real GNP for the country and applying this figure with extreme caution. For the most part, the productivity change will be about 2 to 3 percent per year.

Net migration forecasts can be accomplished by establishing the level of migration in the most recent period and then comparing past to present economic circumstances. The U.S. Department of Treasury, Internal Revenue Service, is now providing address-matched migration data for counties to researchers. This information, taken annually from Form 1040, provides current information that can assist in observing trends. This comparison enables the analyst to judge whether the level and direction of previous migration will continue. Migration analysis was considered in greater detail in Chapter 3.

Assume that the application of good judgment yields the following forecasts:

1. The 1990 mortgage interest rate will be the same as it is today.
2. Household income will increase by 4.5 percent per year until 1990.
3. Construction costs in the county will increase by 6 percent per year because land prices are rising by 9 percent per year while labor and material costs are going up by about 4 percent per year.
4. Net migration will decline to 90 percent of its previous level because there is movement into the adjacent outlying county.

Using these forecasts allows the analyst to develop the values for 1990 in the format of Exhibit 8-7B. First, using simple averages, the minimum price of the house increases to $108,560 ($92,000 × 1.18). Second, the minimum income level to buy that house increases to $42,240 ($108,560 ÷ 2.57). Since the interest rate did not change, it does not enter the calculation. Net migration for the three-year forecast period will be 2,700 (1,000 per year in the past times 90 percent times three years). The migrants can be distributed across the income categories by using the 1979 income distribution, just as it was used in 1986. So, for the $40,000–$44,999 income bracket, net migration for 1987–1989 is 165 (2,700 × 0.061). Any inaccuracy established by using a 10-year-old distribution can be tolerated because an ad hoc juggling of the distribution also will produce inaccuracies.[4]

The increase in income to buy the minimum-sized house in 1990 eliminates the $35,000–$40,000 income-earning bracket from the market. So the total number of households that can buy houses valued above the $108,500 figure in 1990 is 12,085. The shortcut approach shown in Exhibit 8-7B can be used to relate households in each income bracket to a minimum house price. The new house price-to-income ratio is still 2.57 because the analyst assumed it to be so when the necessary income level was calculated. Given this assumption,

---

[4]The difficulties inherent in projections of this nature suggest that the analyst might use scenarios, with "worst case," "most probable," and "best case" forecasts. The client can then assess better the risk in the projections and in any building plans based upon these forecasts.

the number of 1990 households that could afford to buy a house priced at $140,000+ are those in the $55,000+ income brackets. The exact number in the exhibit is 5,097.

This analysis can be combined with an analysis of foreseeable supply. In this application of the unmet demand analysis, the disaggregation of supply may consider the geographic market under analysis and the price range (dwelling unit size). The analyst may utilize information from the pipeline analysis to identify developers. A survey of developers having site plan approvals and projects underway can reveal annual construction plans over the foreseeable future. Telephone companies may provide this information, which is collected for their planning purposes in providing service to developing areas. Some market analysts have established systems for keeping track of all approved and platted subdivisions and apartment projects. This information over time indicates trends and can be a valuable check against future starts reported by developers, who are often overly optimistic. Building permit data disaggregated by location, type of construction, and value also can serve as a check against prospective starts obtained by survey. Care must be exercised in the use of permit data, however, because developers typically understate the building's value when taking out the permit. The best indication of the value of new construction indicated by site plan approvals or permit data is the location of the development and the character of the neighborhood or other nearby projects.

Analysis Using Tenure Disaggregation

In addition to the geographic segmentation by subarea initially established, the analyst may need to disaggregate new construction on the basis of owner- and renter-occupied units, or single-family and multifamily units. To perform this analysis, the analyst must return to the analysis of Exhibit 7-3 and break out construction information on owner- versus renter-occupied construction. The analyst may also use the supply-side data from the past as an indicator of the distribution of owners and renters. Then these past data are forecast into the future.

The analyst starts with information about owner- versus renter-occupied housing units in the most recent census. An example of these data is given in Exhibit 8-9. Then this information is updated to the current period by using building permit data from public records (primary data) or secondary data from a source such as *Construction Review*. The primary data source is much better because it can also provide information on demolitions and net conversions as well as information on the number of permits actually used through the certificates of occupancy. The primary data also provide information on pipeline construction. All these data were put into Exhibit 7-3.

There are several indicators for the distribution of owner- versus renter-occupied housing units. First, the 1980 census gives one distribution. Second,

	1980	1980–86	1987–
Total housing stock	4,000		
Owner units	3,100 (77.5%)		
Renter	900 (22.5%)		
New construction		900	200
Owner		300 (33⅓%)	60 (30%)
Renter		600 (66⅔%)	140 (70%)
Vacancy rates			
Owner	4.1%	4.1%	
Renter	6.6%	6.6%	

Exhibit 8-9 Tenure Disaggregation.

the updating process from 1980 to 1986 provides another figure for the distribution. Building permit information can be divided between single-family and multifamily units (but doesn't list renter-occupied single-family units). Then the updated levels of owner- and renter-occupied units in 1986 gives a fourth measure of the distribution.

Upon which measure is it best to base the forecast? Building permit data give the best distribution because it represents the occurrences of the recent past. However, it must be supplemented with a single-family owner-renter ratio from elsewhere. The pipeline construction information is also important because it tells the analyst what is currently taking place.

If the analyst discovers that 60 of the 200 units in the pipeline for 1987 are owner-occupied units, then the 1987 distribution of owner to renter units will be 30 percent and 70 percent, respectively. Comparing this distribution in the update period with the 1987 data from the pipeline reveals the supply side of the market from 1980 through 1986, judged the appropriate distribution, to be approximately one-third owner-occupied to two-thirds renter-occupied units. This is a first approximation that has to be verified by examining the demand side of the market.

The trend in the vacancy rates of the two forms of housing can be checked. If the vacancy rates stay the same, relative to each other, during the updating period, then the recent distribution of construction activity between the owned and rental housing was accepted by the demand side of the market. However, adjustment in the apartment–single-family split may be required if the apartment vacancy rate has increased above normal, indicating that, in the aggregate, this portion of the market is overbuilt. In this case, the forecast for future construction should be a distribution that is judged sufficient to drop the relatively high rental unit vacancy rate. In the context of this example, the analyst might judge that future production should be distributed in a 50/50 relationship. In this instance, the analyst is assuming that developers will act accordingly over the forecast period.

Disaggregation by Housing Type and Price Range

The disaggregation process may indicate gaps in the market. Some decision makers look for gaps in the market to identify markets to serve.

Assume, for example, that in 1985, the analyst identified the following demand forecast breakdown by type of for-sale unit in the market area:

	1986	1987
Single-family detached	2,000	2,380
Fee-simple townhouses	900	1,100
Condominiums	300	360
	3,200	3,840

Also assume that an analysis of aggregate supply data revealed the following pipeline expectations:

	1986	1987
Single-family detached	1,400	1,200
Fee-simple townhouses	1,400	1,200
Condominiums	350	300
	3,150	2,700

The demand-supply ratios are then as follows:

	1986			1987		
	Units Demanded	Units Supplied	D/S Ratio	Units Demanded	Units Supplied	D/S Ratio
Single-family detached	2,000	1,400	143%	2,380	1,200	198%
Fee-simple townhouses	900	1,400	64	1,100	1,200	92
Condominiums	300	350	86	360	300	120

The demand-supply relationships over the next two years show that fee-simple townhouses and condominiums will be overbuilt in 1986 but that by 1987 the excess inventory will be worked off and there will be unmet demand for condominiums. The single-family detached segment indicates a high level of unmet demand. There are, however, substantial differences in price and location that must be considered so that an appropriate production and marketing strategy can be devised.

Assume that the forecast single-family demand is classified by price ranges established by the local homebuilders' association as follows:

HOUSE PRICE	1986		1987	
	Number	% of Total	Number	% of Total
Less than $100,000	400	22%	452	19%
$100,000–119,999	380	19	452	19
$120,000–129,999	340	17	405	17
$140,000–159,999	300	15	357	15
$160,000–179,999	240	12	309	13
$180,000–199,999	180	9	238	10
$200,000 and over	120	6	167	7
	2,000	100%	2,380	100%

Assume further that a field survey produced the following analysis of the supply situation in the following pipeline:

HOUSE PRICE	1986		1987	
	Number	% of Total	Number	% of Total
Less than $100,000	280	20%	92	16%
$100,000–119,999	252	18	216	18
$120,000–129,999	266	19	240	20
$140,000–159,999	196	14	192	16
$160,000–179,999	182	13	156	13
$180,000–199,999	126	9	108	9
$200,000 and over	98	7	96	8
	1,400	100%	1,200	100%

A comparison of the forecasts indicates the gaps as follows:

HOUSE PRICE	1986			1987		
	Demand	Supply	Gap	Demand	Supply	Gap
Less than $100,000	440 −	280 =	160	452 −	192 =	260
$100,000–119,999	380 −	252 =	128	452 −	216 =	236
$120,000–129,999	340 −	266 =	74	405 −	240 =	165
$140,000–159,999	300 −	196 =	104	357 −	192 =	165
$160,000–179,999	240 −	182 =	58	309 −	156 =	153
$180,000–199,999	180 −	126 =	54	238 −	108 =	130
$200,000 and over	120 −	98 =	22	167 −	96 =	71

The largest gaps exist in units priced below $120,000 and in the $150,000 price range. Larger gaps appear the second year in all price ranges. The builder would do well to compete at the lower price if the organization is geared to such a product.

Some decision makers start with a target market. A production builder would examine the depth of market for the product, as would a luxury homebuilder. In either case, the data desired are the same—the numbers on the depth of demand and depth of supply.

Role of the Competitive Analysis

Since the focus is eventually going to turn to a specific site, primary data must be gathered for the competitive and potentially competitive projects in the market area. The market segmentation process using psychographic analysis will indicate the different market segments or target markets. Thus, if demand and supply are about equal in a given price bracket, there could still be a gap or unsatisfied demand if available units do not contain features many consumers would like to see as substitutes for available amenities.

A competitive analysis will, among other things, be helpful in revealing the preferences of purchasers. By matching various physical characteristics of the unit with a profile of the purchasers, a preferred pattern can emerge. But, sometimes, the builder succeeds despite mistakes in product design and marketing. There may be purchasers who would not live in anything resembling the models as presented but like the basic space and value. The analyst could then look for characteristics of purchasers themselves by interviewing occupants of homes.

The basics of the competitive analysis are, however, in the physical characteristics of the site, the units, and the location. The competitive analysis is based upon project sales rate data correlated with price and features. The key element is a spreadsheet showing the results of the competitive audit. Following is a simplified example of a competitive audit.

A subject property contains a 100-acre site (net exclusive of streets, etc.) developable at 3.5 units to the acre. The site is in the northwest quadrant of the county in the center of a developing area that is neither the highest-priced part of the town nor the cheapest. New projects are coming on line in the $125,000-to-$175,000 price range.

The Survey The analysis of competitive projects may be used to evaluate physical characteristics as they relate to sales rates. The spreadsheet containing information on competitive projects would look like the spreadsheet at the top of page 169.

The analysis focuses on both the project and the individual units. For

SUBDIVISION AND COMMENTS	UNIT TYPE	BED-ROOMS	BATHS	BASE-MENT	FINISHED SQUARE FEET	PRICE	PRICE PER SQUARE FOOT
Westwood Estates,							
Unit I	Split foyer	3	2	Full	1,360	$119,500	$87.87
Good location	Rambler	3	2	Full	1,410	127,500	90.43
and amenities	Split level	3	2.5	Half	1,610	139,500	86.65
Green Valley							
Good location,	Split foyer	3	2	Full	1,380	124,500	90.22
fair amenities	Rambler	3	2	Full	1,390	129,950	93.49
	Two-story	4	2.5	None	1,560	139,500	89.42
Westwood Estates,							
Unit II	Rambler	4	2.5	Full	1,650	149,500	90.61
Good location	Split foyer	3	2	Full	1,580	154,500	97.78
and amenities	Two-story	4	2.5	Full	1,730	159,500	92.20
Clover Ridge							
Poor location,	Split foyer	3	2	Full	1,650	142,500	86.36
poor amenities	Rambler	4	2.5	Full	1,690	154,500	91.42
	Two-story	4	2.5	Full	1,790	159,500	89.11

example, Clover Ridge provides a large house for the price, but the location is less desirable and the amenities are lacking. An analysis of the sales rates of the various types of units may also be made.

Product Analysis A review of the competitive analysis will indicate which projects are selling best. The analysis of competitive projects may first focus on the project as a whole, especially the price range, and on location, as well as extent of amenities and value (e.g., heated or air-conditioned living space per dollar purchase price).

Second-round analysis identifies the most popular amenities and analyzes basic design/construction features such as size in square footage; number of bedrooms and baths; specialized additional rooms such as family rooms, dens, and the like; number of stories; and architectural style. These features are intended to appeal to a targeted segment of the buying public. To predict what features will have the greatest attraction requires an understanding of the buyer's profile. Buyer profile analysis could reveal that there are empty nesters who are buying. Such houses typically have fewer bedrooms and baths than do the average in the marketplace. They also are likely to be single story to eliminate stairs, which become more difficult to climb with advancing years. Starter homes for yuppies (young upwardly mobile professionals) might be in the same price and size class. In this submarket, two stories and cathedral ceilings with impressive living areas are likely to count for more than large kitchens with eating areas or porches and patios.

Absorption   Absorption is the key to the analysis of the market. Absorption is the nexus between the submarket-level disaggregation and segmentation process and the site-specific competitive analysis.

Absorption to the client is the pace at which the product is sold or rented. Sometimes units are purchased by investors or speculators who will use a "for sale" unit as rental property or will contract to buy and then sell the contract before closing. Sometimes there is an intention to sell, but, as has happened in some condominium markets, a decline in demand makes it impracticable. The purchaser could then "breach" or buy for "investment." Units sold and then held for future resale are "absorbed" as far as the builder is concerned, but when the market begins to strengthen—or at the first opportunity—this inventory will again enter the market.

The more relevant concept, but more difficult to measure, is the absorption that is based upon use. Thus, one would look at "for sale" housing to be owner occupied and "for rent" housing to be renter occupied. The depth of demand is based upon use, although the supply of "new units taken" falls into categories such as speculative purchases without tenants, renter-occupied units, and owner-occupied units. The units taken in the nonuse category should not be interpreted as having set historical patterns for use. They should be considered as potential deductions from what could be absorbed in the subject use category in subsequent periods.

To reconcile the disaggregation steps with the competitive analysis, the analyst first allocates the demand to a local area. The analyst allocates demand within the local area to existing and potentially competitive projects as well as the subject. In allocating the demand to a local area, it is useful to consider that growth patterns aid in new construction by (1) moving land development outward, (2) moving development upward, and/or (3) filling in.

Project-level forecasts can be made using rates of absorption for similar projects. Or, with enough historical information, projections may be made on a project-by-project basis, with allowances for new projects.

The projected rates of absorption for the subject project may start with an average absorption rate. Adjustments may then be made for different price segments of the market and possibly even for the ability to market to different target markets. Availability of financing and price competitiveness will also influence absorption rate. After making all such adjustments, the most realistic absorption rate will be forecast.

CONCLUSIONS

While general and specific submarket analysis questions may be addressed, at some point the housing market analysis goes to the site specific, that is, to the project level. When it does, the "hard numbers" (i.e., those most defensible) are sales rates experienced by competitive projects. No matter how good those numbers are, they are not sufficient for forecasting what will be absorbed by the time a new project comes on line and over the time span necessary to market the new project.

The most relevant issues are future overall demand and how that demand will be disaggregated. These numbers get "soft" going far out into the future. But, if the numbers and the assumptions necessary to get to a local market share for a project do not make sense when compared to the historical absorption rates, then the historical rates will not be sustainable.

This market analysis process allows the analyst to examine shifts in demand and substantial changes in supply leading to an overbuilding. Extrapolation of historic trends works when there are no changes in direction, but extrapolation misses the turning points. It is the turning points that count the most in avoiding big losses or making big gains. Thus, market analysis, and absorption analysis, should be sensitive to identifying turning points. This can be done only when proper forecasts, not simple projections, of the absorption rate are made.

READINGS

MCMAHON, JOHN, *Property Development*. New York: McGraw-Hill Book Co., 1976.

PARRY, D., *The Reno Economy and Housing Market*. San Francisco: Federal Home Loan Bank, January, 1978.

PARRY, D., *Sacramento SMSA Housing Markets*. San Francisco: Federal Home Loan Bank, March, 1978.

URBAN LAND INSTITUTE, *Residential Development Handbook*. Washington, D.C.: Urban Land Institute, 1978.

9

MARKET ANALYSIS FOR RETAIL SPACE

INTRODUCTION

Retail space is essentially the floor area and supporting facilities devoted to the retail sale of goods and services to the general public. The floor area where goods are displayed and sold or services provided is a critical measure of retail space, but the retail facility also contains several other spatial components. The normal components of retail space include

1. *Sales area*: the floor area used exclusively for display, service, and checkout, including entrances and exits for customer traffic.
2. *Storage area*: the floor area used to receive, store, and/or process goods arriving at the retail outlet before being placed in the sales area.
3. *Administrative offices and business area*: the floor area excluding checkout facilities, used for internal management functions.
4. *Utility areas*: the floor area devoted to the provision of essential services to the building, such as heating and refuse disposal.
5. *Site areas*: the ground areas covered by buildings and used to provide supporting facilities, including parking, ingress and egress, outside utility areas, landscaping, and other site amenities.

Retail market analysis determines the amount of retail space within a market area that current and forecasted levels of demand for retail goods will justify. The retail space consumer is the business entity that occupies the space to provide retail goods and services to customers. The amount, location, design, and quality of space the retailer occupies is justified by the number, type, and characteristics of customers for the goods and services. Thus, the demand for retail space is expressed by the retailer but is derived from the demand for the retailer's products.

Retail space required to satisfy the current and future level of demand forecast by a market analysis is usually expressed in terms of floor area. Normally, the floor area is defined as gross leasable area (GLA), that is, the total floor area occupied exclusively by a tenant, including accessory utility, storage, and administrative space, as measured from the outside walls of the building. It is important to define the type of floor area used in a market study because it could have several meanings. Some analysts define it to mean only the sales and display area measured from internal walls. A critical concern is that the definition used in the market analysis conform to the client's needs, to local customs regarding the measurement, or to the definition used to calculate the sales per square foot figure in secondary data sources.

Sales per square foot is calculated by dividing the gross annual sales revenue by the square feet of floor area used to generate the revenue. The average or normal sales per square foot for a particular type of retail activity in a specific market area is the standard used. There are different sources for such a standard—local or national trade or industry organization, business periodicals reporting on the particular type of business, government bodies, or professionally compiled data sources. Some of these sources use GLA to calculate sales rates, while others may use only the sales and display area, or some other floor area measure. When translating the sales volume forecast into a floor area requirement, the analyst must be certain that the standard used produces the type of floor area defined in the study.

A second measurement issue is that GLA may be the same as gross building area (GBA) in a single-tenant building, but a lease may exclude some areas from inclusion in GLA in a multitenant building or a shopping center. Gross building area is the total amount of floor area under the roof measured from the outside wall of the building. Thus, when floor area is forecasted using existing leases as a measure of existing floor area, the analyst must determine what proportion of the common areas are included in GLA. Then a ratio for converting GLA to GBA must also be known to forecast total space needed.

In selecting the appropriate sales per square foot standard, the analyst must also make certain the standard applies to the particular type of space being analyzed, such as a free-standing building, multitenant building, small shopping center, or large shopping center.

Major Steps in Market Analysis for Retail Use

To determine the amount of retail space justified by demand for goods and services, market analysis for retail space focuses on consumer characteristics and behavior and on the capability of specific types of retail activities to compete in the market. The analysis consists of four basic steps, as follows:

1. Determination of the retail trade area for the stores located on the property.
2. Analysis of the competitive environment in which the shopping center or commercial district must operate.
3. Determination of the shoppers who currently use the stores on the property, or who would use the stores if the property provided the retail services they desired.
4. Analysis of changes and establishment of forecasts for economic and demographic information developed in the first three steps in the process.

Each of these steps will be discussed in detail in subsequent parts of this chapter.

Preliminary Steps of Analysis

The analyst attempting to identify the quantity and quality of retail space must deal with three issues to identify the demand and supply factors the analysis must utilize. The three issues are classification of (1) the specific type of good and service, (2) the consumers to whom goods and services are targeted, and (3) the type of retail facility. In the sections that follow, each issue is further refined, and a procedure for dealing with each is discussed.

Classifying Goods and Services   It is first necessary to identify the type of retail activity and the activity's basic characteristics since these largely determine the type and nature of space to be occupied. Exhibit 9-1 provides a classification system for most retail goods and services. By focusing on the product lines the retail establishment carries, the analyst groups it into a general category of similar businesses that have similar market characteristics and will appeal to groups of consumers with similar shopping habits. Exhibit 9-1 identifies some basic market and shopping trip characteristics usually associated with each category of retail establishments.

There are two principal questions the analyst should address about the type and general characteristics of the product the retail establishment is marketing:

1. What is the general category or type of goods and services being provided, including a detailed description of any specialization or combination of products and activities that are present?
2. What is the specific nature of the operation, including how frequently is the item normally purchased and what type of shopping is needed to acquire it?

Exhibit 9-1 gives general categories for most products and a more specific classification where more detailed characteristics are listed. In general terms shopping goods (or high-order goods) are durable commodities that are rela-

Exhibit 9-1 General Categories of Retail Goods and Services.

CATEGORY	TYPE OF ITEMS	PRICE LEVEL OF INDIVIDUAL ITEMS	FREQUENCY OF REPLENISHMENT	TYPE OF SHOPPING TRIP	PROXIMITY TO MARKET
A. Shopping or High-Order Products					
1. Personal shopping goods	Clothing, jewelry, dry goods, gifts	Moderate to high	Often—several times per year	Single- or multiple-purpose comparison	Moderate—15 to 30 minutes
2. Household shopping goods	Furniture, appliances, carpets	High	Infrequently—less than per year	Single-purpose comparison shopping	Within driving range—over 30 minutes
3. Automotive products	Automobiles and major accessories, trailers, boats	High	Infrequently	Single-purpose comparison shopping	Within driving range
B. Convenience or Low-Order Products					
1. Convenience goods	Groceries, drugs, hardware, liquors	Low to moderate	Frequently—daily to monthly	Multiple-purpose repetitious shopping	Close by—5 to 15 minutes
2. Personal services	Beauty or barber shops, cleaners, health spas	Low	Frequently	Multiple-purpose repetitious shopping	Close by
3. Repair services	Shoe repair, small appliance repair, furniture repair	Low	Frequently to often	Multiple-purpose repetitious shopping	Close by
4. Personal business and financial services	Branch bank, real estate, insurance	Varies	Frequently to infrequently	Single- or multiple-purpose repetitious or comparison shopping	Close by to moderate
C. Miscellaneous Products—Mixed Characteristics					
1. Eating and drinking establishments	Fast foods, dining services with menu foods, cocktails	Low	Frequently	Single- or multiple-purpose repetitious consumption	Close by
2. Entertainment and recreation	Theaters, bowling arcades	Low	Frequently	Single-purpose repetitious activity	Close by
3. Automotive services and accessories	Gasoline, tires and batteries, engine repair and maintenance	Low to high	Frequently to often	Single- or multiple-purpose repetition or comparison shopping	Close by to moderate

tively expensive and are purchased infrequently, when the desire or the need arises. Consequently, the consumer usually undertakes comparative shopping to investigate the quality and design differences as well as price differences of the various similar products on the market. Since cost and product comparisons are needed, the consumer usually makes a special shopping trip and may travel greater distances to shop.

Convenience (or low-order) products are generally nondurable commodities that are relatively inexpensive and are purchased frequently (daily, weekly, monthly). Because the consumer is in and out of the stores as part of a daily routine, the quality of products and prices are well known. The consumer usually knows in advance which stores he or she will patronize and which products she or he will purchase. As a result, there develops a fairly routine shopping pattern.

To be competitive, the stores must offer a combination of attractions that will, first, get the customer's attention and, then, continue to hold that interest. This is called the "attract and hold" capability of the establishment, or the establishment's "ability to capture." Repeat business and volume are the keys to success in such an enterprise. Thus, the convenience retail establishment must be price competitive, have competitive product lines, utilize advertising and merchandising techniques that motivate customers, offer quick service, provide amenities such as a pleasant display area and good parking, and—critically— be in a convenient, accessible location that is perceived to be, or physically is, close to the customer's residence or place of employment.

All product lines and businesses do not fit conveniently into a retail category. One product may be a specialized product, such as a gift box of food items. In this case the analyst must use judgment to classify it as either a shopping good or a convenience good, or create a new specialized goods category for it. Miscellaneous products may have some characteristics of both shopping and convenience products. Other establishments, such as variety stores, department stores, or discount stores, may carry a large variety of product lines. In these instances, the analyst usually classifies the establishment by its predominant product line, or if the market dictates, by its image.

A major purpose of this implicit step in retail space market analysis is to enable the analyst to identify those types of businesses with which the subject property is most compatible and complimentary as well as those with which it is competitive. The next step is to examine the types of markets the retail operation expects to attract.

Classifying Types of Markets   The next step in the preliminary analysis is to examine the types of potential consumer groups the retail establishment will attract. There are three major questions to be addressed here:

1. Who are the various groups or types of consumers in the general population

that normally purchase the retail establishment's products? This should include an identification of some of their major distinguishing characteristics.

2. How many, and what types of, consumers are needed to generate a sufficient business volume; for example, what are gross annual sales?

3. What are the major consumer characteristics (demographic, economic, psychographic, etc.) that underlie demand for the retail establishment's products? These will be used to understand demand and develop a marketing strategy.

Before specific target markets are selected and their demographic and economic characteristics examined, the analyst must identify why consumers are attracted to the retail establishment. In his classic work on retail locations, Richard Nelson[1] identified three major categories of markets from which retail demand could be drawn:

1. *Generative business*: A retail operation that has such strong market appeal that it is a primary destination for customers in a specific location. Department stores, well-known specialty stores, supermarkets, and anchor stores are examples of this type of market.

2. *Shared business*: Market appeal that is based upon the cumulative attraction of generative and complementary retail operations at a particular location. The individual business may not have sufficient drawing power, but the combination of goods and services available attract customers to the general vicinity where the appeal of individual establishments can be offered.

3. *Suscipient business*: Market appeal from an independent source, such as a major public transportation facility, that attracts customers into an area where the retail operation can position itself and offer its goods or services. This type of market is parasitic or dependent on an external source and is subject to the peculiarities of that particular market, such as a retail business dependent on a "captive market" in an office center that closes on Saturday when most employees do not come to work.

By classifying the type of market appeal the retail operation has, the analyst is subsequently able to identify the source of customers. This step is necessary to identify relevant demographic and economic characteristics. For example, a gift shop operating within a suscipient business environment on a major commuting route near an office/hotel center and an airport may identify nearby employees, commuters and transient traffic, and conventioners as the principal sources of demand. A similar gift shop in a neighborhood strip operating on a shared business concept would identify nearby households and customers attracted by nearby generative businesses as their principal sources of demand. Armed with this information, the analyst can identify the appropriate data sources to quantify demand beginning with sources such as employment figures for local employers, census figures for households in the trade area, or traffic volume figures for commuters.

[1] Richard L. Nelson, *The Selection of Retail Locations* (New York: F. W. Dodge Corp., 1958), p. 53.

Classifying Types of Facilities   Once the type of operation and its basic demand sources have been identified, the final step in the preliminary analysis is to establish the type of facility needed to execute a marketing strategy successfully.

Exhibit 9-2 lists various types of retail locations and facilities. For each type of location listed, the major types of complementary retail tenants are also given. By classifying the retail operation into one of these categories, the analyst is able to provide answers to the three basic preliminary questions and proceed with a detailed analysis of demand and supply characteristics.

ECONOMIC ANALYSIS OF RETAIL MARKETS

Retail market analysis is initially based on the analysis of the demand for the product or service being sold in the retail space. Then, the demand for the retail space is extracted from the analysis of the demand for the product. So the first phase of retail market analysis focuses on the consumers' demand for the product, while the second phase translates the demand for the product into the demand for space on the subject property.

Demand for Retail Products and Services

The demand for a retail product is a function of the number of consumers, consumer income, tastes and preferences about the product, price of substitute products, credit conditions, and payment plans. However, demand for retail products is not as strongly affected by credit conditions as is the purchase of housing. The demand variables that are most important in an analysis of retail services are the number of consumers and their current income level. As an initial step, the level of purchasing power can be calculated by the appropriate multiplication of an income level by the number of customers. If households are the consuming unit (as they are for appliances, furniture, carpeting, etc.), then mean household income should be used to form the purchasing power variable. If individuals are the consuming unit (as they are for food, clothes, etc.), then per capita income should be used in conjunction with population to form the purchasing power variable. As purchasing power increases, the demand for retail goods and services increases. As a consequence, the demand for retail space also increases.

In addition to purchasing power, another important demand-side variable is the consumer's taste and preference pattern for the products that can be purchased. The consumer has tastes and preferences toward several important aspects of a retail establishment. The first aspect affected by taste and preferences is the product being sold. The consumer may consider both real and perceived aspects of the product in the decision to buy. In addition the consumer may react to differences surrounding the sale, such as the availability

TYPE OF MARKET AREA	TYPE OF LOCATION	MAJOR LOCATIONAL CHARACTERISTICS	TYPICAL TYPES OF RETAIL TENANTS
Regional	Central business district	At hub of regional thoroughfares; near center of commercial and residential areas	Department stores; variety stores; personal shopping and specialized goods and services; business goods and services; eating and drinking, entertainment; other supporting goods and services
	Regional shopping center or district	At intersection of two or more regional thoroughfares; near major residential and outlying employment areas	Department stores; two+ variety stores; shopping goods; specialized goods and services; eating and drinking, entertainment and recreation; other supporting goods and services
	Specialized shopping center district	Parasite to central business district or regional center; on location similar to regional center	Fashion apparel; factory outlets; eating and drinking; specialized goods and services
Community	Community shopping center or district	On a major regional thoroughfare, usually at a major intersection; convenient to two or more neighborhoods; entertainment and recreation, personal business, and financial services	Department stores; one or more discount stores; major drug or variety store; personal shopping goods; fast-food outlets; automotive services and accessories; other supporting goods and services
	Discount or off-price center	Same as for community shopping center or specialized shopping	Discount store; factory outlets; personal shopping goods; convenience goods; fast-food outlets; entertainment and recreation; other supporting goods and services
Neighborhood	Neighborhood shopping center or district	On a major thoroughfare close to an intersection; adjacent to at least one neighborhood	Supermarket, convenience goods, some personal shopping goods; personal and repair services; personal business, financial services; fast foods, entertainment, and recreation; automotive services; other supporting goods and services
	Convenience center or cluster	On a major or minor thoroughfare; adjacent to a neighborhood	Convenience food store; convenience goods; automotive services; personal services; repair services
Undifferentiated	Arterial street, commercial strip	On a major thoroughfare between residential and employment areas	Free-standing units; household shopping goods; convenience goods; automotive accessories and services, automotive products; fast-food outlets; numerous other

Exhibit 9-2   Types of Retail Locations.

TYPE OF MARKET AREA	TYPE OF LOCATION	MAJOR LOCATIONAL CHARACTERISTICS	TYPICAL TYPES OF RETAIL TENANTS
Undifferentiated, *cont.*	Highway-oriented commercial strip	On a major highway; usually at outlying locations, but may be same as arterial street, commercial strip	Transient facilities: eating and drinking with fast foods; household shopping goods; automotive services and accessories, automotive products; convenience goods; entertainment and recreation
	Heavy commercial strip	On a major or minor thoroughfare; may be same as highway-oriented or arterial commercial strip	Trucking and storage; building materials; major auto repair; salvage uses; automotive service; limited convenience goods; eating and drinking, with fast foods
	Dependent commercial	Near, adjacent to, or within a major use or market generator	Gifts, souvenirs, and specialized goods and services; eating and drinking, entertainment, and recreation; personal services
	Free-standing structures and uses	On a major thoroughfare; usually in outlying location; occupies large individual site; may or may not be in a cluster or strip	Automotive products; household shopping goods; distributors with retail outlet; supporting eating and drinking or convenience goods

Exhibit 9-2 *Continued.*

of credit, delivery charges, and the attitudes of the sales personnel toward the customer. Regardless of how they are obtained, such perceptions about the product and the circumstances surrounding the sale can affect the sales volume. Change in tastes and preferences causes the consumer to rearrange the combination of retail goods purchased from time to time. For example, as new products are offered for sale (video recorders, personal computers, lightweight cassette players with earphones, etc.), they are added into the consumer's market basket, and the quantity of other products purchased either decreases or the purchase of some other specific product is discontinued. In addition, as the consumer moves through his or her life cycle, different products are bought. For example, the young consumer·may spend proportionally more for clothing, recreation, and entertainment activities, while the older consumer may spend proportionally more for home furnishings, education expenses, and insurance.

Different income groups allocate their expenditures for a particular type of retail product in different ways. For example, the low-income household may buy men's clothing exclusively in discount stores, while the upper-income households may buy clothing exclusively in specialty men's shops.

In addition to purchasing power and tastes and preferences (related to life-cycle variables and income), the price of substitute products is also important.

A substitute product is a product in the same retail category but not identical to the subject product. For example, price differences between high-quality shirts and acceptable-quality shirts can affect the consumer's choice. If the price of shirts that are merely acceptable increases and narrows the price differential enough, the consumer may switch to the purchase of high-quality shirts. Also, a price difference between two stores at the same location can cause the consumer to purchase from the lower-price store given equal quality of the items.

Credit conditions, especially the installment interest rate and the willingness of the vendor to provide the credit, can affect the demand for consumer durable products such as appliances, furniture, floor coverings, and so on. But the demand (the ability to buy) can also be affected for nondurable products if the consumer is short of cash and has reached the credit limit. However, the affect of the interest rate is not as great as it is in the case of the demand for housing.

Since expenditure patterns change over time, the market analyst must obtain information from the past and the present to see what the trends are. Expenditure patterns also change by region of the country, and they change with respect to the size of the urban area in which the consumer resides. Therefore, the expenditure patterns are a function of the (1) consumer's original taste and preferences for different products; (2) income levels, which reflect the ability to buy; and (3) time, which reflects changes in economic variables such as price, income, and preferences.

Demand for Retail Space on the Subject Site

The traditional variables that affect the demand for the retail product also affect the demand for retail space on a specific site. The spatial distribution of purchasing power is an important factor in evaluating site specific demand for retail space. Two adjacent areas (census tracts, neighborhoods, etc.) with different income levels may have different levels of purchasing power. The households in the two areas will also have different employment characteristics, such as single wage earner households versus households with two principal wage earners versus households with one principal and one part-time wage earner. In addition, the two adjacent areas may have different purchasing power because of different spatial factors, such as development densities. One area could have large lots, while the other area has the same size and type of home (a proxy for income) on smaller building lots. One area can be primarily condominiums and apartments, while the other area is single-family detached housing. Consequently, shopping areas located in these two geographic areas will have different sales volumes because the purchasing power based upon its constituent parts is different.

Consumer tastes and preferences also have a spatial context. In addition to the changes in tastes and preferences that can occur because of the spatial distribution of different age groups, income groups, and groups with other characteristics, consumer perceptions concerning the retail store and its amenities can affect the level of demand and, thus, sales volume.

Retail establishments are spatially distributed so the consumers have different travel costs and costs of friction. Consumers try to minimize these costs so the retail stores closer to the point of origin (usually the home) are viewed more favorably, other things being equal.

In addition, retail space can be evaluated on the basis of real differences in accessibility, attractiveness, cleanliness, and spaciousness, for example, or it can be evaluated on perceived differences in these attributes. Consumers prefer to travel along picturesque, safe, and direct routes. Consumers prefer clean, uncluttered, and aesthetically pleasing space. When expressing their demand for the product they will prefer those sites that provide these amenities.

Because retail activity is located at different points in space, the effective price of a substitute can be different even when the shelf price is the same. The difference in price is generated in the mind of the consumer by the real and perceived costs of travel. In addition, the shelf price of the product can be different if the retail establishments located at the different points use a different markup percentage, or if two stores in the same retail chain practice geographic price discrimination.

Supply of Retail Products

The supply of retail products and services can be viewed as being price elastic; that is, a small change in price will result in a more substantial change in the quantity of the product being supplied. This is the same as saying that the producers and sellers of the products are able and willing to supply a large amount of additional product when the price of the product increases slightly due to an increase in demand. The reverse is also true. If the costs of production increase due to wage or rent increases, materials price increases, or labor productivity declines, then producers decrease the amount of the product they are willing to supply at a given price level. This usually results in a price increase as fewer consumers pay more for a commodity in short supply.

Supply of Retail Space

Most market analyses are concerned with the amount of additional retail space current and forecasted levels of sales will justify. This additional space can be satisfied by constructing space at new locations or expanding the space at existing locations. Only rarely is the demand for additional space satisfied by seeking vacant space in the retail resale market. Indeed, most vacant retail space in existing developments is viewed as being obsolete or otherwise noncompetitive with new or expanded retail locations, or it is viewed as undergoing changes in tenants, which reflects not an increase in demand, but a change in the type or nature of space being demanded. Consequently, few market studies focus on the retail resale market. The major determinants of the amount of new retail space that developers are able and willing to produce have to do with the costs of construction. As the price of resources in the construction process increases, the supply of new retail space declines. As the number of developers in the market increases, the amount of new retail space increases. The list of supply factors that were discussed for new residential construction are also applicable for new retail construction.

The supply of existing retail space is similarly affected by the same type of variables that affect the supply of existing residential units. So the volume of new retail construction, retail space demolition, and net conversion are the factors that cause the existing stock of retail space to change.

Analysis of the new retail construction market yields information about the minimum rent that will cover construction costs. This is a supply-side consideration. But when it is coupled with the demand in the new retail space market, the analyst can judge the extent to which the market will pay a premium above this minimum rent level.

Analysis of the stock of existing retail space in conjunction with the demand for retail space determines the rent level for retail space in the market under analysis.

TRADE AREA ANALYSIS

After the type and nature of the retail operation has been appropriately identified and classified, the analyst begins the market analysis for retail space by focusing on the retail trade area. The retail trade area is simply the geographic territory from which customers are drawn to the retail site. The analyst needs to obtain information about the economic, demographic, and psychographic characteristics of potential customers in the trade area to understand the type and the extent of the goods and services they will demand, and what types of facilities and merchandising techniques are needed to capture and increase the demand. But, first, the physical and economic characteristics of the trade area itself must be examined so that proper boundaries can be ascertained and the constraints on satisfying demand can be identified.

Factors Determining Size and Shape of Trade Area

When retail trade areas are considered conceptually, they take on very regular shapes. Trade areas may be circular, elliptical, or hexagonal. When an analyst identifies a retail trade area, several underlying assumptions are made. The primary assumption is that the trade area is located on a "flat, featureless plain" and that consumers are uniformly distributed on this plain. Additional assumptions identify all consumers as having the same economic, demographic, and psychographic characteristics by stating that all consumers have the same income and preferences. As part of the "featureless plain" assumption, transport costs are also assumed to be proportional to distance, and all points in space are readily and equally accessible to the site of the retail establishment.

The real world, however, is not a featureless plain, and a homogeneous population is not uniformly distributed over space. Consequently, even if the economic, demographic, and psychographic characteristics of the consumer in the trade area are the same, or roughly the same, trade areas in the real world are normally not regularly shaped geometric areas. The actual shape and size of the trade area are affected by the following variables:

1. *The transportation system.* This includes the mode of transportation (roads, buses, rapid rail lines), its load-carrying capacity, its accessibility to users, and its quality.
2. *Physical barriers to the flow of traffic.* These barriers include natural phenomena such as rivers, topographic features (cliffs, ridge lines, fault lines), and man-made barriers such as railroad lines and restricted-access land areas.
3. *Psychological barriers.* These barriers can include land uses that are considered hazardous and unsafe, undesirable, and unpleasant.

In addition to these physical variables that point out the lack of reality in the "flat, featureless plain" assumption, the distribution of population and the distribution of purchasing power are also not uniform over space. Consider the following phenomena:

1. Existing patterns of residential development affect the location of households as well as their density.
2. New development of residential space affects the pattern and density of development at the fringes of the city and also within the city as infill construction and rehabilitation take place.
3. Application of eminent domain powers for transportation systems and other public uses affects the distribution and density of population.
4. Households with different income levels are not randomly scattered over space. Households with similar incomes tend to cluster in selected geographic areas. Therefore, purchasing power per household varies over space.

The actual shape and size of the retail trade area more than likely does not conform to geographic areas for which statistical data are readily available. Therefore, the retail trade area is made to conform to geographic areas such as the following for which secondary data can be readily obtained:

1. *Counties.* Counties can be used if the retail establishment is a relatively large entity such as a regional shopping mall or a commercial district in a small rural area.
2. *Census tracts or zip code areas.* These geographic areas are suitable if the retail development is a community shopping center or a commercial district along the main arterial in the metropolitan area. For such retail activities, an adjacent county might be appropriate, but most typically census tracts or zip codes would be better.

3. *Blocks.* Block data become important if the retail development is a neighborhood shopping center whose primary and secondary trade area are both enclosed with the census tract, or if the trade area encloses small portions of two or more census tracts. In addition, block data are important if the market analyst wants a more detailed spatial study.

There is a need for the analyst to match the trade area to the geographic areas for which data are available. If the trade area and census tracts are coterminous, this problem is eliminated. However, this is rarely, if ever, the case. Therefore, the analyst must visualize the relationships between the census tracts and the trade area and then make judgments as to the use of the aggregate census tract data.

Primary, Secondary, and Tertiary Trade Areas

The total trade area is typically divided into three components: the primary trade area, the secondary trade area, and the tertiary trade area. Differentiation of these components is made on the basis of driving time, percentage of total sales, and/or percentage of total customers attracted to the retailer's establishment.[2] The primary trade area has been defined in the following ways:

> The primary trade area is the geographic area immediately adjacent to the property and extending out to driving time of a certain duration. Different retail establishments have different maximum driving times to establish the primary trade area. For supermarkets, driving times of 5 minutes may determine the primary trade area. For large shopping centers, the primary trade area may extend to a driving time of 20 to 30 minutes.
>
> The primary trade area is a geographic area immediately adjacent to the property from which the retail establishment obtains a substantial (60 to 70) percent of its total customers.
>
> The primary trade area is the geographic area immediately adjacent to the property that generates 60 to 70 percent of the retail establishment's total sales.

These statements reveal that the primary trade area is defined on the basis of two principal variables: driving time and total sales. Total sales have been measured on the basis of actual dollars or by the number of customers that serve as a proxy for retail sales. However, the number of consumers is not a good proxy for total sales because of differences in income patterns, expenditure patterns, ease of access to the site, proximity, and so on.

The secondary trade area is defined on the basis of the same two variables. For example, consider the following statements:

[2]Earlier discussions of driving time as a measure of the trade area can be found in Nelson, *Retail Locations*, pp. 209–210, and in James A. Bruner and John L. Mason, "The Influence of Driving Time upon Shopping Center Preference," *Journal of Marketing*, Vol. 32, April 1968.

The secondary trade area is a geographic area adjacent to the primary trade area and extending away from the site for a predetermined driving time. For the supermarket, the secondary trade area could be that area lying between the driving time of 5 to 12 minutes from the site. For the shopping center, the secondary trade area could be that geographic area lying between 20 and 45 minutes of driving time.

The secondary trade area is the geographic area from which the retail establishment is able to obtain an additional 20 percent of its total sales or total customers.

The primary and secondary area together should account for 90 to 95 percent of the retail establishment's total sales. The geographic area that accounts for the remaining 5 to 10 percent is known as the tertiary trade area. It is immediately adjacent to the secondary trade area and extends to the point where the customer with the longest driving time resides.

MODELS FOR DELINEATING RETAIL TRADE AREAS

There are several techniques that help to identify retail trade area boundaries and determine the potential attractiveness of retail sites and operations within those trade areas. Some of the better known techniques are explained in this section. A more detailed description of each model and the mathematical procedures for performing the analysis can be found in the appendix to this chapter.

Reilly's Model of Retail Gravitation

William J. Reilly developed his *Law of Retail Gravitation* to explain how residents of a geographic area located between two cities choose the city in which to shop. The model determines the percentage of that small, intermediate area's population that will travel to each of the retail centers. Reilly defined his law of retail gravitation in the following way.

Under normal conditions two cities draw retail trade from a smaller, intermediate city or town in direct proportion to some power of the population of these two larger cities and in an inverse proportion to some power of the distance of each of the cities from the smaller, intermediate city. In any particular case, the exponents used in connection with population or distance are dependent upon the particular combination of retail circumstances involved in that case. Typically, however, two cities draw trade from a smaller, intermediate city or town approximately in direct proportion to the first power of the population of these two larger cities and in an inverse proportion to the square of the distance of each of the larger cities from the smaller, intermediate city.[3]

[3]William J. Reilly, "Methods for the Study of Retail Relationships" (Austin: Bureau of Business Research, University of Texas, 1929), p. 16.

In mathematical form, Reilly's law is stated as:

$$\frac{B_a}{B_b} = \left(\frac{P_a}{P_b}\right)^N \left(\frac{D_b}{D_a}\right)^n$$

where

B_a = the percentage of the area's consumers who will travel to city a
B_b = the percentage of the area's consumers who will travel to city b
P_a = the population of city a
P_b = the population of city b
D_a = the distance in miles from the area to city a
D_b = the distance in miles from the area to city b
N = exponent showing relative attractiveness of larger population size ($N = 1$ used by Reilly)
n = exponent showing relative attractiveness of shorter distance ($n = 2$ used by Reilly)[4]

When the appropriate data are used in the formula and the calculations are made, the result is a numerical value for the relative drawing power of the two cities. This percentage, or multiplier, results from calculating a numerical value for the B_a/B_b ratio and shows the proportion of total customers in the trade area drawn to city a as compared to those drawn to city b. For example, the ratio could take on the value of 1.5. If this is the case, city a has 1.5 times the drawing power of city b. This translates into the fact that city a attracts 60 percent of the area's population whereas city b attracts 40 percent of the population. Remember that this relative drawing power is based on both distance and population. A numerical example of such a calculation is presented in the appendix to this chapter.

When figures for drawing power are established for several of the areas affected by the two cities, the trade area can be drawn by linking the places with the same numerical drawing power for one of the sites. For example, if the analyst is seeking the primary trade for city a, all places in the vicinity of city a for which B_a is equal to, or greater than, 60 percent are included. The interpretation of this area as a primary trade area is different from the discussion that appeared earlier. Here the primary trade area is the geographic area surrounding the shopping area from which 60 percent or more of the local residents are attracted to the subject site. The difference in definition rests on the fact that more than 60 percent (or less than 60 percent) of the shopping area's customers could come from this geographic area.

A hypothetical example of the use of Reilly's model to determine a shopping area's retail trade area is shown in Exhibit 9-3. The precise position of the trade area boundaries depends on how the analyst uses Reilly's law to

[4]Reilly, *Retail Relationships*, p. 48.

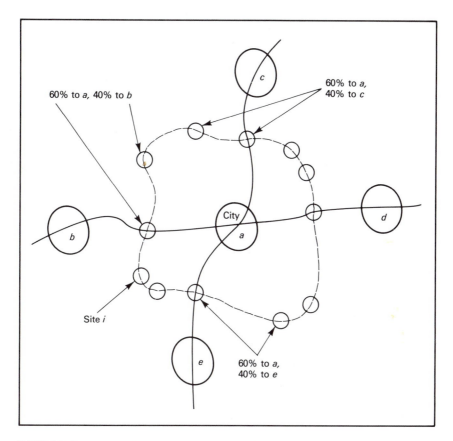

Exhibit 9-3 Determining a Primary Trade Area Using Reilly's Model.

determine distribution of customers. Since the model is only capable of handling two cities at a time, the necessary calculations are made on the following pairs of cities in the exhibit: city *a* and city *b*, city *a* and city *c*, city *a* and city *d*, and city *a* and city *e*.

The impact of a third alternative is felt off the main roads where a resident of a site such as *i* can choose among shopping in the cities *a*, *b*, or *c* depending on the secondary road system in the area. On the major connecting roads between the cities, there is a clear distinction of shopping alternatives for the consumer; the disutility of traveling on the secondary roads, or driving through city *a* to reach another city, is viewed as being too great, so the customer will show a preference for city *a*.

Converse's Modification Converse modified Reilly's formula to obtain an estimate of the distance away from a retail center where its influence was equal to the influence of the competitor.[5] In other words, Converse modified Reilly's law to obtain an estimate of the distance to the "breaking point" where the consumers as a group would split their patronage between the two competitors, 50 percent would travel to city *a* and 50 percent would travel to city *b*.

When the size of the two cities and the distance between them is known, the Converse modification allows the estimation of the point in space where customers are shared equally. The Converse modification can be used to calculate the point in space where city *a* obtains 60 percent, 70 percent, or even 80 percent of the total customers by letting the ratio of $B_a/B_b = 50\%/50\% = 1$ or by substitutions of $60\%/40\% = 1.5$, $70\%/30\% = 2.33$, or $80\%/20\% = 4.0$ for the ratio. A numerical example of this breaking point formulation is given in the appendix.

Ellwood's Modification Ellwood suggested that Reilly's law be modified and restated using different variables. Ellwood's statement of the law is given in the following comment:

> The principal retail districts within a metropolitan trading area attract trade from the residential sections of the area approximately in direct proportion to the size of the retail districts and in inverse proportion to the square of the driving time distance from each residential section to the retail districts.[6]

Ellwood replaced population of the urban area with size of the retail district and distance measured in miles with driving time. Given these changes, Reilly's law under the Ellwood modification takes the following form:

$$\frac{B_a}{B_b} = \left(\frac{S_a}{S_b}\right)^N \left(\frac{T_b}{T_a}\right)^n$$

where

$$N = 1$$
$$n = 2$$
$$S = \text{size of retail area (in square feet)}$$
$$T = \text{driving time (in minutes)}$$
$$a, b = \text{the two shopping areas}$$

Ellwood introduced the gravity model to determine trade areas within a metropolitan area, as seen from the previous quotation from his article.

[5]P. D. Converse, "New Laws of Retail Gravitation," *Journal of Marketing*, October 1949, pp. 379–384.

[6]L. W. Ellwood, "Estimating Potential Volume of Proposed Shopping Centers," *The Appraisal Journal*, October 1954, p. 583.

Huff's Probability Formulation

The next step in the development of the gravity model is Huff's probability formulation of such a model.[7] The first distinguishing feature of Huff's formulation is that the model can handle the interaction among three or more retail districts. The Reilly model, including the Converse and Ellwood formulations, can only handle the interaction between two retail establishments. Therefore, the Huff model is an extension of Reilly's law of retail gravitation, but it is a substantial modification, focusing on the same variables that the Ellwood formulation utilizes, namely, the size of the retail center and travel time.

The Huff model uses the following equation to establish the probability that a consumer located at a given point of origin will travel and shop at a specific shopping center or retail district. The Huff probability formula is

$$P(C_{ij}) = \frac{S_j / T_{ij}^\lambda}{\sum_{j-i}^{n}(S_{ij} / T_{ij}^\lambda)}$$

where

$P(C_{ij})$ = the probability that a consumer living at site i will shop at retail center j
S_j = the size of the retail center j in square feet
T_{ij} = the travel time from site i to retail center j
n = the number of retail centers in the immediate area
λ = a parameter that reflects the effect of travel time on different kinds of shopping trips (Huff discovered values of 3.19 for furniture and 2.72 for clothing.)

When the appropriate data are included into the equation, the result is a numerical value for $P(C_{ij})$ in the 0 to 1 range. For example, if $P(C_{ij})$ is calculated to equal 0.8, then, given the alternative shopping opportunities and the travel times to those shopping areas, 80 percent of the consumers who live in area i will, more than likely, shop at shopping center j. The remaining 20 percent will be divided between the other alternative shopping areas. A numerical example of the calculations and the results for the Huff model are present in the appendix to this chapter.

Exhibit 9-4 depicts the Huff model calculations. Travel times are calculated along the major routes that the consumers use to get from point A, the centroid of cell i, to each of the three (or more if they exist) shopping areas designated S_1, S_2, and S_3. Square footage of retail space is obtained for each of the shopping alternatives S_1, S_2, and S_3, and, given the travel times, the prob-

[7]David L. Huff, "A Probability Analysis of Shopping Center Trade Areas," *Land Economics*, February 1963, pp. 81–90, and "Defining and Estimating a Trade Area," *Journal of Marketing*, July 1964, pp. 34–38.

ability value (or percentage of households expected to patronize S_1, S_2, and S_3) is calculated for each sector of the market area identified by the grid (the squares in the exhibit) for each of the shopping areas. These results are then used to determine the specific trade areas. If shopping area j is the subject site, the analyst might decide to link together all the sectors created by the grid for which $P(C_{ij})$ is equal to, or greater than, 60 percent.

Applebaum's Customer Spotting Model

The models discussed in the previous section rely on both secondary and primary data to generate a geographic trade area. Population data are usually secondary data, while specific data for square feet of retail space, distance, and travel time are primary data generated by the analyst, sometimes using secondary sources such as maps. In contrast, William Applebaum[8] used information received directly from consumers to define primary and secondary trade areas. His process involves the following steps:

1. Develop the customer spotting map.
2. Develop the subarea population.
3. Estimate sales for each subarea.
4. Group subareas into the trade area.

Each of these tasks is discussed next.

The Customer Spotting Map   An interviewer randomly selects individuals as they enter or leave the retail establishment. As part of the interview process, the consumers are asked to identify their place of residence or the point of origin from which they came to the retail establishment. This information is displayed on a detailed street map by placing a pin at the location of the customer's residence or point of origin. Then, the array of the pins represents the geographic distribution of the population that shops at the retail establishment.

If the selection process is random, and if a sufficient number of customers are interviewed, these customer spotting data can be used to develop the primary and the secondary trade areas.

Developing the Population Count   The second step in the process of defining the primary and secondary trade areas is the creation of appropriate small geographic areas. Applebaum utilized a grid that created cells, each one-fourth mile square. An example of his grid system and subsequent calculations

[8]William Applebaum, "Method for Determining Store Trade Areas, Market Penetration, and Potential Sales," *Journal of Marketing Research*, May 1966, and "Advanced Methods for Measuring Store Trade Areas and Market Penetration," in *Guide to Store Location Research*, ed. by C. Kornblau (Reading, Mass.: Addison-Wesley, 1968).

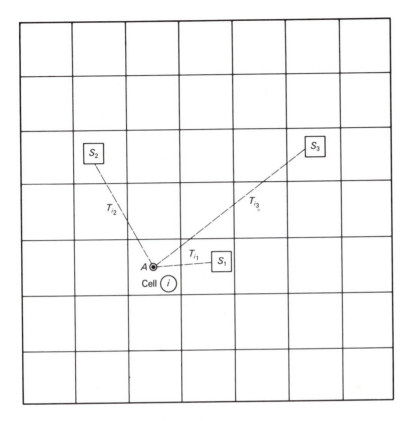

Exhibit 9-4 Trade Area for the Huff Model.

is shown in Exhibit 9-5. This grid is placed over the detailed street map of the area, and the population in each cell is determined.

The ability to determine the population with appropriate accuracy depends on the availability of data for the geographic area represented by each cell. If each cell in the grid represents a city block, and if block data are available, then the population within the cell is easy to determine.

Often, it may be necessary to subdivide the area into geographic subareas that are irregularly shaped and conform to geographic areas for which data are available. For example, if a regional mall is being analyzed, the small area map can be the census tract map or a zip code map.

When detailed land use or subdivision maps can be obtained, the grid pattern can be drawn to the scale of the map, and the number of dwelling units can be counted within each cell and multiplied by the average household size for the census tract to get a reasonably good estimate of the population within that cell.

Estimating the Sales In Applebaum's original study, $32,000 was identified as the adjusted weekly sales of the supermarket. Then, he identified $100

Exhibit 9-5 Grid System in Applebaum's Customer Spotting Technique.

The grid below records, in each cell, the fraction Sales / Population and the resulting per capita sales figure.

				100/475 $.21		100/523 $.19	600/1050 $.57	100/1125 $.09	200/1375 $.15										
						300/1275 $.24	200/1175 $.17	200/1150 $.17	200/1175 $.17	300/725 $.41		100/825 $.12	100/900 $.11						
					200/450 $.44	300/1075 $.28	100/1100 $1.09	400/1025 $.39	200/750 $.27	300/1150 $.26	100/700 $.14	100/950 $.11	200/700 $.29				300/275 $1.09		
100/100 $1.00					100/75 $1.33	300/250 $1.20	100/550 $.18	300/850 $.35	700/900 $.78	300/725 $.41	400/1375 $.29	100/350 $.29	700/1200 $1.58	400/600 $.67		100/75 $1.33			
200/175 $1.14			100/275 $.36	100/375 $.27				100/275 $.36	200/900 $.20	500/625 $.56	100/625 $.16	400/725 $.55	400/575 $.70			100/150 $1.67			
		100/275 $.36	100/300 $.33		300/450 $.67	100/300 $1.33	200/275 $1.67	200/300 $.73	600/475 $1.26	600/925 $.65	500/975 $1.51	300/825 $.36							
			100/200 $.50		100/400 $.25			300/125 $2.40	700/450 $1.55	800/525 $1.52	200/525 $.38	900/775 $1.16	200/800 $.25					100/125 $.80	
100/75 $1.33					100/275 $.36	100/225 $.44		100/125 $.80	1000/300 $3.33	900/250 $3.60	400/275 $1.45		100/250 $.40	100/125 $.80					
								100/25 $4.00	100/50 $2.00	200/325 $.62	300/200 $1.50				100/50 $2.00				
										100/125 $.80	600/375 $1.60								
		100/100 $1.00	100/25 $4.00	200/75 $2.67	200/50 $4.00	300/75 $4.00	400/75 $5.33			100/50 $2.00							100/200 $.50		
												100/175 $.57	300/300 $1.00	300/650 $.46	200/150 $1.33		100/200 $.50		
												100/150 $.67		200/300 $.67			200/175 $1.14		
													100/225 $1.44	100/350 $.29	200/175 $1.14		100/100 $1.00		
											100/50 $2.00								
											100/100 $1.00								

Sales / Population = per capita sales

as the typical weekly purchase of the customer. Using the values of $32,000 for sales and $100 per customer per week, Applebaum identified the need to obtain 320 respondents and thus a customer spotting map containing 320 pins.

Given this information, Applebaum examined each cell in the grid and counted the number of customers within that cell. He multiplied each one of these spotted customers by $100 to obtain an estimate of sales to customers spotted in the cell. Then, he divided this estimate of weekly sales by the population in that grid to obtain the sales per capita in each cell in the grid pattern.

Delineating the Primary Trade Area   Applebaum defined the primary trade area as that geographic area adjacent to the subject property from which 60 percent of the customers, and consequently 60 percent of the sales, are drawn. Using this definition, Applebaum began with the cells nearest the stores, and then, in descending order, he included those cells that showed the highest per capita sales until 60 percent of the customers, or 192 customers, were recorded. These cells were enclosed in the primary trade area. An example of his primary and secondary trade areas are shown in Exhibit 9-6.

The grid pattern with the primary trade area is then superimposed over the detailed street map. Based on the street pattern, geographic barriers, man-made barriers, nonresidential usage, and the location of the competition, Applebaum made adjustments to the shape of the primary trade area.

Exhibit 9-6   Trade Areas Derived from Applebaum's Grid System.

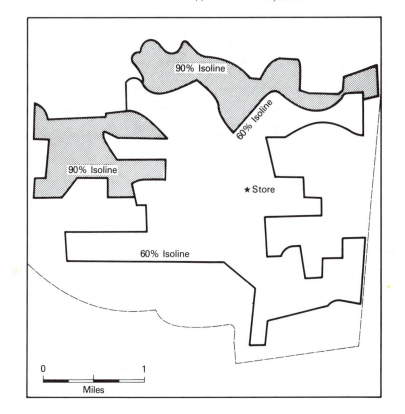

Adaptations of the Customer Spotting Technique

There are several other ways to spot customers without using an interview process. Each of these processes requires internal information from the subject property for which the analysis is being done. The first of these alternative techniques is to spot cars or, more precisely, the license plates on those cars. In states that imprint county names on the state license plate, the parking lot of the retail establishment can be checked to discover the county of residence of the customers. However, the usefulness of county of residence appears to be the greatest for regional shopping centers that attract customers from several counties, and for an area in which the counties are of reasonable size (the smaller the counties, the better). For example, if a shopping center existed at the point in space where four large counties touched, and if the analyst checked the plates in the parking lot, there would be cars from all four counties. But the analyst would not know whether the customers came from the full geographic area of each county, or just from those portions of the county nearest the shopping center. In other states, the registration address can be obtained from the State Registrar of Motor Vehicles. For a fee of, say, 50 cents per plate, the street address and city can be obtained. A much more refined trade area can be defined from this information. In collecting license plate data, the analyst should visit the center at peak shopping hours during the week to obtain a sample of plates sufficient to delineate the trade area.

The second technique uses the check-cashing process of the retail establishment. If the analyst can determine that the customers who pay by check are similar in their purchasing patterns and income level to those who pay by cash, then the addresses that are printed on the check, or requested when the check is cashed, can be spotted on a map to develop the trade area. Important points to keep in mind are the group using checks and the group using cash may or may not be a part of the same population, and may or may not be similar in their actions. Also the relative size of the purchase by customers who pay by check versus those who pay by cash may be different. The analyst must investigate these issues and determine if the two groups are similar or different. When this is resolved, then a large enough sample size and a reasonable amount of geographic dispersion of the people in the trade area (i.e., a stratified sample based on location) must be obtained.

The third technique is a modified form of the second that uses credit card receipts and the generally requested telephone number, which is almost universally requested and written on the receipt. The exchange, the first three numbers, usually convey some degree of locational information. So, if all the credit card receipts carry only four such exchange numbers, and the conditions just discussed are met, then the trade area consists of the geographic area in which those exchanges are used.

For some retail establishments, the credit accounts that they carry as a matter of business can also be used to determine the trade area. However, these data present the greatest problem with regard to comparability to the group of customers who do not use internally provided credit.

FACTORS AFFECTING THE RETAIL TRADE AREA

Trade area delineation models reveal two critical variables in the analysis. In the translation from Reilly's law to Huff's law, the critical variables were initially population and distance in miles. Then, the size variable changed to square feet of retail space and the distance variable changed to travel time. The population of an urban area and the square footage of retail space are proxies for the merchandise mix and selection offered by the retail establishments. Consumers want a variety of items from which to choose when they are shopping. Shopping facilities in larger urban areas—larger population base, larger retail stores—are assumed to provide a greater degree of selection.

Distance and travel time are proxies for the costs and disutility of travel. Consumers attempt to minimize the costs of friction associated with shopping, such as distance and travel time. Since distance and travel are assumed to represent the cost of friction, consumers seek to minimize them.

In addition to square footage (selection) and distance (costs of friction), there are other important variables that affect the retail trade area. This section of the chapter explicitly discusses the underlying concepts of trade area analysis.

Geographic Aspects

Each retail trade area has a geographic component and an economic component. The geographic component, often referred to as the "range" of the trade area, measures the distance or the travel time from the subject property to the edge of the trade area. Changes in the various factors that affect travel time can affect the geographic extent of the trade area. Some of these factors are discussed next.

The Street System and Accessibility Streets and roads can affect the geographic extent of the trade area in several ways. Interstate highways, for example, can reduce travel time and thereby increase the geographic extent of the trade area. In addition, abutting street characteristics can affect the access to the site. For example, heavy traffic congestion may reduce site access significantly from the direction that requires left turning movements, thereby seriously reducing the attractiveness of the site and location for a particular use. Movement along highly congested roads also increases the travel time. Consequently, if the primary access street for a retail use is frequently congested with stop-and-go traffic, the analyst may find that the trade area is not effectively penetrated. Travel time for a given distance along an expressway may be equal to or, at certain times of the day, greater than travel along the secondary road. This can result in expanding trade area boundaries in those directions affected by the expressway.

Other important considerations about the street system are access points to the road, railroad intersections, stop lights, timing or synchronization of signals, numbers of stop signs, and the quality of the road surface. Each of these variables can tend to have a smoother flow of traffic than surface streets. Railroad intersections can create delays. Stop lights and stop signs can slow the flow of traffic. A poor-quality surface also slows the flow of traffic. If the surface is of sufficiently poor quality, it may even discourage travel along the roadway, diverting traffic away from a retail location.

These accessibility factors affect the size of the trade area and, consequently, the number of actual and potential customers. In this way, access affects the sales of the retail establishment and, consequently, demand for retail space at a particular location.

Access onto the Site   In addition to the travel time variables, there are variables that must be considered that affect the customer's ability to get from the street system onto the site itself. For example, the number and placement of curb cuts, the existence of workable, left-turn lanes, and the slope of the access ramp leading from the site to the street can limit site access. These variables affect the customer's willingness to utilize the site and may drive customers toward alternative shopping opportunities.

The Route Environment and Travel Anxiety[9]   In addition to physical factors, there are psychological factors that also can affect the geographic extent of the trade area. These psychological factors are related to the customer's perceptions of the route that is being traveled. People prefer to drive along scenic and clean (litter-free) streets. Consequently, given the quality of all other factors, people will drive farther along a scenic route. Junk yards, industrial areas, and areas of sign pollution and roadside clutter are considered unsightly. In addition to the visual appearance of the street, safety and health issues can also affect people's willingness to use a travel route. People will avoid areas that present traffic hazards and areas plagued with smoke and dust.

Economic Aspects

In its simplest form, the economic aspects can be stated by the following rule: sales must cover all explicit costs or expenses of the retail operation and leave a sufficient return to the owner for the risk involved in the operation (the entrepreneur's profit). This same simple principle can also be stated in the

---

[9]See discussions by Richard B. Andrews, "Situs: Variables of Urban Land Use Location," in *Urban Land Economics and Public Policy* (New York: The Free Press, 1971), pp. 45–47; and James A. Graaskamp, *A Guide to Feasibility Analysis* (Chicago: Society of Real Estate Appraisers, 1970), p. 77.

following way: the retail operation must have a trade area that allows it to reach and exceed the market threshold. In this context, the threshold is a level of product sales equal to the full cost of operation.

Even when the geographic extent of a trade area is fixed, the overall sales levels of that trade area can improve. The market threshold can be reached and even exceeded as the purchasing power in the trade area increases. In turn, the purchasing power of the trade area is a function of the income level of households in that trade area and the number of those households. Consequently, the analyst performing a market analysis focuses upon measures of purchasing power in the trade area by analyzing its two components: income and the number of consumers (population for some studies, households for other studies).

In evaluating the economic aspects of the trade area, the analyst should also consider the extent of competition. In some cases, the location of competitors helps to define the subject establishment's trade area. In other cases, competitors are located in and have the trade area as the subject property. The analyst must determine which of these is true for the analysis at hand.

Purchasing power and competition determine the success of a retail establishment. For the retailer to meet essential economic goals, there must be sufficient purchasing power to generate expenditures, and the subject establishment must be sufficiently competitive to assure an adequate capture rate.

Interrelationship between Geographic and Economic Aspects

When the analyst considers geographic and economic aspects jointly, there are three major points involved. First, there are spatial variations in purchasing power. High-income areas are usually separated from poorer areas. In high-income areas, product lines offered for sale are different from those sold in low-income areas. For example, high-income areas are likely to have boutiques instead of discount family clothes stores, new car and luxury car dealers instead of used car lots, gourmet food outlets and "fancy" restaurants instead of diners and cafeterias, and so on.

Second, as the purchasing power increases, the geographic extent of the retail trade area needed to achieve a market threshold shrinks. In this case, fewer people with higher incomes can generate the necessary level of sales.

Third, if the income level stays constant but the population density increases in the geographic area, the retail trade area can also shrink and still provide a market threshold. In this case, more people with lower incomes generate the necessary level of sales.

The issue of purchasing power and population density also come into play for the topic of overlapping retail trade areas. As population density increases, travel times become shorter and thresholds are reached in smaller retail trade areas.

Nature of Retail Products

In general, there are distinct categories of retail goods. These product categories are shopping goods and convenience goods.[10] Recently, they have been referred to as high-order goods and low-order goods, respectively. Shopping goods abound in markets where consumers desire a wide selection of goods from which to make a choice.

Moreover, the expenditure for the product is a relatively large percentage of the consumer's budget. For example, automobiles, appliances, and clothing are considered to be shopping goods. Each of these makes up a different percentage of the consumer's budget, but each expenditure is large enough to require special attention by the consumer.

Finally, the products may be similar, but they are differentiated in the mind of the consumer. That is, either the consumer knows that real differences exist among products or believes that there are differences among them. There may also be differences in merchandising such as credit arrangements, layaway plans, free delivery, attitude of the sales personnel, merchandise return policy, and so on.

Convenience goods or low-order goods are products that appear in markets where selection or diversity of merchandise is not important to the consumer. These goods are not only frequently purchased; they are relatively undifferentiated in the mind of the consumer. Moreover, the cost of individual items is a relatively small percentage of the consumer's budget.

Image (Nature) of the Retailer   In addition to the geographic, economic, and product considerations previously discussed, other factors can affect the retail trade area. These involve a comparison between the consumer's image of self and the consumer's image of the store. In a single sentence, "consumers tend to patronize those stores which they feel are somewhat like themselves." "In turn,[11] the consumer's image of a store is the summation of his attitudes toward various aspects of that store."[12]

The factors that affect the consumer's attitudes toward a retail establishment are identified in Exhibit 9-7. Notice that the classification scheme provided in Exhibit 9-7 incorporates some of the geographic and product-related factors previously discussed. However, it also lists other factors that the analyst may have to consider when the subject property and the competition are being evaluated.

---

[10]Earlier discussions of convenience and shopper's goods appears in Brian Goodall, *The Economics of Urban Areas* (Oxford: Pergamon Press, 1971), pp. 136–137.

[11]Robert Wyckham, "Consumer Images of Retail Institutions," in *Handbook of Marketing Research* (New York: McGraw-Hill, 1974), p. 4–304.

[12]Wyckham, "Consumer Images."

Locational convenience
  Access, travel time, parking availability
  Traffic barriers
Merchandise suitability and availability
  Quality of items, breadth and depth of the assortment
  Number of brands in stock, number of departments in a store
  Number of stores in a mall
Value and price concerns
  Price of the products in subject property in relation to the price of the same product in a competing
    store, price discounts, sale prices and policies
Sales effort and service policies
  Courtesy and helpfulness of the sales staff, availability of service personnel, reliability and usefulness
    of advertising, credit arrangements, billing procedures, nature of delivery services, availability of
    on-site food vendors
Design features
  Floor plans and space utilization, decor, merchandise displays, customer traffic patterns, actual
    and perceived congestion
Clientele characteristics
  Perceptions regarding the type of customers
Posttransaction satisfaction
  Satisfaction with the quality of the products, price paid, return policy

SOURCE: Adapted from Table 1 in Robert Wyckham, "Consumer Images of Retail Institutions," *Handbook of Marketing Research*, by Robert Ferber (New York: McGraw-Hill Book Company, 1974).

Exhibit 9-7 Factors Affecting the Image of a Retail Establishment.

Trade Area Overlap

The nature of the product (shopping versus convenience goods, etc.), the level of purchasing power in the trade area, consumer attitudes toward travel, and the concept of product differentiation determine the existence of trade area overlap. Each of these topics will be discussed in this section.

As an introductory statement to the discussion, trade area overlap is a function of the consumer's reaction to the product and travel to get the product. The consumer seeks information about price, quality, service, and monetary and nonmonetary cost of travel to make the selection of the shopping site. Then, based on a comparison of these factors, the consumer may go to a more distant shopping facility even though other consumers in the same area go to the nearby facility. This overlap tends to decline as the actual distance between the shopping facilities increases, and it tends to increase for those goods for which the consumer wants greater selection.[13]

Product Characteristics: Shopping Goods   When acquiring shopping goods, consumers want a wide selection; thus retail trade areas for competitive outlets may overlap. In fact, retail establishments often locate next to each other so that

[13]Louis P. Bucklin, "Trade Area Boundaries: Some Issues in Theory and Methodology," *Journal of Marketing Research*, February 1971, pp. 30–37.

each establishment can benefit from the increased volume of potential customers drawn to the cluster of retail establishments, a principle known as "cumulative attraction." The market areas for competitors who sell similar products are, for the most part, coterminous: they draw their customers from the same geographic area. To clarify this point, consider the case of a cluster of automobile dealerships.

Several dealerships, offering different makes of cars, will cluster along a certain street or in a certain area of town. Customers will come to this cluster and inspect the product of at least two or three of these dealerships. If a customer spotting map for each dealership were undertaken, the trade area for each dealership will overlap to a great extent.

A second situation in which the trade area for shopper's goods overlaps is the case in which the consumer travels to a second cluster of stores to broaden the selection. Customers may travel to a second cluster of car dealerships to see the offerings available at that location. The second cluster of dealerships may contain more dealerships that not only sell the same kinds of cars as in the first cluster but also offer other selections. If a customer spotting map were created for each cluster, the trade area for the second cluster should overlap with the closest of the fringe of the trade area for the first cluster.

What is true for the cluster may also be true for individual retail establishments in that cluster. For example, the Chevrolet dealership in cluster 1 may have a trade area that intersects the trade area for the Chevrolet dealership in cluster 2. In this event the consumers are differentiating between the dealerships that sell the same product.

Product Characteristics: Convenience Goods   Because selection of a particular item from the shelf is not important for the convenience good buyer, and because the product is undifferentiated in the mind of the customer, retail establishments for convenience goods have a general tendency to locate away from each other. The nature of the product establishes a repelling force between the retail establishments providing the product. However, establishments selling convenience goods are often found in the same geographic area, and often have overlapping retail trade areas. This phenomenon is contrary to the results expected when repelling forces exist.

There are several reasons for convenience good establishments having overlapping trade areas:

1. Even though the products are seen as being undifferentiated, the consumer differentiates among the retail establishments that sell the products. For example, consumers may be loyal to a certain grocery store chain, drug store, or dry cleaner. This loyalty can be based on the consumer's perception regarding price and quality of the merchandise being offered, circumstances surrounding the sale, perceived differences in the convenience associated with a specific retail establishment, or the consumer's perception of the facility (attractiveness, cleanliness, age, etc.).

2. The purchasing power of the geographic area must be sufficiently high to allow the attainment of a market threshold for the retail establishments. In other words, the combination of population density and the income level must be sufficiently high to generate a level of purchasing power in the geographic area to support two or more of the same type of establishments in the trade area.[14]

Consumer Attitudes toward the Shopping Trip Retail trade areas can overlap because of consumer attitudes toward travel as well as their reaction to specific shopping trips. Many consumers perceive little difference between a 1-minute drive and a 5-minute drive, or between a 15-minute drive and a 20-minute drive. Once the initial disutility of starting the trip is considered, the marginal disutility of an additional minute or two on the road is unimportant. Consequently, the consumer may pass one retail establishment if the second store is relatively close. Or the consumer may choose to drive to the store 5 minutes north of the house instead of the store that is 2 minutes south of the house because the travel time difference is insignificant.

Other attitudes can also cause trade area overlap. These include

1. *The frequency of the trip.* If the trip is not frequent, the consumer may drive to a more distant retail establishment.
2. *The urgency of the need.* If the product (medicine) or service (dental care for a toothache) is needed immediately, the consumer will travel to the place at which it is available regardless of distance or travel time.
3. *The specialized nature of the product or service.* The product might be so specialized that it is not stocked by the typical retail establishment. So the consumer must drive past one store to reach the store that carries the product.

Retail Clustering

There are several familiar retail clusters such as shopping centers, a cluster of auto dealerships, or a cluster of furniture stores. A discussion of major principles reveals that clustering occurs for different reasons among various types of establishments.[15]

Clusters of Stores Selling Similar Shopping Goods Auto dealerships, furniture dealers, and appliance dealers often group themselves in "specialized" clusters along principal arteries or in a small geographic area. These establishments locate in close proximity to each other so their combined drawing power can generate increased traffic or potential customers to the area. More people come to the stores when they are part of the cluster than if they were located

---

[14]Goodall, *The Economics of Urban Areas*, p. 135.

[15]Discussions of clustering and cumulative attraction appear in Nelson, *Retail Locations*, "The Theory of Cumulative Attraction," pp. 57–64, "The Principle of Compatibility," pp. 65–78, and "Shopping Center Types," pp. 173–181.

independently in different parts of town because it is easier for them to perform comparative shopping.

The Shopping Center   The shopping center is a second type of cluster. It is different from the cluster of retail establishments selling similar shoppers goods because it contains stores that are complementary with each other as well as competitive. There are several principles that help to explain the success of shopping centers as a viable retail entity.

First, shopping centers are based on the theory of cumulative attraction. They generate an increased consumer traffic flow for each individual retail establishment. This increased traffic flow arises because of the nature of shopping goods such as clothing, shoes, housewares, jewelry, and home furnishings. Product differentiation and a desire for a wide selection of merchandise still exist in the minds of the consumers.

Second, the composition of shopping centers changes as their size changes. Typically, smaller shopping centers (neighborhood and community centers) contain a greater proportion of convenience goods establishments (specialty shop malls in high-income areas are an exception to this). Larger shopping centers (regional and superregional malls) contain a larger proportion of shopping goods establishments.

Third, each store in a shopping center is affected by the existence or the actions of the other stores in the shopping center in three ways:

1. Deliberate actions to generate customer traffic.
2. Affinity relationships and the principle of compatibility.
3. Consumer perceptions of the shopping center's image.

The shopping center often selects tenants on the basis of the retail establishments' ability to attract customers. Major attractors, often called "anchor stores," generate the vast majority of the customers. In addition, there are shopping goods stores that either broaden the selection or complement the products sold in department stores. There is the third category of store that does little to generate traffic, but depends on the consumer traffic flow for its business. This category includes convenience goods sellers and fast-food establishments.[16]

A second way in which one store in a shopping center is affected by the other stores is through affinity relationships,[17] where the compatibility[18] between and among the retail establishments is important. These stores are located most often in close proximity to each other so the consumer will conveniently find stores whose product lines supplement and complement each other.

[16] Nelson, *Retail Locations*, pp. 53–54.

[17] Arthur Getis and Judith M. Getis, "Retail Store Spatial Affinities," *Urban Studies*, November 1968.

[18] Nelson, *Retail Locations*, pp. 65–78.

Some stores seen as compatible for a large shopping center are:

1. Department stores—compatible with all apparel stores, shoe stores, variety stores, jewelry stores, knitting and linen stores.
2. Women's apparel stores—compatible with men's and children's apparel stores, and vice versa.
3. Women's shoe stores—compatible with men's and children's shoe stores, and vice versa.
4. All apparel stores—compatible with all shoe stores.

Because of internal clustering within a shopping center based on these compatibility relationships, the consumer finds an extended merchandise mix that allows for comparison shopping among retail establishments such as clothing stores. It also allows one-stop shopping trips to buy other products.

The third way in which the stores in a shopping center can affect each other is through their effect on consumer perceptions. In the physical sense, for example, an independent men's clothing store located in a shopping center that is deteriorating and suffering from economic obsolescence can have a different image and a different customer profile from the same establishment selling the same product but located in a new shopping center in a rapidly growing area.

In a marketing sense, the consumer's image of the other stores in the center can reflect on a specific store. For example, if consumers believe that some stores in the shopping center stock low-quality/low-price merchandise, they may well view every store in the same light, even if the merchandise is not low quality. On the other hand, if a favorable image exists toward the center as a whole, it may also exist toward each store in the center.

Distance: Perceptual or Psychological Aspects

Beyond the information provided by actual distance and travel time, several researchers have discovered that the consumer is affected by his or her estimate of that actual distance and travel time. Thus two retail establishments that offer the same products at the same actual distance or travel time can be perceived to be located differently in the mind of the consumer. Early research identified negative impressions of the retail establishment as one factor affecting perceptual or subjective distance, biasing the consumer's estimate of driving time upward and making the estimate of driving time greater than the actual time.[19]

The market analyst may need to determine the extent to which these negative factors exist vis-à-vis the retail establishment's access characteristics, its design and attractiveness features, its pricing-versus-quality rating by the consumers, and other factors discussed in this chapter. The analyst should determine

[19]Donald L. Thompson, "New Concept: Subjective Distance," *Journal of Retailing*, 1963, pp. 1–6.

the need to investigate the impact of perceptual distance in the market being analyzed at the time of the analysis.

Multipurpose Shopping Trips

When consumers plan their shopping trips, they typically plan to visit several retail establishments. Shopping centers are designed to accommodate this multipurpose orientation by bringing several of the possible desired combinations under a single roof, or into a single area. This is the case for the shopping good as well as the convenience good. Research has determined that multipurpose shopping trips are undertaken to minimize the costs of travel in its monetary and nonmonetary aspects and that people are willing to travel farther if the saving in time and effort in combining stops at one place is greater than the increased cost of travel.[20]

Supermarkets, and those shopping centers anchored by supermarkets, present a slight exception to the multipurpose shopping trip. One study found that 30 percent of trips to the grocery store were single-stop shopping trips and, like the other studies, people will travel farther for the advantage of combining several stops into a single trip.[21] Another study found that stops averaged 2.7 on the multipurpose trip. In addition to the original supermarket (included in the 2.7 stops), the most frequently visited retail stores were variety stores, drugstores, another supermarket, gasoline stations, and a financial institution.[22]

[20]Anthony Downs, "A Theory of Consumer Efficiency," *Journal of Retailing*, Spring 1961, pp. 6–12; and David L. Thompson, "Consumer Convenience and Retail Area Structure," *Journal of Marketing Research*, February 1967, p. 37.

[21]Jac Goldstucker, *New Development in Retail Trade Area Analysis* (Atlanta: Publishing Services Division, College of Business Administration, Georgia State University, 1978), p. 77. These authors report on an unpublished study by John D. Systoen.

[22]David B. MacKay, "A Microanalytic Approach to Store Location Analysis," *Journal of Marketing Research*, May 1972.

READINGS

APPLEBAUM, WILLIAM, "Method for Determining Store Trade Areas, Market Penetration, and Potential Sales," *Journal of Marketing Research*, May, 1966.

BRUNNER, J., and J. MASON, "The Influence of Driving Time Upon Shopping Center Location," *Journal of Marketing*, April, 1968.

BUCKLIN, L., "Trade Area Boundaries: Some Issues in Theory and Methodology," *Journal of Marketing Research*, February, 1971.

CONVERSE, P. D., "New Laws of Retail Gravitation," *Journal of Marketing*, October, 1947.

ELLWOOD, L. W., "Estimating Potential Volume of Proposed Shopping Centers," *The Appraisal Journal*, October, 1954.

HUFF, D., "A Probabilistic Analysis For Shopping Center Trade Area," *Land Economics*, February, 1963.

KANE, BERNARD J., *A Systematic Guide for Supermarket Location Analysis.* New York: Fairchild Publishers, 1966.

LAZER, W., and A. WYCHMAN, "Perceptual Segmentation of Department Store Markets," *Journal of Retailing*, Summer, 1969.

MANDELL, L., "Quality of Life Factors in Business Location Decisions," *Atlanta Economic Review*, January, 1977.

MASONS, J., and C. MOORE, "An Empirical Reappraisal of Behavioristic Assumptions in Trading Area Studies," *Journal of Retailing*, Winter, 1970–71.

NELSON, RICHARD L., *The Selection of Retail Locations.* New York: F. W. Dodge, 1958.

REILLY, WILLIAM J., *Methods for the Study of Retail Relationships.* Austin: Bureau of Business Research, University of Texas, 1929.

Appendix

REILLY'S LAW OF RETAIL GRAVITATION

A numerical example of Reilly's law reveals the results of the formula's calculations. To solve Reilly's equation, use the values for the exponents specified by Reilly; that is, $n = 2$ and $N = 1$.

Let

$$P_a = 10,000 \qquad D_a = 20$$
$$P_b = 15,000 \qquad D_b = 30$$
$$\frac{B_a}{B_b} = \left(\frac{10,000}{15,000}\right)^1 \left(\frac{30}{20}\right)^2$$
$$= (0.067)\left(\frac{3}{2}\right)^2$$
$$= (0.67)\left(\frac{9}{4}\right) = (0.67)(2.25) = 1.5$$

so

$$B_a = 1.5B_b$$

and

$$B_a + B_b = 1 \quad \text{or} \quad B_b = 1 - B_a$$

so

$$B_a = 1.5(1 - B_a)$$
$$= 1.5 - 1.5B_a$$
$$B_a + 1.5B_a = 1.5$$
$$B_a(1 + 1.5) = 1.5$$
$$B_a = \frac{1.5}{2.5} = 60\%$$

and

$$B_b = 100\% - 60\% = 40\%$$

This leads us to the conclusion that 60 percent of the residents of the small, intermediate city will shop in city a and 40 percent will shop in city b. This division of customers occurs in the example, under the specifications given; that is, city a is smaller and closer than city b to the area under analysis. Changes in the magnitude of the population and distance variables can be evaluated by reworking the formula. Consider the following changes from the initial conditions:

1. Population of city a increases from 10,000 to 15,000 while P_b, D_a, and D_b remain the same. In this case the percentage of shoppers going to city a will increase to 71.4 percent.
2. The distance to city a declines from 20 miles to 10 miles while the distance to city b increases from 30 to 40 miles and P_a and P_b remain unchanged. In this case the percentage of customers going to city a will increase to 91.5 percent. The analysis of these changes reveals that a larger city will draw a greater percentage of the consumers from a given location and that a greater percentage of customers will be drawn to a city from locations that are closer to the city.

CONVERSE'S MODIFICATION OF REILLY'S LAW OF RETAIL GRAVITATION

Converse modified Reilly's formula to obtain an estimate of the distance away from a retail center where its influence was equal to the influence of the competitor. In other words, Converse modified Reilly's law to obtain an estimate of the distance to the "breaking point" where the consumers as a group would split their patronage equally between the two competitors, 50 percent would travel to city a and 50 percent would travel to city b.

The modification was accomplished by letting the ratio of $B_a/B_b = 50\%/50\% = 1$. The mathematics of the calculation are

Let

$$\frac{B_a}{B_b} = \frac{50\%}{50\%} = 1$$

so

$$1 = \left(\frac{P_a}{P_b}\right)\left(\frac{D_b}{D_a}\right)^2$$

$$\frac{P_b}{P_a} = \left(\frac{D_b}{D_a}\right)^2$$

$$\frac{P_b}{P_a} = \frac{D_b}{D_a}$$

but

$$D_a + D_b = D_T$$

so

$$D_b = D_T - D_a$$

and

$$\frac{P_b}{P_a} = \frac{(D_T - D_a)}{D_a}$$

$$= \frac{D_T}{D_a} - 1$$

$$1 + \frac{P_b}{P_a} = \frac{D_T}{D_a}$$

$$D_a = \frac{D_T}{(1 + P_b/P_a)}$$

$$= \frac{50}{(1 + 15{,}000/10{,}000)}$$

$$= \frac{50}{(1 + 3/2)}$$

$$= \frac{50}{(1 + 1.22)}$$

$$= \frac{50}{2.5} = 20$$

When the size of the two cities and the distance between them is known, the Converse modification allows the estimation of the point in space where customers are shared equally. Utilizing the values of $P_a = 10{,}000$, $P_b = 15{,}000$, and $D_T = 50$, we find that the breaking point for the retail center located in city a is 20 miles. The Converse modification can be used to calculate the point in space where city a obtains 60 percent of the total customers. This is accomplished by setting the following equality:

$$\frac{B_a}{B_b} = \frac{60\%}{40\%} = 1.5 = X$$

$$X = \left(\frac{P_a}{P_b}\right)\left(\frac{D_b}{D_a}\right)^2$$

$$(X)\left(\frac{P_b}{P_a}\right) = \left(\frac{D_b}{D_a}\right)^2$$

$$(X)\left(\frac{P_b}{P_a}\right) = \frac{D_b}{D_a}$$

but

$$D_a + D_b = D_T$$

This example points up the fact that the Converse modification can be used to establish the breaking point for any rate, not just 50 percent of the customers being attracted to a specific site. Rates such as 60 percent, 70 percent, or even 80 percent of the customers are possible. This simply requires a calculation for the value of X as shown in the previous example and its inclusion into the formula.

THE ELLWOOD MODIFICATION OF REILLY'S LAW OF RETAIL GRAVITATION

Reilly's law of retail gravitation under the Ellwood modifications takes the following form:

$$\frac{B_a}{B_b} = \left(\frac{S_a}{S_b}\right)^N \left(\frac{T_b}{T_a}\right)^n$$

where

$N = 1$
$n = 2$
$S = $ size of retail area in square feet
$T = $ driving time (in minutes)

The Elwood specification of the gravity model lends itself to solution just as the Reilly model and the Converse modification of the model were solved. As an example of this case, solve for B_a using the following values:

$S_a = 150{,}000$ square feet
$S_b = 200{,}000$ square feet
$T_a = 5$ minutes
$T_b = 12$ minutes

$$\frac{B_a}{B_b} = \left(\frac{150{,}000}{200{,}000}\right)^1 (12/5)^2$$

$$= (0.75)\,(2.4)^2$$

$$= (0.75)\,(5.76) = 4.32$$

$$B_a = 4.32 B_b$$

$$= 4.32(1 - B_a)$$

$$B_a = 4.32 - 4.32 B_a$$

$$B_a + 4.32 B_a = 4.32$$

$$5.32 B_a = 4.32$$

$$B_a = \frac{4.32}{5.32} = 0.812 = 81.2\%$$

Using this same example to calculate the 50/50 breakpoint yields

$$T_a = \frac{T_T}{(1 + S_b/S_a)}$$

$$= \frac{(12 + 5)}{(1 + 200,000/150,000)}$$

$$= \frac{17}{(1 + 1/33)}$$

$$= \frac{17}{(1 + 1.155)}$$

$$= \frac{17}{2.155} = 7.89 \text{ minutes}$$

Given these values for retail space and driving times, the trade areas break approximately 8 minutes from retail center a and 9 minutes from center b.

THE HUFF PROBABILITY MODEL

The Huff model uses the following equation to establish the probability that a consumer located at a given point of origin will travel and shop at a specific shopping center or retail district. The Huff probability calculation is

$$P(C_{ij}) = n \frac{S_j}{T_{ij}}$$

$$j = 1 \frac{S_i}{T_{ij}}$$

where

$P(C_{ij})$ = the probability that a consumer living at site i will shop at retail center j

S = the size of the retail center j in square feet

T_{ij} = the travel time from site i to retail center j

n = the number of retail centers in the immediate area

k = a parameter that reflects the effect of travel time on different kinds of shopping trips (Huff discovered values of 3.19 for furniture and 2.72 for clothing).

The calculation of the probability estimates becomes clear utilizing the following example. Exhibit 9-4 is a simplified version of a grid pattern that establishes a series of geographic subareas. Three shopping centers or commercial districts S_1, S_2, and S_3 are located in this space. The point indicated in A is the geometric center of the subarea known as i. In addition, the following facts are known about the size of the shopping centers and the travel time from point A in subarea i to each respective shopping center:

$$S_1 = 150{,}000 \text{ square feet}$$
$$S_2 = 200{,}000 \text{ square feet}$$
$$S_3 = 300{,}000 \text{ square feet}$$
$$T_{i1} = 5 \text{ minutes}$$
$$T_{i2} = 12 \text{ minutes}$$
$$T_{i3} = 18 \text{ minutes}$$

Given these data, the probability that a consumer located in subarea i will purchase products at shopping center S_1 can be calculated. This calculation is

$$P(C_{i1}) = \frac{(S_1/T_{i1}^k)}{(S_1/T_{i1}^k) + (S_2/T_{i2}^k) + (S_3/T_{i3}^k)}$$

$$= \frac{(150{,}000/5^3)}{(150{,}000/5^3) + (200{,}000/12^3) + (300{,}000/18^3)}$$

$$= \frac{(150{,}000/125)}{(150{,}000/125) + (200{,}000/1{,}728) + (300{,}000/5{,}832)}$$

$$= \frac{1{,}200}{(1{,}200) + (115.7) + (51.4)}$$

$$P(C_{i1}) = \frac{1{,}200}{1{,}367.1} = .878 = 87.8\%$$

This calculation reveals that 87.8 percent of the customers residing in subarea i will shop at shopping center S_1. Once this probability is calculated, the probabilities for consumers living in subarea i shopping at S_2 and S_3 are easy to calculate. They are simply

$$P(C_{i2}) = \frac{115.7}{1{,}367.1} = 0.0846 = 8.46\%$$

$$P(C_{i3}) = \frac{51.4}{1{,}367.1} = 0.0376 = 3.76\%$$

Since only three competing shopping centers exist, the sum of the three probabilities must equal 1.

At the instructor's discretion, several additional cases can be presented to highlight the use of this procedure.

1. What happens to $P(C_{i1})$ if S_1 expands from 150,000 square feet to 300,000 square feet?
   Answer: $P(C_{i1}) = 93.49\%$.
2. What happens to $P(C_{i1})$ if travel time to S_2 declines from 12 minutes to 6 minutes because of road improvements?
   Answer: $P(C_{i1}) = 55.1\%$.

3. What happens to $P(C_{i1})$ if a new shopping center S_4 opens? ($S_4 = 300{,}000$ and $T_{i4} = 8$ minutes.)
   Answer: $P(C_{i1}) = 61.4\%$.

The Huff model can be used to delineate a trade area by choosing a desired level for the probability of consumers utilizing the subject property. For example, the primary trade area for shopping center S_1 could be those subareas for which $P(C_{i1})$ is greater than or equal to 50 percent. The secondary trade area could be those subareas for which $P(C_{i1})$ is greater than 30 percent.

10

FORECASTING THE DEMAND FOR RETAIL SPACE

ESTIMATING PURCHASING POWER AND EXPENDITURE
    PATTERNS
    Purchasing Power
    Expenditure Patterns
ANALYZING THE COMPETITION
    Surveying the Competition
ESTABLISHING COMPETITIVE DIFFERENTIALS
EVALUATING CONSUMER CHARACTERISTICS
ESTIMATING RETAIL SALES AND JUSTIFIED
    SQUARE FOOTAGE
    Unmet Demand for Retail Products and Services
    Sales Estimation
    Estimating Warranted Square Footage
    Estimating Site Size Requirements

This chapter presents an integrated discussion of the techniques used to forecast the demand for retail space. The discussion starts with an estimation of purchasing power followed by an analysis of retail expenditures. Then, a discussion of two supply-side issues—evaluation of the competition and determination of competitive differentials—is presented. These discussions lead to consideration of the next major topic—the estimation of retail sales—which in turn allows for the calculation of justified square footage of retail space and estimation of size requirements for the site.

ESTIMATING PURCHASING POWER AND EXPENDITURE PATTERNS

After establishing the boundaries of the retail trade area and the basis on which secondary data are available, the analyst then shifts the focus of the analysis to the consumers in the trade area and their purchasing power. If the census tract is the basis for secondary data, then the population in the market area can be described by

1. Per capita income.
2. Appropriate household income (mean, median, or other midpoint).
3. Total population.
4. Number of households.
5. Age composition of the population and households.
6. Income composition of the population and/or households.
7. Size of the households in the census tract.

Purchasing Power

Various measures of purchasing power can be developed. First, total purchasing power in a census tract or trade area can be estimated as the product of the mean household income value times the number of households, or as the product of per capita income times the population. These two purchasing power figures, one based on household income and the other on per capita income, will differ because some individuals are not included in households (those living in group quarters). To minimize any such difference, the analyst must be certain that the data for households include single-person households.

An important conceptual issue enters the picture at this point. The distribution of household income is skewed, in almost every trade area. The extent of skewness can be seen by the difference between the mean and median incomes. The mean income value is always pulled in the direction of the outlying income figures. In a trade area with some very high relative incomes, the mean will be greater than the median. In a trade area with some very low relative incomes, the mean will be less than the median.

This information is important because the use of the mean income figure can exaggerate the effective purchasing power in the trade area even though the actual purchasing power is being reported. For example, assume that the trade area has a small group of very-high-income households. Their existence pulls the mean above the median income figure. Now assume that the analyst is forecasting sales, say, in a community shopping center. The actual total purchasing power is the number of households times the mean income value. But the high-income group may have no need or desire to shop at this shopping center because the shops will serve the needs of the typical resident of the area. In this instance, the effective purchasing power is represented better by the number of households times the median income figure. This same line of reasoning can be applied to a trade area in which there is a group of low-income households. The actual purchasing power figure may underestimate the effective purchasing power.

The second aspect of purchasing power estimation that warrants attention by the analyst is the issue of estimating purchasing power for different income categories in the same market area. Depending upon the analysis, income segmentation may be recommended. In this case the analyst may be able to obtain data on the number of households in the trade area that earn between $15,000 and $24,999 as well as the number of households in the other income categories.

How does the analyst estimate the purchasing power of this income group? It is always the mean income times the number of households, but in this situation, the mean and the median income for the income group are not provided. The analyst must invent an income figure. The easiest such value to invent is the midpoint income value. In this example, it is the income figure in the center of the range between $15,000 and $24,999, namely, $20,000. The estimate of purchasing power for this income group would be $20,000 times the number of households in the income category. But the midpoint income for the category is neither the mean nor the median income for the households in that income category. The midpoint income value is only a mathematical concept related to the range of possible incomes; it does not describe the income distribution except by happenstance. In reality, the midpoint income will be above the mean income for the income category when the income category itself lies above the mean income for all households in the trade area.

To visualize this point, examine Exhibit 10-1. Notice that the use of the midpoint income overestimates the actual purchasing power for the $15,000-to-$24,999 income category. Also notice that the distribution of households in the income category is skewed, even though the population as a whole is not skewed.

The third issue regarding purchasing power is the distribution between total purchasing power and purchasing power disaggregated by retail category and by point of expenditure. Total purchasing power is a means to an end. The analyst is primarily concerned with the manner in which the households use their purchasing power to acquire different types of products and the point in space, the retail site, at which those expenditures are made. So, the analyst must also develop a method for disaggregating total purchasing power by retail category and allocating it to the retail sites where the dollars can be spent. These two concerns will be addressed in later sections of this chapter.

Expenditure Patterns

Households in different income categories maintain different expenditure patterns across all types of goods and services. Sometimes, these differences are very marked; at other times, they are only moderate. For example, examine

ACTUAL INCOME	NUMBER OF HOUSEHOLDS	INCOME CATEGORIES	NUMBER OF HOUSEHOLDS
4,000	1		
6,000	2		
8,000	4	$0–9,999	7
10,000	6	10,000–14,999	24
12,000	8	15,000–24,999	21
14,000	10	25,000 and above	0
16,000	8		
18,000	6		
20,000	4		
22,000	2		
24,000	1		

Mean = $14,000
Median = 14,000

Purchasing Power (PP) in the $15,000–24,999 Category

Midpoint income	=	$20,000
Median income	=	18,000
Mean income	=	18,286
Actual PP	=	384,000
PP estimate using midpoint	=	420,000
PP estimate using mean	=	384,000
PP estimate using median	=	378,000

Exhibit 10-1 Trade Area Purchasing Power Analysis: Hypothetical Case.

Exhibit 10-2 Selected Estimated Distribution of Expenditures by Income.

INCOME CATEGORY	MIDPOINT	FOOD		CLOTHING	
		At Home	Away	Men's	Women's
All	$11,419	10.1%	3.7%	1.89%	2.70%
Under $3,000	2,000	29.9	5.7	2.20	4.27
$3,000–3,999	3,500	21.9	5.0	1.92	3.76
$4,000–4,999	4,500	19.4	4.6	1.75	3.32
$5,000–5,999	5,500	17.8	4.1	1.95	3.16
$6,000–6,999	6,500	14.7	4.4	1.68	3.05
$7,000–7,999	7,500	14.1	4.1	1.87	2.97
$8,000–9,999	9,000	12.7	3.8	1.83	2.76
$10,000–11,999	11,000	11.0	3.9	1.96	2.55
$12,000–14,999	12,500	11.1	4.0	1.92	2.57
$15,000–19,999	17,500	8.5	3.4	1.82	2.40
$20,000–24,999	22,500	7.4	3.2	1.82	2.31
$25,000 and over	30,000	5.8	3.4	1.84	2.66

SOURCE: *Consumer Expenditure Survey: Integrated Diary and Interview Survey Data*, U.S. Department of Labor, Bureau of Labor Statistics, 1978.

Exhibit 10-2, which presents information taken from the *Consumer Expenditure Survey: Integrated Diary and Interview Survey Data,* U.S. Department of Labor, Bureau of Labor Statistics, 1978. When the survey was performed in 1972, households in the lowest-income categories ($3,000 to $5,999) spent 22.0 percent of their income for food at home and 5.0 percent of their income for food away from home. Contrast this with the expenditure of the upper-income group (over $15,000) for these two categories of food expenditure—approximately 7.0 percent to 3.3 percent, respectively. The higher-income group spends much less of its total income on food than does the lower-income group. The higher-income group also spends twice as much on food at home as food away from home. Members of the lower-income group spend four times as much on food at home as they do on food away from home.

The differences in expenditure percentages across income groups for men's and women's clothing is not as great as the difference in the food category. But, when these percentages are applied by income category, the upper-income groups spent much more in dollar terms than the lower-income groups. For example, the $20,000–24,999 income group spend 1.82 percent of its income, or $409.50 (1.82% × $22,500), for men's clothing per household. The $7,000–7,999 income group spends a similar 1.87 percent, or $140.25 (1.87% × $7,500), for men's clothing per household. In addition to the difference in dollars spent, these two income groups tend to make their expenditures for different types of clothes and different quality levels of clothes. These expenditure patterns can translate into different types of retail stores.

From this discussion and the example, it can be safely assumed that different income groups spend different percentages of their income on the same retail category of goods and services. In general, necessities (food, clothing, and shelter) make up a larger share of the lower-income group's budget. But the quality of the product purchased also tends to diminish for lower-income groups. This kind of information may be important when analyzing market areas characterized by income groups at the end of the income distribution (either upper or lower income) because the actual percentages are not like the values for the middle-income group or the population as a whole.

ANALYZING THE COMPETITION

Once purchasing power of the trade area and the level of expenditures for the particular products under investigation have been established, the analyst estimates the amount of retail space that is supported by market demand. The next steps involve an evaluation of the competitive environment and the capability of the subject property for successfully operating within that environment. The competition consists of other similar retail operations that are located in the trade area and will share major portions of the trade area with the subject property, as well as similar retail operations located outside but adjacent to the trade area. These external retail establishments have their own trade areas that overlap the trade area being analyzed.

Once the competition has been properly identified, the analyst collects information about each competitive outlet that reveals its strengths and weaknesses and identifies its pertinent operational and physical characteristics. A similar analysis is conducted for the subject property. The subject and each competitive outlet is then analyzed point by point for the purpose of identifying the competitive capability of the subject and each competitor. Based on this comparative evaluation, the analyst exercises judgment in estimating sales levels, market shares, factors that may precipitate changes in these conditions, and other aspects of competitive operations. These judgments are subsequently used to support the analyst's forecasts of the amount of total retail space for the specific products being studied in the trade area and how much of that space can reasonably be expected to be captured by the subject.

In summary, the first step after examining the purchasing power of the trade area is a survey of the competition followed by an analysis of the competitive differential. These topics will be discussed in the next sections.

Surveying the Competition

Several steps are required to determine the nature and impact of competition on the sales potential of the retail operation. These steps are described in Chapter 5, Analyzing the Subject Property and Its Competitive Environment, specifically the survey and evaluation of the competition.

Performing a survey of the competition requires the analyst, first, to identify existing competitive retail establishments in, as well as near, the subject property's trade area. Second, the analyst must identify the competition that is under construction or in the planning stage; that is, the analyst must identify the competition "in the pipeline." Third, the analyst must identify the potential for future expansion of retail establishments in, as well as near, the trade area.

Once the distinguishing features of the subject property and its retail establishment(s) are outlined, each competitive retail establishment in and near the trade area should be investigated with the same degree of thoroughness. The end result of the analysis should be the construction of a table that allows the analyst to compare each property and each establishment with regard to each factor used in the evaluation. This type of table is the starting point for the analysis of the competitive differential and the "gap in the market."

After careful consideration and outlining of the factors to be included, the analyst then performs a survey of the competition. As part of the survey, the analyst determines the amount of retail space under construction and the amount of space being planned for construction in the near future. By driving the main traffic arteries the analyst may observe retail space under construction. Checking building permits will supplement the field research and reveal the amount of retail space in the planning or site approval process.

As a third part of this analysis, information is gathered about the availability of vacant land in, or adjacent to, the trade area that would allow for the future construction of a new facility. After identifying the amount of vacant potential commercial space in the trade area with adequate access characteristics, the analyst must then identify which parts of that vacant space are zoned for commercial activity and have the required sizes and shapes to meet current development standards. As part of this analysis, existing commercial developments should also be checked to see whether or not additional retail space can be constructed in adjacent areas. As a final part of the evaluation of the existing facilities, the analyst should also make a determination of the renovation potential of the structure.

In this manner, the analyst takes into account potential competitive space that is not directly considered through an analysis of building permits and other publicly recorded development intentions. In making estimates of the amount of probable development that may occur, the analyst must again exercise keen judgment and exhibit an understanding of how commercial development activities most often occur in the area. Additional development of retail space shouldn't be anticipated simply because zoned land is vacant, or because there is room for an existing facility to expand. The judgment that commercial development is probable in these locations should be based on well-supported indications of the need or demand for expansion, who might be capable of expanding, and when and how the expansion should take place.

These supply-side data are used in conjunction with demand forecasting. If purchasing power is forecast to increase and available space exists, then development will more than likely occur. This expansion of competition will diminish the impact of growth on the subject property. If purchasing power does not grow, existing inventories of potential commercial land will probably not undergo development.

ESTABLISHING COMPETITIVE DIFFERENTIALS

After identifying the competition, estimating the probable expansion of existing facilities, and taking into account permitted and planned competitive developments, the analyst is ready to determine the competitive differential that can exist between the subject and its competition. The analysis starts with a consideration of the data generated from the survey of existing, planned, and prospective competitive retail establishments. The data collected for each competitive site identify

1. The physical features of the competition.
2. The neighborhood in which the competition is located.
3. The on-site amenities they provide, such as special parking facilities, landscaping, pedestrian facilities, or special architectural features.

4. Their accessibility characteristics.
5. Characteristics of the products being sold.

Once this information is known, the analyst can compare the characteristics of the existing retail establishments to see whether the subject property is better or worse than the competition using procedures such as those described in Chapter 6. From these data, the analyst can identify the advantages and disadvantages of the subject property and recommend which characteristics can be exploited and which should be avoided.

If the analysis is performed for a new enterprise, the analyst can advise the client about the nature of the competition so that the client can provide space, structure, amenities, accessibility, and product lines that are better than those offered by the market or at least on par with the competitive facilities.

As part of the analysis of the existing competition, a retail activity that is not being adequately provided within the trade area can be identified. For example, the survey might reveal that the closest retail establishment selling children's clothing is outside of the subject property's trade area. A store specializing in infant wear and children's clothing would fill a "gap in the market" that exists in the trade area. To determine if there actually is a "gap in the market," the survey of competition may have to be very extensive.

Another way of determining the gap in the market is to take a look at the competitive environment within product categories. In this instance, the analyst may discover that all the men's clothing stores in the trade area and the adjacent areas sell nothing but traditional men's clothing. Even though there is ample retail space provided to meet the needs for men's clothing, a special need may exist for high-fashion, faddish, or contemporary men's clothing.

EVALUATING CONSUMER CHARACTERISTICS

The next aspect of the process of evaluating the competitive differential is an understanding of the consumers who reside in that trade area. There are no secondary data sources with regard to the psychographic variables of the population. For example, secondary data do not identify the attitudes, life-style, tastes, and preferences of the consumer. To obtain such information, the analyst needs to undertake consumer research. (The topic of consumer research was introduced in Chapter 5; questionnaire design and sampling are discussed in Chapter 14.)

In this phase of the analysis, consumer research is directed toward the discovery of consumer attitudes and preferences that may be directed toward the existing and proposed retail establishment(s) on the subject property vis-à-vis the existing and proposed competitive operations. The analyst should try to determine consumer attitudes, preferences, habits, and so on regarding

1. Operational characteristics of the subject and competitive retail establishments, including
   a. Quality of merchandise
   b. Diversity, selection, and mix of merchandise
   c. Sales policy (credit, refund, sales staff attitudes, etc.)
   d. Cleanliness and attractiveness of the store(s)
   e. Types and characteristics of displays
2. Site amenities of the retail establishments, including
   a. Parking features such as adequacy of spaces, proximity to entrance, condition of surface, overcrowding
   b. Lighting (especially its role as a security feature)
   c. Access to and from major streets
   d. Cleanliness of the lot
3. Physical characteristics of the structure
   a. Physical condition
   b. Access from parking lot
   c. Floor plan and layout
4. Neighborhood/locational features
   a. Prestige
   b. Cumulative attraction
   c. Access to trade area

These data can help the analyst to make judgments about competitive differentials and competitive capability in the trade area. The demand for retail products is determined by purchasing power (number of consumers times income), taste/preference, and so on. The demand for a specific retail product on a particular site is determined, first, by the percentage of consumers with purchasing power who wish to purchase that product. Then, the analyst considers the percentage of consumers who choose to shop at the subject site. Consumer tastes and preferences are an important determinant of each of these consumer decisions.

The information about tastes and preferences is used by the analyst to support judgments underlying the forecasts of sales for particular items. The sales forecasts form the basis for estimating the amount of floor space required.

ESTIMATING RETAIL SALES AND JUSTIFIED SQUARE FOOTAGE

The process of estimating retail sales and the justifiable or warranted square footage for a specific retail development involves gross sales estimation, retail square foot estimation, and required necessary site-size determination. Each of these topics is a necessary part of retail trade area analysis for a specific new site. Often, a preliminary technique that analyzes unmet retail demand in the trade area also is useful.

Unmet Demand for Retail Products and Services

The economic potential for the construction of new retail space and the expansion of existing retail space can be obtained by establishing the level of unmet demand (also known as market vacuum) within the trade area. The level of unmet demand for each category of products sold in the retail space under study is estimated and then aggregated to get an estimate of total demand on sales potential for the site. To measure unmet demand, the analyst usually starts by obtaining secondary data from which total income of all households in the trade area can be calculated. For example, if the analysis focuses on men's clothing, information about the percentage of household income spent for men's clothing must be obtained. Information about expenditures for specific products is available from the following sources:

1. *Consumer Expenditure Survey*
2. *Relative Importance of Components in the Consumer Price Indexes* (RICCPI)
3. *Census of Retail Trade*

The Consumer Expenditure Survey is published about every 10 years by the U.S. Department of Labor, Bureau of Labor Statistics. The last two editions provide data for 1980–1981 and 1971–1972. The data in Exhibit 10-2 are taken from this source. The data in the 1980–1981 version are not as extensive as those provided in 1971–1972. The 1980–1981 edition provides extensive data only for food at home, food away from home, energy consumption, and selected items—personal care products and services, nonprescription drugs and supplies, and housekeeping supplies.

The second source for data on the percentage of income spent for different retail goods is the *Relative Importance of Components in the Consumer Price Indexes*, an annual publication of the U.S. Department of Labor, Bureau of Labor Statistics. The 1982 data are used to generate the percentage figures given in column 2 in Exhibit 10-5.

Both the *Consumer Expenditure Survey* and the *RICCPI* just described provide the percentage figures for expenditures directly. The *Census of Retail Trade*, on the other hand, can be used to estimate such percentages. Data for sales in broad retail categories are given for counties for the most recent census period—1982. (The earlier census data were presented for 1977.) The analyst can take the sales data from this publication and divide it by an estimate for total county income (obtained by multiplying population/times the mean per capita income) for the corresponding time period—1982. When this division is made, the analyst has a percentage figure that reflects the expenditure pattern for county residents. This estimate will more than likely require population and income updating.

Using two data sources to generate the percentage of income spent on a product such as men's clothing permits the analyst to verify the magnitude of the percentage of income spent on that particular item. As part of this data selection process, the shortcomings of each data set must be kept in mind. The data in each source are compiled so that only highly aggregated figures are available. Data from *The Consumer Expenditure Survey* are presented for broad income groups, age groups, and regions of the country. The price index data (*RICCPI*) are national in scope and are not disaggregated in any way by income group or region. The *Census of Retail Trade* data are given by county and MSA but are aggregated for the income categories. In addition, the data from each of these sources are at least two years old in the best of cases, and there is no feasible way to update the percentage distribution to reflect changes in tastes and preference and the relative prices of consumer goods that may have changed since the data were gathered.

The final decision on which data source or sources to use, and what percentage of income spent on each retail category to establish, ultimately rests with the analyst. The factors that must enter the decision involve the appropriateness and reliability of the data. The fundamental question in the analyst's mind is, Which data set best reflects the economic phenomenon in the market being analyzed? The underlying reality is that all market areas are not the same at a point in time, and a market does not remain static over time. Thus, a single approach may not be appropriate in all instances.

Once the percentages of income expended for the various retail categories are obtained, they can be multiplied by purchasing power in the trade area. This provides a dollar figure for annual expenditures in the trade area for each retail category (e.g., a category such as men's clothing). This figure can now be compared to actual expenditures for men's clothing in either of two ways.

The first way the analyst can approximate such an expenditure is to begin with the square footage of retail space devoted to men's clothing. This information is already contained in the survey of the competition. Then, using information provided in *Dollars and Cents of Shopping Centers* (published by the Urban Land Institute), the analyst obtains an estimate of the average sales per square foot of showroom space in men's clothing stores. A simple multiplication of the number of square feet devoted to men's clothing in the trade area times the median sales per square foot provided by *Dollars and Cents of Shopping Centers* gives a rough approximation of total sales of men's clothing in the trade area. The analyst can now compare this sales figure with the figure for consumer expenditures on men's clothing derived from other sources. If the sales and the expenditures were about the same, the analyst could conclude that stores in the trade area were capturing virtually all men's clothing consumers who reside in this trade area. If sales were higher than expenditures, then sales are also being made to consumers outside the trade area. It would then be desirable to determine who these customers are and include their purchasing power in the forecasts. If the calculated potential expenditures were higher than estimated sales, this would be the basis for obtaining a reasonable, but not an extremely accurate, estimate of the probability of new retail space being constructed in the trade area.

For example, the survey of the competition could reveal that there are four men's clothing stores in the trade area, with 9,000 square feet of cumulative showroom space. Using the average sales per square foot figure of $105 per square foot taken from *Dollars and Cents of Shopping Centers*, these stores would sell $945,000 in merchandise. Now, if the level of income in the trade area were $84 million, and if 1.45 percent of this sum is spent for men's clothing, the trade area will support approximately $1,218,000 in sales of men's clothing. In this instance, there is room in the market for another men's clothing shop with sales of approximately $273,000 and 2,600 square feet of retail space. The $273,000 represents the sum currently being spent in men's clothing stores outside the trade area.

On the other hand, if the trade area contains four stores with estimated cumulative sales of $1,155,000 from 11,000 square feet of cumulative store space, and if income in the trade area is only $60,000,000, then the households in the trade area can only support sales of $870,000. This relationship between sales and the percentage of income expended for men's clothing reveals that sales of $1,155,000 exceed spending of $870,000. The men's clothing stores in the trade area are supplying the needs of consumers in the trade area plus selling to customers from outside the trade area.

Does this mean that a new men's clothing store cannot enter the market? No! It simply means that the new entrant must take advantage of location in the trade area and consumer preferences. In this case primary data should be gathered to check consumer preferences concerning the product to be sold and to check their reaction to the location for the store. For example, the existing stores may sell traditional, conservative men's wear while the survey reveals that men travel out of the trade area to buy more faddish, trendy, avant garde styles. Consequently, there is a gap in the market.

Sales Estimation[1]

An illustration of how to estimate sales for a retail establishment begins with a consideration of Exhibit 10-3. The exhibit represents a hypothetical census tract map of a geographic area. The symbols that appear on this map have the following meaning:

X = the subject site. It is classed as a K_1 establishment.

---

[1]The estimation techniques presented in this and subsequent sections have been created to reflect the best practices found in unpublished consultant reports to clients who shared the reports with the authors.

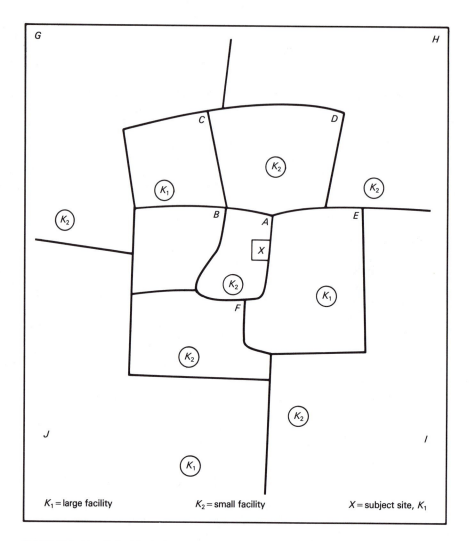

Exhibit 10-3 Hypothetical Trade Area.

K_1 = a competitive retail establishment of equal or greater size than the subject property. In this instance, size is a proxy for the product choices offered by the establishment (i.e., the merchandise mix existing within the establishment).

K_2 = competitive retail establishments of smaller physical size.

A, B, C, D, E, F = the census tracts that are considered as the primary trade area. (This trade area is defined on the basis of driving time, which represents the distance away from the site that can be reached over the same time period on the existing street system at a nonrush hour, but typically traveled, time of day.)

G, H, I, J = The census tracts that are considered as the secondary trade area. In this example, the tertiary trade area is combined with the secondary area.

To classify competitive shopping centers as either K_1 or K_2, the analyst evaluates the characteristics of each center. A system for classifying competitive centers was presented earlier in the discussion on survey of the competition. For present purposes, the survey of competitive space should identify the strengths and weaknesses as well as other distinguishing characteristics of the competition. The retail establishment on the subject site should develop an operating strategy that permits it to compete and achieve a required level of sales recognizing both favorable and unfavorable aspects of the competition. Part of this strategy should focus on site, locational, and architectural factors, while other aspects of it deal with the marketing and operational factors.

The primary trade area in the example presented in Exhibit 10-3 is established by driving time within the census tracts. However, the analyst will have to use judgment about the effect of geographic mismatches between the trade area and the census tract. In our example (Exhibit 10-4), a census tract is included in the primary trade area if it is entirely contained within the line representing equal driving time away from the subject site or if more than 50

Exhibit 10-4   Estimated Total Purchasing Power in Trade Area and Purchasing Power Captured by Subject Site for Current Period.

CENSUS TRACT	(1) NUMBER OF HOUSEHOLDS	(2) INCOME	(3) (1) × (2) TOTAL PURCHASING POWER (IN $000'S)	(4) DRAWING POWER OR THE PENETRATION RATE OF THE SITE	(5) (3) × (4) PURCHASING POWER TO SITE (IN $000'S)
Primary					
A	1,800	$20,000	$36,000	40%	$14,400
B	1,200	14,000	16,800	25	4,200
C	1,500	18,000	27,000	25	6,750
D	1,400	19,000	26,600	25	6,650
E	1,200	12,000	14,400	40	5,760
F	1,500	11,000	16,500	20	3,300
				Subtotal	$41,060
Secondary					
G	1,000	$12,000	$12,000	5%	600
H	900	10,000	9,000	10	900
I	800	10,000	8,000	5	400
J	700	10,000	7,000	5	350
				Subtotal	$2,250

Total purchasing power for trade area (sum of column 3) = $173,300,000.
Purchasing power to the site from the primary and secondary trade area (sum of column 5) = $43,310,000.

percent of its geographic area is contained within that line. The primary trade area becomes the geographic area defined by census tracts *A* through *F*.

In this instance, the percentage would represent the probability that a representative consumer residing in a specific census tract would shop at the subject property. The probability estimate is calculated using total square footage of this specific type of retail space in the trade area, including the subject property and its competitors, and the travel time to get from each census tract to the subject property and to each of the competitors.

Second, the percentages in column 4 can be derived intuitively. For purposes of the example, the intuitive approach is used so that the percentages in column 4 are estimates based on the analyst's understanding and interpretation of the following generalized relationships:

1. *The distance to the subject site.* For example, the households residing in census tract *F* are farther away than the households residing in census tract *A*. Therefore, other things being equal, the retail establishment on the subject site should attract more people from census tract *A* than from census tract *F* as consumers strive to reduce distance or travel time.

2. *The characteristics of the competition.* The size of the competition and their location should affect the drawing power of the subject site. For example, the retail establishment on the subject site should draw more people from census tract *F* than it would from census tract *D* because there is a retail establishment in census tract *D* that is of equal or greater size and carries at least an equivalent selection of merchandise.

3. *The competitive differential.* One obvious competitive advantage that the retail establishment on the subject site might have is its newness. If the analyst is studying the market for the creation of a new shopping center, the fact that it is new and, it is hoped, physically attractive will draw people to it at least once. However, to maintain high levels of consumer patronage and sales, the developer must generate the competitive advantage discussed in an earlier section and avoid creating any disadvantages.

4. *Accessibility to the site.* If the street pattern is different among the census tracts, the retail establishment on the subject site may attract a different percentage of consumers from census tracts that are the same distance from the site. For example, more people can be drawn to the subject site from census tract *D* because the subject site is served by a major artery while the households in census tract *E* must use secondary roads or roads that are narrow and congested. If the consumers in census tract *E* have better access to other retail sites, they will go there.

5. *Physical and psychological barriers.* The retail establishment on the subject site may attract more individuals from one census tract than another because of the physical barriers that deter their travel in that direction. The list of these physical barriers includes bridges, railroad crossings, excessive stoplights, inconvenient intersections, steep grades, winding roads, and poor quality of the road surface. Psychological factors such as the impact of the route environment and perceptions of hazardous conditions can also affect the travel patterns of consumers. People are more willing to drive along pleasant, picturesque streets than along cluttered and noisy streets. People will try to avoid areas that they feel present health or safety hazards, or are simply dirty, dingy, or otherwise aesthetically unpleasing.

When the drawing power percentages are obtained and represented in column 4 of the table, they can then be used to calculate the values in column 5. These figures represent the purchasing power from each census tract that can be attracted to the site. The total for column 5 represents the purchasing power of the trade area (all census tracts in the primary and secondary area) that the subject property can capture.

Once the final value for column 5 in Exhibit 10-4 is calculated, it fits into the analysis presented in Exhibit 10-5. Column 2 in Exhibit 10-5 shows that each household spends a percentage of its income for selected categories of items such as food, clothing, furniture, appliances, and so on.

Further insight into expenditure patterns can be obtained from a review of Exhibit 10-2, which shows that households in different categories spend different percentages of their income on the same retail product. Within each category it can be safely assumed that households tend to spend their income in roughly the same manner for broad categories of retail products. However, as noted earlier, this statement may not be true for specific items. For example, households in the same income group may spend approximately the same percentage of their income for clothing. However, two specific households may spend their funds on different types of clothing identified by style, price range, and so on.

Realizing these facts, the analyst faces the problem of data availability discussed earlier. For example, the analyst may use data in the *Consumer Expenditure Survey* with the assumption that households in a given income category spend approximately the same percentage for a broad retail category of goods, such as clothing. However, the most recent publication provides detailed categorization by income only for food. There is no breakdown for clothing and other retail categories. On the other hand, the *Relative Importance of Components in the Consumer Price Indexes* presents a very detailed breakdown of retail categories or product types but only presents an overall percentage figure for each income category, age group, or region of residence.

The percentage figure taken from the Retail Census is also a single percentage figure that reveals no segmentation. So it is akin to the data from *Relative Importance of Components in the Consumer Price Indexes* because it represents all income groups.

The analyst must choose one of these data sources to generate the figures that appear in column 2 of Exhibit 10-5. Values from relative importance of components in the CPI were selected for this example. If the trade area is not representative of the national distribution of households by income category, the analyst can use judgment to adjust the percentage figure. For example, if the subject trade area has a higher mean household income than does the nation, the analyst can reduce the percentage figure for a category such as men's and boys' clothing from 1.44 percent to a lower value because the percentage spent on clothing decreases as income levels rise. This adjustment was not used in the example.

EXPENDITURE ACTIVITIES	(2) % OF DISPOSABLE INCOME	(3) ESTIMATED SALES	(4) SALES PER SQUARE FOOT OF GROSS OR LEASABLE AREA*	(5) JUSTIFIABLE SPACE (SQUARE FEET)	(6) GROSS LEASABLE AREA (SQUARE FEET)	(7) LOWER AND UPPER DECILE FOR GROSS LEASABLE AREA (SQUARE FEET)
Retail Activity						
Supermarket (food at home)	12.87%	$5,574,000	$265.13	21,024	25,368	17,040–36,464
Food away from home	6.11	2,642,000				
Restaurant w/liquor			115.84	22,807	3,600	1,618– 8,302
Fast food/carry out			146.04	18,090	1,750	606– 3,185
Liquor/wine	0.84	363,800	200.96	1,810	2,562	1,125– 4,783
Dry cleaners/laundry	0.52	225,200	61.62	3,655	1,680	900– 3,200
Clothing, men's and boys'	1.44	662,600	101.96	6,499	2,704	1,429– 6,325
Clothing, women's and girls'	1.59	688,630	105.00†	6,558	2,000–3,000‡	816– 6,576‡
Footwear	0.68	294,500	130.00§	2,265	1,700–1,369‖	900– 4,000‖
Furniture	1.30	563,000	74.69	7,538	4,352	1,650–24,900
Major appliances	1.21	524,000	82.02	6,389	2,500	960– 7,600
Personal car services	1.01	437,430	122.13	3,587	7,500	3,000– 9,153
Subtotal	25.56%					
Other Expenditures						
Housing (shelter),	21.34					
Fuel, and utilities	8.38					
Health care service	5.02					
Transportation	20.25					
Subtotal	55.00%					
Misc. expenditures and savings¶	19.44					
Total	100.00%					

*Median sales volume per square foot in a community shopping center.

†Ladies' specialty is $110.41 and ladies' ready to wear is $98.62. The $105 is a judgment to represent these values.

‡Gross leasable area is 2,000 square feet for ladies' specialty and 3,000 square feet for ladies' ready to wear. The lower and upper deciles are 816 and 6,576 for specialty and ready to wear, respectively.

§$130 used as an approximation for the $123.43-to-$135.29 per square foot sales from men's and women's shoe stores.

‖GLA is 1,369 for men's and 1,700 for women's shoe stores.

¶This contains expenditures for retail categories not specifically identified, namely, insurance (nonmedical) and savings.

Exhibit 10-5 Forecasted Sales and Justifiable Subject Store Floor Area.

To continue the analysis, the "purchasing power to the site from the primary and secondary trade areas" calculated in Exhibit 10-4 ($43,310,000) is multiplied by the percentages of income spent on retail activities given in column 2 of Exhibit 10-5. The product of this multiplication, displayed in column 3 of Exhibit 10-5, represents the sales estimate for retail establishments that can be located on the subject property. For example, a supermarket located on the subject site will have estimated annual sales of $5,574,000. A men's and boys' clothing store will have estimated annual sales of $623,664.

The analyst must keep in mind that the figures in column 3 and, thereby, column 5 in Exhibit 10-4 must be based on current estimates of households and income. To get these current estimates, the updating techniques discussed in Chapter 3 apply.

Moreover, the analysis is not completed until the data in column 5 are forecast into the near future. This will affect the level of future sales (column 3 in Exhibit 10-5).

Estimating Warranted Square Footage

The information from *Dollars and Cents of Shopping Centers 1984* about median sales per square foot of gross leasable area is presented in column 4. These figures are derived for the community shopping center that typically contains 150,000 square feet of gross leasable area but can vary in size from 100,000 to 300,000 square feet. When the figures in column 4 are divided into the figures in column 3, the result is an estimate of "justifiable square footage" (i.e., the square footage that can be supported by the retail trade area's purchasing power that will be directed toward the site).

To continue the analysis, the information in the last two columns of Exhibit 10-5 is also extracted from *Dollars and Cents of Shopping Centers 1984*. These data allow for a comparison of square footage data for the site with square footage data for existing retail establishments. For example, the figures gathered for our analysis lead to a justifiable square footage of approximately 21,024 for supermarket space. Based on a comparison with the data in columns 6 and 7, the analyst can determine that the site can only support a small supermarket that is below the average size of 25,368 square feet and slightly larger than the stores in the lowest 10 percent of the size distribution (i.e., stores with square footage figures below 17,040 square feet).

The analyst can also compare this store size to the size of competitors. (Currently supermarkets have added sections that have previously been free-standing operations. The most noticed examples are the beer and wine sections, the drug and notions sections, and the deli section. Some supermarkets have also added flower shops and clothing sections.) The 21,024 square feet may be too small in comparison to the competition, so a larger store may have to be built to suit the prospective tenants.

Similar comparisons can be made for each of the other categories. The strength of the information, or its accuracy and reliability, depends on the assignment of the penetration percentages and the study of the competition that underlies it. If the penetration percentages are conservative, then, based on current data only, the following recommendations can be made:

1. The supermarket may be marginally successful. Its ultimate success depends on the growth of households and purchasing power in the census tracts that comprise its primary trade area. A forecast of purchasing power is needed.
2. The site will support approximately 20,000 square feet of restaurants (the cuisine of the restaurant to be developed from the competitive evaluation and consumer research). This is some combination of restaurants and fast-food operations. For example, there could be two moderate-sized restaurants (5,000 square feet each) plus three fast-food outlets (2,000 square feet each).
3. One small liquor store is possible. (This could be part of the supermarket.)
4. One dry cleaner/laundry is justified.
5. Men's and women's clothing stores are justified. The site could support two shops with above-average footage in each product line.
6. A furniture and appliance store is justified. This could be a single operation with approximately 14,000 square feet or two separate entities of 8,000 and 6,000 square feet for furniture and appliances, respectively. However, the analyst should carefully consider if this type of operation is compatible with the other tenants in the shopping center or if it should be constructed as a free-standing structure nearby.

If the anchor store can be justified as a supermarket by analyzing the future trends, then the justifiable square footage could be

35,000	Supermarket (based on future sales and the inclusion of some high-volume grocery sections such as a beer/wine section, a deli, and a health and personal care section, but not including some low-volume nongrocery section)
10,000	Restaurants (6,000 and 4,000 square feet, respectively)
6,000	Fast food (3 @ 2,000 square feet each)
6,000	Men's clothing (2 @ 3,000 square feet each)
6,500	Women's clothing (2 @ 3,200 square feet each)
14,000	Furniture/appliances
2,200	Shoe store
2,500	Dry cleaning
3,500	Drug store (prescription center)
85,700	Total justifiable square footage by retail category
12,000–20,000	Speculative space
97,700–105,700	Total space provided

The speculative space is based on the analyst's judgment about the following factors:

1. Miscellaneous expenditures and savings are a residual category of the expenditures shown in Exhibit 10-5. First, a typical savings rate is established. House-

holds in the United States have historically saved between 5 and 8 percent of their incomes. A savings rate of 7 percent was selected, leaving approximately 12 percent for miscellaneous retail purchases.

2. Sales per square foot of $150 was selected to reflect the nongrocery items. This value is a high-side estimate for sales per square foot and will lead to a conservative estimate for speculative space.

3. A weighting factor of 35 to 60 percent is used to represent the possibility that the retail activity will be found in a shopping center. These values are judgments that should be based on the analyst's knowledge of the market.

The mathematical calculation is

$$\$43,300,000 \times 12\% = \$5,196,000$$
$$\frac{\$5,196,000}{\$150} = 36,640 \text{ sq. ft.}$$
$$36,640 \times 35\% = 12,124 \text{ sq. ft.}$$
$$36,640 \times 60\% = 20,784 \text{ sq. ft.}$$

So, speculative space is approximately 12,000 to 20,000 square feet.

The speculative square footage will provide space for those activities that are not explicitly enumerated in column 1 of Exhibit 10-5 but are aggregated in the "Miscellaneous Expenditure and Savings Category." This space could be designed for the following activities that can be supported by current sales estimates, given the existing competitive structure.

RETAIL ACTIVITY	MEDIAN GLA	SALES PER SQUARE FOOT
Bank	2,500	—
Jewelry store	1,200	185
Liquor store	1,800	200
Camera shop/film processing	1,600	180
Beauty shop	1,200	81
Barber shop	700	82
Arts and craft	1,500	62
Shoe repair	700	95
Toys	4,000	76
Card and gift shop	2,400	74
Bookstore	2,000	100

The size of Phase II development is a function of growth in purchasing power. For example, the area may grow in five to eight years so that a future marketability study of the site will show its capacity to support a third women's clothing shop, a second shoe store, and a branch bank. If this development is to take place, a plan to accommodate it must be included in current plans. Additional land for the expansion of retail space and extra parking may be bought today and warehoused for a reasonable period of time.

Estimating Site Size Requirements

Once a forecast of retail floor area is obtained, it is simple to convert the retail space to gross building area (GBA) or to total site area with the use of ratios. The analyst may obtain local statistics, such as the ratio of sales area to total floor area, the ratio of gross leasable area (GLA) to GBA for certain building and tenant types, or the ratio of GBA to total site area. For example, the analyst may find that a small neighborhood shopping center is expected to support 84,000 to 97,000 square feet. Local sources indicate that comparable centers have a GLA that is 90 percent of GBA, and there is a 1:4 ratio of retail floor area to site area. The analyst could recommend the following:

$$\frac{100,000 \text{ sq. ft. GLA}}{0.9} = 111,112 \text{ sq. ft. GBA}$$

$$111,112 \text{ sq. ft. GBA} \times 4 = 444,448 \text{ sq. ft. site}$$

Thus, a 100,000-square foot center would require an additional 11,100 square feet of building area for support services and 280,000 square feet for parking, access, amenities, et cetera, for its own operation.

The total site size required is 10.2 acres (444,448 square feet divided by 43,560 square feet per acre). The structure would sit on 2.55 acres while the remaining 7.65 acres would include space for all necessary activities.

If 106,000 square feet is used as the retail space that the site can currently support, then site size will have to be 10.82 acres. If excess acreage is going to be purchased for possible Phase II development, then any additional 10,000 square feet of future retail space development will require 44,444 total square feet of site (1.02 acres).

READINGS

APPLEBAUM, WILLIAM, *Guide to Store Location Research*. Reading, Mass.: Addison-Wesley, 1968.

BARRETT, G. V., *How to Conduct and Analyze Real Estate Market and Feasibility Studies*. New York: Van Nostrand Reinhold Co., 1982.

COHEN, SAUL, B., and GEORGE R. LEWS, "Form and Function in the Geography of Retailing," *Economic Geography*, January, 1969.

GENTRY, J., and A. BURNS, "How Important Are Evaluative Criteria in Shopping Center Patronage," *Journal of Retailing*, Winter, 1977–78.

GETIS, ARTHUR, and JUDITH M. GETIS, "Retail Store Spatial Affinities," *Urban Studies*, November, 1968.

HUFF, DAVID L., "Defining and Estimating a Trade Area," *Journal of Marketing*, July, 1964.

NEVIN, J., and M. HUSTIN, "Image as a Component of Attraction of Intraurban Shopping Areas," *Journal of Retailing*, Spring 1980.

ROCA, R., *Market Research for Shopping Centers*. New York: International Council of Shopping Centers, 1980.

THOMPSON, DONALD L., "Future Direction in Retail Area Research," *Economic Geography*, January, 1966.

THOMPSON, DONALD L., "New Concept: Subjective Distance," *Journal of Retailing*, 1963.

URBAN LAND INSTITUTE, *Shopping Center Development Handbook*. Washington, D.C.: Urban Land Institute, 1985.

WEALE, W. B., "Measuring the Customer's Image of a Department Store," *Journal of Retailing*, Summer, 1961.

11

OFFICE MARKET ANALYSIS

INTRODUCTION

The methodology of an office market analysis is deceptively simple. The judgment and assumptions necessary to implement the analysis, however, require a
thorough understanding of the factors shaping the local economy (discussed in
Chapter 3) and the nature of the markets for office space. More than for any
other real estate, the market for office space is subject to extreme fluctuations
in supply—a point of discussion in the next paragraph. No matter how carefully
analyzed and planned, the success of a proposed office building development
or acquisition may ultimately be determined by the timing of the investment in
the swings of local office market demand and supply conditions. Consequently,
the market analyst should provide the client with an analysis of current market

conditions and the outlook for the local office market in the foreseeable future. Since office construction can require two years or more from permit to opening, followed by a rent-up period, the analyst is concerned with market conditions over the next three or four years from the date of the study.

Historically the addition to the supply of office space in major American cities has fluctuated dramatically, with high volumes of construction followed by prolonged lulls when little new supply is added to the local stock. A factor contributing to the high rate of construction in recent years has been the rising proportion of white-collar service-related jobs in our economy. This basic demand for office space has been augmented by investors who consider office buildings in the central city to be a preferred real estate investment. Pension funds, insurance companies, and foreign investors have a marked preference for office building investment. Such investors have "deep pockets" (a relatively large amount of equity capital available) and can afford to carry the property through years of operating losses. A history of rising rents and construction costs can induce these investors to supply space in a market with excess supply and suffer current low occupancy rates. The need to be first into the market as a deterrent to competition also can result in simultaneous development and contribute to an oversupply.

Office buildings have been the choice product of syndicators. Tax laws that gave a rapid write-off of investment and that gave tax incentives for historic preservation and for the rehabilitation of older commercial buildings contributed to the demand for syndication "product" in the office market. Other demanders of office space, such as major corporations needing a national or regional headquarters office, often provide not only the space that they require for immediate use, but additional space for future expansion. In the interim, this space is part of the speculative supply in the market and is offered for rent to a general tenancy. The provision of such space may be made even when market conditions are not favorable for additional speculative space and can contribute to an oversupply condition.

An overbuilt market will eventually slow the rate of new construction until demand and rents have risen to levels that once again provide financial feasibility. The lull in provision of office space in a local market may last from a few months to several years or longer, depending upon the economic growth of the local economy and the degree of overbuilding.

LINKAGES IN AN OFFICE MODEL

Office space users can be segmented into two broad groups. The first consists of office users who serve a local market such as doctors, dentists, lawyers, accountants, insurance agents, real estate brokers, bankers, and residential appraisers. The second group is concerned with activities that serve a nonlocal market, for example, regional offices of major corporations, financial service companies with nonlocal clientele (banks, brokerage houses, investment bankers), insurance service companies, and others.

The links to customers are important. The nearby commercial areas may provide such links. Other businesses and facilities upon which the office activity is dependent are usually nearby, as are shopping facilities, eating establishments, and other services needed by the office employees.

The linkage requirements of the service employment group, the first group mentioned, are similar to the linkage requirements for retail space. Many of these users will readily shift between storefront space and office building space. Such office space is frequently on the second floor or in the back arcade of a shopping center because it also needs exposure to passing retail traffic.

The second group of basic office space users is somewhat more flexible in the sense that its members may have a wider choice of alternative locations; that is, they are not tied to the need for direct customer exposure. The basic locational choice may deal only with which city or sector of the metropolitan area they need. The choice of a specific location beyond that may be based upon such factors as (1) proximity to the downtown area (source of numerous business contacts) or the airport, (2) access to the local expressway or thoroughfare system for easy commuting or mobile business operations, (3) being in a location that is prestigious or has high visibility for the purpose of image building, and (4) being proximate to needed business services or related business functions. Thus, these office users shop for available locations that best fulfill their particular requirements from the stock of office locations available within the general area in which they have decided to locate.

The quality-of-life factors that make for pleasant residential areas and living conditions, especially those that appeal to the top executives making the locational decision, are increasingly important in office location analysis. Good living conditions, along with a reasonable availability of sites and services, are more and more becoming critical determinants of office locations.

Given the complexities of office location decision making among the various office users, no satisfactory office space classification currently exists. One of the tasks of this chapter, therefore, is to present a system for office market disaggregation that contains most of the distinctions needed and can act as a model for classification systems that may be developed.

MARKET DISAGGREGATION: CLASSIFICATIONS FOR OFFICE SPACE

Office space is constructed and supplied to the market on a speculative or a nonspeculative basis. Nonspeculative office space consists of that space custom-designed and built for the exclusive occupancy of a particular office user. The office space is either built or acquired by the owner-occupant, such as a corporation constructing offices for its own use, or it is built to be occupied on a long-term basis by a single tenant, such as a corporation arranging to occupy offices built to its own specifications under a sales-leaseback agreement. Regardless of how nonspeculative space is owned and operated, it is not available to general tenants seeking to occupy office space available on the market at competitive rental rates. Speculative office space, on the other hand, consists of that space offered to general tenants in the market at competitive rents. It is designed to accommodate general office users who are seeking nonspecialized space or certain types of conventional specialized space (medical, etc.) and who will bid up rental rates to gain locational advantages and amenities that may be available. In this manner, the profit levels and value generated by rental income provide incentives to owner-investors to provide speculative office space with competitive advantages that meet the requirements and expectations of many office users rather than the specific design requirements of a single tenant or highly specialized tenants.

Some office users may switch occasionally between speculative and nonspeculative space, but by and large most will remain in one particular sector of the market for a long period of time. Office market analyses are usually performed only for speculative space, since nonspeculative space does not represent competitive space available to satisfy general market demand. However, in calculating office demand from secondary data, the analyst is usually unable to distinguish initially what proportion of aggregate office demand will be satisfied with nonspeculative space. To make the distribution of demand between the two categories, the analyst is forced to make assumptions that may not be readily verifiable using available secondary data. Similarly it is difficult to distinguish on the basis of building permit data or other measures which office space is nonspeculative. Further, some office space may be speculative, occupied partially by the owner-occupant, with remaining space for rent or some way switched from intended nonspeculative occupancy to market occupancy after construction begins. It is often necessary to try to make this distribution for the analysis to focus only on the market for speculative space.

Exhibit 11-1 provides a simple classification system for nonspeculative office space. The principal purpose of classifying nonspeculative office space into these categories is to permit the analyst to develop an inventory of total office space (both speculative and nonspeculative) by major type. Later in this chapter, a similar classification for speculative office space with compatible categories will be presented. Once such an inventory is created, changes in the amount of each type of office space can be monitored. The amount of office space available or planned for nonspeculative occupancy along with the amount already occupied indicates to the analyst what proportion of total office demand by type is satisfied outside the competitive office market in a local area. The analyst can then use this information to estimate absorption or other market outcomes for speculative space.

Prestigious office space	Usually houses a prestigious professional or headquarters-type operation in a prominent location. The structures contain architectural features designed to display an impressive image and contain a high level of amenities.
General office space	Functionally designed office space that houses a wide variety of office operations to support business operations located elsewhere. Often located in accessible but not highly visible locations, these structures have various amenity levels and can be subcategorized as (1) high amenity, (2) normal amenity, and (3) low amenity.
Supportive office space	Functional office space designed to support other types of operations within the same building or complex. Location and amenity levels depend on the requirements of the dominant operations housed in the structure, but the office space is generally secondary and not as visible or accessible as primary operations subcategorized as (1) offices with retail; (2) offices with warehousing; (3) offices with light, industrial, or technical operations; and (4) offices with industrial production facilities.

Exhibit 11-1 Nonspeculative Office Space Categories.

Alternatively, the analyst might derive the speculative/nonspeculative ratios or adjustments to the ratio from other empirical or nonempirical sources. Standard ratios from national, regional, or local industry may be available, although these standards frequently need adjustments for specific local conditions or specific type of space. If time and budget permit, the analyst can conduct a survey among specific types of employees to ascertain their conditions and plans for occupying specific types of office space. While these surveys provide extremely important information, occupancy statistics derived from the inventory method are usually a better measure of actual distribution.

Central-City and Suburban Markets

The local office market in a metropolitan area can also be disaggregated into the central-city and the suburban markets. The two markets attract generally different tenants, although the distinction is not clear-cut and similar tenants may be found in both suburban and central-city markets. The central-city office market is characterized by high-rise buildings serving as the home offices of industrial corporations, insurance companies, and financial institutions. Speculative construction in the central city attracts firms that are willing to pay premium rents for the prestige of address and for maximum accessibility to a dispersed clientele. Other firms locate in the central city because of the need for face-to-face contacts or access to public records.

The suburban office market attracts tenants who do not require the visibility, accessibility, and prestige of a central-city location. These office users include the "back rooms" of companies that may have their selling floors in a downtown location. Computer operations, for instance, can be separated from the front office and located in less expensive suburban locations. The suburban market also contains tenants who serve clientele from a more limited geographic area. Real estate and insurance brokers, for instance, may primarily serve clients residing in or seeking a residence in certain suburbs. The central-city market is not the exclusive choice for the location of corporate headquarters. Companies are increasingly choosing a more campuslike atmosphere of a suburban location over the congestion of the central city.

Although speculative space in the suburban market can be analyzed separately, and the central-city and suburban markets may be observed at any one time to have significantly different occupancy rates, the analyst realizes that the two markets are linked. The construction of speculative space in the central city is sometimes attractive to prospering tenants in suburban locations who are ready to upgrade their consumption of office space. The attraction of the central city increases when overbuilding results in depressed rents and rent concessions to tenants. This movement to the central city can transmit the vacancies from that market to the suburban market. Similarly, some downtown office tenants may migrate to suburban areas when depressed conditions in the suburban market overcome the attractiveness of a central location.

Nodes of Development

The local office market can be conceptualized as containing nodes of office space scattered over the metropolitan area. The major node, of course, is the central business district. Other nodes develop around hospitals and other health care facilities, near public buildings such as a courthouse, at the intersections of major traffic routes, and in and near concentrations of retail land uses. Office parks and mixed-use developments create other concentrations of office space. These nodes of office space, because of proximity, may contain space in direct competition with the subject property. When the subject property is part of a node that has developed near a specialized land use, such as a hospital, the relevant competition may be contained only within the node. However, the market analyst must keep in mind that many tenants of speculative suburban office space are relatively indifferent about their specific location if accessibility and other amenities among possible sites are similar. Thus, properties in a suburban node located on a beltway on the other side of the central city may be competitive with the subject property.

Quality Aspects of Office Markets

Traditionally, the quality of office space has been categorized into three major classifications as follows:

1. *Class A*: The property has an excellent location and access; the building is in good to excellent physical condition and meets or exceeds building code requirements; rents are competitive with new construction.
2. *Class B*: The property has a good location; construction and physical condition

are good and meet code, but the building suffers from some functional obsolescence and physical deterioration; rents are below those for new construction.

3. *Class C*: The property is an older building (15–25 years) and may not meet code; the building suffers physical deterioration and functional obsolescence, but remains part of the active supply, with reasonable occupancy rates at generally lower rents than Class B buildings.

This classification system requires the analyst to evaluate and aggregate at least five comparative aspects of office buildings:

1. Quality of location.
2. Age or newness of structure.
3. Physical condition of structure.
4. Quality level of general amenities.
5. Rental range.

Most local metropolitan areas have trade organizations that compile office market data using a system of major classifications, so most office market analyses dependent on secondary data are forced to utilize those classifications. Unfortunately, there are several problems with such an aggregative evaluation. The lack of precise standards or guidelines for classifying each element evaluated often results in classes of office space that are inconsistent. Further, changes in conditions over time, such as changes in rent levels and amenity standards, complicate subsequent evaluations and inhibit comparison of times-series data.

If comparisons are needed between one market and another, one frequently finds that the different classes of office space are defined differently in each area, making the comparison difficult, meaningless, or impossible. While the use of the Class A, B, C system at least provides some system for office space data, there is ample room to improve the data base so that occupancy and rent statistics can be consistently and comprehensively utilized in market studies.

Exhibit 11-2 suggests a system for classifying office space amenities that will enable the analyst to make judgments about the comparative quality of office space under study. This system can be used with the classification system suggested for disaggregation (discussed later with reference to Exhibit 11-3) so that comparisons can be made by location and type of office space as well as amenity level. In addition, these categories lend themselves to a system of weighting and ranking, as demonstrated in Chapter 6, so that a point system for evaluation can be developed.

Thus, the central-city or suburban office markets, or buildings in identifiable nodes, can be disaggregated by quality as well as type and location. Again, the structures in the different quality levels are linked by firms moving to upgrade space in response to their own prosperity and to market conditions affecting properties in the various classes. The analyst, who most often is concerned with one portion of the market, must not ignore competition from different quality structures in linked markets.

A. Site Amenities
   1. Parking adequacy
      a. Number of spaces
      b. Size and angle of spaces
      c. Location of spaces
   2. Adequacy of internal circulation
      a. Width and configuration of internal roadways
      b. Accessibility to connecting streets
      c. Driving and pavement conditions
   3. Special site facilities
      a. Separate pedestrian facilities
      b. Outside recreation facilities
      c. Special landscaping
B. Special architectural features
   1. Special design for approaches and entranceways
   2. Special treatment of public spaces/common areas
   3. Specialized exterior design for visual effects
C. Interior facilities
   1. Special technical facilities for operations
   2. Environmental controls and safety features
   3. Internal views and open spaces
D. Quality level of internal finishings
   1. High quality
   2. Medium quality
   3. Low quality

Exhibit 11-2 Classification of Office Space Amenities.

Disaggregation for Speculative Office Space

Competitive aspects of speculative office space are of primary interest to the office market analyst. There are three major factors that differentiate the major competitive elements of office space: (1) type of office space, (2) general amenity level, and (3) location. Exhibit 11-3 shows a comprehensive matrix system for classifying speculative office space into various categories using these three major factors. Most often, the analyst will be concerned with only two or three linked or competitive categories of office space. However, it is often necessary to conceptualize, if not actually calculate, how various segments of demand may be satisfied with alternative forms of office space. Properly utilized, the suggested classification system can help to identify the characteristics and amount of office space capable of satisfying the particular requirements for most types of office space demand.

The speculative office space classification system provides much greater detail than does that suggested for nonspeculative office space. The following is a discussion of some of the major differences.

General Types of Office Space   In addition to the three general types of office space for nonspeculative markets, a fourth category, mixed-use office development, is provided for speculative space. A mixed-use office development consists predominantly of office use of exhibition/convention space and contains

Exhibit 11-3 Location and Amenity Classification System for Speculative Office Space, by Type.

TYPE AND AMENITY CATEGORIES	Prestige		General Office Space						Supportive Office Space		Mixed-Use Office Development		
			Specialized			Nonspecialized							
Locational Categories	Specialized	Non-specialized	High Amenity	Normal Amenity	Low Amenity	High Amenity	Normal Amenity	Low Amenity	With Warehousing	With Technical Facilites	With Retail	With Hotel	Multiuse
Central city													
Office district													
Restricted													
Unrestricted													
Free standing													
Individual													
Mixed use													
Suburban													
Office district													
Restricted													
Unrestricted													
Free standing													
Individual													
Mixed use													

significant supportive secondary uses (retail, hotels, etc.) that add measurably to the environmental qualities of the office space and that are designed to enhance the amenity and marketability of the office space. Unlike supportive office space, the office use comprises the dominant character or at least a co-dominant image for the mixed-use development.

Secondary Types of Office Space   Each of the four major types of office space are subcategorized into more specific types of space. Both prestige and general office space can be further divided into specialized and nonspecialized categories. Specialized refers to conventional office space that is equipped with special design or facilities commonly required by certain categories of tenants, such as medical practitioners or high-tech operations. Nonspecialized space is speculative space that has no special facilities and is suitable for general office tenants. In the general office space category, both specialized and nonspecialized categories are subdivided further on the basis of amenity levels, as identified in Exhibit 11-2. All prestige space is normally considered to have a high amenity level, and further subdividing is not needed. Both supportive office space and mixed-use office development are sub-categorized by the major type of dominant or co-dominant uses contained in the office complex. The amenity level within each category of mixed-use development is assumed to be similar.

Locational Categories   The location for each type of office space may be further identified on the basis of (1) its geographic position, (2) the relative intensity of office uses in the immediate vicinity, and (3) the degree of developmental and operational control exercised by the property managers.

The first level of classification, central city versus suburban, deals not only with the general urban location but also with accessibility and often with developmental restrictions. Because of the geographic centrality of many central business districts and in-town development nodes, most central-city office developments are better served by arterial routes and mass transit systems than are suburban developments. Also, because of intense competition for scarce sites among various urban land uses and traditional public investment in the infrastructure, some requirements for the provision for supporting facilities and site development are often less stringent or are subsidized in central-city locations.

The second level of locational classification identifies if the space being evaluated is situated in a geographic area defined (by zoning, development boundaries, or both) as a specialized office area, designated as office district, or if it occupies an independent office site in a nonspecialized office area, designated as free-standing.

A third level of locational classification then distinguishes office district locations as restricted, meaning internal developmental and operational controls are in force (as in most office parks), or unrestricted, where no formal set of internal controls exists. Also, free-standing locations are similarly subcategorized as individual, meaning an independent office use, relatively unconstrained by other adjacent or nearby land uses, or mixed-use, which indicate the site and/or structure functions as the single office element within a larger complex containing other uses.

Again, while most office market analysts are normally concerned with only one or a few categories of space, unless they are performing a comprehensive office market study, the starting point for most analyses is estimating aggregate office demand and supply. Consequently, the analyst must segment demand and disaggregate supply to focus on the specific sectors of the office market with which the analysis is concerned. The classification system described in this chapter helps to facilitate that focus. The system may be used as a conceptual tool, to narrow the type and amount of space under analysis. Alternatively, it may be used to perform actual calculations that provide a comprehensive inventory of space by type, calculate ratios with which to distribute aggregate levels and demand and supply, or make adjustments to standardized ratios.

Often the analyst may deal with other specialized segments of the office market and need to distinguish office space on the basis of other characteristics. Some of the more common distinctions include

1. *Building height*—low rise versus elevator office buildings.
2. *Type of occupancy*—single tenant versus multitenant buildings, or tenant profiles by standard industrial code (SIC) category.
3. *Scale of tenant space*—large flexible tenant spaces versus limited rigidly partitioned.

COMPONENTS OF AN OFFICE MARKET ANALYSIS

Theory about the demand for office space is not as well developed as is theory about residential or retail space. Unlike demand for residential space, which can be envisioned as a function of households and their income levels, or the demand for retail space, which can be envisioned as a function of customers and their purchasing power, the demand for office space comes from both the household sector seeking services and the business sector seeking to house certain employees. From the simplest perspective, office space demand results from the functional requirements of those business, professional, administrative, and other activities that require office space to house their operations. In that sense the analyst often considers that the demand for office space is derived from the expansion of businesses and other office-dependent activities found in employment statistics. However, employment data must be manipulated and measured against other factors to obtain that portion of the community's total labor force that requires accommodation in offices.

Once an estimate of total office demand is obtained, it is then necessary to determine how that demand is distributed among the various types and locations of office space available. The analyst must be able to deal with the functional and environmental requirements of the various office users to estimate how demand is distributed.

The following sections of this chapter describe a conventional methodology for estimating demand for office space using employment data. The discussion will also review how demand can be segmented by types of industry and will identify a methodology for estimating the amount of space needed to accommodate office users.

Delimiting the Geographic Market Area

Office markets typically do not have boundaries that circumscribe the geographic area in which customers or clients are located. Exceptions are doctors, dentists, and other professionals, whose clients are attracted to their offices by the reputation of the professional or by proximity of the office. For some professional tenants, a market could be defined that contains the majority of their clients, although their markets may be diffused over the metropolitan area when the specialists, law firms, and clinics enjoy outstanding reputations.

For many firms that occupy office space constructed on speculation for rent to a general tenantry, geographic submarket areas are not particularly relevant. In an aggregate market demand analysis of such properties, the analyst uses the geographic area that constitutes the appropriate local economic area. It is often helpful in large markets to break the market down in geographic sectors that represent the major office districts and nodes of development, but this may not be used except for particular steps in the analysis. Given that many demanders of office space may not have strong requirements or preferences for a specific location (although they often do require a location in the general area), the economic area chosen is typically large (i.e., a central city, county, or MSA). The need for an employment forecast is another practical reason to work initially with a larger economic area. Employment forecasts, using data by place of employment, may be obtained for larger economic areas from planning agencies, state development agencies, and private firms, such as the National Planning Association, Washington, D.C. Allocating a portion of total employment to specific geographic areas or to a subject property to estimate absorption rates is handled later in the analysis, if the assignment requires demand at a particular location to be estimated.

Demand Analysis

Major steps in an analysis of the aggregate local demand for office space include (1) delimiting the geographic area to be analyzed, (2) deriving "white-collar" office employment from total local employment, (3) forecasting this office employment, and, possibly, (4) allocating to the net new demand for space in new or renovated buildings an additional component of demand resulting from an internal market shift of existing office tenants from lesser to better quality space.

Other information required are the square feet currently needed per office employee and, if the square feet per employee is expressed as net rentable area, the average efficiency ratio that expands rentable square feet to gross building area. Gross building area is the total area of the building in square feet. Net rentable area is the amount of space available to rent to tenants. Common elements such as hallways, entryways, and so on are generally excluded from the net rentable area unless the tenants have the exclusive use of such areas. The efficiency ratio is net rentable area divided by gross building area.

When the assignment involves assessing the demand at a particular site or for a given project, a forecast must be made of the capture rate that allocates a portion of aggregate local demand to a specific property or geographic area. The client will want an assessment of the absorption rate for the proposed project (i.e., the number of spare feet expected to be rented per year). The client will also need recommendations regarding the most probable market rent, lease terms, and package of amenities required to maximize the marketability of the property.

Supply Analysis

An aggregate supply analysis requires analyzing competitive properties in the local market, including (1) existing occupied properties, (2) properties that are vacant and available for rent, (3) properties under construction, (4) properties under permit, (5) properties planned for construction, and (6) properties that can be used for office construction in the future.

When the analysis is on the aggregate level, the analyst should document the level and trend of (1) square footage of competitive space added to the existing stock, (2) market absorption rates, and (3) vacancy rates. The assumptions and judgment required in the demand analysis make the supply side analysis of office markets extremely important. Past and recent occupancy and absorption experiences in the market should be examined for confirmation of demand forecasts. A demand forecast must be carefully examined and documented if it suggests future market absorption rates and vacancy levels significantly different from an observed level and trend.

Absorption

When the assignment involves a particular site or project in a metropolitan area, the analyst often selects properties that are judged to be directly competitive with the subject property and obtains detailed information on this component of the aggregate local supply. The classification system for market disaggregation helps to focus on specific market sectors. Then, planned construction, permits issued, and properties under construction or vacant and available also are ascertained for that portion of the local market judged directly competitive with the subject property. The characteristics of the subject property are carefully compared to the immediate competition. Rental terms, amenities provided, locational attributes, and physical characteristics of the competition are compared with their absorption rates and vacancy levels to recommend attainable rental terms and the necessary amenity package that will enhance the marketability of the subject property. Observed absorption rates are reviewed in the context of overall market conditions and with respect to this property's ability to attract a share of forecast aggregate demand. Again, if the analysis indicates an absorption rate for the subject property that deviates significantly from the actual experience of competitive properties, the analyst must carefully review the assumptions, the facts, and the analysis. To avoid the "volitional fallacy," the analyst should exercise extreme caution in assuming that the subject property will capture more than its indicated share of forecast demand. The share for a single project, even in small markets, will rarely exceed 10 to 15 percent, and usually is well below that proportion.

The absorption analysis is the nexus between the results of disaggregation of demand matched against supply and the results of the competition analysis. The former indicate basic changes in the market; the latter only indicate recent experience.

SUMMARY

Once the specific characteristics of office space under analysis have been identified and the geographic and economic dimensions of the market taken into account, the analyst moves to an analysis of aggregate demand and supply. Following observations about the level and strength of market outcomes, the site-specific elements can then be explicitly considered. In the next chapter, methods for estimating aggregate demand and supply and for evaluating site-specific elements required for an office marketability study are discussed.

READINGS

BIBLE, DOUGLAS, and JOHN W. WHALEY, "Projecting an Urban Office Market: A Source of Information for Appraisers," *The Appraisal Journal*, October, 1983.

DETOY, CHARLES J., and SOL L. RABIN, "Office Space: Calculating the Demand," *Urban Land*, June, 1972.

DOWNS, ANTHONY, "How Much Office Space Will We Need In The Future?," *National Real Estate Investor*, February, 1983.

KELLY, HUGH F., "Forecasting Office Space Demand," *Real Estate Review*, Fall, 1983.

JENNINGS, CHRISTOPHER R., "Predicting Demand for Office Space," *Appraisal Journal*, July, 1965.

12

TECHNIQUES OF PERFORMING OFFICE MARKET ANALYSIS

Survey of the Competition

Assumptions and Limitations
Methodology
Competitive Differentials

SUMMARY

INTRODUCTION

Once the analyst identifies the specific product, defines the geographic extent of the market area, and thoroughly understands the nature, characteristics, and data sources of the local office market, it is time to undertake the analyses and forecasts required to estimate relevant market outcomes. The analyst is interested, first, in evaluating the local office market supply and demand conditions. The first step in the analysis will indicate if absorption of office space on the market adequately supports prevailing rent levels, and if there is adequate support for the scale and type of office development activities present in the market. Second, the analyst investigates the sector of the market within which particular projects are competing. This second phase will deal with specific characteristics that underlie a project's ability to compete in the market. Upon completion of these steps, the analyst is able to address questions that deal with the amount of space, type of space, timing of the offering, location of the projects, amenity level and design features to be included, and, critically, rental levels that can be supported. Many more detailed questions may be addressed along with specific investment and feasibility aspects of a particular project.

There are three basic tasks the analyst undertakes in performing an office market analysis. The tasks are

1. Evaluate supply and demand of office space generally in the market and forecast salient absorption characteristics.
2. Focus on specific sectors of the market and determine supply and demand conditions along with competitive characteristics and differentials that help to explain how specific tenant groups and specific developments contribute to the absorption and successful operation of the office market.
3. Address specific questions about market conditions, operation of the specific sector of the market and other market factors that are needed to devise strategies and programs required for feasibility analyses, operational plans, and other pertinent actions.

AGGREGATE ANALYSIS OF THE OFFICE MARKET

The following analysis assumes that the analyst has decided to perform a marketability study for a "business park" project. A "business park" development is one in which the tenant is offered office space with supporting warehousing space, research and development facilities, or production space. The space is developed on a speculative basis as unfinished space, but it is marketed to tenants at rent levels for finished space, giving the tenants an ample allowance for finishing and other tenant improvements. Thus the project is competitive with other Class A speculative office space and office-industrial space, but the tenant has the opportunity to specify the amenity level and other critical features and still lease at competitive rents. The initial general market demand analysis considers the aggregate demand for all categories of office space. The site-specific analysis narrows the focus down to those developments directly competitive with the business park concept.

Aggregate Demand Analysis

The market analyst is initially concerned with the demand for speculative office space available for rent or for sale to a general tenantry. Conceptually, this office space demand is the net result of

Local firms expanding
    plus
Local firms upgrading
    plus
New firms originating locally
    plus
Firms relocating into the market
    less
Local firms contracting
    less
Local firms ceasing business
    less
Local firms exiting the market[1]

The principle source of this demand are firms seeking quarters for clerical, supervisory, and management personnel engaged in providing services and products to the consumer. Accountants, attorneys, insurance and real estate agencies, advertising and public relations firms, doctors, dentists, government agencies not in public buildings, stock brokerage firms, and mortgage companies are among the users of speculative office space.

A component of aggregate market demand comes from local firms expanding employment or upgrading the quality of their office space as the demand for their services and products increases. Some of these firms serve the

[1]This concept of office space demand is a modification of a concept initially cited by Charles J. Detoy and Sol L. Rabin, "Office Space: Calculating the Demand," *Urban Land*, June 1972, pp. 4–13.

local economic area and comprise part of the nonbasic or service component of the local economic base; other local firms may serve regional and national markets and are part of the basic or export component of the community's economic base. The analyst must understand the nature of the local economy, for local prosperity is basic to any forecast of the demand for office space.

Other office space users include the headquarter offices of local and nonlocal firms. When headquarter offices are constructed new for owner-occupancy, the firm is classified as nonspeculative and is not part of the demand for speculative space. Headquarter offices that locate or expand by purchasing or renting existing space are components of the demand for speculative space. The analyst cannot easily forecast the entry of nonlocal (regional, national) headquarter offices into the market. Certain communities have the attributes that are attractive to these companies, which are responding to the structure of their markets for products and services and to the geographic dispersion of their plants and subsidiaries. While factors such as the cultural, social, educational, and economic attributes of a community, the availability of a trained labor force, climate, and transportation can be important in the decision to locate a headquarters office, at times the site may simply be the location preferred by top management. When possible, the market analyst should isolate the component of past demand for space attributable to new nonlocal headquarters operations and estimate whether this source of office employment will continue to materialize in any office employment forecast. An inventory of office space distinguishing between speculative and nonspeculative categories will help to provide the proportion of total demand that should be targeted for speculative space. If no such inventory is available, alternative means of proportioning must be employed.

Owner-occupants that construct new space for their own use are not part of the demand for speculative office space. However, not all owner-occupants are excluded: firms that purchase and occupy space that has been constructed on speculation are a component of the local demand. Such companies may acquire all or part of an existing building for their own use, perhaps leaving a part of their acquired property available for rent until they need the excess space. The expansion of an owner-user into space previously available for general tenancy is part of the total local demand for office space when it takes available space off the market.

Practically all firms require some amount of office space. The analyst, however, is not generally concerned with the demand for auxiliary office space from industrial plants, warehouses, and retail stores which provide offices for management as an integral part of the building that comprises their plant or store. When the offices connected with these enterprises are separated from the plant or store, they become part of the demand for speculative space and the analyst should incorporate these needs into forecasted aggregate local demand. However, specifically identifying the contribution to aggregate demand from manufacturing office employment in detached space is tenuous. Further, the proportion of office employment in local manufacturing will vary with the mix of manufacturing employment by industry.[2]

Forecast of Local Employment by Industry The geographic area for local employment forecast in an office market study is typically the county or MSA. The area chosen is large enough to contain all significant office developments and represents a geographic area for which employment data are available. The market analyst may purchase employment forecasts from a respected research organization, such as CACI or the National Planning Association. For instance, the National Planning Association provides regional employment forecasts for all Bureau Economic Areas (BEAs), Metropolitan Statistical Areas (MSAs), states, and counties. Keeping in mind that the real estate market analyst typically is not a population forecasting demographer or an employment forecasting economist, reliance on expert opinion is suggested. However, the analyst may prepare employment forecasts for independent use or as a check on estimates obtained from other sources. Such forecasts can be done by a proportionate analysis that relates county employment to available state or national forecasts. A two-stage employment forecasting model can be used to perform these tasks. The model first correlates past state and national employment, and then forecasts state employment by taking the indicated proportion (past state employment/past national employment) times an independent forecast of national employment. National employment projections are available from the Bureau of Labor Statistics and the Bureau of Economic Analysis. The local employment forecast is then accomplished by using an independently obtained estimate of future state employment times the historic ratio of local employment to state employment. When an independent forecast of state employment is available, the process reduces to the single-stage relationship of local to state employment. These single-stage (local/state) proportionate techniques are shown in Exhibit 12-1.

Proportionate analysis assumes that past trends in local employment relative to the state will persist into the short-run forecast period. Proportionate share analysis can be modified by using a three-year average of local to state employment to establish past relationships. The three years selected are spaced at five-year intervals and produce an average that helps to avoid misstatement of a proportionate share based on a single year's data. Local employment fluctuations could distort the relationship at a point in time.

Another modification of proportionate share utilizes a multiplier that indicates whether the local area has been increasing in population at a more (or

---

[2]In one study, 22 percent of manufacturing employment in southeastern Virginia was estimated to be office workers, with 55 percent of these workers assumed to be in detached space. Douglas S. Bible and John Whaley, "Projecting an Urban Office Market: A Source of Information for Appraisers," *Appraisal Journal*, October 1983, pp. 515–523. Another study estimated that white-collar jobs accounted for 37 percent of all New York City manufacturing employment in 1980, with white-collar ratios varying widely from industry to industry (from 88 percent in the tobacco industry to 33 percent in furniture). Hugh F. Kelly, "Forecasting Office Space Demand," *Real Estate Review*, Fall 1983, pp. 87–95.

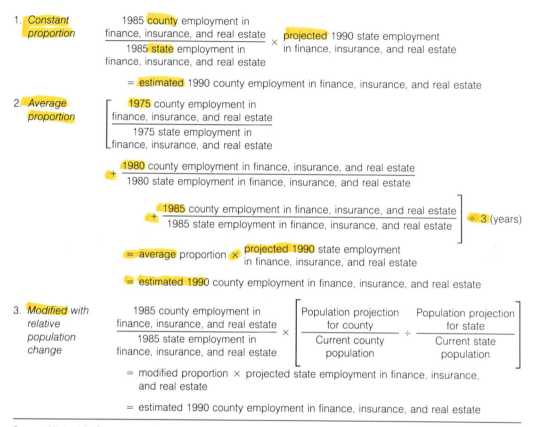

1. *Constant proportion*

$$\frac{\text{1985 county employment in finance, insurance, and real estate}}{\text{1985 state employment in finance, insurance, and real estate}} \times \text{projected 1990 state employment in finance, insurance, and real estate}$$

= estimated 1990 county employment in finance, insurance, and real estate

2. *Average proportion*

$$\left[\frac{\text{1975 county employment in finance, insurance, and real estate}}{\text{1975 state employment in finance, insurance, and real estate}} \right.$$

$$+ \frac{\text{1980 county employment in finance, insurance, and real estate}}{\text{1980 state employment in finance, insurance, and real estate}}$$

$$\left. + \frac{\text{1985 county employment in finance, insurance, and real estate}}{\text{1985 state employment in finance, insurance, and real estate}} \right] \div 3 \text{ (years)}$$

= average proportion × projected 1990 state employment in finance, insurance, and real estate

= estimated 1990 county employment in finance, insurance, and real estate

3. *Modified with relative population change*

$$\frac{\text{1985 county employment in finance, insurance, and real estate}}{\text{1985 state employment in finance, insurance, and real estate}} \times \left[\frac{\text{Population projection for county}}{\text{Current county population}} \div \frac{\text{Population projection for state}}{\text{Current state population}} \right]$$

= modified proportion × projected state employment in finance, insurance, and real estate

= estimated 1990 county employment in finance, insurance, and real estate

SOURCE: Michael R. Greenberg et al., *Local Population and Employment Projection Techniques* (New Brunswick, N.J.: Center for Urban Policy Research, Rutgers University, 1978).

Exhibit 12-1 Forecasting Local Employment by Industry.

less) rapid rate than the state (also shown on Exhibit 12-1). A population multiplier greater than 1.0 would indicate a local population growth rate in excess of the state population increase. In this instance, employment would be expected to increase, particularly in employment categories that serve the local population (nonbasic employment). This latter variation of proportionate analysis can be appropriate for an analysis of the demand for office space, since nonbasic employment are users of speculative office space. Alternatively, a simple linear regression also can be used to estimate future employment. Historical employment data (a three-year moving average is suggested to minimize local fluctuations in employment) is regressed against time using least squares linear regression. At least five years of employment data should be used in projecting the trend (seven years of data will provide five three-year moving averages).

The examples in Exhibit 12-1 assume that a state forecast of employment by industry is available (or can be derived from a national forecast). If such detail is not available, the local total employment must be forecast and then distributed by industry using historic local proportions. Sufficient past data should be examined to reveal any changes in the structure of local employment by industry. Classification of employment by industry in the 1970 and 1980 Census of Population can reveal changes in local employment patterns.

In Exhibit 12-2, a single-stage constant proportion forecast of county wage and salary employment is accomplished. The 1980 local employment in each industry is divided by the 1980 state employment in that industry to obtain the 1980 percentage of state employment in the industry accounted for by the county. That percentage is then multiplied times an independently obtained forecast of state employment by industry for 1990 to obtain the 1990 county employment in that industry.

The employment data used for the forecast given in Exhibit 12-2 are from the U.S. Department of Commerce, Bureau of the Census, *County Business Patterns. County Business Patterns* does not cover (1) government workers, (2) self-employed persons, (3) farm workers, (4) domestic service workers, and (5) railroad workers. Of these occupations, self-employed persons and government

Exhibit 12-2   Forecast of Wage and Salary Employment by Industry.*

	1980			1990	
	County Employment†	*State Employment†*	*% State Employment*	*Forecast State Employment‡*	*Forecast County Employment*
Agricultural, forestry and fisheries	810	10,282	0.079	10,500	830
Manufacturing	12,457	1,267,600	0.010	1,436,100	14,360
Mining	618	30,800	0.020	40,200	800
Construction	13,862	180,100	0.077	211,000	16,250
Transportation and public utilities	21,549	254,400	0.085	280,500	23,840
Wholesale trade	27,854	148,200	0.188	171,500	32,240
Retail trade	81,719	740,800	0.110	861,400	94,750
Finance, insurance, and real estate	37,132	206,000	0.180	250,200	45,036
Services	90,027	1,500,500	0.060	1,742,900	104,575

*The breakdown of employment in this exhibit uses categories of economic divisions from the Standard Industrial Code. SIC classifications are based on establishments classified by their major activity. Employment is first divided into broad economic divisions A–K. Economic division I is services and includes establishments primarily providing services for individuals; business and government establishments; hotels and lodging places, establishments providing personal, business, repair, and amusement services; health, legal, engineering, and other professional services; educational institutions; and others. Economic divisions are broken down into major groups (two-digit code), industry groups (three-digit), and industry definitions (four-digit). Economic division I (services), for instance, has a Major Group 70 (hotels, rooming houses, camps, and other lodging places), an Industry group 701 (hotels, motels, and tourist courts), and an Industry definition 7011 (hotels, motels, and tourist courts). The SIC Manual is published by the U.S. Technical Committee on Industrial Classification.
†U.S. Department of Commerce, Bureau of the Census, *County Business Patterns.*
‡State Department of Development.

workers can constitute demand for office space, although only government workers in nonpublic buildings are part of the demand for speculative space. Employment reported in *County Business Patterns* can be increased to an estimate of total employment by industry by developing a multiplier from information in the Census of Population:

$$\frac{\text{1980 U.S. total employment in industry A}}{\text{1980 U.S. wage and salary employment in industry A}}$$

$$\times \text{ Estimated 1990 wage and salary employment in industry A}$$
$$= \text{total estimated 1990 employment in industry A}$$

Use of this multiplier assumes that the relationship between total employment and wage and salary employment remains constant over time and that the local area is typical of the United States as a whole.

Government employment must be separately forecast. To include government workers, sum the service and public administration industries as reported in the *Census of Population* in developing the numerator of the employment multiplier shown. Use only United States service industry wage and salary employment in the denominator. The resultant multiplier, when taken times the service employment projection developed using *County Business Patterns* ratios, will provide an estimated combined employment in service and public administration. Alternatively, the U.S. Department of Labor, Bureau of Labor Statistics, "Employment, Hours and Earnings, States and Areas" provides government employment for MSAs, or the *Census of Population*, 1970 and 1980, may be used to independently forecast 1990 employment in public administration.

Exhibit 12-3 transforms wage and salary employment shown in Exhibit 12-2 into total employment for the county. The multipliers in Exhibit 12-3 vary by industry with the proportion of self-employed and other workers not included in wage and salary employment. The 1980 *Census of Population* provides the information for derivation of the multipliers. For example, the 1980 wage and salary employment in agriculture, forestry, and fisheries in the United States was 1,342,247; total employment in that industry in the United States was 2,913,589, indicating a multiplier of 2.17. Agriculture, forestry and fisheries, construction, and transportation and public utilities are categories with relatively large proportions of self-employed. Mining, manufacturing, and wholesale trade have significantly smaller proportions of workers not classified as wage and salary employees.

Office-User (White-Collar) Employment A component of the employment in each industry is engaged in occupations that require office space. Such workers are usually referred to as "white-collar" employees. However, not all white-collar employees are users of office space. Retail sales workers, for instance, are a major white-collar occupation which often does not require desk space.

Exhibit 12-3 Total County Employment Forecast by Industry.

INDUSTRY	1980			1990		
	Wage and Salary Employment	Employment Multiplier*	Total Employment	Wage and Salary Employment	Employment Multiplier*	Total Employment
Agricultural services, forestry, fisheries	810	2.17	1,760	830	2.17	1,800
Mining	618	1.04	640	800	1.04	830
Construction	13,862	1.32	18,300	16,250	1.32	21,450
Manufacturing	12,467	1.08	13,460	14,360	1.08	15,500
Transportation and public utilities	21,549	1.30	28,010	23,840	1.30	30,990
Wholesale trade	27,854	1.06	29,530	32,240	1.06	34,170
Retail trade	81,719	1.10	89,940	94,750	1.10	104,220
Finance, insurance, and real estate	37,132	1.11	41,220	45,036	1.11	49,990
Services and public administration	90,027	1.98	178,250	104,575	1.98†	207,060

*Multiplier adjustment for self-employed:

$$\frac{1980 \text{ U.S. total employment in industry}}{1980 \text{ U.S. wage and salary employment in industry}} \times \text{estimated county wage and salary employment in industry} = \text{estimated total 1990 county employment in industry}$$

†Multiplier adjustment for self-employed in services and to add employment in public adminstration:

$$\frac{1980 \text{ U.S. total employment in services and public adminstration}}{1980 \text{ U.S. wage and salary employment in services}} \times \text{estimated total county employment in services}$$
= estimated total county employment in services and public administration

To estimate the proportion of office-using workers from each industry, the cross-classification of state industrial employment by occupation in the 1980 *Census of Population* is used. Cross-classification of industry employment by occupation also is available in previous censuses, but without the detail of the 1980 census.[3] Because of the greater detail in the 1980 census, it is preferable to use the 1980 cross-classifications to derive office-using employment by industry and to retain that ratio over the employment forecast period, rather than projecting a trend in the ratio of white-collar employment by industry based on changes in the ratios observed from previous decennial censuses. Using a ratio derived only from 1980 data will capture the shift up to 1980 in the increased proportion of white-collar workers in the structure of employment. Not permitting the ratio to change over the employment forecast period will provide a conservative estimate of office-using workers.

Exhibit 12-4 provides the office-using, white-collar employment by industry for the state. The proportions of office using occupations range from 6.2 percent in agriculture, forestry, and fisheries to 67.1 percent in finance, insurance, and real estate. The major categories of occupations accumulated as office users are portions of managerial and professional specialty occupations and technical, sales, and administrative support occupations. Employment from other occupational categories could be included for a more complete estimate. However, the proportion of office workers for these categories is extremely small, and these office users are not usually tenants in speculative space. Except in specific instances, they do not add measurably to the demand for speculative office space. Also, several subcategories of occupations are not included in the estimate of office workers because the occupations generally do not constitute tenantry in speculative office space.[4]

Modifications to Office-Using Employment   The market analyst may refine the forecast number of office-using workers by recognizing that the office-using employment in an industry, such as manufacturing, are not all occupants of speculative office space. A portion of white-collar manufacturing employment occupies offices which are part of the company's plant. Further, a large component of public administration employment will be found in public buildings and not in speculative space provided by the private sector for general tenantry.

[3]The 1970 *Census of Population* reports, by industry, employment in the occupation groups of Professional, Technical, and Kindred; Managers and Administrators; and Clerical and Kindred, which comprise the major categories of office space users. Other categories in the 1970 Census are Sales Workers; Craftsmen and Kindred; Operatives, Except Transport; Transport Equipment Operatives; Laborers, Excluding Farm; Farm Workers; and Service Workers, Including Household. The greater occupational detail in the 1980 Census permits refinement in the judgment required to select categories that represent office workers.

[4]Subcategories removed are public administration and education administration administrators; health-related occupations; teachers; writers, authors, entertainers, and athletes; sales occupations; and supervisors. All "blue-collar" categories are omitted (service occupations; farming; construction trades; etc.).

Exhibit 12-4 Office Users (occupation of employed persons) by Industry, State Data, 1980.

OCCUPATION*	AGRICULTURE, FORESTRY, AND FISHERIES	MINING	MANUFACTURING	CONSTRUCTION	TRANSPORTATION, COMMUNICATION, AND PUBLIC UTILITIES	WHOLESALE TRADE	RETAIL TRADE	FINANCE, INSURANCE, AND REAL ESTATE	SERVICES AND PUBLIC ADMINISTRATION	TOTALS
Managerial and professional specialty occupations†	2,575	3,100	164,403	19,313	31,633	30,759	78,854	48,708	153,350	425,847
Technical sales and administrative support‡	2,541	2,988	169,325	14,257	84,238	40,984	70,405	105,547	243,872	565,171
Total office users	5,116	6,088	333,728	33,570	115,871	71,743	149,259	154,255	397,222	991,018
Total all employed persons	82,525	30,989	1,373,172	209,447	302,310	186,605	742,698	229,779	1,400,867	4,170,438
Percent office users	0.062	0.196	0.243	0.160	0.383	0.384	0.201	0.671	0.283	0.237

*Occupations not included are service occupations; farming; forestry and fishing; precision, production, craft, and repair occupations; construction trades; extractive occupations; precision production; operators, fabricators, and laborers; transportation and material moving; handlers, equipment cleaners, helpers, and laborers.

†Occupations not included are public administration administrators; education administration administrators; health diagnosing; health assessment and treating; registered nurses; teachers; writers, authors, entertainers, and athletes.

‡Occupations included are administrative support occupations, including clerical; not included are sales occupations and supervisors.

SOURCE: 1980 U.S. Census of Population, *Detailed Characteristics*, Table 224.

Also, in the services industries, only the industry categories of business services and professional and related services generate office users likely to be found in speculative office space.

The analyst may refine the 20,880 expected increase in office-using workers, 1980–1990 (Exhibit 12-5), by allocating only portions of the increase in manufacturing employment and services and public administration employment to the final demand for office space. Bible and Whaley suggest that approximately 50 percent of the office-using manufacturing employment is in the market for detached space.[5] Other location specific ratios based on local occupancy data may be more appropriate in specific applications.

Service industries comprise about 51 percent of total 1990 industry employment shown in Exhibit 12-5 as "Service and Public Administration," or 140,570 of the total 207,060 employees in the combined category. The categories of business services and professional and related services account for approximately 83 percent of all service industries employment (excluding repair services, but including private households, hotels and lodging places, and entertainment and recreation services). In this county, about 20 percent of public administration employment has been occupying office space provided by the private sector. This percentage can differ substantially among communities, and the analyst must determine the proper allocation from information provided by federal, state, and local authorities. In many communities, public administration employment may not be a significant share of total local employment, or they may be almost entirely housed in public buildings. In these instances, the analyst may choose to omit public administration employment altogether from the forecast of office-using employment.

As shown below, modifying the office user forecast of 20,880 employees to reflect the foregoing factors results in a net increase of 16,720, after removal of the manufacturing, service industries, and public administration office users not expected to be in speculative office space. (Calculations are rounded.)

Manufacturing:

$$
\begin{array}{rl}
500 & \text{office-user increase total} \\
\times 0.50 & \text{in speculative space} \\
\hline
250 & \text{office users in speculative space}
\end{array}
$$

Services and public administration:

$$
\begin{array}{rl}
8,160 & \text{office-user increase} \\
\times 0.51 & \text{services industry employment} \\
\hline
4,160 & \text{service industry increase} \\
\times 0.83 & \text{in speculative space} \\
\hline
3,450 & \text{service industry office users in speculative space}
\end{array}
$$

[5]Douglas S. Bible and John W. Whaley, "Projecting an Urban Office Market: A Source of Information for Appraisers," *The Appraisal Journal*, October 1983, pp. 515–523.

Exhibit 12-5 Office User Forecast for County 1980–1990.

INDUSTRY	1980			1990			1980–1990
	Industry Employment*	Percentage of Office Users†	Number of Office Users	Industry Employment*	Percentage of Office Users†	Number of Office Users	Change in Office Users
Agriculture, forestry, and fisheries	1,760	0.062	110	1,800	0.062	110	—
Mining	640	0.196	120	830	0.196	160	40
Construction	18,300	0.160	2,930	21,450	0.160	3,430	500
Manufacturing	13,460	0.243	3,270	15,500	0.243	3,770	500
Transportation and public utilities	28,010	0.383	10,730	30,990	0.383	11,870	1,140
Wholesale trade	29,530	0.384	11,340	34,170	0.384	13,120	1,780
Retail trade	89,890	0.201	18,070	104,220	0.201	20,950	2,880
Finance, insurance, and real estate	41,220	0.671	27,660	49,990	0.671	33,540	5,880
Services and public administration	178,250	0.283	50,440	207,060	0.283	58,600	8,160
Total							20,880

*Exhibit 12-3.
†Exhibit 12-4.

```
 8,160  office-user increase
×0.49  public administration employment
 4,000  public administration increase
×0.20  percent in speculative space
   800  public administration office users in speculative space
```

```
 8,660  total manufacturing, services, and public administration increase
 4,500  less portion in speculative space (250 + 3,450 + 800)
 4,160  employee increase not in speculative space
```

```
20,880  total office-user increase
-4,160  not in speculative space
16,720  office users in speculative space
```

These modifications have been presented to show the reasoning of the analyst. In the report to the client, the analyst may choose to show these modifications in office-using employment without the detailed analysis. For instance, in the report, the percentage of office users in the services and public administration category, shown in Exhibit 12-5 as 28.3 percent, would be converted to office users in speculative space and shown as 14.7 percent (3,450 + 800 = 4,250 ÷ 8,160 = 0.521 × 0.283 = 0.1474). Then, the number of office users in 1980 would be reported as 26,270 (178,250 × 0.1474) and in 1990 as 30,520 (207,060 × 0.1474), for an increase in office users taking speculative space of 4,250 rather than the 8,160 total office users shown in this category in Exhibit 12-5. Similarly, the 500 increase in office users in manufacturing would be shown as approximately a 250 increase by using a 12.2 percent factor rather than 24.3 percent given in Exhibit 12-5.

Office Space per Employee   Estimated office-using employment must be converted into the needed square feet of office space. Office space per worker varies by occupational classification, with managers and professional individuals occupying more square feet of space (300–500 square feet) than clerks and secretaries (65–80 square feet). Government workers occupy 10 to 15 percent less square feet per worker than their private sector counterparts. The changing character of business operations also affects the square foot per employee ratio, with the provision of employee lounges, libraries, space for computers, and other amenities tending to increase the amount of square feet per employee. On the other hand, the rising cost of construction presses for design standards that reduce the square feet needed per employee while maintaining an aura of spaciousness. All these factors combine to affect the average square feet per employee, which can range from 200 to 220 square feet. The average changes over time, and the market analyst must verify the ratio used in the study. Professional organizations, such as the Builders-Owners-Managers Association (BOMA), Realtors National Marketing Institute, or the Institute for Real Estate Management, are sources of information to develop the ratio. The market analyst also should verify the assumed ratio by observation of typical local office buildings.

The number of square feet per employee provides a measure of occupied office space. Hallways, foyers, storage rooms, and other common areas of office buildings must be accounted for to estimate the gross building area (total area of the building in square feet). To estimate total building area, an average efficiency ratio is applied to the average square feet per employee. The efficiency ratio is net rentable area divided by gross building area. Net rentable area is the amount of space available to rent to tenants and may be measured differently among localities (BOMA has one definition; the "New York" convention is another). In general, the tighter the office market, the more building area landlords are able to include in net rentable area. For purposes of this analysis, occupied area (200 square feet per employee) is assumed to equal net rentable area. An efficiency ratio of 85 percent converts 200 square feet of occupied area to a gross building area of about 235 square feet (200 sq. ft. ÷ 0.85 sq. ft. = 253.3 sq. ft.). Efficiency ratios generally range from 80 to 85 percent.

Aggregate Need for Office Space In our example, the adjusted increase of 16,720 office users in the county provides an estimated total need for 3,929,200 gross square feet of office space (16,720 × 235 sq. ft. per person) over the 10-year projection period. On the average, the market will demand approximately 393,000 square feet per year, 1980–1990. This indication of aggregate need for speculative office space must be combined with an analysis of existing and potential supply to speculate about absorption levels and other future market conditions.

Aggregate Supply Analysis

An analysis of aggregate demand for speculative space must be combined with an analysis of existing and potential supply to make supportable estimates about overall market conditions in the foreseeable future. The analyst may conduct surveys of existing office buildings and obtain permit data and information from planning agencies and developers to estimate planned construction and construction in progress. A variety of other sources provide information about local office markets, including Coldwell Banker; *Black's Guide to Office Space* (332 Broad Street, Red Bank, N.J. 07701); *National Office Market Report* (The Office Network 3200, One Shell Plaza, Houston, Tex. 77002), as well as large local commercial brokerage firms. The information varies in coverage (selected cities) and in detail.

If secondary data sources are available and the data are considered reliable and accurate, the aggregate inventory of current office space can then be included in the analysis. In larger markets, the local sources compiling an inventory of office space often subdivide the data by local geographic sectors but generally do not include office data by type of space or amenity level, except on the basis of locally defined Class A, B, or C categories. The analyst may update secondary sources or, in a few instances, perform a new survey using office space categories suggested earlier that provide more specific information about the attractiveness and marketability of the office space under analysis. However the inventory is obtained, certain additional information about each type of space is needed:

1. Gross square feet of space supplied per year.
2. Gross square feet under construction and in permits issued.
3. Locational qualities.
4. Proportion that is single-user space (multiple tenant).
5. Leased space (percentage occupied and vacant).
6. Absorption rate (thousands of square feet per year offered and occupied).
7. Rental ranges (with tenant concessions taken into account).
8. Comments (recent trends in typical rents, etc.).

This information permits the analyst to conclude that demand and supply in the market are in balance or that conditions of oversupply or excess demand exist. For the analyst to speculate about market conditions in the forseeable future, several pieces of information are needed, particularly;

1. Present levels of occupancy.
2. Recent trends in occupancy rates.
3. Levels of absorption by rental range or class.
4. Expected levels of new construction.
5. Forecasts of aggregate demand.

Within the context of these general market conditions, the prospects for a particular property can be analyzed.

Existing Office Space Analysis   The properties indicated in Exhibit 12-6 constitute the existing Class A space in the defined market area. The information was compiled from a field inspection of each property and data obtained from several secondary data sources.

The dividing line for Class A space was difficult to distinguish because of the quality of new business parks and research and development office buildings. There is a considerable amount of space which is borderline Class A and therefore might be considered as competition. However, the properties indicated in Exhibit 12-6 satisfy the physical characteristics and market rents and are considered competitive.

The data in Exhibit 12-6 reflect a total of approximately 1,534,524 square feet of rentable office space. As of the survey date, there were 666,222 square feet leased, reflecting an existing occupancy rate of 43.4 percent.

LOCATION/ BUILDING		TOTAL RENTABLE AREA	TOTAL RENTABLE LEASED	TOTAL RENTABLE VACANCY	OCCUPANCY PERCENT
L-1	Building A-1	112,500	0	112,500	0%
	Building A-2	112,500	20,000	92,500	18
L-2	Building B	124,850	95,733	29,117	77
L-3	Building C	72,500	56,300	16,200	78
L-4	Building D	60,000	20,000	40,000	33
L-5	Building E	88,274	35,000	53,274	40
L-6	Building F*	55,000	0	55,000	0
L-7	Building G	60,000	56,000	4,000	93
L-8	Building H	60,000	57,000	3,000	95
L-9	Building I*	140,000	30,000	125,000	21
L-10	Building J	160,900	35,900	125,000	22
L-11	Building K1	42,000	37,345	4,655	89
	Building K2	42,000	38,897	3,103	93
	Building K3	95,000	88,100	6,900	92.7
	Building K4	95,000	55,447	39,553	58
	Building K5*	103,000	0	103,000	0
L-12	Building L	111,000	30,500	80,500	
	Totals	1,534,524	666,222	878,302	

*Indicates space in final completion stages.

Exhibit 12-6   Class A Office Market Comparable Summary.

As a supplement to this information, one 1985 secondary data source indicates that there are 2,900,000 square feet of existing Class A office space in a larger geographic area that includes the study area. Their review further shows that there are approximately 1,210,000 square feet vacant, amounting to a 58.3 percent occupancy rate. Although the report accounts for a broader market area than that identified in this analysis, the vacancy percentage is worth noting.

Another secondary data source further reports that space built prior to 1985 maintained an 82 percent occupancy level. Office space made available in 1985 had a 22 percent occupancy level. Their aggregate supply forecast indicated a 47 percent occupancy level in the market, based on an estimate of 1,750,000 square feet of Class A space available.

The secondary data estimates of Class A space available were considerably greater than the primary data shown in this report. These variations are primarily due to a broader definition of market area and classification of Class A space. Therefore, for the purpose of this analysis, the amount of existing Class A space is estimated at 1,550,000 square feet. Utilizing 1,550,000 square feet as the amount of existing space, there is approximately 880,000 square feet of existing space for lease, or about 57 percent of the total space. This estimate reflects a high percentage of new space in the total inventory. The percentage used is consistent with that developed in Exhibit 12-6.

LOCATION/ BUILDING	TOTAL RENTABLE AREA (SQUARE FEET)	PRELEASED RENTABLE AREA (SQUARE FEET)	COMPLETION DATE
C-1 Building M	30,000	4,500	Summer '86
C-2 Building N-1	50,000	0	Summer '86
C-2 Building N-2	40,000	0	Summer '86
Total	120,000	4,500	

SOURCE: Field inspection.

Exhibit 12-7   Class A Office Construction Activity Summary.

Analysis of Projects under Construction   To determine an estimate of construction activity in the submarket, a field inspection of the area was conducted. There were only three sites identified as projects under construction, as shown in Exhibit 12-7.

Conversations with developers indicated that of a total of 120,000 square feet under construction, only 4,500 square feet was preleased. Thus, when construction is complete, an additional 115,500 square feet of speculative space will be introduced into the market.

Estimation of Future Projects   Performing an accurate estimation of future projects is a difficult task which has many limitations. Obtaining information within a limited time frame, developers that are less than completely open about sharing their plans for the future, and changing market conditions are just some of the problems which complicate compiling information about future office developments. Despite these difficulties, a field inspection of possible development sites and interviews with respective landowners are needed to supplement other data.

In Exhibit 12-8, a recap of identified development sites is shown with corresponding location references to Exhibit 12-6. Several projects, shown as locations D-2, D-3, D-4 and D-7 respectively, are all planned as business park developments included in Exhibit 12-7 or elsewhere, and their floor area is not included in this forecast.

Conversation with the developer of the D-1 Project indicated that the property would have 11 additional buildings upon completion, with 110,000 to 120,000 square feet in each. The start-up dates for construction are not definite at this time and will be determined by market conditions.

Development of the D-5 project is scheduled to start at the end of 1986. The property will bring another 650,000 square feet into the market. The developer also indicated that it will begin building 400,000 more square feet at a nearby site in 1986.

The D-8 developer indicated that the development is planning to introduce 2,000,000 more square feet of Class A office space. The starting date for this would also be dictated by market conditions. In addition, developers of the

LOCATION	TOTAL RENTABLE AREA (SQUARE FEET)	NUMBER OF BUILDINGS	START-UP DATE
D-1	1,100,000	11	Market determined
D-2	0	0	N/A
D-3	0	0	N/A
D-4	0	0	N/A
D-5	650,000	?	1986–87
D-6	400,000	?	1986–87
D-7	0	0	N/A
D-8	2,000,000	?	Market determined
D-9	300,000	?	Market determined
D-10	100,000	1	1986–87
	1,000,000	?	Market determined
Total	5,550,000		

SOURCE: Field inspection.

Exhibit 12-8 Class A Office Proposed Development Summary.

D-9 project plan to add another 300,000 square feet as the market adjusts. Also, the developer of the D-10 project stated, "There is another 100,000 square feet planned at the site for 1986," and the development has the potential to add another 1,000,000 square feet of space.

In summary, this analysis identifies approximately 1,150,000 square feet of space which will begin construction by late 1986. There is also another 3,400,000 square feet of space planned. If the D-10 property is fully developed, another 1,000,000 square feet of space could be introduced into the market. There also appear to be possibilities for expansion at the L-11 development (on Exhibit 12-6); however, exact figures were not available. As a result, the submarket potentially has over 5,550,000 square feet of future office space planned in the next five years.

Land Zoned or Purchased for Office Development The county follows a policy of not zoning land until a bona fide plan is presented and a firm commitment to development is made. In view of the high level of office development activity on sites already acquired and zoned and the potential oversupply that exists, further identification of potential office sites was considered too speculative to include in the report.

Supply Forecast and Conclusion The report has identified that there is approximately 880,000 square feet of Class A office space vacant out of a total of 1,550,000 square feet of Class A space. There is also another 120,000 square feet under construction. By late 1986 or early 1987, 1,150,000 square feet of new construction would be started. In addition to these figures, 4,400,000 square feet or more are planned for the future.

A secondary data source reports that the market absorbed approximately 300,000 square feet of space in 1985, while an alternative secondary data source stated that 440,000 square feet were absorbed.

If the existing space vacant of 880,000 square feet and the new construction square footage of 120,000 are combined, there would be 1,000,000 square feet of space available in 1986. Considering past absorption trends, this would leave 600,000 to 700,000 square feet vacant by year end. The 1986–1987 new construction would then add another 1,150,000 square feet to the market by the end of 1987. If the 1987 absorption is similar to past trends, there would be 1,450,000 to 1,550,000 square feet available by the beginning of 1988.

Further predictions would depend on definite determination of the 3.4 to 4.4 million square feet of possible new construction and an accurate absorption forecast. The latter will be the subject of the product demand segment of this analysis.

Absorption Analysis of the Submarket

As previously pointed out, the current supply of Class A space totals 1,550,000 square feet, of which 725,000 square feet is leased. The current available supply is therefore 825,000 square feet. An additional 120,000 square feet in three buildings is under construction. The total existing supply of 825,000 square feet constitutes over a two-year supply of space if it is absorbed at the rate of 393,000 square feet per year.

An additional 1,150,000 square feet of space is scheduled to begin construction in late 1986 and 1987 and, if that space is indeed built, constitutes an additional three-year supply. This potential five-year supply of Class A office space in this suburban area far exceeds what is considered a healthy supply.

ANALYSIS OF SITE-SPECIFIC FACTORS TO EVALUATE MARKETABILITY

Subsequent to the analysis of the general supply and demand factors for the local office submarket, the analysis becomes more narrowly focused on the subject property and its immediate competitors. First, an in-depth evaluation of the subject property's physical and functional characteristics is performed. Then an analysis of the competition is undertaken to determine their competitive characteristics and competitive differentials. Based on these analyses, the analyst is able to estimate the competitive strength of the subject property and to ascertain a capture rate that can be used to help evaluate the feasibility of the project.

Analysis of the Subject Property

This part of the analysis looks at the individual aspects of the subject site that affect its capacity for development and its competitive position in the general market. These aspects include accessibility, linkages, visibility, physical characteristics of the site, and legal constraints. The financial and managerial capabilities of the site's developer and owner are also important factors to be considered.

This part of the study is intended to provide three sets of evaluations:

1. An evaluation of the site's suitability for development. What constraints and opportunities for development are there on this particular site?
2. An evaluation of the site's competitive advantages and disadvantages, as a base for competitive analysis in the next step.
3. An evaluation of the capacity of the owner to finance, develop, and manage a project on this site, based upon prior performances on other projects.

The method of analysis consists of two steps. First, each site-related aspect is broken down into individual factors and measurable components. Components are then compared against a standard considered to be "normal" or "desirable" in terms of function and performance. After this comparison is made, each component is evaluated as to its overall importance. The results are combined into an evaluation of the individual factor's performance and its importance to the particular site-related aspect under consideration.

The second step evaluates each aspect's impact on the overall physical development and marketability of the site, based upon the ranking and weighting evaluation in step 1. The combined results of analyzing each aspect form the basis for the first and second steps in the evaluation. Step 3 is based upon owner-supplied information.

Analysis of Regional Access   There are presently two major routes from the freeway system to the project site. These routes are (1) Industrial Boulevard from I-200 to Industrial Parkway, which leads to the site, and (2) Commuters Boulevard from I-100 to Industrial Boulevard, connecting into Industrial Parkway. It is also possible to reach Industrial Parkway from I-100 via Hill Road, but this route benefits only the northeasternmost sections of the metro area. Mass transit does not service Able County, and any form of mass transit is unlikely to be put into service in the near future, so this factor is not considered.

Study Factor 1—Industrial Boulevard

MEASURABLE COMPONENTS	PERFORMANCE STANDARD	PERFORMANCE AS MEASURED/OBSERVED
Traffic volume	20,000 v.p.h.	60,800 v.p.h.
Road capacity	25,000 v.p.h.	—
Congestion level	Low, no or minor delays	High, excessive delay
Bottlenecks/obstacles	No delays at intersections	Five major bottlenecks at intersections

*Performance Ranking**
Ranking = −2. Industrial Boulevard suffers from extreme overloading magnified by the effects of

Study Factor 1—*Continued*

traffic bottlenecking at major intersections. Driving time between Industrial Parkway and I-200 can reach 30 minutes during peak periods.

Importance to Overall Access†
Weight = 5. Industrial Boulevard is the primary connector between the market area and the metro freeway system.

Commentary   Major improvements to this roadway are planned, with a projected completion date of 1990. See Study Factor 5.

v.p.h = vehicles per hour.
*Ranked −2 to +2: 0 = "standard" or "nominal" performance level.
†Weighted 1 to 5: 1 = unimportant, 5 = critically important.

Study Factor 2—Commuter's Boulevard

MEASURABLE COMPONENTS	PERFORMANCE STANDARD	PERFORMANCE AS MEASURED/OBSERVED
Traffic volume	20,000 v.p.h.	41,000 v.p.h.
Road capacity	25,000 v.p.h.	—
Congestion level	Low, no or minor delays	High, excessive delays
Bottlenecks/obstacles	No delays at intersections	Limited intersections; capacity creates congestion and delay

Performance Ranking*
Ranking = −2. Overloaded far beyond capacity. Major bottlenecks particularly in the I-100 area, at Cross County Highway, and at Industrial Boulevard (limited intersection capacities).

Importance to Overall Access†
Weight = 3. Provides access from I-100 and portion of Able and Baker Counties; Industrial Boulevard provides a more direct route to the site from most of the metro area.

Commentary   Already heavily developed with commercial and light industrial uses. May require additional traffic signal control points (10 currently exist between I-100 and Industrial Boulevard) that would further impede traffic flow. Limited room for additional lanes.

*Ranked −2 to +2: 0 = "standard" or "nominal" performance level.
†Weighted 1 to 5: 1 = unimportant, 5 = critically important.

Study Factor 3—Industrial Parkway

MEASURABLE COMPONENTS	PERFORMANCE STANDARD	PERFORMANCE AS MEASURED/OBSERVED
Traffic volume	8,000 v.p.h.	16,000 v.p.h.
Road capacity	10,000 v.p.h.	—
Capacity level	Low, no or minor delays	Low normally, low to moderate at peak
Bottlenecks/obstacles	No delays at intersections	Minor delays at Old Bridge Road at peak

Performance Ranking*
Ranking = +2. Roadway carries a high traffic volume without major delays, relatively smooth traffic flows.

Study Factor 3—*Continued*

Importance to Overall Access†
Weight = 4. Industrial Parkway connects Industrial Boulevard (the primary access roads) to the site. Access to 95% of services (e.g., banks, restaurants) is via this road.

Commentary   This roadway has been recommended for widening from two to four lanes within the next five years. This recommendation is found in the "Able County Transportation Improvements Program" study recently conducted by the Regional Planning Commission in cooperation with the county and the state D.O.T. At present, the project has no official status.

*Ranked −2 to +2: 0 = "standard" or "nominal" performance level.
†Weighted 1 to 5: 1 = unimportant, 5 = critically important.

Study Factor 4—New Bridge Road

MEASURABLE COMPONENTS	PERFORMANCE STANDARD	PERFORMANCE AS MEASURED/OBSERVED
Traffic volume	8,000 v.p.h.	4,500 v.p.h.
Road capacity	10,000 v.p.h.	—
Congestion level	Low, no or minor delays	Low
Bottlenecks/obstacles	No delays at intersections	No delays

Performance Ranking*
Ranking = 0. Not overloaded; no apparent functional problems.

Importance to Overall Access†
Weight = 2. New Bridge Road serves as a local access road from Industrial Boulevard and from Able City. In terms of regional access to the site, it has little significance at this time.

Commentary   The county and state D.O.T. are considering the extension of Connector Road to Industrial Boulevard along the present New Bridge Road right-of-way. This would provide the site with an additional route to I-100. There are no current plans or timetables for construction at present.

*Ranked −2 to +2: 0 = "standard" or "nominal" performance level.
†Weighted 1 to 5: 1 = unimportant, 5 = critically important.

Study Factor 5—Roadway Improvements (within next 5 years)

MEASURABLE COMPONENTS	MAJOR IMPROVEMENTS NEEDED?	IMPROVEMENTS STATUS (3-1-86)
Industrial Boulevard	Yes	Underway
Commuter's Boulevard	Yes	Minor Improvement at I-100
Industrial Parkway	Near future	Indefinite
New Bridge Road	No	—

Performance Ranking (adequacy of proposed improvements)*

Industrial Boulevard	+2
Commuter's Boulevard	−1
Industrial Parkway	+1

Study Factor 5—*Continued*

MEASURABLE COMPONENTS	MAJOR IMPROVEMENTS NEEDED?	IMPROVEMENTS STATUS (3-1-86)
New Bridge Road	N.A.	
Overall	+1	
Importance to Overall Access†		
Industrial Boulevard	5	
Commuter's Boulevard	3	
Industrial Parkway	4	
New Bridge Road	N.A.	
Overall	4	

Commentary   Industrial Circle is not considered as a means of regional access, although the residential areas that feed into this road may generate some commuter traffic (and shopping traffic) into the site.

*Ranked −2 to +2: 0 = "standard" or "nominal" performance level.
†Weighted 1 to 5: 1 = unimportant, 5 = critically important.

Analysis of Site Access

Analysis of Site Access   Plans for the site show major access into the site from both adjacent roadways. Due in part to the irregular shape of the site, a number of lesser access points are provided to allow development of the site to its maximum potential.

MEASURABLE COMPONENTS	PERFORMANCE STANDARD	PERFORMANCE AS MEASURED/OBSERVED
Number of entrances	Two major access points minimum	Two planned plus secondary access
Location of entrances	Easy access to major thoroughfares	Location of one entrance at the intersection of Industrial Parkway and Industrial Circle; one entrance onto New Bridge Road
Entrance capacity	609 v.p.h. onto Industrial Parkway, 685 v.p.h. onto New Bridge Road plus 25% reserve	850 to 1,000 v.p.h. if left turn arrows are provided at entrance intersections
Integration into traffic flow	Major access points located away from existing intersections or incorporated into them	At Industrial Parkway, existing road extended into development; at New Bridge Road, access is 1,200 feet from nearest intersection

*Performance Ranking**
Ranking = +2. Based upon owner's development plan. As proposed, the site access appears to meet all anticipated traffic flow requirements.

Importance to Overall Access†
Weight = 4. Lack of central access points and the associated internal site roads would limit development of the site to areas near the road frontage.

Commentary Traffic signals will likely be required at the Industrial Parkway entrance to control congestion created by vehicles making left turns and to permit vehicles on Industrial Circle to reach the adjacent shopping center safely.

*Ranked −2 to +2: 0 = "standard" or "nominal" performance level.
†Weighted 1 to 5: 1 = unimportant, 5 = critically important.

Analysis of Visibility The primary viewpoints into the site are along Industrial Parkway and from Industrial Circle. This can be considered the "front door" of the property due to its exposure to the heavily traveled thoroughfare.

MEASURABLE COMPONENTS	PERFORMANCE STANDARD	PERFORMANCE AS MEASURED/OBSERVED
Elevation of site versus elevation of roadway	Site elevation at or slightly above roadway	Elevation of Industrial Parkway = approximately 1000.0 ft.—range 982.5 to 1017.5 ft. elevation adjacent site areas = approximately 980.0 to 1030.0 ft. Elevation of New Bridge Road = approximate elevation of adjacent site areas = 1020.0 to 1030.0 ft.
Major obstacles and "clutter"	No water towers, billboards, etc.	None
Obstruction from adjacent buildings	No negative impacts	Village shopping center may break up visual unity of office park as seen from Industrial Parkway
Required setbacks from right-of-way	Varies with owner and owner government aesthetic goals	50 foot setback required under 0-I zoning
Foliage	Existing trees enhance site without hiding best views of development	Likely with existing trees—narrow trunks with high branches
Viewpoints from roadway	Good visibility from all major approach directions	Moderately good; see commentary below
Visibility of entrance points	Good visibility from all major approach directions	Moderately good; see commentary below

Performance Ranking*	Elevations	+2	Site mostly equal to or slightly higher than roadway will lend prominence to buildings
	Obstacles	+2	None
	Adjacent buildings	−1	Village shopping center identity may be imcompatible with proposed office parks
	Setbacks	0	Setbacks required have little effect on building visibility
	Foliage	+1	Thin trunks and high branches; easy to see through
	Viewpoints	+1	Good with one exception; see comment
	Entrance visibility	0	Good with one major exception; see comment
	Overall	+1	
Importance to Overall Visibility†	Elevations	4	Major factor in promoting site visibility
	Obstacles	1	"Clutter" tends to irritate more than obscure
	Adjacent buildings	2	Areas next to the shopping center have higher elevation

MEASURABLE COMPONENTS		PERFORMANCE STANDARD	PERFORMANCE AS MEASURED/OBSERVED
Importance to Overall Visibility† Continued	Setbacks	1	Applies to all similar sites this area
	Foliage	2	Landscaping can be changed if needed
	Viewpoints	4	Major factor
	Entrance visibility	4	Locus of park identity
	Overall	3	

Commentary Main entrance into site is hidden by trees and a curve in the road when one approaches on Industrial Parkway from the south. This situation may change when the southernmost part of the site is developed.

*Ranked −2 to +2: 0 = "standard" or "nominal" performance level.
†Weighted 1 to 5: 1 = unimportant, 5 = critically important.

Analysis of Physical Characteristics and Site Features The site is a roughly triangular parcel, heavily wooded with moderately rolling terrain and a small lake. A small strip shopping center is being built on 9.6 acres of the property. About 72 acres are available for office-industrial and office development.

Study Factor 1—Shape of Parcel

MEASURABLE COMPONENTS	PERFORMANCE STANDARD	PERFORMANCE AS MEASURED/OBSERVED
"Peninsula" intrusions by other parcels	No major intrusions	Three significant intrusions
Effect of land use and site plan areas	No significant restrictions	Intrusions divide site into three areas—moderate impact on circulation and efficiency

*Performance Ranking**
Ranking = −1. Shape of the site is a handicap to creation of a cohesive and efficient site plan.

Importance to Overall Site Development†
Weight = 3. The shape reduces the "developability" of the site. However, all but a small portion of the site remains usable.

Commentary One or both of the adjacent undeveloped "peninsula" parcels may eventually be acquired by the owner. These parcels can be incorporated into the present plans for the site without major disruptions or addition to site infrastructure.

*Ranked −2 to +2: 0 = "standard" or "nominal" performance level.
†Weighted 1 to 5: 1 = unimportant, 5 = critically important.

Study Factor 2—Topography

MEASURABLE COMPONENTS	PERFORMANCE STANDARD	PERFORMANCE AS MEASURED/OBSERVED
Slopes	Between 5% and 10% slopes over developable area of site	10% to 20% slopes over most of site; 20%+ near lake and site boundaries

Study Factor 2—*Continued*

MEASURABLE COMPONENTS	PERFORMANCE STANDARD	PERFORMANCE AS MEASURED/OBSERVED
Drainage and holding capacity	No flood plains or swampy areas; no extensive grading to create runoff storage required	Generally good drainage; not in flood plain; existing drainage swales can be used as additional storage ponds

*Performance Ranking**
Ranking = 0. Topography is typical for the Industrial Parkway area.

Importance to Overall Site Development†
Weight = 3. Site topography is most suitable for smaller-scale structures (20,000 to 50,000-square foot footprints) or buildings that can "step up and down" with the terrain. There are several "flatter" areas that can support 60,000 to 70,000-square foot single-floor footprints, near the existing lake, near New Bridge Road, and north of the main roadway through the site. Larger office-industrial type uses will require major cut-and-fill operations to level the land.

Commentary   Care should be taken to try to adapt the buildings to the land, and not vice versa. This will preserve the site's amenity value (its mature trees) and reduce the cost of earthwork and landscaping.

Study Factor 3—Utilities to Site

MEASURABLE COMPONENTS	PERFORMANCE STANDARD	PERFORMANCE AS MEASURED/OBSERVED
Power	Adequate capacity (Standard for all components listed)	Adequate service
Water		Adequate service
Sewer		Inadequate capacity
Gas		Adequate service
Telephone		Adequate service

*Performance Ranking**

Power	0		Gas	0
Water	0		Telephone	0
Sewer	−1	(see commentary below)	Overall	5

Importance to Overall Site Development†

Power	5	Gas service is not essential, but is an attractive feature to prospective tenants.
Water	5	
Sewer	5	
Gas	2	
Telephone	5	
Overall	5	

Commentary   The site is located in the Able Creek Basin sewage district. A moratorium on development in this area was lifted recently, but capacity for hookups is limited. The current 2.0-million-gallon-per-day capacity of the system is being enlarged to 6.5 m.g.d., with the additional capacity due on line April 1987.

*Ranked −2 to +2: 0 = "standard" or "nominal" performance level.
†Weighted 1 to 5: 1 = unimportant, 5 = critically important.

Study Factor 4—Other Characteristics

MEASURABLE COMPONENTS	PERFORMANCE STANDARD	PERFORMANCE AS MEASURED/OBSERVED
Foliage	75% of site covered with mature trees	90% coverage of site, 20-year pines
Soils	Sufficient bearing capacity to support spread footings for low- and midrise building approximately 5,000 p.s.f. capacity	3,000 p.s.f. typical in market area. Pilings or other deep foundations required above three stories
Water table	Stable, well below footings and frost line (8–10 ft. +)	5- to 10-ft fluctuation yearly
Property zoning	No changes in zoning needed	Zoned 0–I: office industrial
Adjacent land use	Compatible office or commercial	Residential, buffer required

*Performance Ranking**

Foilage	+1	Good coverage, mature trees, no major hardwoods
Soils	0	Average for this area
Water table	1	Fluctuation causes ground swelling; extra foundation expense
Zoning	+1	Variance required for midrise construction
Adjacent land use	1	Established neighborhood requires buffer and other measures to avoid conflicts
Overall	0	

Importance to Overall Site Development†

Foilage	3	Mature trees have good amenity value
Soils	4	Cost of foundations required for substandard soil conditions can be a major cost factor
Water table	4	Direct impact on cost of basements, foundations and site drainage
Zoning	5	Legal requirement
Adjacent land use	2	Allow for buffer, light shields, etc.
Overall	4	

Commentary 1986 revised county land-use map shows R-M residential property north of the site as future commercial area.

p.s.f. = pounds per square foot.
*Ranked −2 to +2: 0 = "standard" or "nominal" performance level.
†Weighted 1 to 5: 1 = unimportant, 5 = critically important.

Analysis of Linkages Office users typically require a variety of support services and facilities, such as printing, personnel services, and places to eat. The ready availability of such services can play an important part in the locational decisions of potential tenants. Important office linkages include not only nearby support services, but also the availability of facilities such as airports.

"Ready availability" can be considered in terms of the time it takes to reach a destination and how often one needs to make the trip.

TYPE OF LINKAGE	PERFORMANCE STANDARD	PERFORMANCE AS MEASURED/OBSERVED
Thoroughfares	1 minute	1 minute to reach Industrial Parkway
Restaurants	5 minutes	14 fast-food and sit-down restaurants available
Printing services	5 minutes	3 available
Travel offices	5 minutes	1 available
Office supplies	5 minutes	2 available
Banks	5 minutes	7 available
Computer and business machines supply/service	15 minutes	5+ available
Private commercial airports	20 minutes	20 minutes in off-peak traffic
Major airport	30 minutes	45 minutes in off-peak traffic

*Performance Ranking**
Ranking = 0. Adequate services available for day-to-day office and employee needs.

Importance to Overall Site†
Weight = 4. Not all potential tenants/clients require extensive support services nearby, but most find them convenient.

Commentary   Number and quality of services in the market area are likely to improve as the area develops. Improvements in progress on Industrial Boulevard and I-100 will improve access to the airport.

*Ranked −2 to +2: 0 = "standard" or "nominal" performance level.
†Weighted 1 to 5: 1 = unimportant, 5 = critically important.

Consolidated Analysis   This part of the analysis evaluates the effect of each site-specific aspect upon the development potential of the site and the effect on its marketability. Aspects are evaluated using a scale of −2 to +2, with negative numbers indicating deleterious effects, zero indicating no significant effect, and positive numbers indicating an improvement or beneficial effect. The following provisos pertain:

1. The evaluation of development impacts is based upon whether factors analyzed in the last section serve to increase or decrease the cost or difficulty of building a project on the site.
2. The evaluation of marketability impacts is based upon whether the factors analyzed in the last section act to reduce or improve the competitiveness of a project built on the site.

SITE-RELATED ASPECT	EFFECT ON DEVELOPMENT POTENTIAL	EFFECT ON MARKETABILITY
Regional access	0	−2
Site access	+1	+1
Visibility	0	0
Physical characteristic	0	+1
Linkages	0	+1

Analysis of Owner Financial and Managerial Characteristics   The developer of the subject property is a major development corporation. Its properties in the market area include the New Bridge Business Park, Old Bridge Centre, and Luxury Towers. The company acts as the owner, developer, and manager of its properties. The company had developed 875,000 square feet of office space in the area by 1984.

The company plans to develop the subject site using little or no leveraging. Most or all of the costs of development will be paid out of pocket, using cash generated by other corporate properties. The company will borrow long term against the development if extremely favorable financing terms are available, but the goal would be to take advantage of a financial opportunity, not to leverage equity.

The company intends to exercise tight control over the development of the subject property. The goal is to maintain a high level of quality and consistency in the architecture and landscaping of the total development. The company will build on a speculative basis and on a build-to-suit basis, acting as construction manager for each building.

Conclusions   Three major conclusions can be stated at this point, although the analysis of the competitive differentials will follow subsequent analysis. The three conclusions based on the analysis of the subject property are:

1. *Suitability for development.* The subject site is handicapped by irregular shape, uncertain soils, and adjacent residential land use. This is offset somewhat by superior accessibility and potential for integration into the surrounding street patterns.
2. *Competitive advantages.* The site suffers from being difficult to reach during peak traffic periods and from visibility difficulties along the major thoroughfare approach to the project. This is balanced by good visibility once you are near the entrance, good access onto the site, and adequate availability of services. The presence of the shopping center can be positive or negative, depending upon how well it integrates into the surrounding project. The completion of the Industrial Boulevard improvements in the next five years should greatly improve the marketability of this site.
3. *Owner's capabilities.* Based upon the owner's cash-basis financing and successful track record with other projects, there appear to be problems in this area.

Survey of the Competition

The objective of this analysis is to, first, determine the competitive projects within the market area of the subject parcel and, then, to define in relative terms the attributes of each in relation to standards set within the market. This information, coupled with the Analysis of the Subject Property, will allow the analyst to predict the amount of time it will take to lease the proposed office facilities. The project absorbtion, or capture, rate is the amount of space which is expected to be leased in a one-year period of time within a specific development.

To determine this capture rate, input must be taken from several sources. The General Market Analysis has provided the analyst with the type of space to be constructed (Class A office space), the market area to be studied, and the level of market absorbtion. Using this information and conducting further primary and secondary research, this section of the study attempts to answer the questions,

1. Should the project be built?
2. If built, how fast will it lease?
3. If not built, how long before a similar project can hope to be successful?

Assumptions and Limitations   This survey of the competition was limited to Class A projects that were available for occupancy, under construction, or announced at the time of this analysis. There are, however, several parcels in the area owned by major national and local developers which, at the time of this study, have no published plans for development. These potential developments could be a major factor in the future, although the amount of land held by these entitites was not explicitly taken into account.

Given that the subject property is a new project providing first-generation space, it is logical that this study assumes that the primary competitors of the subject project would be other Class A developments within the same market area. The study has also included some business park space that has been constructed to a level of 90 percent or greater pure office space, with a triple net rental rate, comparable to rents for Class A office space less operating expenses.

Methodology   Based on rental rates and dates of completion, the market was disaggregated into buildings fitting the definition of Class A office space within the local market area. To reiterate, Class A office space is defined as buildings that are new or in excellent condition, designed to provide high-amenity office space with rental rates well above those for lesser-quality space.

The business park space in the survey was limited to entire buildings which were built out to a percentage of 90 percent or more office space, with equivalently high rental rates (greater than $9.00 per square foot on a triple net basis, in this instance).

Primary research (field surveys) conducted to determine the relative attributes of each of the competitive facilities further confirms that the buildings identified in previous exhibits would be potential competition for the subject project. Each building was surveyed and ranked on a scale of 1 to 5 for the following attributes:

1. Financial factors
2. Physical features

Exhibit 12-9   Definitions of Terms for Analysis of the Competition.

Rate	Quoted rental rate as published to the market: 5 = $20.00, 4 = $20.00–18.50, 3 = $18.50–17.00, 2 = $17.00–15.50, 1 = $15.50 or less.
Factor	Common area factor added to adjust for tenants' percentage share of the common building facilities (lobbies, restrooms, maintenance rooms) and utility areas.
Build-out	Allowance for tenant improvements paid by landlord.
Escalation	Manner in which rent is adjusted yearly to adjust for increase in operating expenses.
No. of stories	Height of the building being studied, in stories: 5 or greater = 5, 1 = 1.
Construction	Perceived quality of construction: 5 = very high, 1 = poor.
Dock	Existence of a loading facility: 5 = 1 or more docks, 3 = loading area or door, 1 = none.
Glass	Subjective view of the building assuming that more glass provides the better views.
View	Rating of the views from the tenant space within the building.
Finish	Ranking of building on levels of finish within the common areas.
Parking	Relationship of the amount of parking and its accessibility to the building. Covered parking increases the ranking by 1 point.
Landscaping	Ranking of the general appearance and upkeep of the grounds.
Corner	Ranking of the building's ability to provide two-way visibility from corner spaces.
Offices	Prestigious space within the building: 5 = 5 or more corners, 3 = 4 corners, 1 = less than 4.
Amenities	Amenities within a reasonable driving range, such as restaurants, fast-food establishments, banks, hotels, convenience shopping, and supplier of office materials: 5 = within a 2-minute drive, 3 = within a 5-minute drive, 1 = greater than an 8-minute drive.
Residential	Ranking of the mileage between the project and the major residential neighborhoods in the area with homes valued in excess of $150,000.
Commuter routes	Distance from major commuter routes.
Visibility	Visibility of the building from area's major thoroughfares.
Identity	Recognizability of building (takes into consideration visibility and signage).
Food	Availability of food or snacks in building: 5 = sandwich shop, 3 = vending area, 1 = none.
Security	Existence of a security system: 5 = electronic entry or manned service, 3 = locked doors after hours and motor patrol of the parking lots, 1 = unlit parking and 24-hour access.
Conference	Conference rooms available to tenants: 5 = available at no charge, 3 = available at some charge, 1 = none.
Health facility	Presence of health facility: 5 = health club/workout area, 3 = jogging trail, 1 = none.
Age	Age of building in years: 5 = 1 or less, 4 = 2 years, 3 = 3 years, 2 = 4 years, 1 = greater than 4 years.

3. Locational features
4. Building project amenities

These four areas were broken down further, as can be seen in Exhibit 12-9, to present a comprehensive view of the factors that may be weighed in the mind of the decision maker. A detailed definition of each of these factors is also presented in Exhibit 12-9.

The next step assigns a weight to each of the individual characteristics. Those factors having the greatest influence on the decision-making process should be given greater attention than those of lesser importance. If time and budget permit, a survey of the decision makers within companies currently occupying competitive space should be made to ascertain just what is important to them in their decision to relocate. This survey would provide not only the weighting needed but also valuable input concerning desirable amenities. This information would help provide direction for the marketing effort of new office buildings.

Financial factors loom as the single most important consideration for most companies when planning a relocation. The rental rate is always a major determinant of whether a move is possible or not, but other factors also affect a firm's financial willingness to move. The focus here, however, is on what causes a firm to choose one office space over another.

While the rental rate may be the single most important factor decision makers initially review, a better indication of the actual cost of occupancy can be obtained by considering a building's loss factor, the base building condition, and build-out allowances. To obtain an accurate comparison of the cost of occupancy, rental rates are presented as a usable number that eliminates differences in loss factors from project to project.

Exhibit 12-10 Weighting of Comparative Factors.*

Rental	5	Build-out	5
Escalation	3	No. of stories	2
Construction	2	Dock	1
Glass	3	View	2
Finish	4	Parking	3
Landscape	3	Corner offices	2
Amenities	5	Access	5
Proximity to		Residential	4
Commuter routes	4	Visibility	4
Identity	3	Food	3
Security	2	Conference	1
Health facilities	1	Age	4

*5 = critically important
4 = very important
3 = average importance
2 = somewhat important
1 = unimportant (however, all else being equal, this item could come into play.)

Build-out allowances are adjusted to show the base building condition (the condition of the tenant space prior to the construction of tenant improvements) with the finished ceiling already in place. An adjustment (equal to $3.75 per square foot in this case) is subtracted from the allowance of a building with a base building condition quoted slab to slab (that is, where the tenant must pay for the installation of all improvements made above the finished ceiling, including the actual installation of the ceiling).

Exhibit 12-11   Analysis of the Competition. (Weighted Rankings)

COMPETITIVE BUILDINGS	FINANCIAL FACTORS	Rate	Factor	Buildout	Escalation	PHYSICAL FEATURES	# Stories	Construction	# Elevators	Dock	Glass	View	Finish	Parking
Building A		25		4			4	4	—	1	12	2	8	9
Building B		25		4			4	4	—	1	12	4	8	9
Building C		15		12			10	8	—	1	12	4	12	9
Building D		15		12			10	8	—	1	12	4	12	9
Building E		5		12			10	8	—	1	12	6	12	9
Building F		25		12			10	8	—	1	12	4	8	6
Building G		5		12			8	8	—	3	9	8	16	9
Building H		10		12			10	8	—	3	9	8	16	9
Building I		10		12			10	8	—	5	9	8	16	9
Building J		20		8			8	4	—	3	6	4	8	3
Building K		15		12			4	2	—	1	6	2	12	3
Building L		20		8			4	2	—	4	9	2	12	8
Building M		5		8			10	4	—	2	9	6	16	9
Building N		10		12			10	8	—	1	15	4	12	9
Building O		20		8			4	4	—	1	6	2	12	6
Building P		25		12			6	4	—	2	12	4	4	15
Building Q		10		12			10	6	—	2	12	4	16	15
Building R		15		12			4	4	—	2	6	2	12	6
Building S		5		16			8	8	—	2	12	8	20	12
Total														

The second step of the analysis assigns weights to the financial features, building features, locational features, and building amenities categories, depicting their perceived importance in the decision-making process. These weight-

Exhibit 12-11 *Continued.*

Landscape	Corner Offices	LOCATIONAL FEATURES	Amenities	Access	Proximity to Residential	Commuter Routes	Visibility	Identity	BUILDING AMENITIES	Food	Security	Conference	Health Facilities	Age	TOTAL PER BUILDING
6	6		25	20	8	16	8	9					3	4	174
6	6		25	20	8	16	8	9					3	4	176
6	6		20	20	8	16	8	3		5			3	8	181
6	6		20	20	8	16	8	3					3	16	189
6	6		20	20	8	16	8	3					3	20	193
3	6		25	25	8	20	20	6		5				4	208
12	8		10	10	12	12	12	12						20	186
12	8		15	10	8	12	15	15						20	205
12	8		15	10	8	12	15	15						20	207
3	8		25	25	8	8	20	6						4	171
3	6		10	15	8	8	12	3						20	142
6	6		10	15	8	8	4	3						20	162
9	8		15	10	12	12	4	3						20	162
6	10		15	25	16	12	4	3						16	188
9	10		10	10	8	12	16	6						20	164
6	8		10	15	8	8	4	3						4	165
6	8		10	15	12	12	8	3				3		20	184
6	8		10	20	8	12	16	9						16	168
12	12		10	15	12	12	4	9		15	10	3		20	225
															3412

ings are presented in Exhibit 12-10. The weighted rankings for each feature are summed to a single gross figure and used to make comparisons among competitive properties.

Two problems preclude a comparison of absorption rates at this point. First, 66 percent (12 out of 18) of the Class A projects surveyed were completed within the last 18 months, which resulted in extended lease-up periods because of the tremendous influx of space to the market. Second, project-specific data were not available for space existing before 1984.

The final step was to consolidate the information on product absorption for the next five years.

Competitive Differentials   Results from the tabulations in Exhibit 12-11 show that within a given year, the projects in the survey could each expect to receive between 4.16 percent and 6.60 percent of the market's yearly absorption for Class A office space. This conclusion is obtained by examining the last column of Exhibit 12-11 (total per building) and finding the percentage each building is of the total for all competitive buildings. Building K scored lower than any competitive building with 142 points, which represents 4.16 percent of the total 3,412 points for all competitive buildings. Building S scored 225 points, representing 6.60 percent of the total for all competitive buildings. In a market that is as competitive as the market area, turnovers could be very high and cause individual capture rates to fluctuate greatly. As the market becomes tighter, the percentage share of the product absorption should stabilize. Forecast capture rates for reach of the competitive projects are shown in Exhibit 12-12. The

Exhibit 12-12   Expected Percentage Annual Project Absorption.

COMPETITIVE BUILDINGS	
Building A	5.1%
Building B	5.2
Building C	5.4
Building D	5.4
Building E	5.7
Building F	6.1
Building G	5.5
Building H	6.2
Building I	6.2
Building J	5.0
Building K	4.23*
Building L	4.7
Building M	4.8
Building N	5.6
Building O	4.8
Building P	4.9
Building Q	5.4
Building R	5.0
Building S	6.7*

*Extreme points in the analysis.

forecast shows expected absorption without the introduction of the space that would be offered by the subject property.

Sixty-six percent of the projects in the survey are less than two years old, and only one has reached an occupancy level greater than 40 percent. Obviously, lease-up periods in the current market are extending beyond a two-year period.

Using projected absorption figures for the market and distributing these to individual projects, the analyst can identify the following results. Demand for Class A office space in the market area for the next five years is about 393,000 square feet per year. This market represents approximately 1.55 million square feet of existing office space, of which 880,000 square feet is currently vacant. This represents less than a 45 percent occupancy rate in the market. Projecting a yearly absorption of 393,000 square feet, the market has over a two-year supply of space.

On the project level, competitive projects in the market can expect absorption rates in the range of 13,500 square feet to 26,800 square feet per year for the next two years. This assumes that no additional space will be brought on line during the period. Assuming that space was existing at the present, and given the attributes of the site as stated in the analysis of the subject property, the subject property could expect to be in the higher end of the range.

Due to the nature of the severe oversupply on the market of Class A office space, it would be unwise for the developer to begin the new project at this time. This does not preclude the possibility of development as early as late 1987. By building a quality structure with facilities such as sandwich shops and space for exercise facilities and by providing a relatively high amenity level for both the exterior and interior finish, the developer can expect to be competitive with the most successful projects in the market.

SUMMARY

When the market analyst must estimate the capture rate for a particular project, such as a suburban office building to be constructed, an implicit allocation of aggregate demand to the subject property is made. The ability of a project to capture a portion of the aggregate local demand for office space will depend upon the marketability of the property. The analyst judges the general prospect for absorption of vacant space in the market by relating aggregate market demand to the present and expected supply of available space. However, the analyst recognizes that the subject property, as a new building, competes most directly with vacant Class A space. The critical question is, "What portion of aggregate demand will be attracted to available Class A surburban space, including the subject property?" To answer this question, the analyst relies upon recent absorption trends in this portion of the market.

If the absorption rates of Class A properties judged to be directly competitive with the subject property have been at a pace where typical buildings have recently been achieving a "normal" occupancy in two years, and if the aggregate demand and supply analysis is expected to be in balance in the short run, the analyst might conclude that the subject property should achieve normal occupancy in two years. If present and expected supply is forecast to outstrip demand and the market is expected to become dull, the analyst will moderate the absorption rate estimated for the subject property.

In formulating an opinion about the absorption rates for a particular Class A property, the analyst did not have a basis for predicting shifts among segments of the office market such as existing office users moving from Class B to Class A space.

Obtaining market information about the potential magnitude of shift in demand from intramarket moves of existing office users can be obtained from a survey of tenants now occupying space in the local market. Large commercial real estate brokerage firms, such as Coldwell Banker, often collect and keep current such data. The "office prospect file" of such firms may show each tenant by SIC code, indicate the office space needs of the tenant, and provide lease expiration dates. The analyst who specializes in a given local market may conduct such surveys annually.

The foregoing site-specific analysis used only information that was readily available from a field survey. A more thorough analysis of competitive properties would have enhanced the analyst's ability to judge competitive differentials. Exhibit 12-13 provides a more complete listing of data that could be obtained for each competitive property.

A survey conducted to obtain the data shown in Exhibit 12-13 would reveal the annual lease expirations and the number of square feet potentially sought by those tenants. Knowing the SIC classification of the tenant would also permit insight into the type of office space that will be sought. The analyst may note that an additional component of demand for Class A space will come from some portion of these tenants whose leases are expiring within the near future. While this fact may be considered in the absorption rate expected for the subject property, caution must be exercised in attributing specific results to upgrading tenants. The proportion of existing tenants who actually move varies greatly over the business cycle and among communities, with older cities having a larger component of demand for better quality space attributable to upgrading tenants.[6]

The assumption that the subject property will perform as well as the typical property in its class and location is the first approximation of an absorp-

---

[6]Detoy and Rabin, "Office Space." This article has a thoughtful discussion of the intra-market shift in demand for office space. The authors report that "generally, for every square foot of space demanded by new tenants, 1.6 square feet is demanded by upgrading tenants. It is important to note that this ratio varies from 1:0.80 to 1:2.4 (although these are not the lower and upper bounds), so *extreme caution must be exercised in choosing an appropriate ratio*. This choice is heavily influenced by the stock of second class office space in the community."

Property name
Address
Age (occupancy date)
Building description
  Total square feet, GFA: GLA:
  Retail space (GFA):
  Number of stories:
  Elevators:
  Materials and quality of construction:
  Overall exterior-interior condition:
  Quality, adequacy, cleanliness of common areas:
  On-site tenant amenities:
  Visibility:
  Accessibility:
  Percent vacant: Square feet vacant:
Parking
  Garage:
  On-site:
  Adequacy:
  Ingress/egress:
Neighborhood/district
  Types of properties:
  Overall condition:
  New construction:
  Available land:
  Adequacy of transportation:
  Convenience of shopping, restaurants, etc.:
  Major office tenants in area:
Tenant information*
  Firm name:
  Date of occupancy:
  Firm business: Prelease: Owner-occupant:
  Type of tenant   Signature tenant: Government tenant:
  Lease expiration:
  Square feet occupied (indicate if full floor):
  Rent per square foot (total):
  Tenant finishing allowance:
  Tenant pays:
  Other (future relocation or expansion plans, etc.?
      new firm? previous location? reason for move?):

---

*Information may be collected for all or a sample of tenants; when obtained from a single source (developer, property manager), the names of all tenants, the square feet occupied by each, whether a prelease or owner-occupant, and a "typical" rent per square foot and "typical" lease terms are ascertained. Typical rent and lease terms can be inferred from tenant interviews.

Exhibit 12-13 Competitive Property Survey.

tion rate for the property. Further analysis may result in the conclusion that the property will outperform (or not) the average experience in the market. The analyst must exercise caution in reaching such conclusions, taking care to maintain the objectivity of the analysis.

Selection of directly competitive properties requires an understanding of the nature of a local office market. Do competitive properties exist in the suburban or central-city market? What class of property competes with the subject property? Are the competitive properties in an identifiable node? The analyst considers, for both the subject property and competitive projects, such factors as

1. Overall architectural appeal.
2. Materials used and quality of construction.
3. Spaciousness of common areas.
4. On-site tenant services.
5. Parking adequacy.
6. Visibility.
7. Ease of ingress and egress to and from the site.
8. Accessibility of the site; adequacy of highways, streets, public transit.
9. Type and condition of properties in the neighborhood.
10. Construction trends in the neighborhood and the availability of land for future construction.
11. Availability of restaurants, banks, shopping, and other establishments of importance to office workers.

After selection of competitive properties based on the foregoing attributes, the analyst surveys the properties to determine their "average" rent per square foot, what operating expenses are paid by the tenants, the age of the property, the property rental experience, the present amount of vacant space, space preleased prior to construction, owner-occupied space, and the characteristics of other tenants. To the extent possible, this information should be obtained for properties proposed or under construction as well as for existing buildings. The information is obtained by inspection of the properties and by questioning developers, property managers, building owners, and tenants.

A survey form, to be completed by the analyst, is useful when conducting inspections of competitive properties and when interviewing. The use of a form, such as the one in Exhibit 12-13, assures that all pertinent questions are asked and that no relevant information is overlooked. From these forms, the analyst composes the information reported to the client.

READINGS

BIBLE, DOUGLAS S., AND JOHN W. WHALEY. "Projecting an Urban Office Market: A Source of Information for Appraisers," *The Appraisal Journal*, October 1983, pp. 515–523.

DETOY, CHARLES J., AND SOL L. RABIN. "Office Space: Calculating the Demand," *Urban Land*, Urban Land Institute, June 1972, p. 4–13. Reprinted in *Readings in Market Research for Real Estate*, James D. Vernor, ed., pp. 243–257. Chicago: American Institute of Real Estate Appraisers, 1985.

DOWNS, ANTHONY. "How Much Office Space Will We Need in the Future?" *National Real Estate Investor*, February 1983, pp. 28–106.

KELLY, HUGH F. "Forecasting Office Space Demand in Urban Areas," *Real Estate Review*, Fall 1983, pp. 87–95

MCMAHAN, JOHN. *Property Development*. New York: McGraw-Hill, 1976. See particularly Ch. 9, pp. 177–202.

SELDIN, MAURY, CRE. "A Reclassification of Real Estate and Market Analysis: Toward Improving the Line of Reasoning," *Real Estate Issues*, Spring/Summer 1984, pp. 44–49.

URBAN LAND INSTITUTE. *Office Development Handbook* (Community Builders Handbook Series). Washington, D.C.: Urban Land Institute, 1982.

WEAVER, WILLIAM C. "Forecasting Office Space Demand with Conjoint Measurement Techniques," *The Appraisal Journal*, July 1984, pp. 389–398.

13

DATA FOR MARKET AND MARKETABILITY STUDIES

INTRODUCTION

An analysis of market supply and demand factors requires the analyst to undertake a thorough data specification and data collection program. Once the purpose and scope of the study have been defined, the physical elements of the project taken into consideration, and economic environment identified, the crucially important step of examining specific market factors must be broached. The analyst must specify the particular market variables to be used in the analysis, how these variables will be measured, and what sources of information will be used to accomplish these tasks. In other words, the market analyst must develop a complete data program, which is the heart of the market analysis activity.

The two types of data, primary data and secondary data, must be understood, and the sources of the data identified. All data should be current, relevant, reliable, accurate, and conceptually correct. Finally, the nature of the potential error that can arise in each type of data should be understood. These issues are explored in this chapter.

PRIMARY AND SECONDARY DATA

Primary data are facts (information) explicitly gathered by the researcher in pieces aggregated for exclusive use in the analysis at hand. Secondary data are facts initially gathered by others for other purposes but applicable to the analysis of the subject property. In general, secondary data already exist in published or other form and are gathered by the investigator from available sources.

Methods for Obtaining Primary Data

Since primary data are facts gathered explicitly for a particular analysis, data identification and collection intentionally focus only upon the specific question the analysis is attempting to answer. Primary data must be gathered by the analyst as part of the study process. The analyst can obtain the data either through the process of observation or by questioning people directly. Using observation techniques will require inference from people's actions or other items the analyst has observed.

Observation   As a data gathering technique, observation can reduce human error. An observed action on the part of a shopper, for instance, is a true fact (unless the shopper is deceiving the observer). In contrast to questioning techniques, observation does not misinterpret responses; it avoids interviewer and nonresponse biases. Observation occurs at the place and time of the action, and proper recording of all pertinent facts by the observer should prevent loss of information due to forgetting or overlooking of facts. Also, individuals who may object to questioning may often be observed without a problem.

Information that can be gathered by observation includes pedestrian and automobile traffic counts, directions of traffic flow at intersections, male and female shoppers, congestion in parking lots, assessment of the types and overall physical condition of neighborhood properties, vacancies in apartment complexes, queuing problems at checkout counters, and other items which can be counted.

Observation cannot provide accurate psychographic data. For instance, attempting to sort shoppers by age category is difficult unless very broad age groupings are used. Accurate inference of family income from manner of dress or automobiles driven to a shopping center is not possible. Attitudes and preferences of shoppers cannot be ascertained by observation. Any inferences from observed data are subject to the biases and misinterpretation of the observer. Observation not only provides data on current behavior; it cannot identify what will be done or what has been done.

Questioning   The questioning process can provide data on the economic and demographic characteristics of the consumer and can provide the analyst with information on consumer attitudes, opinions, habits, tastes, and preferences. Data obtained from questioning can be inaccurate because a question may be misunderstood, an answer may be fabricated, or the subject may choose not to reply. The question may be improperly phrased, the sample may not be representative of the population, or interviewer bias may creep into the questioning process. The importance of survey research in market and marketability analysis requires the analyst to be aware of these potential problems. Chapter 14 addresses proper questionnaire construction, questioning techniques, and sampling procedures.

Sources of Secondary Data

The sources of secondary data that can be used to handle a market analysis assignment are identified in the chapters where secondary data are required. The discussion of economic base analysis in Chapter 3 is punctuated with references to the data sources. Then, in Chapters 7 through 12, where the topics of housing market analysis, retail trade analysis, and office market analysis are discussed, appropriate data sources are also mentioned.

Several authors have written articles or monographs detailing secondary data sources. These materials should be available to the reader in most college and university libraries.

CATEGORIES OF DATA

The analyst must identify the data needed to provide answers to the research questions posed by the analysis. The analyst establishes research objectives and specific questions to be answered only after a thorough understanding of the nature of the study and the users of the information. As the research continues, the need for additional data often arises. The analyst develops the lists of data required for each type of analysis. Repetitive projects reduce data selection and gathering to a relatively routine task, although the analyst should continually review and update data sources. The data needed for a typical market study can be generally categorized into five types of information: economic, demographic, psychographic, locational, and physical. These five categories of data are listed in the first column of Exhibit 13-1.

The market analysis has two principal focal points: the consumer and the product. These two foci are presented as column headings in Exhibit 13-1. Under each of these general headings, the analyst may be required to consider a specific factor, such as the individual consumer or the subject site. The analyst may also be required to consider groupings of these data; that is, the demand side of the market (aggregate consumers), or the supply side of the market composed of new construction and a survey of the competition, or the resale market and a survey of the relevant competition.

The analyst can place each research task into the format shown in Exhibit 13-1. The analyst conceptualizes the categories of data that are the most important to the study and eliminates less important variables to reflect time and budget constraints imposed on the study. Three cells in the table are not used because the data combinations are illogical: cell D2 would contain demographic variables for the property in the market, and cells A5 and B5 would be concerned with physical features of the consumer. An interesting question is raised about cell E2. Are there demographic features to resale property? Based on the discussion in Chapter 4 about the supply side of the resale market, the answer is "yes"; that is, households that offer resale units may have distinctly different

Exhibit 13-1 Categories of Market and Subject Property Data.

	CONSUMER ORIENTED		CONSUMER AND PROPERTY ORIENTED	PROPERTY ORIENTED	
	For Each Individual	Market Demand	Subject Property (The Site)	Market Supply	
				New Construction	Resale
Economic	Cell A1 (P)	Cell B1 (P/S)	Cell C1 (P)	Cell D1 (P/S)	Cell E1 (P/S)
Demographic	Cell A2 (P)	Cell B2 (P/S)	Cell C2 (P)	Cell D2 not applicable	Cell E2 (P/S)
Psychographic	Cell A3 (P)	Cell B3 (P/S)	Cell C3 (P)	Cell D3 (P/S)	Cell E3 (P/S)
Locational	Cell A4 (P)	Cell B4 (P/S)	Cell C4 (P)	Cell D4 (P/S)	Cell E4 (P/S)
Physical/legal	Cell A5 not applicable	Cell B5 not applicable	Cell C5 (P)	Cell D5 (P/S)	Cell E5 (P/S)

P = primary.
S = secondary.

reasons for selling, and the demographic characteristics of these households could be meaningful.

After the categories of data required for the study are identified, the analyst must determine whether primary or secondary data will be used. Also, the analyst must decide upon the mix of data sources in those cases where a mix is possible. For example, the data in cell A1 in the exhibit can only be obtained using primary data techniques. This is represented by the "P" in the upper right-hand corner of the cell. The data for cell B1 can be obtained from either primary or secondary sources so the cell contains the symbol "P/S." As a general rule, data pertaining to a specific individual or site can only be gathered as primary data. Data for a market can be assembled from primary data or obtained from secondary sources.

At this point the analyst must decide the best possible source of data to answer the research questions. The choices made at this point are highly dependent upon the analyst's judgment. Data characteristics associated with each cell illustrate some of the problems of choice for each type of data.

The first principal difference presented in Exhibit 13-1 is the distinction between consumer orientation and product orientation. Consumer orientation deals with characteristics of the individual consumer, the market, and the reactions of the individuals and the market toward the subject property. Property orientation deals with characteristics of the property, space users on the property, and the nature of the properties and space users in the market. The subject property serves as the focus of the analysis. The subject site is the bridge between the consumer-oriented and the property-oriented side of the exhibit.

Data Cells for Characteristics of Individuals

When the analyst obtains information about specific individuals, primary data must be collected. There are two decisions that must be made before the analyst undertakes data collection. First, the analyst must determine which variables are important and are to be included in the analysis. From a complete listing of the economic, demographic, psychographic, and locational variables which can be used, the analyst must select those that are relevant and important. Once the variables have been selected, the analyst must then determine which data gathering technique will be used—observation or questioning.

If the decision is made to obtain primary data about the individual consumers, it is important to identify the type of information that can be obtained. Simply stated, the analyst may require information about economic phenomena (cell A1), demographic characteristics (cell A2), psychographic characteristics (cell A3), and locational phenomena (cell A4) variables. Following are lists of variables to serve as a checklist for the kind of information that the analyst may wish to obtain. Depending upon the nature of the analysis, different variables and different combinations of these variables will be important. The list of variables is not exhaustive but represents a reasonably comprehensive set of factors used in real estate market research.

Economic Variables (cell A1)

Income (current, disposable, household, family, per capita, etc.)

Wealth (savings in the form of savings accounts, financial assets, real property assets, etc.)

Consumption patterns (purchases by product line, budget allocation, time of purchase, etc.)

Mortgage payment factors (interest rate, type of loan, term of loan, rent payments)

Expenses (ownership costs for principal residence, total operating expenses for income property)

Demographic Variables (cell A2)

Age

Sex

Marital status

Household size

Occupation

Educational attainment

Ethnic characteristics

Psychographic Variables (cell A3)

Attitudes

Cognitive component: the beliefs, perceptions, opinions, or information about the object

Affective or emotional component: the feelings of like or dislike about the object

Behavorial component: the actions or predisposition toward the object

Preferences (intentional, conscious ordering of the objects)

Habits (unconscious, fixed responses to the objects)

Desires (stated, inferred)

Locational Variables (cell A4)

Linkages (in existence and potential for change)

Proximity measures for the linkages (distance, travel time, transport costs, etc.)

Externality effects of adjacent and proximate activities (mix of location and psychographic aspects)

Data Cells for Market Demand

The variables contained in the next set of cells are directly related to the variables contained in the cells for the characteristics of individuals. To a large extent the summation of the information for the individuals is represented here. Thus, the list of variables is similar to the variables list under the "A" cells, but the former represents the market rather than the individuals.

Economic Variables (cell B1)

Number of consumers (population, households, families)
Income (per capita, mean and/or median household, mean and/or median family)
Income distribution
Rent (mean, median, and distribution)
Consumption expenditures

Demographic Variables (cell B2)

Age profile
Sex distribution
Marital status
Household sizes
Occupational profile
Educational profile
Ethnic characteristics

Psychographic Variables (cell B3)

Descriptive statistics (for the population's attitudes, preferences, tastes, habits, and desires)

Locational Variables (cell B4)

Linkage patterns (converted to a market or trade area)
Descriptive statistics (about proximity measures and the evaluations of the externalities)

Economic and Demographic Data Cells for the Subject Property

The data in these two cells take on a special significance because they consider the property and the actual and potential inhabitants of the property. The inhabitants can be residential space users if the property is an apartment building; they can be retail space users, if the subject property is a shopping center; or they could be office space users in the case of office buildings. So, the data in these cells refer to the economic characteristics of the property, its actual or current inhabitants, the customers of the inhabitants, the potential inhabitants, and the customers of the potential customers. These variables include the following:

Economic Variables

Subject property variables
    Rental income
    Vacancy rates
    Operating rates
    Operating expenses
    Debt service
Variables for inhabitants (residential properties)
    Occupational characteristics
    Income characteristics
Variables for consumers (retail properties)
    Number of consumers
    Income
    Income distribution
    Expenditures

Demographic Variables

Variables for inhabitants (residential properties)
    Age characteristics
    Sex characteristics
    Marital status
    Household size
    Educational characteristics
    Ethnic characteristics

Variables for customers (retail properties)
    Age profile
    Sex distribution
    Marital status
    Household sizes
    Educational profile
    Ethnic characteristics

Psychographic Data for the Subject Property

The psychographic data in cell C3 refer to the actual and potential inhabitants of the property and their attitudes, preferences, and so on toward the property. The psychographic data also refer to the attitudes and opinions of customers regarding the property.

Locational and Physical Data for the Subject Property

Chapter 6 contains a list of variables that would comprise data needed in cells C4 and C5.

Economic Data for New Construction

The data that belong in cell D1 pertain to the supply side of the new construction market and focus on the economic factors. Based on the discussion in Chapter 4, the variables are input prices (such as the cost of the land), construction labor, materials, construction loans, and builder overhead and profit. Based on the discussion in Chapter 5, data derived from the survey of competition are also included in this cell. Cell D2 is not used.

Psychographic Data for New Construction

Cell D3 contains the psychographic factors that enter the supply side of the new construction market. The principal factor is builder expectations toward market activity, discussed in greater detail in Chapter 4. In addition, data derived of the evaluation of the competitive characteristics of the subject property, discussed in Chapter 5, are combined in this cell.

Locational Data for New Construction

Cell D4 contains data about the locational characteristics in the market for new construction of housing units, retail space, or office space. If the market is a small geographic area, its access to job sites, shopping opportunities, entertainment, and so on are important. If the market is a small retail trade area, customer travel time and route environment, for example, are important.

Physical and Legal Data for New Construction

The data in cell D5 comprise physical and legal information that affects new construction in the market. This information includes characteristics of zoning regulations, subdivision regulations, and the like, as well as drainage patterns, soils, and other site features.

Economic, Demographic, and Psychographic Data for the Resale Market

The data in cells E1, E2, and E3 were discussed in detail in Chapter 4, where the focus was on the supply side of the residential resale market. That discussion contains information about life-cycle and economic variables of the households selling units in the resale market.

When the focus of the study is on resale of retail property, the information in these cells is focused on the current space user or occupant. For example, if free-standing retail space is being offered for sale by its current owner/occupant, data regarding this owner may be important.

Locational, Physical, and Legal Data for the Resale Market

The data in cell E4, and cell E5, represent locational and physical characteristics of the competitive properties in the market. The cells rely heavily on the survey of the competition discussed in Chapter 5 as well as on the locational and physical characteristics identified in Chapter 6.

BIAS AND ERRORS IN SECONDARY DATA

Secondary data are often gathered to provide a body of descriptive statistics, such as the U.S. Census publications. Other secondary data were developed to answer more specific questions, which are not necessarily the same questions being addressed in the market analysis. Secondary data may be available to the general public or may be obtainable by subscription or membership in trade organizations. Often, private data sources provide summarized versions of raw data collected by organizations involved in various types of research. These groups generate and make available the data as a by-product of their work. In other instances, the private proprietary organizations compile and market a data base specifically to supplement secondary data available from public sources.

Secondary data are often available from both the original source, which collects and organizes the data, and from sources that simply summarize data collected by others and market the information. For example, the original source of secondary data for population characteristics is the *U.S. Census of Population*. When data are obtained directly from census publications, all the backup information is provided about data collection techniques, statistical methodologies used, possible inaccuracies, and other valuable background inputs. A detailed breakdown of all population characteristics for numerous geographical subdivisions is available. However, the analyst may find it more convenient to use summarized versions of this population data in the *U.S. Statistical Abstract*, which does not collect and organize, but simply distributes the secondary data. Organizations that perform the task of summarizing and distributing data are referred to as secondary sources. In any event, the analyst should be aware of the advantages and disadvantages of using original sources of secondary data or obtaining the data summarized by others elsewhere.

The use of secondary data exposes the analysis to a variety of possible errors and bias, but precautions are available to deal with them. The analyst will not be able to remove or overcome some of the errors, but knowledge of their existence will help in making informed conclusions and establishing some level of confidence in the judgments which result.

The analyst strives for accuracy by reducing the error in his or her investigation. Four categories of potential error that can reduce accuracy in secondary data are

1. Sampling and nonsampling errors.
2. Errors that invalidate the data reformulation.
3. Errors that require data reformulation.
4. Errors that reduce reliability.

Secondary data should be checked for errors to verify their accuracy. If such validation cannot be accomplished, then secondary data should be regarded as suspect. Whenever it is possible, statistical techniques should be employed to eliminate or explicitly take errors into account.

Issues Concerning Secondary Data

Both primary or secondary data should be accurate, valid, unbiased, precise, reliable, appropriate, and timely. The following discussion will explore these concepts further.

Accuracy and Validity Both accuracy and validity of data should be checked for each group of data being studied. The analyst generally collects primary data from a sample, and in specifying and selecting the sample, the analyst must be careful to reflect the nature of the true population accurately. This same principle underlies the use of secondary data; it must accurately reflect what is taking place. Validation is the process of checking to make sure proper procedures were followed in collecting, organizing, and analyzing the data. Data that have been validated are considered more accurate because more is known about their origin and characteristics. Consequently, more confidence can be placed in the use of validated data.

Bias Bias is the deviation of a statistical estimate from the true parameter the statistical procedure is designed to estimate. It is the systematic error introduced into an analysis by the failure to follow proper procedure or by other errors in the data program. The analyst strives for unbiased estimates.

Reliability Reliability refers to reproducibility or replication of estimates. If the analyst uses two or more techniques to measure the same value (i.e., population) and the estimates are close together, the estimates are judged to be reliable. Similarly, if the analyst draws two or more samples from the same population and the results are close, then there is reliability in the sampling process.

The analyst is concerned with the removal of inaccuracy, bias, and imprecision. Several concepts are discussed in the following section of this chapter which provide background information needed to combat these problems.

Appropriateness In addition to the concepts discussed in the previous paragraphs, the analyst is also concerned that the data are the appropriate data. The data must measure what they are supposed to measure; the sample must be taken from the correct population.

Timeliness The data must reflect the time period that governs the analysis. If current sales are the issue, 1980 income levels and customer counts are not timely. This issue was handled in the discussion of updating in Chapter 3, but it can arise in more subtle ways that are discussed in the next section.

Sampling and Nonsampling Errors

When primary data are generated by means of either the observation or questioning techniques, the resulting data contain whatever bias and error that arose in the process of data gathering. The questioning process can produce both sampling and nonsampling error. These errors are present when the data are summarized as secondary data. Sampling error arises when the sample chosen by the analyst does not accurately reflect the facts, attitudes, and so on of the total group (the population) being studied. This could arise because the sample selected comprised an unrepresentative portion of the full population.

Five general types of nonsampling errors arise in the primary data gathering process:

1. *Frame error* occurs when the list that the analyst generates to represent the population omits certain individuals, whose opinions, attitudes, or other characteristics are not represented.

2. *Measurement error* arises when the individuals who respond to the questions give information that is not true.

3. *Sequence bias* occurs when the questionnaire suggests or induces an idea or opinion in the mind of the respondent as a direct consequence of questions on the questionnaire.

4. *Interviewer bias* occurs because of the presence or influence of an interviewer in a personal and telephone interview. The interviewer may unknowingly bring out an untrue response to sensitive questions (i.e., the respondent may answer to please the interviewer instead of giving the truth). Or the interviewer might record a verbal response incorrectly because the statement is interpreted with the interviewer's bias.

5. *Nonresponse bias* occurs because a certain group of individuals is not reached even though the analyst tried to contact them, or individuals are contacted and they refuse to participate or do not answer certain questions.

The sampling or nonsampling errors that underlie the generation of primary data may be carried forward when the data are summarized and presented as secondary data. Such errors are often undetectable when the secondary data are employed and can cause errors in the analysis. A full understanding of these errors requires an understanding of the nature and components of primary research, topics which are more fully explained in Chapter 14.

Errors That Can Invalidate the Data[1]

Secondary data may be contaminated and rendered invalid for use because of actions or attitudes of personnel or the organization performing the data program. The organization gathering the data may manipulate or reorganize the data to meet some specific purpose that is not known by others. Also, the organization collecting the data may be inept. In other instances, the data may have been "adjusted" so that the collecting agency can show that its organizational goals are met, such as portraying the organization in a more favorable light. Or the data must be manipulated purposely to generate adverse conclusions about situations which the collecting agency opposes. If any manipulation occurs, the data are not valid for use.

Other organizations may collect, organize, and distribute data without properly specifying it or, even worse, not caring about its validity. Whenever ineptness, confusion, or carelessness is suspected, the analyst should not use the data.

In addition to the contamination errors that arise because of manipulation, ineptitude, confusion, or carelessness, there is a second broad class of error, called concept error, that can invalidate the data. Data containing concept error may still be used, however, if the analyst can obtain information about the nature of the error. Concept error is defined as the error that arises because of the difference in meaning between the concept, or general idea, that is to be measured (an abstract item) and the indicator or specific item that provides a usable measurement of that concept (a concrete item). A direct measure of a complex concept may not be feasible.

Market analysis is replete with indicator variables that are surrogates for the data which the analyst cannot obtain. For instance, the analyst may be seeking information about household income, which includes wages, salaries, rental income, interest income, and dividends. The indicator used to measure household income may only report wage and salary data. In this case, the indicator contains a large component of household income but has not included all sources of income that the household sector can receive. Or the analyst may seek information on the number of families that reside in the market area. In this sense,

---

[1] The material presented in this section and the subsequent sections on errors are synthesized from: Herbert Jacob, *Using Published Data* (Beverly Hills, CA: Sage Publications, 1984) and David W. Stewart, *Secondary Research* (Beverly Hills, CA: Sage Publications, 1984).

the analyst is seeking information about groups of individuals that are related by blood, marriage, or adoption. The indicator variable used is households. The indicator overstates the number of families because it includes "primary individual households" in addition to "family households." In this instance, while there is a distortion because of the concept differences, adjustments may be made to bring the indicator data closer to the concept idea. The analyst may discover that the average family household comprises 3.5 persons and 92 percent of all households are families. Adjustments could then be made based on these percentages. The indicator data are made more useful, but the nature of the adjustment and the extent of any error in the adjustment should be identified so that others may judge the reliability of the conclusions.

In another example, the analyst is seeking information about the "cost of living" in the market area. The analyst is attempting to discover the "real" expenditures for goods and services of households residing in the market area. The indicator variable used is national consumer price index (CPI) data. In this case, the indicator may not accurately represent the local expenditure because the market basket purchased by the typical household nationwide may not be the same market basket purchased by the typical household residing in the market area. Moreover, there may be a substantial difference between the typical national household and typical local household.

Concept error may, but does not necessarily, invalidate the data and the analysis. The analyst may decide to use the data, even though concept error is present, and deal with it with a variety of techniques. The decision to use the data depends upon the following considerations:

1. *The size of the discrepancy between the concept and the indicator.* If the size of the discrepancy is small, and if the indicator responds similarly to the some causal factors that affect the concept, then the discrepancy in the data could be utilized.

2. *The purpose of the analysis.* An exploratory study is able to tolerate larger errors than a study that is designed to test rather explicit hypotheses.

3. *Availability of valid or accurate data.* If accurate data exist, they should be used. But this statement must be tempered by the cost of accurate data and the time constraints under which the study is being made. If accuracy is costly and cannot be obtained in a timely manner, then the analyst may decide to use data that contain some degree of concept error. In such instances, the analyst should understand both the nature of the concept error as well as its magnitude and direction.

Errors That Require Data Reformulation

The situation may arise where secondary data are not directly useful to the analyst because the data do not adequately measure what the analyst is seeking to measure. The following four errors are commonly found in secondary data that may require reformulation to correct:

1. Errors arising from changing circumstances.
2. Errors arising from inappropriate transformations in the data.
3. Errors arising from inappropriate extrapolation of past data into the future.
4. Errors from inappropriate updating techniques.

Errors Caused by Changing Circumstances This type of error is caused by a change which has not been reflected in the data series. For example, there could have been a change in the geographic boundaries for which the data were gathered. If the geographic size of an MSA increased between 1970 and 1980, MSA population statistics for each of these years would not be comparable until the analyst either added to the 1970 SMSA figure the counties used to expand the 1980 boundaries or removed those counties from the 1980 MSA figure to return to the original 1970 SMSA base.

A change in the underlying unit of measurement can occur. For example, a data series which presented monthly statistics is now presented on a bimonthly basis. The analyst must either combine previous monthly data into bimonthly groupings as currently used or split the bimonthly data in the appropriate way into monthly statistics. The unit of measurement could also have changed because of a shift in the collection time period. Sales that were initially measured from September 1 to August 31 of the following year are now given for the calendar year. In this instance, there is a point in the data where a 9-month unit of measure is followed by a 15-month unit of measure.

An error can arise because the concept being measured is redefined over time. For example, gross leasable area may have been presented as an interior measure in the past, but current standards utilize the exterior dimensions of the structure. Moreover, the concept of net leasable area can also change with the inclusion or exclusion of common areas into the definition.

An error can result from an indicator variable which does not grasp the complexity of the concept variable. A minimum number of customers in a trade area may have been postulated for success. However, the critical issue is not the number of customers; rather, it is the purchasing power directed toward the product or service being provided by that store. The 6,000 people living in the store's trade area may be irrelevant as a success criterion if the tastes and preferences of the people change, or if the price of the product or service changes relative to their income level, or if the prices of substitute products change relative to their income level, or if the price of substitute products changes relative to the price of the product being offered.

Errors That Arise from Inappropriate Transformations Original data are often presented in secondary data sources in categories that were created to make the data more presentable in a tabular format. Data may be presented as, say, a ratio that made sense for the original purpose for which the data are gathered, but does not make sense in the context of the analyst's study. Or the original categories do not reflect the analyst's needs to handle the task at hand. To make this type of error more specific, consider the following.

The indicator variable can utilize the wrong base measurement. For example, the data source might be housing occupancy costs (utility payments, insurance, property tax) per capita when in fact housing occupancy costs are more appropriate on a household basis, not a per capita basis. Another example would be educational expenses per capita, when the more appropriate measure would be educational expenses per student. In each instance, the "per capita" base is not the most appropriate measure.

Secondary data may be presented in groupings by income or rent. The categories may change from one report to another. For example, the top income category in the series may have been $25,000 and up; then a decade later, the top income category may be $50,000 and up. In this instance, a new category, or categories will have to be created for the $25,000 to $50,000 range. This classification problem can exist within a data series and/or between data series. Sometimes the analyst can reassemble one set of categories to resemble the categories or classification scheme used in another data series. Inappropriate base measures or inappropriate and possibly changing classification of data result in data that do not perfectly provide the information needed to resolve the analyst's problem. Unless the analyst transforms the data, the analysis can be flawed.

Errors from Inappropriate Extrapolations   Secondary data often are not available for the intervening years between published reports. Data for intervening years have to be interpolated from the two nearest reporting years. For instance, if the analyst needs information for 1976, the data obtained from the 1970 census and the 1980 census may have to be used. Utilizing only these two points, the interpolation can be made as a straight line or as an exponential rate of change at an increasing or decreasing rate. Without knowing the true path of change between these two points, any one of three answers can be obtained.

Typically, the interpolation is made using an average annual straight-line rate of change, unless the analyst is able to obtain a third point which suggests the shape of the curve. The shape of the curve may also be estimated by analyzing another related data series in which the variable moves at approximately the same direction and magnitude.

Errors from Inappropriate Updating   An obvious error can occur if one of the updating techniques is used incorrectly. For example, the housing inventory method might be used without the vacancy-level adjustment, or the ratio technique might be used without making the adjustment for changing household size. However, the most common error in the updating process arises from a misunderstanding of the nature of the secondary data. The 1980 census reports information as of April 1, 1980 for almost all of the variables. The most notable exception is the income variable, for which data are gathered as of 1979. Very often these data are used as 1980 income, which can either overestimate or underestimate the true income for the individual and the market area. An even more glaring error is the use of data in the year of its publication instead of the year it was gathered. For example, data from *Dollars and Cents of Shopping Centers* was published in 1984, but it is 1983 information, and should not be presented as 1984 information.

Errors That Reduce Reliability

A data set is reliable if successive counts produce the same result. Reliability is not accuracy; the data set is accurate only if it is free from procedural and measurement errors. An inaccurate data set can be reliable if it maintains the same degree of inaccuracy.

The reliability of data is a function of the organization that gathers, organizes, records, and publishes the secondary data. Several issues should be considered when evaluating the organization collecting and disseminating the data, such as whether data collection is the stated purpose of the organization, or whether data collection is merely a secondary or adjunct function. Another issue is whether the individuals and staff that undertake data collection are trained and experienced in data collection procedures. The analyst should also determine whether the organization has adequate resources to do a thorough job.

Errors causing the analyst to question the reliability of the data fall into three categories:

1. Clerical.
2. Changes in collection procedures.
3. Failure to use correct data.

Clerical Errors   To detect the existence of blatant clerical errors, the data might be displayed in an easily comprehended manner (e.g., a scatter plot diagram or a simple table). In this way, "outliers" (data entries that are substantially different from the rest of the data set) can be more easily detected. This procedure will allow the analyst to catch the misplaced decimal, the added zero, or the extra digit.

Error Due to Changes in Collection Procedures   When error results from a change in collection procedure, the data generated may be quite different from previous data in the same data set. This may arise because of the different methods or times (time of day, day of week, season or the year, etc.) used to collect the data. The use of the scatter plot or a simple review of the raw data may reveal discontinuity or a jump in the data points attributable to the change in the collection procedures.

Error Due to Corrected Data   Data can be inconsistent from 'one report to another in the same series because of errors that have been discovered, corrected, and then reflected in subsequent versions of the data set. Most often, these are clerical errors. The analyst needs to use the most recent version to reduce errors. Also, if possible, the analyst should know when data are checked, and when the "clean" version of that data is printed. Whenever secondary data gathered or reorganized at some point in the past are used, the data should always be checked against the newest versions of that data set.

SUMMARY

This chapter deals with issues the analyst must face when beginning the task of designing a data program for real estate market analysis. As a first task, a decision must be made whether to use primary or secondary data. That decision is often based on the type of data needed for the study, and whether or not the data are available from secondary sources. Then the data must be examined to determine if they are sufficiently accurate and reliable to be used. This chapter presents a method for establishing the categories of data needed and the potential sources for that data. Methods of determining the adequacy of secondary data are discussed.

Primary data collection techniques are far more complex. A more detailed discussion of methods of developing and utilizing primary data for real estate market analysis follows in Chapter 14.

READINGS

ELDRED, GARY, and ZERBST, R., "Consumer Research and the Real Estate Appraiser," *The Appraisal Journal*, October, 1976.

RABIANSKI, J., and J. VERNOR, "An Overview of Financial Synthesis of Market Analysis Data," in *Readings in Market Research for Real Estate*, ed. James D. Vernor. Chicago: American Institute of Real Estate Appraisers, 1985.

REDMAN, ARNOLD L., and C. F. SIRMANS, "Regional/Local Economic Analysis: A Discussion of Data Sources," *The Appraisal Journal*, April, 1977.

STEWART, DAVID W., *Secondary Research*. Beverly Hills, Calif.: Sage Publications, 1984.

14

PRIMARY DATA

INTRODUCTION

Real estate analysis relies on marketing strategies and market research, that is, the "systematic gathering, recording and analyzing of data about problems relating to the marketing of goods and services."[1] Since every real estate research problem is in some way unique, individual research protocols are usually custom tailored.

The market research process for real estate analysis involves six steps, as follows:

1. *Problem formulation.* Here is where the client's objectives need to be clarified. What are his or her measures of success? What alternatives are acceptable? What hypotheses are being tested?

2. *Development of the research design.* What is the appropriate level of measurement? Issues of reliability and validity must be considered. Will the study be descriptive, or do we expect causal relationships to exist?

3. *Design of the actual data collection method and questionnaire.* Will only secondary data be used, or will primary data need to be collected? Should data collection be by observation or by questionnaire?

4. *Sample design and the actual data collection.* What is the proper sampling frame? What is the correct sample size? Which sampling methodology is appropriate? How will the questionnaire be administered? If a field force is utilized, how will the team be trained and supervised?

5. *Data analysis and interpretation.* Who will be responsible for key punching, editing, coding, and tabulating the data? Will univariate or multivariate statistical techniques be utilized?

6. *Development of the final report.*

Numerous questions need to be answered in this process, and this chapter will address the subject of questionnaire design and sampling as a means of

[1] Report of Definitions Committee of the American Marketing Association (Chicago: AMA, 1961).

asking the questions that must be raised and answered. First, however, is a discussion of the use of focus groups to assist in the design of research questionnaires.

Focus Groups

In primary research, the data collection is either qualitative or quantitative. Qualitative research involves small groups of people and is generally exploratory in nature. The most commonly used form of qualitative research is the focus group. Because of the group's relatively small size, usually 8 to 12 people, it cannot provide a statistically significant sample. As a result the outcomes cannot be used to describe the population as a whole. Used properly, focus group analysis can assist in identifying research questions for inclusion in the questionnaire, for generating new ideas, and for disaster checking (i.e., determining if questions or answers produce misleading results).

Focus group interviews are usually conducted in a large room that is set up especially for that purpose. Generally, there is a one-way mirror, a conference table, comfortable chairs, and microphones. The client for whom the analysis is being prepared is seated in a dark room behind the one-way mirror where he or she can observe the focus group. The sessions are usually tape recorded and may be videotaped. The focus group participants are told of the one-way mirror and the taping.

The focus group participants are chosen because they have something in common. They may have the demographic characteristics of the target market, or they may be potential users of the project. They are typically homogeneous to the extent possible. Men and women can be included in the same session.

Participants have been told to expect to stay for about two hours and that refreshments will be served. Compensation or other types of incentives may also have to be provided to certain groups of participants, such as builders or representatives of major tenants.

A moderator is required for a focus group. The moderator should be someone who is trained in qualitative research. Prior to the focus group meeting, the moderator will prepare a discussion guide, which is a detailed outline of the questions and the main points to be discussed by the focus group. The discussion guide is reviewed and approved by the client prior to the actual session. The moderator can then utilize the discussion guide (without the knowledge of focus group members so that a stylized format does not stifle or bias responses) and lead participants through the areas that have been agreed upon. A good moderator will look for comments by the participants that might lead to new areas not considered in the discussion guide. Flexibility, without losing sight of the main objectives, is a critical element of any successful focus group.

Usually within two to three weeks after the focus group sessions have been completed, the moderator will listen to the tapes and provide a written report. An experienced moderator can use marketing and research expertise in making observations about why certain things developed during the sessions and suggest future actions. For effective use of the focus group results, the researcher needs complete analysis, not just a summary of the tapes.

Qualitative research techniques are acquired principally from experience rather than in the classroom. Prior to using a particular moderator, try to ascertain his or her level of experience. Experience in the research technique is more important than is knowledge of a particular project. A good moderator should also have a good knowledge of marketing.

In most cases, qualitative research is undertaken as a first step to quantitative research. Remember, an analyst cannot draw statistical inferences from the results of focus groups since they are too small to represent the population as a whole. The analyst can, however, gain insights that will assist with new ideas, questionnaire design, and disaster checking.

QUESTIONNAIRE DESIGN

Primary data are collected by interview, self-administered questionnaires, and direct observation. Regardless of the method of data collection, the analyst must design the format for recording responses and observations in advance of the actual data collection process. Even in direct observation, the analyst has a checklist to ensure complete and orderly collection of data and to facilitate later coding and aggregation.

The content of the questionnaire or checklist will vary with the problem under consideration. The instrument should be designed to facilitate writing the report; that is, the content of the questionnaire or checklist is determined after the problem to be addressed by the report has been defined and after the methodologies to be used are determined. At that point, the data requirements are isolated, and the instrument can be designed to provide the needed information. Tables and other information gathered by the analyst should be easily derived from the questionnaire or survey instrument and should fit logically into an orderly presentation of the report.

Questioning Techniques

Several methods can be used to ask questions. The information desired and the strengths and weaknesses of the individual techniques will determine their use. In selecting a particular technique, the analyst should involve the use of structured or nonstructured questions as well as disguised or nondisguised questions, and whether a personal interview, telephone interview, or self-administered questionnaire sent by mail would be more appropriate. Other considerations include using open-end or closed-end questions and the proper wording of specific questions.

Structured and Unstructured Questionnaires A structured questioning procedure focuses upon a fixed list of predetermined questions. These questions are then asked, and there is no deviation from either the list of questions or the wording within those questions. The nonstructured questionnaire has no fixed list of questions, and an attempt is made to develop a free interchange between the interviewer and the respondent about a specific problem or issue. The interviewer asks questions that flow freely and easily within the conversation and attempts to focus the direction of the conversation to obtain responses that are pertinent to the analysis. For the most part, the questioning procedure used in real estate market analysis is more structured than nonstructured. However, the use of nonstructured interviews is growing; it is frequently a better technique to use when attitudes and preferences are being investigated.

The degree to which the questioning process is structured depends on the data required in the analysis. Factual data, such as age, marital status, income, household characteristics, and spending patterns, can be obtained using a structured questioning process. Perceptual information also can be obtained by means of a structured process. However, if the analyst wishes to know why the perceptions are formed or how they can be changed, then an unstructured or partially structured process might be more suitable for the study. The degree to which the process is structured also varies according to the type of instrument and method of communication that is used.

Disguised and Nondisguised Questioning In a disguised questioning procedure, the objective of the study is not made known to the respondent. In an undisguised questioning process, the objective of the study is made clear to the respondent before the interview begins. For the most part, the questioning procedures involved in real estate market analysis are nondisguised. Disguised procedures are most often used in instances where the subject may be controversial or emotional, and when disclosure could provoke a biased response.

An example of undisguised questioning is that done for marketability studies designed to obtain data about a specific project. The project has to be identified for the respondent. This identification can be handled in several ways:

1. The project can be explicitly identified for the respondent by using phrases such as "are you familiar with the ACME subdivision?" "Do you shop at the Bentwood Plaza?"
2. The project can be implicitly identified for the respondent by using phrases such as "I would like you to consider a single-family subdivision that possesses the following characteristics . . ."; "I would like to ask you questions about your shopping patterns and habits in the vicinity of Broad and Main Streets."

The use of a disguised questioning process in this type of research would cover up the nature of the study and render a large part of the data obtained irrelevant and unusable.

Method of Communication   Three methods of communication are the personal interview, the telephone interview, and the self-administered questionnaire, usually sent by mail. The personal interview is a face-to-face contract between the interviewer and the respondent. The questions can be totally structured because the interviewer can simply hand the respondent a fixed list of questions. In this instance, the interviewer is employing a self-administered questionnaire. The interviewer gives the instrument to the respondent and collects it upon completion. Or the personal interview can be nonstructured, with the interviewer and the respondent entering into a conversation. However, the personal interview is most likely to be partially structured. The interviewer has a predetermined list of questions that are somewhat fixed in the order of presentation, but also has the capability of probing to obtain more complete responses.

The telephone interview also can be structured, partially structured, or nonstructured. The mailed questionnaire by its very nature can only be a structured instrument. It is self-administered by the respondent; the respondent sees the fixed list of questions and responds. When the document is completed, it is returned in a self-addressed envelope.

The choice of method of communication is related to the problem to be addressed and to the budget and time available. If consumer shopping preferences at a particular shopping center are sought, a personal intercept interview would be appropriate. If factual demographic and economic information is required, any of the three methods could be used, typically employing structured or partially structured questions. In-depth probing of attitudes and perceptions requires a personal or telephone interview. Often, time and budget considerations are primary determinants of the method of communication. The mailed questionnaire is often the least expensive, but the most time-consuming. Other methods are more labor intensive and expensive, but costs can be controlled by sampling.

The next section focuses on the type of questions that can be included in the questioning technique. The question forms that will be discussed can be used in any of the three methods of communication: personal interview, telephone interview, and self-administered questionnaire. However, the form of the question is often dictated by the degree of structure utilized in the questioning process. For example, the closed-end question is not a useful question form in the nonstructured questioning process.

Open-End and Closed-End Questions   Only two general types of questions can be asked on the questionnaire. One type is the open-end question in which the respondent fills in a blank with a response that is considered appropriate. Examples of open-end questions are:

1. How much do you typically spend in this store?_____

2. What do you think about condominiums?_____

3. What rent would you pay for a 1200 square foot two-bedroom apartment?____

Open-end questions can be good first questions on a questionnaire when they introduce the subject and obtain general reactions from the respondent. On a structured, mailed questionnaire, an open-end question can serve as an attention-getting device that piques the respondent's interest in completing the questionnaire. An open-end question can bring forth a variety of answers. This can be an advantage because the answers from the respondents may be different from the answers that the analyst might expect to receive.

An open-end question presents certain advantages, but it also creates disadvantages. For example, whereas the open-end question permits the respondent to give the most important or the most appropriate response, the resulting generation of a multitude of responses makes tabulation of the responses difficult.

The first step in dealing with varied responses is to categorize them in some systematic manner, so the analyst-interviewer has to interpret and group the statements that have been made. Sometimes the interpretation reflects the true feeling of the respondent. At other times the interviewer's interpretation may misspecify the respondent's true feelings. For example, the interviewer may have asked the question "What do you like about this shopping center?" The following two responses could have been obtained, "I like the convenience of shopping here" and "There is plenty of parking." The analyst must now determine whether these two responses are the same or whether they are different. More than likely, the analyst would assume that these two statements are not the same. "Convenience" might mean accessibility to the site, but it could also mean proximity of the shopping center to the home. "There is plenty of parking" more than likely means exactly what is stated. A third response might have been, "It's close to home." In this case, it is likely that the respondent saying that the shopping center is "close to home" and the respondent saying that it is "convenient" are both saying the same thing. Such problems of interpretation always arise when open-end questions are used.

An implicit weighting system can appear in open-end questions. They favor the better educated segment of the population, whose members are capable of expressing themselves in writing or orally. Often, the less educated and the less extroverted will only respond in one or two words and will not express their true feelings. In a self-administered questionnaire, the open-ended question requires a greater amount of individual energy and motivation on the part of the respondent than required by a closed-end question. Finally, the nature of the responses to an open-end question typically precludes the use of statistical procedures.

The closed-end question is constructed by presenting the responses assumed to be the most appropriate, most popular, or most frequently given as part of the question. At one end of the spectrum of closed-end questions is the yes/no question, such as

"I like to shop at this shopping mall because the parking lot is adequate."
Yes   No

Here the interviewer makes the assumption that there are only two appropriate responses: "yes" and "no." However, a problem can arise when the respondent may not know the answer, or the fact stated in the question is not relevant to the respondent. Consequently, there is a third option that might be provided: "I don't know." The yes/no or dichotomous question cannot be used in any instance where the respondent may wish to qualify the response.

The most familiar form of a closed-end question is the multiple-choice question, such as

1. "Why do you shop at this mall? Please give the most appropriate response."
   a. There is plenty of parking.
   b. It is close to home.
   c. The facility is clean.
   d. It's on my way home from work.
   e. I like the mix of stores contained in the mall.

The same closed-end question can be asked by having the respondent pick all of the appropriate responses. The question can be reworded in the following way:

2. "Why do you shop at this mall? Please *identify all* of the appropriate statements."

More elaborate forms of a closed-end question often appear on questionnaires. Exhibit 14-1 provides examples of the style and format of such questions. Notice that the question just given has been rewritten in Exhibit 14-1 to differentiate the intensity of the respondent's feelings.

Care must be taken that the responses listed in a closed-end question are mutually exclusive. The possible responses should not have the same meaning or represent the same thing. For example, the phrases "wide selection of goods" and "extensive merchandise mix" would mean the same thing in a question about a retail store. If two responses are requested, the respondent may check both of these and thereby not provide any real information about a second factor. All of the important and appropriate alternatives should be contained within the list of responses. The use of the "other" option can turn a closed-end question into an open-end question if the printed options are not complete and do not contain the most appropriate responses.

Advantages of closed-end questions include the fact that they can be asked quickly and typically require less effort to answer. A properly worded

1. The following statements are provided to obtain your reaction to their importance in exploring why you shop at this shopping mall. Please use the following scale in your response.

a = this factor is very important

b = this factor is moderately important

c = this factor is not important

d = this factor is not part of my decision

There is plently of parking	a	b	c	d
It is close to home	a	b	c	d
The facility is clean	a	b	c	d
It is on the way home from work	a	b	c	d

2. The following statements are provided to obtain your reaction to their importance in explaining why you shop at this shopping mall. Please put an "X" at the point on the line that best represents your opinion.

	very important			not important		
There is plenty of parking						
	1	2	3	4	5	6
It is close to home						
	1	2	3	4	5	6
The facility is clean						
	1	2	3	4	5	6
It is on the way home from work						
	1	2	3	4	5	6
The mix of stores in the mall						
	1	2	3	4	5	6

Exhibit 14-1 Closed-end Questions.

closed-end question facilitates a response by making the respondent willing to provide an answer and by triggering the respondent's recall capabilities about the important or appropriate answer. The closed-end question also eliminates bias in recording the answers, in tabulating the responses and in assembling the data. The predetermined form of the response makes tabulation and analysis relatively quick and permits the use of statistical analysis.

Disadvantages of closed-end questions include the fact that the prede-termined responses can eliminate the spontaneity, diversity, and independent thought of the respondent. Also, the list of choices may be incomplete, inap-propriate, or not mutually exclusive, affecting the quality of the information obtained. Closed-end questions may present too many alternatives to the re-spondent. If the list of responses is too long, the respondents are not able to remember the items when that list is read to them. Consequently, a question with a long response list works better on a written questionnaire than on a personal interview or telephone interview. A closed-end question can also create a response bias because of the order in which the alternatives are presented to the respondent. This bias of position can be overcome by alternating the order in which alternatives are listed. However, this solution requires the printing of several forms of the questionnaire. Often it is not clear to the respondent that more than one answer is possible or requested. If uniformity of response across all respondents is desired, it is necessary to make the number of choices that should be selected clear to the respondents. This avoids the problem of one respondent selecting two answers while another respondent selects six. Finally, the phrase "select the best answer" should not be used to cover up a poorly worded question.

Choice of Words for a Question

There are a number of important ideas that the analyst must keep in mind when choosing words for a specific question. The ideas presented here are rules of thumb to be followed, not fundamental principles. However, an understanding and utilization of these points can avoid confusion and misunderstanding in the mind of the respondent. The researcher assumes the burden of conforming to the respondent's level of understanding and of using language and vocabulary that the respondent can correctly interpret. Each question should focus on the respondent's previous knowledge or experience. For example, the following question can lead to a misunderstanding: "Given your understanding of the typical household's current need for living space, which of the following design features should be included in homes of the future?" This question presupposes that the respondent knows the space needs of the typical household. If the respondent does not know, and guesses, then the answer to the question will be unreliable and may be useless. If the analyst is seeking the respondent's desires about space needs, the question should be written in the following manner: "What design feature would you like to see in the home of the future?" If the analyst is seeking the respondent's opinion about the desires of the typical household, the analyst should first determine if the respondent is able to answer the question.

Each question should be a single question. The analyst should check each question and look for the word "and." When the word "and" is found in a question, there is a danger that two questions are being asked instead of one. For example, "Would you use this shopping mall if there were more parking and the appearance of the mall were improved?" If the answer is yes, does that mean that the respondent would frequent the mall if more parking were made available or only if both changes were made? Analyzing the question reveals that it is really two questions and, thus, should be avoided.

Questions should use simple words. The words should only have one meaning, and that meaning should be universally known. However, if the word can be misinterpreted, its meaning should be clarified by the context of the question or by some additional explanation. To the best of the analyst's ability, the words used should be common, everyday words. However, "slang" or "street talk" should not be used. The researcher should also stay away from technical and specialized terms that are familiar to the analyst but not to the respondent.

The question should not be ambiguous. Words such as "usually," "normally," "frequently," "regularly," and so on are ambiguous because what is "frequent" to one person may be "infrequent" to another.

The question should not lead the respondent to an answer, nor should it influence the respondent in any way. An example of a leading question is the following: "Most experts agree that the house of the future will be smaller. When choosing your next house, which of the following will be least important to you?" This question could lead the respondent to say things such as square footage, or the number of rooms, because "the experts" are predicting smaller homes.

Loaded questions should be avoided. Words to which strong emotional feelings or reactions are attached should not be used. Such words can produce a reaction to the loaded term but not to the concept or issue of the question. Contrast the loaded question "Do you approve of the city's new bureaucracy to control land uses?" with the question "Do you approve of the city's new zoning procedure to control land uses?" The term "bureaucracy" can lead to a biased response.

Questions should not be long and complicated. The respondents should be able to read a question quickly, understand its content, and select an answer without difficulty. The respondent should not have to reread or have the question repeated before an answer is given. The single focus of each question should be clearly identified so the respondent is not mislead. The questions should specify whether the analyst is seeking the respondent's opinion about a topic, or whether the analyst is seeking the respondent's opinion about the general, public reaction to a selected item.

Consider the following questions: "Is the single-family, detached house a better housing alternative than a condominium?" and "Do you think that a single-family detached house is a better housing alternative than a condominium?" It is possible that a respondent will give a different response to each of these two similar questions. The first question might elicit the respondent's opinion about what the general public thinks is the better alternative. The second response is directed at the respondent's opinion. Notice that it asks, "Do you think . . . ?" To eliminate the confusion about the proper focus, the two questions should have been written as "Do you think that single-family, detached housing is a better housing alternative than a condominium?" and "In your opinion, do you think that the general public views the single-family, detached house as a better housing alternative than the condominium?"

Questionnaire Design

Three major issues are involved in the design of questionnaires. The first is the nature of the introductory and instructional material. The second is the sequencing or ordering of the questions as they appear on the self-administered questionnaire, or as they are asked in either the personal or telephone interview. The third is the physical layout or design of the self-administered questionnaire.

Introductory Material The opening statement introduces the respondent to the nature of the project and to the purpose of seeking responses. Thus, this opening statement makes the questionnaire a nondisguised questioning process. The introduction should instill a desire to participate and should clarify the process and the procedures of the instrument.

If the researcher can tap underlying motives, both the degree of participation by a single individual and the degree of participation within the group or sample can be increased. Participation can be increased if one of the following is present: (1) the respondent finds the topic to be interesting or important; (2) the respondent is impressed by the prestige or visibility of the research agency; or (3) the potential respondents' self-esteem or egos are flattered by having their opinions and views sought. A good introductory statement will identify the purpose of the study. If an interview is being conducted, the interviewer identifies himself or herself and the purpose of the interview. The introduction should establish the interviewer's friendliness and interest in the respondents and their views. The introduction will help to develop a rapport between the respondent and the interviewer. As part of this process, the name of the agency should be used if it is appropriate for the study. In real estate market analysis, the name of the agency or the research group is often a neutral factor, and little is to be gained by using the name and the affiliation. But, if the agency is important, it should be presented to the respondent in the questionnaire and in the interview.

The researcher must know and understand the concerns of respondents that reduce their willingness to participate. Respondents are usually concerned about the use to which the information will be put. This is a general concern about all the information they provide, but it is especially true for questions which they consider to be embarrassing or threatening. This concern must be diminished at the beginning. The usual way to alleviate the concern is a guarantee of anonymity, given verbally in the interview and in written form on the self-administered questionnaire.

Respondents may be apprehensive about participating because they think that the questions will be embarrassing, threatening, difficult, meddlesome, or personal. It is useful to disspell this worry by giving the respondent an idea about the nature of the questions that will be asked. The following statements can be used to accomplish the desired purpose:

1. "For the most part the questions are designed to obtain your opinions concerning housing attributes. We do not feel that the questions are personal or difficult."

2. "We will be presenting you with a series of straightforward questions about the attributes of new housing units. The questions are not personal or difficult."

The respondents would like to be assured that their time commitment will not be inordinate if they agree to participate. This concern can be eliminated by giving them an approximate time for completion. The following statement could be made: "We have tested this questionnaire (or interview) and it usually takes 5 minutes to complete."

The introductory statement also clarifies the questioning process and procedures. Each questionnaire should contain clear instructions and introductory statements to minimize confusion and to elicit straightforward, unbiased responses. The objective of the introduction is to attract the respondent's attention and to provide the direction to feel competent and comfortable in giving honest answers. If the respondents are not interested in the subject matter, or if the respondents feel that their contributions to the process are insignificant, there will be a marked reduction in the willingness to cooperate in the questioning process. Therefore, this opening statement should clarify the purpose of the interview and draw out the respondent's desire to participate. Self-administered questionnaires must have the greatest clarity because the respondent cannot ask for clarification and direction.

Each self-administered questionnaire should begin with the basic instructions that are required to answer the questions and to complete the questionnaire. The information that is typically contained in such an introduction consists of statements concerning the purpose and content of questionnaire. The information also contains instructions to guide the respondent in answering the questions. For closed-end questions, the instructions could say, "Place a checkmark or an 'X' in the box next to the appropriate response." If the question is open-ended, the instructions should give guidance about the length of the answer. In addition to the introduction and instructions for the questionnaire as a whole, it is often useful to present introductory material and special instructions at the beginning of each major section of the questionnaire. These shorter introductions can help the respondent make sense of the questionnaire and show the logic of the questioning pattern. Moreover, good instructions for each major section can make the respondent willing to continue with the questionnaire.

Instructions may also be necessary within the body of a question to aid the respondent to provide an answer. Special instructions inside a question are required when the question contains a list of possible responses and the researcher desires some fixed number of actual responses. In this instance, the special instructions should tell the respondent to select one answer, three answers, or some other definite number. The wording might be, "From the list below, please identify the most important reason for your decision," or "From the list below, please identify the three most important reasons for your decisions." Instructions may also be needed when a list of options is given inside the question. The respondent may be requested to identify several options and then to rank order those options. In this instance, the instructions within the question might read, "Please read all the options below and then select the three most important reasons underlying your decision. Number the most important reason as '1', the second most important reason as '2', and the third most important reason as '3'."

Sequencing Questions

Proper sequencing of questions is essential both to ensure unbiased responses and to provide order in analyzing responses. Several issues related to sequencing follow.

Opening Questions   After the introductory information is presented, the opening questions appear on the questionnaire. They should logically follow the introductory statement. These opening questions should heighten the respondent's interest in participating in the questioning process and be simple and easy to answer. In addition, they should deal with topics that are important in the mind of the respondent. In this way, the opening questions help to justify the time and effort required for participation.

The exact nature of the opening question is dependent upon the method of questioning. The opening questions on a self-administered questionnaire should not be the same as the opening questions on an instrument designed for personal interviews or telephone interviews. For the self-administered questionnaire, the opening questions should pique the respondent's curiosity and heighten the respondent's interest in participating in the questionnaire. Typically, questions that ask for the respondent's opinion are good opening questions on a self-administered questionnaire. If the respondent can handle the relatively simple first questions, he or she develops a sense of confidence about being able to handle the task and do it well.

The opening questions for either a personal or telephone interview should focus on the development of ease of expression and conversation between the respondent and the interviewer. The interviewer should first make a short statement that introduces the potential respondent to the nature of the study and the respondent's contribution to that study. Then, after this short introduction, the interviewer can ask questions about demographic data. These questions cannot be threatening. They should establish a rapport and conviviality between the individuals. The following questions capture the nature and tone of questions that elicit demographic information:

1. "Can you tell me how many people are in your family?"
2. "How old are the children?"
3. "What are their names?" (This can be a somewhat reliable way of getting to the sex of the children.)
4. "Can you give me the approximate age of your wife or husband?"

The nature of these questions is nonthreatening. They focus on the type of information that new acquaintances might exchange as they get to know each other. The tone of the question is friendly and exhibits an interest and a curiosity on the part of the interviewer.

Middle and Ending Questions   The middle questions in the self-administered questionnaire and in the interview focus on the information that is required in the analysis of the subject property. These questions can be questions of preference, attitude, and opinion. Requests for demographic and economic data should generally be placed at the end of the instrument, since these facts are the least interesting for the respondent to provide in written form. If requests for demographic and economic information appear at the beginning, the respondent may quickly lose motivation to complete the form.

In the interview, embarrassing or threatening questions should be placed in the middle or ending sections of the questionnaire, after interest and rapport have been established. This rule-of-thumb is appropriate for an interview because, if the respondent terminates, at least some useful information has been gathered from previous questions. For a self-administered questionnaire, the rule-of-thumb may have negligible benefits. If the respondent stops responding, the questionnaire is usually discarded. It is returned unfinished in only a small number of cases.

Difficult or complex questions should be placed in the middle portion of the questionnaire. They are not good opening questions because they establish the wrong frame of mind; they are not good ending questions because they require concentration and a desire to compete on the respondent's part. Difficult and complex questions should be asked after the respondent is comfortable with the process but not too tired to answer.

Logical Ordering of Questions   Whether the questionnaire is self-administered or an interview, the questions within that instrument should be presented to the respondent in a logically ordered fashion. The analyst should identify major areas of similarity among the questions and group those questions. For example, suppose the analyst wishes to obtain three different categories of data: (1) demographic information about the respondent, (2) preferences and opinions about the dwelling unit in which they reside, and (3) opinions about the structural characteristics of a new townhouse community being developed in the neighborhood. The questionnaire could be divided into these three broad categories. When the interviewer is asking for preferences and opinions about the existing unit in which the respondent lives, there are no questions in the logical flow about either demographic data or opinions concerning the new development.

A respondent who becomes frustrated with a confusing sequence of questions increasingly responds, "I don't know" or "I am indifferent." Notice that the logical sequence is really in the mind of the respondent. The analyst has to be able to put himself into the mind of the respondent and to develop the logical sequence that the respondent would like to see.

Funnel Method   Some researchers who accept the need for a logical pattern and order to the questions often advocate the use of general questions to start the investigation, and then the use of specific questions. This approach is called the funnel method. It is usually used for a sequence of questions in a questionnaire. It can be used for the entire questionnaire, but this is less likely. The funnel process starts with a question or a short series of questions designed to obtain information about the respondent's knowledge, attitudes, feelings, or concerns toward the issue. These questions allow the researcher to discover the respondent's frame of reference and level of knowledge before the specific aspects of the issue are disclosed. These questions also allow the researcher to filter or screen out the uninformed or disinterested respondents.

After the filter or screening questions separate the respondents into two or more groups, the appropriate specific questions can be directed at each group. This approach increases the accuracy of the information received from each group and allows the researcher to make comparisons among the distinct groups.

The inverted funnel method reverses the sequence of questions in the funnel approach. Specific questions are asked first, and general questions follow. The inverted funnel method may be used when the initial reaction of a respondent is desired before any type of group identity is suggested. Once respondents perceive themselves as part of a group, which the thinly veiled general questions often suggest, the responses may contain less personal opinion and become imbued with the respondent's opinion of group values.

Sequence Bias   Sequence bias is concerned with the effect that one question can have on the answers to subsequent questions. For example, a questionnaire may be designed to obtain information about preferences regarding the physical layout of single-family, detached housing. The researcher may go through a series of questions that focus on the design features of the structure and the layout of the rooms within that structure. Three, four, or five questions of this nature can appear one after another. Then, the next question might ask for the most important features that the consumer is looking for in the selection of a single-family detached dwelling unit. The response to this last question could be biased by the preceding questions which focused the consumer's attention on the layout of the rooms within the structure.

Sequence bias can be eliminated by randomizing the questions within the questionnaire. Randomization, however, is contrary to the need for a logical order of questions in the questionnaire. Also, upon close examination, even the randomly generated questionnaire may have a sequencing of questions that generate bias. However, the nonlogical sequencing makes identification of the direction of the bias difficult. The analyst must decide whether a logical ordering of the questions or a random list of questions is to be used in the questionnaire. The logical ordering seems preferable for most real estate market research problems. After making every attempt to eliminate sequence bias in the questionnaire, whatever sequence bias may appear can be partially predicted and used to adjust the actual responses received.

An issue related to the sequence bias is the ability of the respondent to change the response to an earlier question based upon the response or thought process involved in a later question. For example, the third question on a questionnaire might be

3. What is your preferred housing choice?
   a. Single-family detached house
   b. Townhouse
   c. Low-rise condominium
   d. High-rise condominium
   e. An apartment

The respondent may have chosen townhouse as the response to this question. Then subsequent questions appear on the questionnaire, and at some point the following question is asked:

15. Given that many townhouse communities have management and association fees just like condominiums, but the townhouse owner must insure and maintain the dwelling, do you think that this difference will influence consumer acceptance of these two forms of housing? Specifically, answer the following question: Do you feel that the low-rise condominium is preferable to the fee-simple townhouse surrounded by communal property?

If the respondent chose to answer "yes" to this subsequent question, he or she may then wish to go back to question 3 and change the response in that question based on the information given in question 15. The trained analyst could look at the responses to these two questions, see that they are contradictory, and make the valid assumption that the respondent did not know the difference between a fee-simple townhouse development and a condominium development. This would signal the need to educate the consumer about the product if the subject property is designed as a fee-simple townhouse community or if the subject property is a mixed-residential-use development containing both condominiums and fee-simple townhouses. The builder does not want someone buying a townhouse, paying lower maintenance and association fees, but not realizing that the burden of maintaining and insuring the property rests with the owner of the fee-simple townhouse.

Returning to the main issue, the respondent in this example may go back and change the response to question 3 given the information contained in question 15. If he or she does, then there has been a bias generated in the responses to question 3. In the self-administered questionnaire, this bias may not be detectable if the individual can easily erase the original response to question 3. To deter this bias in a self-administered questionnaire, it may be wise to imprint the questions on nonerasable paper stock.

The problem of changing answers does not exist in the interview because the interviewer can make a note of the original answer and then also make a note of the change. Moreover, the interviewer can also indicate at what point in the questioning process the change was made.

Questionnaire Format

There are several issues about the format of the questionnaire to be used. Some of these are addressed next.

The Physical Layout and Format The physical layout or format of the questionnaire is important. If the questionnaire is improperly printed, several problems may arise. Respondents can miss questions, they may be confused about the nature of the answer that is requested, or they may become frustrated enough to stop responding. As a general rule, the questionnaire should be neat and uncluttered. Designing an uncluttered questionnaire format involves:

1. Leaving sufficient white space on the page to permit the respondent to see each individual question and to read the instrument without strain. The uncluttered format allows the analyst to direct the respondent's attention to each question individually and to the overall flow of the questions.
2. Specifying sufficiently large typeface or lettering to allow the respondent to read the question without strain.
3. Never placing two different questions on the same line in the questionnaire.
4. Avoiding abbreviations of questions and words.

The physical layout of the questionnaire must permit the respondents to indicate clearly their choices of response to a closed-end question. Exhibit 14-2 provides several forms for collecting the responses to a very simple question. The format chosen should produce the least confusion when the data are tabulated.

Providing only the blank line for a response can lead to the most confusion in tabulating answers because individuals may place a checkmark that crosses over several lines. Therefore, either a "box ☐" or a "circle-the-letter" format should be used. In a questionnaire where the responses are tightly grouped, it may be best to use the box ☐ as the response format.

Contingency Questions Certain questions may only be relevant for a subset of the respondents to a previous question. This topic was initially discussed conceptually in the section on the funnel method, but questionnaire format also is involved. In Exhibit 14-3 the first question the respondents are asked is whether

What is your age? Please indicate the appropriate age group by placing a checkmark next to the age group.

_____	under 18
_____	18 to 25
_____	25 to 34
_____	35 to 44
_____	45 and above

What is your age? Please indicate the appropriate age group by putting an "X" inside the square next to the age group.

☐	under 18
☐	18 to 24
☐	25 to 34
☐	35 to 44
☐	45 and above

What is your age? Please indicate the appropriate age group by putting a circle around the letter in front of the age group.

a.	under 18
b.	18 to 24
c.	25 to 34
d.	35 to 44
e.	45 and above

Exhibit 14-2 Questionnaire Formats.

they belong to the local PTA. Some respondents will answer "yes," others "no." For those who answer "yes," a follow-up question is asked. This question only has reference to the "yes" respondents. Notice how the researcher directs the respondent's attention to this second question, which is known as the contingency question. The respondent reads question 10, answers "yes," and then immediately encounters the arrow that leads to the contingency question.

The second example in Exhibit 14-3 shows a double contingency question. Notice in this instance that the respondent is shown that a "yes" answer to question 16 leads to contingency question "a" and contingency question "b." But, in the event that contingency question "b" receives a "yes" response, there is a second contingency question to which the respondent is directed by an arrow.

10. Have you ever belonged to the local chapter of the American Institute Real Estate Appraisers?

☐ Yes ─────────────────────┐

☐ No

> **If yes:** Have you ever held an office
> in the local chapter?
>
> ☐ Yes
>
> ☐ No

16. Have you ever heard anything about Enterprize Zones?

☐ Yes ─────────────────────┐

☐ No

> **If yes:**
>
> a. Do you generally approve or
>   disapprove of that program?
>
>   ☐ Approve
>   ☐ Disapprove
>   ☐ No opinion
>
> b. Have you ever attended a
>   seminar on this topic?
>
>   ☐ Yes ──────┐
>
>   ☐ No
>
>   > **If yes:** When?
>   >
>   > _____

Exhibit 14-3 Contingency Questions: Self-Administered Questionnaire.

The questions in Exhibit 14-3 are relevant for self-administered questionnaires where the respondent cannot ask the researcher what to do. The directions must be clear and not confusing. The use of the contingency question format provided in Exhibit 14-3 is one of the better procedures for contingency questions, with the contingency question put inside a box and indented away from the main flow of the questions. In this way, the respondent knows that if a "no" response is given to a question, the contingency question does not apply and he or she can move on to the next question.

In the interview format, the flow of contingency questions can be more complex because the interviewer can be trained to record the responses properly. Exhibit 14-4 provides a contingency question format that would be appropriate for a personal interview or a telephone interview. This form of the contingency question would be very confusing if it appeared on a self-administered questionnaire. Individuals who respond "yes" to question 38 are taken along one

Q-38

Have you purchased a house during the last year?

(1) Yes ─────────┐

Q-38.A ◄──────────┘

   What was the age of the
   property?

   1. New
   2. Less than 2 years old

Q-38.B

   Did you purchase the property
   direct from the builder?

   1. Yes
   2. No

Q-38.C

   Who served as middleman in
   your purchase?

   1. My agent or attorney
   2. A licensed real estate agent/broker
      (other than the builder's employee)
   3. Nobody

Q-38.D

   What was the price range of
   the property you purchased?

   1. Under $40,000
   2. $40,001 to $80,000
   3. $80,001 to $120,000
   4. Over $120,000

(2) No ─────────┐

Q-38.E ◄──────────┘

   Had you seriously shopped for a property
   during the year even though you didn't
   make a purchase?

   1. Yes ─────────┐
   2. No

Q-38.F ◄──────────┘

   Why did you not purchase?

   1. Haven't yet found the right property.
   2. Couldn't qualify for financing due to
      income.
   3. Couldn't qualify for financing due to
      down payment.

Q-38.G

   Do you think you will purchase a property
   in the next year or so?

   1. Yes ─────────┐
   2. No

Q-38.H ◄──────────┘

   What is the probable price range of the
   property you will purchase?

   1. Under $40,000
   2. $40,001 to $80,000
   3. $80,001 to $120,000
   4. Over $120,000

TURN TO NEXT PAGE

Exhibit 14-4 Contingency Questions: Interview Format.

path; those who responded "no" to question 38 are taken along a separate and different path. Then, the individuals who responded "no" to question 38 are directed along different contingency paths according to their responses to questions 38e and 38f.

Interviewer Influence

When a personal interview or a telephone interview is undertaken, the presence of the interviewer can affect responses. These interviewer effects can arise from two sources. First, the effects can arise from the respondent's reaction to the presence of an interviewer and to the perceptions he or she may have about this specific interviewer. Second, the effects can occur because of the attitudes, bearing (body language), tone of voice, or vocabulary of the interviewer.

Traits of the interviewer are important because they often determine the quality of the information. The researcher must be alert to this problem, but a thorough discussion of the selection and training of interviewers is beyond the scope of this text.

Favorable effects from the interviewer's presence include the following:

1. The interviewer has the ability to probe and secure additional information that is not readily volunteered but is available through subsequent questioning.
2. The interviewer may be able to gauge the truthfulness of the response, especially in a personal interview, when observation can be relied upon for supplemental data. For example, if the personal interview is taking place at the residence, the size, location, and appearance of the house can be used to support the respondent's answer to a question about income, wealth, or asset holdings.
3. The presence of an interviewer eliminates the respondent's ability to change early responses based on facts or perceptions provided by later questions.
4. The presence of an interview can eliminate misunderstanding on the part of the respondent. The interviewer can clarify any confusing point that may arise with regard to a question on the questionnaire.

Disadvantages from the interviewer's presence include the following:

1. The presence of an interviewer can cause the respondent to fabricate answers. The respondent may feel a need to impress the interviewer and as a result exaggerate income levels. Or the respondent may give the kind of response that the respondent thinks the interviewer would like. The respondent may even give answers that build self-prestige or enhance his or her ego.
2. The presence of an interviewer reduces the feeling of anonymity and may reduce the respondent's willingness to participate in the interview.
3. The presence of an interviewer can cause recording error when the interviewer must translate a verbal response into a short, written statement that is placed on the questionnaire.
4. The interviewer can fake responses or fill in the questionnaires without actually undertaking the questioning procedure. This problem can be minimized by having the project supervisor warn the interviewer that returned questionnaires will be checked and the responses verified. It is advisable to verify a randomly selected number of interviews.

Questionnaire Pretest

After the questionnaire is developed, the researcher should select a small representative sample of respondents to pretest the questionnaire or interview. The pretest permits deficiencies in the instrument to be detected. Problems and troublesome areas in the introductory material, the selection of question types, the wording of the questions, and the sequencing of the questions can be identified.

Several hints can be offered for the pretesting process:

1. It may be useful to pretest a self-administered questionnaire in an interview format to give the interviewer a chance to probe, clarify, and discover any confusion. Then, each question on the questionnaire should be pretested in the form in which it will be given.

2. An open-ended format for a question in the pretest can help identify the list of responses for a closed-end question. However, the actual closed-end questions should also be pretested.

3. Different versions of a question, or different sequences of questions, can be tried to see which works best.

4. It might be necessary to pretest several times if the instrument is complicated or substantive changes are made after the previous pretest.

5. Several options for indicating responses can be utilized and compared for recording answers.

6. Several options for establishing contingency question formats can be tested.

The researcher should examine the pretest questions for

1. Confusing instructions about the nature and format of the responses.

2. An overly high response rate in the "I don't know," "indifferent," and "other, please specify" choices in closed-end questions.

3. A high rate of no response or no answer given to individual questions.

4. An extreme diversity in open-end questions. This means that the responses are not in the same general area or train of thought. For example, a question such as "What do you feel about low-cost housing?" could elicit two diverse sets of answers if the context of the question is not clear. Some respondents might say, "Yes the housing industry should attempt to lower the costs of building housing." Other respondents might say, "I'm opposed to those types of federal government handouts."

5. A high incidence of multiple answers to closed-end questions seeking a single answer.

6. An inability to follow the paths established in a contingency question. This can be signaled by a high degree of missing answers.

7. A high incidence of write-in responses where none are called for, a high incidence of direct comments concerning wording, and a high incidence of qualified responses.

8. No variance in responses when such variation is logically anticipated and needed for the analysis. And the opposite situation, great variance in response when very little is anticipated.

9. Difficulty in reading the responses to closed-end questions.

Pretesting is a most critical step in the process of questionnaire design and should not be skipped or ignored. In each case, the task is to make the questioning process applicable to the respondent. The characteristics of the population and sample under investigation change from study to study, and the interpretation of the same questions may change among the groups. Yesterday's experience is helpful to the researcher, but it is not definitive.

Sample Selection

Once the issues surrounding the type of questions to use, the wording of the questions, the sequencing of the questions, the structure of the questionnaire, and pretesting of the questionnaire have been addressed, the sample must be selected. Major issues in the sample selection process include (1) defining the population or universe to be sampled, (2) deciding whether to use a probability or nonprobability sample, (3) determining sample size, (4) handling nonresponses, and (5) recognizing the very practical budget and time constraints for the research at hand.

Determining the Population   Depending on the specific assignment that the analyst is undertaking, there is a definite group of people, households, firms or properties—the population—that is of interest. If the analyst is delineating a trade area for an existing, small-neighborhood shopping center, then the population consists of those people who frequent the shopping center as well as those who are potential customers of the shopping center. This population can be identified by determining the geographical extent of the trade area. The households that reside within the trade area are the population for the study.

Interviewing every household in the trade area would be very costly and time consuming. Consequently, the analyst selects a sample from the population. Properly accomplished, the characteristics of the population can be inferred from the characteristics of the sample.

Frame Error   To start the sampling procedure, the analyst identifies each element (household, firm, property) in the population. If each element is not identified, the analyst commits a nonsampling error which is often called "frame error." The following example explains the nature of frame error.

Assume that the analyst is attempting to discover the attitudes and the level of use that households in a metropolitan area have for their telephones. To undertake the study, the analyst identifies the telephone directory as the list that enumerates each element of the population. However, even though the telephone directory is the most readily accessible source of information, if it is used to select the sample, frame error is committed. The error, and its consequent bias on the results, arises because certain significant groups of the population are not listed in the telephone directory.

First, the telephone directory does not contain the elements of the population who cannot afford a telephone or, for some reason, have chosen not to possess a telephone. Second, the telephone directory does not contain the elements of the population who have chosen to maintain unlisted telephone numbers (random-digit dialing may overcome problems with unlisted numbers). Third, the telephone directory is published at a specific point in time. Therefore, the information in the telephone directory can be a year old. If this occurs, people who moved into the area are not listed. If the analyst chooses a sample from the telephone directory, these three groups of individuals have no choice of making their attitudes and use levels known.

To avoid frame error or to minimize its impact, the analyst must make certain that the list is as thorough and as complete as possible. If close scrutiny of the list (the telephone directory) reveals that certain elements of the population are not represented, then the analyst must attempt to obtain information about these individuals and include them in the enumerated population. In practice, the real estate analyst often cannot identify all elements of the population to be sampled. The analyst may make the assumption that the elements which have been located constitute the population. If this is not true, this assumption may lead to another problem—results are biased without the analyst's knowledge.

Selecting the Sample   When the analyst has the list of the population, a decision must be made between a random sample and a nonrandom sample. For the most part, a random sample is preferable because it allows the analyst to use statistical analysis to determine the magnitude of sampling error that can arise. If a nonrandom sample is selected, then the analyst is unable to determine the effect of sampling error on the results of the study.

Sampling error occurs when the sample selected from the population does not provide information about the exact nature of the population's cumulative responses. For example, if the analyst were to ask the question, "Do you shop at the Acme grocery store?" 60 percent of the population would respond "yes." Therefore, a 60 percent "yes" response is the true population response. However, this question is not asked of all households in the population, so the analyst does not know the true response.

If a sample is drawn from the population and 57 percent of the elements in the sample respond "yes," they shop at the Acme grocery store, the sample does not reflect the true population response. There is sampling error. However, in this instance, the error is not large. If a second sample were drawn from this population, a response of 30 percent "yes" might be obtained, or a response of 90 percent "yes" might be obtained. In these two instances, the sampling error is large. The use of the random sampling process and statistical inference allows the analyst to make the judgment that the information obtained from the first sample, that is, the one in which the "yes" response was 57 percent, is a reliable estimate of the true population response. The 30 percent response from the second sample is not a reliable estimate of the true population.

Nonrandom samples drawn from the population do not allow the analyst to test for the reliability of the estimate generated by the sample. Thus, the analyst may not be aware of the magnitude of the sampling error.

Probability Sampling Techniques   Probability sampling is based on the principle that each element in the population has a known chance of being selected into the sample. A consistent example is used in the following paragraphs to discuss the various types of probability samples.

An analyst is asked to study a neighborhood shopping center and identify the population as all households who live in the trade area. The analyst obtains a list of mailing addresses for each dwelling unit in the trade area. Then, the analyst checks the list to make certain that frame error does not occur. In this instance, frame error can occur if there are basement apartments in single-family housing units and the tenants receive mail at the same address as the home-owners. It can also occur if previous commercial units were converted into residential dwellings and did not appear on the list of housing units or if certain addresses are apartment buildings. In these instances, the frame error occurs because the list is not a one-to-one correspondence with the households. In the case of the apartment or the apartment building, two or more households exist at the same point in space while the list only identifies one housing unit. After the analyst checks the list to eliminate frame error, there are several ways that a random sample can be drawn from the population.

There are four forms of probability sampling that can be used: simple random, systematic random, stratified random, and cluster. Once random selection is utilized to establish a probability sampling technique, the researcher can rely on statistical analysis to make judgments about the impact of sampling error in the study. If the random selection process is not utilized, then statistical analysis yields unreliable results. Also, when the population cannot be completely identified, statistical analysis or sampling error may give unreliable results.

Regardless of the use of the random selection process, nonsampling errors are not eliminated by probability sampling. Therefore, the researcher should be aware of both frame error and nonresponse error.

The Simple Random Sample The analyst can use the simple random sampling technique by cutting the list of mailing addresses into separate pieces of paper so that one mailing address occurs on each piece. The pieces of paper are dropped into a hat and are shaken vigorously to make sure that the slips of paper are randomly distributed. Then, the analyst selects the appropriate number of slips of paper to be drawn from the hat. (The selection of the sample size will be discussed in a later section.) Assume that 4,000 slips are in the hat and that the analyst decides to select 300 elements for the sample. The procedure requires the analyst to draw a slip of paper out of the hat one at a time and then replace it until 300 slips of paper have been drawn. This procedure may also be used without replacement. In this manner, each slip has an equal and known probability of being drawn before it is in fact drawn. As an alternative, the analyst may number each element in the population and use the table of random numbers to select the sample.

The Systematic Random Sample For the most part, the analyst will not cut the population list into strips and place them into a hat in order to select the sample. Instead, the analyst recognizes that there are 4,000 housing units identified on the list and that 300 of them are needed for the sample. A quick calculation is made; 4,000 divided by 300 reveals that every thirteenth element in the list would have to be drawn to obtain a sample of 300. The random selection process can be insured by undertaking several actions. First, the analyst writes the numbers 1 through and including 13 on individual slips of paper and places these slips of paper into the hat, shakes the hat vigorously, and then selects one slip of paper out of that hat. If, for example, number 7 is withdrawn, the systematic random sample procedure would require that the seventh name on the list is selected for the sample and then every thirteenth element after that. So, the sample would consist of elements 7, 20, 33, 46, and so on.

A second way of performing a systematic random sample could involve the selection of a fixed number of elements from each one of a fixed number of papers in the list. For example, if the 4,000 households were printed on a list of 50 pages, the analyst could randomly select items to be drawn from each page. For example, 50 pages would contain 4,000 names if 80 names appear on each page. The analyst could randomly select five numbers between 1 and 80 and then take that entry on each page. So, the fourth, sixteenth, twenty-first, thirty-eighth, sixty-seventh, and seventy-fifth names on each page could be selected by the random selection process.

There is an inherent danger in the systematic random sample in that it can distort the results. Consider the following example. The analyst wants information about the level of satisfaction of the tenants in a 10-story, high-rise apartment building with 10 apartments on each floor. Each floor is exactly the same, so apartment 101 lies directly below 201, which lies directly below 301. Moreover, apartment 108 lies directly below 208 and 202 lies directly below 302. Also, the floor plan in each apartment is identical. The analyst chooses a systematic sample of placing the numbers 1 through 10 in a hat and withdraws numbers 1 and 8. Based on this procedure, the dwellers of apartments 1 and 8 on each floor are interviewed. If apartment 1 on each floor is located next to the laundry room and the trash collection facility, while apartment 8 on each floor is located next to the elevator, the information concerning the attitudes and level of satisfaction with the apartment will be based on the opinion of the dwellers of the least desirable units on each floor. In this instance, a systematic random sample should not have been chosen and performed in the manner that the analyst established. The random selection process exists, but the numbering system in the structure created a bias in this case. It would have been better for the analyst to have taken a simple random sample of the tenants.

The Stratified Random Sample The stratified random sampling procedure starts with the recognition that there is an important characteristic that differentiates among the elements in that population. For example, the households in the northern section of the trade area may reside in large new, single-family housing units on large lots, while the households in the southern portion of the trade area reside in small, older, single-family housing units on small lots. In this situation, the analyst would like responses from individuals who live in newer, larger houses as well as elements of the population that live in the smaller, older houses.

Other important demographic and economic characteristics can differentiate between elements in the population. There may be different age, income, and ethnic groups residing in the trade area. There may be individuals with different life-styles, attitudes, and preferences living in the trade area. If the researcher identifies an important characteristic, it can be used to create different groups or strata in the population.

Returning to the first example, the researcher would identify two strata in the population: those households living in large new units and those households living in old, small units. Given this twofold categorization, the researcher extracts a simple random sample from each of the two stratas to get the necessary sample. In this way, the researcher guarantees that there will be sufficient information about both groups. A simple random sample of the entire population can lead to a situation where one group is underrepresented. A random sample drawn from the entire population could produce 90 elements drawn from the southern portion of the trade area and only 10 elements drawn from the northern portion of the trade area. In this instance, a sample size of 10 may not adequately represent the attitudes, desires, or purchase patterns of the housing living in large, new housing units.

The size of the random sample taken from each strata can be determined in one of two ways: proportional allocation or disproportional allocation. As a rule, proportional allocation is used when the analyst only knows the size of the strata. If the standard deviation of the observations is known for each strata, the disproportional allocation can be used. In real estate market analysis, proportional allocation is typically the most relevant procedure.

Proportional allocation simply means that the necessary sample is divided in proportion to the relative size of the strata. For example, if the sample size is determined to be 500, and strata 1 is 25 percent of the population while strata 2 is 75 percent of the population, then the sample from strata 1 is $500 \times 0.25 = 125$ while the sample from strata 2 is $500 \times 0.75 = 375$.

Cluster Sampling Procedure Cluster sampling is analogous to stratified random sampling since both processes establish subgroups of the population. In stratified random sampling, the individual members of the subgroups are similar to each other, but there is a difference between the subgroups, such as living in different neighborhoods. In cluster sampling, the subgroups, or clusters, are set up in such a way that there is a great deal of similarity between the clusters, and each cluster reflects the population as a whole. Dissimilarity occurs within each of the clusters.

For example, in the trade area, assume there are households of varying size, from one through four members per household, distributed in space with no apparent pattern to the distribution (i.e., the distribution of household size may be random over space). In this instance, the trade area could be divided into clusters of residential blocks, and, in each cluster, household size is distributed without any apparent pattern.

Given this example, the analyst subdivides the trade area into 16 clusters. Then, the analyst randomly selects 3 of these clusters for the sample. Once these 3 clusters are identified, the analyst must decide on the extent to which the elements in each cluster are studied. If each element in the 3 clusters chosen for the sample is studied, the analyst is using one-stage cluster sampling. The term "one stage" refers to the fact that only one step is used to obtain the elements in the sample. This form of cluster sampling works if the clusters are small relative to the necessary sample size. For example, each cluster could contain 120 to 140 elements, while the necessary sample size is 300. A good response rate from the households in three clusters will yield the 300 respondents.

On the other hand, if the cluster size is large relative to the necessary sample size, "two-stage" cluster sampling can be used. In this case, assume that each cluster contains 1,000 elements while the necessary sample size is 300. The analyst could

1. randomly select 1 cluster from the 16 clusters in the population (first stage) and, *then*
2. randomly select 500 households from the 1,000 households in that cluster (second stage).

The selection of 500 elements will yield 300 responses if 60 percent of the sample respond. The two-stage sampling procedure could also work in the following way:

1. randomly select 2 (or more) clusters from the 16 clusters in the population and *then*
2. randomly select 250 (or less if more than 2 clusters are chosen) households from each of the clusters.

Nonprobability Sampling Nonprobability sampling techniques include convenience sampling, judgment sampling, and quota sampling. The distinguishing feature between probability and nonprobability sampling is absence of the random selection process and the consequent use of statistical inference in nonprobability sampling.

With regard to the accuracy of information in general, nonprobability sampling techniques do not generate less reliable or inherently inaccurate data. The information received from nonprobability sampling can be as good as and, on occasion, even better than the information received from a probability sample. In both probability and nonprobability sampling, frame error and nonresponse error can occur. The researcher should not develop a bias against nonprobability sampling, which is a useful technique even if the extent of sampling error cannot be gauged. It is often used in real estate market analysis, but the analyst must be aware of its limitations and not use it improperly.

The Convenience Sample   In a convenience sample, the researcher identifies the elements in the population that are most accessible, most willing to respond, or simply more convenient to interview. Consider a situation where the researcher is attempting to obtain preference information about products and the shopping habits of people who are leaving a shopping center. A simple random sample procedure would require the researcher to determine, by means of a random selection process, the individuals that will be interviewed as they leave a randomly selected entry way to the shopping center. In the convenience sample, the researcher stands in front of the entrance or exit that has the greater traffic flow. Then the researcher approaches individuals to see if they are willing to respond to the questionnaire and, if they are, solicits their responses. In this way, either the willingness of the respondent to answer questions and/or the accessibility of the potential respondent to the interviewer determine the composition of the convenience sample.

The problem with the convenience sample lies in a misunderstanding that the researcher may have. The convenience sample does not generate the same elements from the population as a simple random sample. This occurs for many different reasons, but the most significant reason is the interviewer's freedom to choose the elements of the population that are approached. At the extremes, a male interviewer may choose to seek responses only from females. An older interviewer may choose to seek only the responses of senior citizens. A female interviewer may only seek the responses of women because she may feel it is inappropriate to approach male shoppers. In each of these extreme cases, the convenience sample generated elements that are markedly different from the elements that a random selection process might provide.

Judgment Sample   In the judgment sample, the interviewer selects the elements based on prior knowledge. For example, the researcher could be attempting to obtain information about the shopping habits of women between the ages of 20 and 45. In this instance, the researcher may know that the willingness to respond is highly related to the number of children accompanying the shopper and the size of the bundle she is carrying. Women with more than one child are reluctant to stop and donate the time to the interview; women carrying bundles are in a hurry to put them in the car. Armed with this prior knowledge, the interviewer chooses to restrict the interview process to women without bundles and accompanied by only one or no children.

In this instance if a problem occurs, it stems from the assumption that the shopping habits of women with one child are similar to the shopping habits of women with more than one child. Any such assumption must be verified by prior knowledge and not merely an educated guess. Then, if there is a difference in the shopping habits, the researcher may know of the differences and be able to weigh the answers received from women with only one child to reflect the attitudes of all shoppers.

The Quota Sample   The initial steps in the quota sampling procedure are similar to the stratified random sampling procedure. However, in the final stage of the quota sampling procedure, a convenience sample is chosen instead of a random sample. Quota sampling starts with the identification of important distinguishing characteristics in the population. Then, the researcher identifies a quota of the number of elements that must be drawn from each distinct group in that population. This procedure is analogous to the establishment of the sample size to be drawn from each strata in a stratified random sampling procedure. However, when the elements in the quota are drawn, they are usually drawn on a convenience basis.

Confusion can occur in a quota sampling procedure because, on the surface, it appears to follow the same steps as the stratified random sampling procedure. However, because of the absence of the random selection process, quota sampling cannot rely on statistics to judge the incidence of sampling error.

Nonresponse to the Questionnaire

There will always be individuals who will not respond to a personal interview, a telephone interview, or a mailed questionnaire. Others will not respond to a particular question or to the process as a whole. This second group is the focus of discussion in this section.

The primary problem with this form of nonresponse is its impact on the sampling procedure. The first effect of the nonresponse phenomenon is an increase in the sample size to be drawn from the population to get the necessary number of responses. Assume that an analyst calculates that 500 responses are necessary in the study. If the analyst also knows that 40 percent of the people will not respond, while 60 percent will respond, then the necessary sample size would have to be $500/0.6 = 833$. To receive 500 responses, the interviewer would have to contact 833 people.

A perplexing problem arises with regard to this matter. What if the analyst did select 833 people for the sample because 500 responses were needed, but the response rate was not 60 percent, but only 40 percent? This means that instead of having the desired 500 responses, the analyst only has 333. How should the additional responses be obtained? There are two ways that this can be done. First, the analyst could have anticipated receiving a lower response rate than the typical response rate for such surveys. In this event, more than 833 people could have been interviewed. If a 50 percent response rate were obtained instead of the 60 percent response rate, 500 respondents would exist.

The other solution requires a reinterview, or callback process, to raise the 40 percent response rate to the desired 60 percent response rate. The way to accomplish this reduction in nonresponses is to identify the nonresponders. Typically, the nonresponse group is divided between people who are *not at home* and those who are home but *refuse to answer*.

The individuals who are not at home vary by day of the week, time of day, season of the year, age, and sex. For example, young males are not likely to be at home. Other groups, such as families without children, employed women, high-income families, and individuals who live in urban areas, are also likely to be not at home at certain times of the day and evening.

Since these characteristics are not randomly distributed in the general population and, more important, in the population under analysis, failure to deal with nonresponse can introduce bias or error in the results obtained from the survey. In general, the lower the response rate from the original sample, the greater the chance for the existence of nonresponse error, and possibly, the greater the magnitude of the resulting error. However, the existence of a low response rate does not necessarily mean that a significant nonresponse error exists.

Reducing Nonresponse in Personal and Telephone Interviews The most common way to handle the issue of people not at home is to set up a procedure to call back at a different time or on a different day. In this way, the not-at-home group can be contacted, and, if they are willing, they can be included in the study. Based on research in this area, the following conclusion can be drawn with regard to the not-at-home problem in general: it is highest in the afternoon (i.e., 2:00 P.M. to 5:00 P.M.) and lowest in the early evening (7:00 P.M. to 10:00 P.M.) for housewives, female heads of households in particular, and male heads of households in general.

Focusing attention on individuals who refuse to answer the questionnaire presents a different problem. Refusals to answer are often the result of the potential respondent's attitude. In this sense, it can be argued that these factors occur randomly within the population and, therefore, are of no consequence because they will not bias the results of the survey. However, there is evidence that high refusal rates are concentrated among the high-income and the low-income groups. Refusal rates are lowest among specialized, homogeneous groups of people. When these different groups exhibit different refusal rates, nonresponse error is highly probable. One key to determining why nonresponse has occurred is to review the characteristics of the sample to determine if nonresponders represent a group that has been inadvertently or systematically excluded from the sample.

Refusal rates can be affected by questionnaire design factors. In the interview process, the majority of refusals occur after the interviewer's introductory remarks. So the introductory remarks, the interviewer's appearance, and the interviewer's tone of voice, mannerisms, and method of approach can be critical variables.

A callback procedure can be used to reduce refusals if they occurred due to a potential respondent's mood. Approaching the individual at a different time or in a different manner could generate a response. If the refusal is due to a personality difference or a personality clash between the potential respondent and the interviewer, the refusal may be eliminated when a different interviewer is sent to the residence. Sometimes a more personal approach can bring out a response. In addition, refusals to answer may be a result of an explicit decision not to provide information. Sometimes a more detailed procedure to assure anonymity can lessen the resistance. However, this refusal often cannot be overcome. The problem of nonresponse can never be completely eliminated from a study.

Nonresponse must be minimized even if it cannot be eliminated. Callbacks must be used. However, the callback often does not eliminate the not-at-home problem or the refusal problem. In the personal interview, many analysts will substitute neighboring dwelling units for the nonrespondent. In the telephone interview, another phone number in the same geographic area is substituted for the person who is not at home. However, when simple switches are employed, then convenience rather than random techniques are being used, and this could seriously bias the sample. Such substitutions are satisfactory only if the substitute possesses the same economic, demographic, and psychographic characteristics. This assumption is usable only in a few situations. More often, the results will not be statistically reliable. It is better to use another technique to assure randomness.

Influences on the response rate in self-administered questionnaires other than the respondent's interest in the topic and analysis include

1. *Follow-up procedures or second mail-outs.*
2. *Monetary incentives.* In general, promised incentives of $2 to $5 paid upon receipt of the completed questionnaire have been shown to be effective. But a *prepaid incentive* of $1 seems to work just as well in increasing the response rate.
3. *Prior notification.* An advance letter or telephone call introducing the study and informing the potential respondent of the questionnaire's arrival helps to increase the response rate.
4. *A return envelope with prepaid first class postage on the return or personal pick-up.*

Less important in affecting the response rate are

1. *Length of the questionnaire.* Even though the page length may not be a significant factor, length of time to complete is a significant factor.
2. *Respondent anonymity and assurances of confidentiality.* These factors produce inconclusive results or variable effects with regard to the response rate.
3. *Identification of the sponsoring entity.* Noncommercial sponsors obtain relatively higher response rates.
4. *Nonmonetary incentives.*

Setting a deadline date for the return of the questionnaire has no apparent effect.

Strategies for Overcoming Nonresponse Several strategies or procedures can be used to overcome the effect of nonresponse, including

1. *Substitution of another potential respondent if a callback does not yield a response.* This technique only solves the problem if the substitute is a good match for the original.
2. *Subjective estimation of the probable effects of nonresponse error based on knowledge from other studies.* The researcher anticipates the possible error.
3. *Imputing attributes to nonrespondents based on the characteristics of the respondent.* This technique requires that the researcher have some comparative information about the respondents and the nonrespondents. For example, nonrespondents are given imputed income figures based on the comparison of their other economic and demographic characteristics to those of the respondents.
4. *Imputing attributes to nonrespondents based on response trend for the respondents.* This technique assumes that nonrespondents are more similar to the respondents who responded to a third or second mailing than are those who responded to a first mailing.
5. *Imputing attributes to nonrespondents who are in the not-at-home category based on actions of the respondents.* This technique requires asking respondents to a telephone or personal survey about their stay-at-home habits. The nonresidents are assumed to be more like the individuals who do not stay home than those who do stay home.
6. *Measuring nonrespondent characteristics.* This technique requires the researcher to develop a sample of the population of nonrespondents and to survey them.

Sample Size Determination

A detailed discussion of the determination of sample size is somewhat beyond the scope of this book, since it is not a textbook on statistics. This chapter does contain a series of tables (Exhibit 14-5) that will assist readers in determining the required sample size, given a desired level of reliability.[2] To be able to use the tables effectively, it is necessary first to understand certain terms.

A confidence interval tells how far away the unknown population parameter the analyst is trying to measure can be from the sample statistic. In other words, it tells how confident one can be that he or she is correct. A 95 percent confidence interval means that if one had taken 1,000 samples of size 300 and then constructed 1,000 separate confidence intervals, or one for each sample, one would expect that 950 of them would have contained the unknown population mean.

This chapter has already considered nonprobability sampling techniques. When the analyst uses one of those methods, the sample may include

[2]Tables in Exhibit 14-5 are taken from Herbert Arkin and Raymond R. Colton, *Tables for Statisticians*, 2nd ed. (New York: Barnes and Noble, 1968), pp. 145–152. These tables were adapted from and extended from tables in H. P. Hill, J. L. Roth, and H. Arkin, *Sampling in Auditing* (New York: The Ronald Press, 1962).

Exhibit 14-5 Tables for Determining Appropriate Sample Sizes.

Table A Table of Sample Sizes Required for Finite Populations, for Selected Confidence Levels, and Various Sample Reliability Limits for Sampling Attributes (95% confidence level; percent in population assumed to be 50%*)

SIZE OF POPULATION	SAMPLE SIZE FOR RELIABILITIES OF				
	±1%	±2%	±3%	±4%	±5%
1,000	†	†	†	375	278
2,000	†	†	696	462	322
3,000	†	1,334	787	500	341
4,000	†	1,500	842	522	350
5,000	†	1,622	879	536	357
10,000	4,899	1,936	964	566	370
20,000	6,489	2,144	1,013	583	377
50,000	8,057	2,291	1,045	593	381
100,000	8,763	2,345	1,056	597	383
500,000 to ∞	9,423	2,390	1,065	600	384

*This section of this table should be used *only* when the sampler is unable or unwilling to estimate a maximum (or minimum) occurrence rate to be expected. The use of this section of the table, while conservative, will result in a much larger sample size than found in other sections of the table where such an estimate is used.

†In these cases more than 50% of the population is required in the sample. Since the normal approximation of the hypergeometric distribution is a poor approximation in such instances, no sample value is given.

Table B Sample Sizes (95% confidence level; expected rate of occurrence not over 5% or not less than 95%)

SIZE OF POPULATION	SAMPLE SIZE FOR RELIABILITIES OF			
	±0.5%	±1%	±2%	±3%
1,000	*	*	313	169
2,000	*	954	371	184
3,000	*	1,134	396	190
4,000	*	1,253	409	192
5,000	*	1,336	418	195
10,000	4,220	1,543	436	199
20,000	5,348	1,672	446	201
50,000	6,370	1,760	452	202
100,000	6,803	1,791	454	202
500,000 to ∞	7,196	1,818	456	203

*In these cases more than 50% of the population is required in the sample. Since the normal approximation of the hypergeometric distribution is a poor approximation in such instances, no sample value is given.

Exhibit 14-5 *Continued.*

Table C Sample Sizes (99% confidence level; percent in population assumed to be 50%*)

SIZE OF POPULATION	SAMPLE SIZE FOR RELIABILITIES OF				
	±1%	±2%	±3%	±4%	±5%
1,000	†	†	†	†	400
2,000	†	†	959	683	498
3,000	†	†	1,142	771	544
4,000	†	†	1,262	824	569
5,000	†	2,267	1,347	859	586
10,000	†	2,932	1,556	939	622
20,000	9,068	3,435	1,688	986	642
50,000	12,456	3,830	1,778	1,016	655
100,000	14,229	3,982	1,810	1,026	659
500,000 to ∞	16,056	4,113	1,836	1,035	663

*This section of this table should be used *only* when the sampler is unable or unwilling to estimate a maximum (or minimum) occurrence rate to be expected. The use of this section of the table, while conservative, will result in a *much* larger sample size than found in other sections of the table where such an estimate is used.

†In these cases more than 50% of the population is required in the sample. Since the normal approximation of the hypergeometric distribution is a poor approximation in such instances, no sample value is given.

Table D Sample Sizes (95% confidence level; expected rate of occurrence not over 15% or not less than 85%)

SIZE OF POPULATION	SAMPLE SIZE FOR RELIABILITIES OF			
	±1%	±2%	±3%	±4%
1,000	*	*	353	235
2,000	*	760	428	266
3,000	*	870	461	278
4,000	*	938	479	284
5,000	2,474	984	491	289
10,000	3,288	1,091	516	297
20,000	3,935	1,154	530	302
50,000	4,461	1,195	538	304
100,000	4,669	1,210	541	305
500,000 to ∞	4,850	1,222	544	306

*In these cases more than 50% of the population is required in the sample. Since the normal approximation of the hypergeometric distribution is a poor approximation in such instances, no sample value is given.

Table E Sample Sizes (99% confidence level; expected rate of occurrence not over 5% or not less than 95%)

SIZE OF POPULATION	SAMPLE SIZE FOR RELIABILITIES OF			
	±0.5%	±1%	±2%	±3%
1,000	*	*	441	260
2,000	*	*	565	298
3,000	*	*	624	314
4,000	*	1,763	658	322
5,000	*	1,934	681	327
10,000	*	2,397	731	338
20,000	7,730	2,721	758	344
50,000	10,063	2,963	776	348
100,000	11,189	3,056	782	349
500,000 to ∞	12,289	3,132	787	350

*In these cases more than 50% of the population is required in the sample. Since the normal approximation of the hypergeometric distribution is a poor approximation in such instances, no sample value is given.

Table F Sample Sizes (95% confidence level; expected rate of occurrence not over 30% or not less than 70%)

SIZE OF POPULATION	SAMPLE SIZE FOR RELIABILITIES OF			
	±1%	±2%	±3%	±5%
1,000	*	*	473	244
2,000	*	*	619	278
3,000	*	1,206	690	291
4,000	*	1,341	732	299
5,000	*	1,437	760	303
10,000	4,465	1,678	823	313
20,000	5,749	1,832	858	318
50,000	6,946	1,939	881	321
100,000	7,465	1,977	888	321
500,000 to ∞	7,939	2,009	895	322

*In these cases more than 50% of the population is required in the sample. Since the normal approximation of the hypergeometric distribution is a poor approximation in such instances, no sample value is given.

Exhibit 14-5 *Continued.*

the unknown population mean, but one can never be sure since it cannot be assigned a confidence level.

Reliability refers to the plus or minus percentage points that the sample mean will adequately represent the population parameter. It is a measure of precision.

Table G Sample Sizes (99% confidence level; expected rate of occurrence not over 15% or not less than 85%)

SIZE OF POPULATION	SAMPLE SIZE FOR RELIABILITIES OF			
	±1%	±2%	±3%	±4%
1,000	*	*	485	346
2,000	*	*	640	418
3,000	*	1,241	716	450
4,000	*	1,384	761	467
5,000	*	1,487	791	478
10,000	4,583	1,746	859	502
20,000	5,946	1,913	898	515
50,000	7,237	2,029	923	523
100,000	7,801	2,071	931	526
500,000 to ∞	8,320	2,106	938	528

*In these cases more than 50% of the population is required in the sample. Since the normal approximation of the hypergeometric distribution is a poor approximation in such instances, no sample value is given.

Table H Sample Sizes (99% confidence level; expected rate of occurrence not over 30% or not less than 70%)

SIZE OF POPULATION	SAMPLE SIZE FOR RELIABILITIES OF			
	±1%	±2%	±3%	±5%
1,000	*	*	*	360
2,000	*	*	873	436
3,000	*	*	1,021	470
4,000	*	1,862	1,116	489
5,000	*	2,053	1,182	502
10,000	*	2,584	1,341	527
20,000	8,213	2,967	1,437	542
50,000	10,898	3,257	1,502	551
100,000	12,231	3,367	1,525	554
500,000 to ∞	13,557	3,460	1,544	557

*In these cases more than 50% of the population is required in the sample. Since the normal approximation of the hypergeometric distribution is a poor approximation in such instances, no sample value is given.

Exhibit 14-5 *Continued.*

Percentage of population assumed and expected rate of occurrence both refer to the proportion of the population having the attribute being estimated. The conservative approach, which would yield the largest possible sample size, would be to use 50 percent. If you can make an informed judgment or if you have data from past studies, then use one of the other tables in Exhibit 14-5.

One caveat needs to be mentioned at this time. The proper determination of the correct sample size is a complex statistical procedure. It must be performed properly to be able to make appropriate inferences about a population from a sample.

If the market researcher does not have the knowledge and skills to utilize properly tables such as those in Exhibit 14-5, or if the researcher is not able to employ proper statistical techniques in collecting and analyzing the data, then a statistician with proper skills needs to be retained as an associate analyst for the project.

READINGS

ARKIN, HERBERT, and RAYMOND R. COLTON, *Tables for Statisticians*. New York: Barnes and Noble, Inc., 1968.

BABBIE, EARL, *Survey Research Methods*. (Belmont, Calif.: Wadsworth Publishing Co., 1973.

HILL, H. P., J. L. ROTH, and H. ARKIN, *Sampling In Auditing*. New York: The Ronald Press, 1962.

RABIANSKI, J., and J. VERNOR, "The Use of Questionnaires in Marketability Research," in *Readings in Market Research for Real Estate*, ed. James D. Vernor. Chicago: American Institute of Real Estate Appraisers, 1985.

TULL, DONALD, and DEL HAWKINS, *Marketing Research: Measurement and Methods*. New York: MacMillan, 1980.

INDEX